THE INCREDIBLES

JACK-JACK

ELASTIGIRL

MR. INCREDIBLE

VIOLET

DASH

	ROBERT PARR	HELEN PARR	VIOLET PARR	DASHIELL PARR	JACK-JACK PARR
ALIAS					
ABILITIES	SUPER STRENGTH	FULL-BODY ELASTICITY	INVISIBILITY AND FORCE-FIELD GENERATION	SUPER SPEED	TELEKINESIS, MIMICRY, DIMENSIONAL TELEPORTATION, SPONTANEOUS COMBUSTION, LEVITATION, SELF-CLONING, MONSTROUS TENDENCIES
WEAKNESSES	BIG EGO	FREEZING TEMPERATURES	INEXPERIENCE	IMPULSE CONTROL	UNKNOWN

NOTES: The Incredibles prove that the only thing stronger than a Super is a family of Supers!

FROZONE

ALIAS

LUCIUS BEST

ABILITIES

- ► CAN GENERATE ICE FROM MOISTURE IN THE AIR
- ► MASTER SPEED SKATER ON ICE PATHWAYS THAT HE CREATES

WEAKNESSES

- ► REQUIRES MOISTURE TO CREATE ICE

NOTES: In addition to his amazing freezing powers, Frozone has his own clothing line and music label.

VOYD

ALIAS

KAREN (LAST NAME UNKNOWN)

ABILITIES

► DIMENSIONAL TELEPORTATION

WEAKNESSES

► WORMHOLE DESTINATIONS CAN BE UNPREDICTABLE

NOTES: Voyd's ability to generate wormholes makes her a formidable hero and perfect for missions that require long-distance travel and quick escapes.

HE-LECTRIX

ALIAS

UNKNOWN

ABILITIES

► ABILITY TO CONTROL AND PROJECT ELECTRICAL CURRENTS
► IMPERVIOUS TO ELECTRICITY

WEAKNESSES

► EXPOSURE TO WATER CAN TEMPORARILY SHORT OUT HE-LECTRIX'S POWER. ALSO, HIS POWERS HAVE NO EFFECT ON NONCONDUCTIVE MATERIALS.

NOTES: Villains who encounter this high-voltage hero are in for the shock of their lives!

BRICK

ALIAS

CONCRETIA. "CONNIE" MASON

ABILITIES

► CAN EXPAND TO THE SIZE AND STRENGTH
OF A BRICK WALL ON COMMAND

WEAKNESSES

► WILL SINK IN WATER

NOTES: When Brick arrives, evildoers find themselves between a rock and a hard place.

REFLUX

ALIAS	*GUS BURNS*
ABILITIES	► CAN REGURGITATE HIS MOLTEN STOMACH ACID
WEAKNESSES	► TIRES EASILY AND OVERHEATS ► MOTION SICKNESS

NOTES: When Reflux goes on the offensive, he is the most offensive hero around.

SCREECH

NOTES: Screech's ability to fly is natural and not a function of his suit, which serves to enhance his owl-like features.

KRUSHAUER

ALIAS	*UNKNOWN*
ABILITIES	► CAN CRUSH OBJECTS WITHOUT TOUCHING THEM
WEAKNESSES	► CAN ONLY CRUSH INANIMATE OBJECTS

NOTES: When Krushauer battles the bad guys, he never fails to leave a lasting impression and a trail of rubble in his wake.

INCREDIBLES 2

ISBN 979-11-86701-84-3 14740

Longtail Books

Prologue

Inside a windowless room, a **stark** white light **flood**ed the darkness.

"File 82-712, **Agent** Rick Dicker **interrogating**," the **straight-faced** secret agent said into a microphone. His deep voice showed no emotion as he prepared to question the **awkward**-looking **teenage** boy sitting before him. "**State** your name, please."

The boy **squirm**ed in his chair and **winced**, **squint**ing at the **blind**ing light. "Uh . . . ," he began. "Tony. Tony Rydinger."

"Tell me about the **incident**," Dicker said.

"Well, there was this girl. . . ." As Tony began to **recount** the story, he saw the memory play out in his mind. He remembered it clearly—walking up to a girl from his school during a **track meet** and talking to her.

"You're, uhh—Violet, right?" Tony had said.

"That's me," said Violet, smiling at him.

"You look . . . different," said Tony.

"I feel different," said Violet **confident**ly.

Tony told Dicker he sort of knew her, but it seemed like she had changed.

"She was more sure of herself than before," he said. "Cool. Cute." He **blush**ed a little, then quickly **clear**ed **his throat** and continued to **relay** the story, explaining how he and Violet had made plans to see a movie together. Then they'd gone back to their seats to watch the track meet.

Everything had seemed normal until Tony and his friends were walking through the **parking lot** on their way home. The ground suddenly began to **rumble** and **quake**! The shaking became more and more **violent**—then an **enormous armor**ed **vehicle** with a **powerful earthmover**

drill attached to the front **exploded** from the ground! It **flip**ped cars out of its way, and Tony and his friends ran in different directions, trying to escape.

Tony **squat**ted behind a car and **peer**ed around it to watch as **chaos envelop**ed the city. Through the **thicket** of cars and **panic**ked **crowd**s, he saw a **platform** slowly **extend** from the vehicle, rising into the air. Then a **hulking** super **villain** appeared, standing on it. He was **cover**ed in armor, had **clamp**like metal hands, and wore an **oversized mining** helmet. His voice **boom**ed across the city as he introduced himself with an **evil cackle**.

"**Behold** the Underminer!" he said. "I am always beneath you, but nothing is beneath *me!*"

Tony tried to stay hidden as the Underminer continued.

"I **hereby declare** war . . . on peace and happiness!"

Tony began searching for an escape **route** and **scrambled** behind another car. Then he **notice**d a strange pair of tall boots over red spandex.★

"You two stay here," said a man's voice.

★spandex 스판덱스. 고무와 비슷한 탄성을 지닌 폴리우레탄 합성 섬유. 잘 늘어나고 가볍고 질겨서, 각종 스포츠 의류 등의 재료로 쓰인다.

"Wait—should we be doing this? It is still **illegal**?" a woman said.

Tony told Dicker that at the time, he had thought the man and woman were Superheroes.

Tony listened as they continued to argue **back and forth** for a few moments. Then the Underminer disappeared into the **tunnel**ing vehicle, and it began to drill down into the **earth**.

"One of you **patrol** the **perimeter**, keep the crowds back and safe. The other watch Jack-Jack!" said the woman.

"But I thought we were gonna go with—" said a girl.

"You heard your mother!" said the man.

Tony **recall**ed seeing the two adults **taking off** after the Underminer.

"I **call** perimeter!" said a boy.

"You're not going anywhere, you **maggoty** little **creep**!" said the girl.

Tony saw his chance to get out, but as he listened to the kids argue, he **recognize**d the girl's voice.

"Oh, great," the girl said. "He gets to be a hero while

I'm stuck ALONE in a parking lot, **babysit**ting like an *idiot!*" She pulled off her **mask** and threw it to the ground. Tony **stare**d at her, **taking in** the **sight** of the Super**suit**. He told Dicker he knew she had sounded familiar. . . . It was Violet! He couldn't believe it.

Violet saw Tony. She tried to tell him everything was fine, but the situation was too **weird** for him to **handle**. So without knowing how to **react**, he just **ran away**.

In the interrogation room, Dicker **switch**ed **on** a strange machine that was **mount**ed to the **ceiling**.

"I feel kinda bad about it," said Tony as Dicker pointed a laser* **beam** between Tony's **eyebrow**s. "Maybe I should've said hi or something? It's not her **fault** Superheroes are illegal. And it's not like I don't like strong girls. I'm pretty **secure** . . . **manhood**-wise. . . .*
What is that?" Tony asked, finally noticing the strange **gadget**.

"Have you told anyone else about this?" asked Dicker, **ignoring** his question. "Your parents?"

★laser 레이저. 증폭기 안에서 유도 방출을 반복하여 증폭된 빛 또는 그러한 빛을 내는 장치.
✻-wise '~에 관하여', '~의 면에서는'이라는 뜻을 나타내는 접미사.

"No," said Tony. "They'd only think I was hiding something. You know what I mean?"

"Sure, kid," said Dicker.

"I like this girl, Mr. Dicker," said Tony. "I'm supposed to go out with her Friday night. Now things are just gonna be . . . weird. I wish I could forget I ever saw her in that suit."

"You will, kid," said Dicker. "You will."

Just then, a small **suction** cup **fire**d from the machine and stuck to Tony's **forehead**. His eyes **flutter**ed for a moment, and everything went black.

Mr. Incredible **clung** to the top of the Underminer's **massive tunnel**er as it **chew**ed through the **earth**. He held on with all his strength, but the machine soon shook him loose, **fling**ing him to the ground! He **gag**ged as dirt and **debris** flew into his mouth.

The giant **drill** cut an **enormous cavern** right below the **financial district**. Once it stopped, a **hatch** opened and the Underminer **emerge**d. He pointed a **detonator** at the newly **carve**d cavern and laughed. "Consider yourselves **UNDERMINED!**" He **press**ed a button, and within seconds, there was a **tremendous explosion!**

Bank buildings dropped straight down to the cavern floor, sending clouds of dust into the air. The tunneler began moving again—this time drilling directly through the walls of the banks and their **vaults**!

BWOOP! BWOOP! BWOOP! The **deafening alarm**s rang out from the vaults, and bright-red **emergency** lights **flicker**ed **urgent**ly. But none of that stopped the Underminer from his work. He pulled a long, wide **tube** from the tunneler and **drag**ged it into the vaults. **Plant**ing himself in the center of the room, he turned on the **powerful suction**. Mountains of cash, **bond**s, and **deed**s were **suck**ed up through the tube and into the tunneler!

Mr. Incredible appeared. With his hands on his **hip**s, he said, "Underminer. We meet again—"

Startled, the Underminer, still holding the **vacuum**, turned toward him. In a **flash**, Mr. Incredible was sucked inside! The tube **bulge**d and **twist**ed as the Super's body **snake**d its way through.

"Oh, GREAT!" **bark**ed the Underminer, **irritate**d. "Now *he's* on the **agenda**."

The **pressure** built as Mr. Incredible **clog**ged the tube until the strength of it finally **force**d him through. He flew out the other side, **tumbling** into the tunneler's vault. A **blizzard** of coins and cash followed, falling into the **pile**s around him.

The Underminer **scowl**ed as he heard a **bang**ing sound from deep inside the vault. A **dent** appeared, growing bigger and bigger with each *bang*. The Underminer threw the **control**s to **autopilot**. Suddenly, Mr. Incredible **burst** through the metal wall, and the Underminer **whack**ed him on the head! The Underminer flashed his **claw**like hands and **punch**ed them up and down like jackhammers.*

"INCREDIBLE!" the Underminer shouted. "Meet JACK HAMMER!"

Mr. Incredible and the Underminer fought, tumbling around the tunneler until Mr. Incredible threw the Underminer against the control **panel**, breaking it! The massive machine began tunneling out of control, drilling upward, toward the **surface**. The Underminer **duck**ed into the vault, and it **separate**d from the tunneler—the

---

★jackhammer 소형 착암기. 압축 공기의 힘을 이용하여 암반이나 암석에 구멍을 뚫는 기계.

vault was actually an escape **pod**! Its **miniature** driller quickly **burrow**ed into the dirt floor and **vanish**ed. Mr. Incredible was left inside the tunneler, which continued to **zigzag haphazard**ly toward the surface.

Mr. Incredible **pound**ed every button and **flip**ped every **switch** and **lever** as he attempted to stop the tunneler. A screen next to the control panel **blink**ed a message: **BREACH** IN THREE . . . TWO . . . ONE . . .

"No, no, no, NO NO NO NO!!!!!!" he **yell**ed, banging his **fist**s against the panel.

With a loud *CRASH*, the tunneler exploded through the asphalt★ and burst onto the streets near the **stadium parking lot**!

A few **block**s away, Dash was keeping the **crowd** back. He **notice**d the **plume** of dust in the near **distance**. "Stay back!" he shouted. Then, using his Super speed, he **zoom**ed off toward the action.

Violet wanted to help, too. When she **spot**ted Dash **whip**ping by in a **blur**, she shouted, "You're not sticking

---

★asphalt 아스팔트. 도로 표면을 덮는 데 쓰이는 혼합물.

me with **babysit**ting!" She ran after Dash, pushing Jack-Jack along in his **stroller**. It was always a **challenge** to keep their baby brother *and* the city safe when a **villain** **struck**.

Elastigirl **stretch**ed, **swing**ing across the city, **making** **her way** to the top of the tunneler. Mr. Incredible emerged from inside the machine.

"I can't **steer** it or stop it!" he said. "And the Underminer has escaped!"

"We'll have to stop it from—" Elastigirl's eyes **widen**ed as she noticed the monorail* approaching. It was too late. The tunneler **slam**med into a **column** holding up the **track**s! The tracks **crumble**d apart and the train began to **dive** toward the ground. Just then, an icy **breeze swept** in. It was Frozone! The newly arrived Super used his ice powers to create a track that **guide**d the monorail **smooth**ly out of **harm**'s way.

But the tunneler continued its **destruction** through the city.

★monorail 모노레일. 선로가 한 가닥인 철도로 차체가 선로에 매달리거나 선로 위를 구르는 방식으로 이동한다.

"We have to stop this thing before it gets to the **overpass**!" shouted Elastigirl.

"I'll try and keep it away from the buildings!" Mr. Incredible yelled back as he **jam**med a **lamppost** into the **tread**s of the tunneler. But the enormous machine kept going, **scraping** against the sides of buildings and **crush**ing anything in its path.

As Dash **race**d through the **scatter**ed debris, the tunneler flung a car into the air. He **swift**ly swept an older woman out of the way.

"Thank you so much, young man—" she said.

Dash saw Jack-Jack rolling toward him in his stroller, **giggling** and **babbling**. Dash **grunt**ed, **realizing** the **responsibility** of babysitting was back on him. Now he was responsible for keeping Jack-Jack safe while also fighting the forces of **evil**!

"Violet!" he shouted, knowing his sister was hiding somewhere **nearby** with her power of **invisibility**. But he stayed focused, always **up for** a challenge.

Violet reappeared and **shield**ed herself with force **field**s as she **chase**d after the tunneler. Mr. Incredible continued to **struggle**, using all his strength to try to stop the machine.

Elastigirl swung her way up to the overpass and stretched her arms in both directions, stopping cars from entering the bridge as the tunneler **took down** its **support**s. The bridge **collapse**d, and Elastigirl stretched to **grab** a **streetlight**, pulling herself to safety.

Mr. Incredible jammed a fallen **pole** into the tunneler's treads, stopping the machine only for a moment before it **snap**ped the pole in half. Dash blurred past him.

"**Heads up**, Dad!" he yelled. Suddenly, Mr. Incredible found himself holding Jack-Jack!

Violet threw force fields on the other side of the tunneler to protect **bystander**s.

Elastigirl saw her. "VIOLET? WHO'S WATCHING JACK-JACK?"

"Dash is watching him!" answered Violet.

Mr. Incredible **sprint**ed past Violet and handed her Jack-Jack. "Violet, here! You take him!"

Elastigirl **leap**ed down from a streetlight and flipped into the open hatch of the tunneler.

As Mr. Incredible and the kids chased after the tunneler, they noticed what was sitting directly in its path: **city hall**. They climbed up to the hatch and hurried inside.

Elastigirl snaked her body through the tunneler's **machinery**, stretching to her **limit**s, trying to **spill** the engine's coolant* to force it to **overheat**. Mr. Incredible appeared.

"Help me with the boiler!*" Elastigirl **urge**d. He **rush**ed in to help her **pry** it loose, **toppling** it over. "That should do it!" She turned to go—and saw her children standing there. **Panic**king, she screamed, "What are you kids doing? GET OUTTA HERE! This thing's gonna **blow**!"

"THERE'S NO TIME!" shouted Violet. She handed Jack-Jack to her mom and created a force field around the family just as a massive **boom rippled** throughout the tunneler. The giant machine **stall**ed—right in front of city hall! The Incredibles **huddle**d together on the floor of the tunneler, laughing with **relief**.

★coolant 냉각수. 높은 열을 내는 기계를 차게 식히는 데 쓰는 물.
✻boiler 보일러. 물을 가열하여 증기를 발생시키는 장치.

"We did it!" **cheer**ed Dash.

"**Freeze**, Supers!" The family looked up through the open hatch to see a team of **cop**s with their **weapon**s **draw**n and **aim**ed at them.

"Ahh, what did we do?" said Mr. Incredible.

Agent Rick Dicker from the National Supers **Agency** drove the Incredibles home. The family, now back in their regular clothes, sat silently listening to the **hum** of the **armor**ed police **van**'s motor.

"Well, that went poorly," said Mr. Incredible, finally breaking the silence.

"Dad—" Violet said softly. "This is probably not the best time to tell you, but something else happened today . . . with a kid . . . and my **mask**. . . ." She told Bob that Tony had seen her.

They soon **pulled into** the **parking lot** of their **current** home: the Safari Court Motel. The small brown-and-orange motel had a **sign** above it with lights that **flicker**ed weakly. When the **rear** doors of the van opened, the Parr family **pour**ed out. Helen and the kids slowly walked toward their room as Bob **linger**ed behind to tell Dicker about Violet's **incident** with Tony.

"**Talkative** type?" asked Dicker through the van window.

"Don't know. Last name is Rydinger," answered Bob.

Dicker **whip**ped out a **pad** and **scribble**d down the name. Then he told Bob he would **check** it **out**.

Bob moved off to join Helen and the kids, but Dicker called him back. "Bob, Helen . . . ? A word, if you don't mind?" Dicker**'s face fell** as they approached the van. "The program's been **shut down**," he said with a **sigh**. He knew how important the Super **Relocation** Program was to the Parr family. Ever since Supers were **force**d **underground**, it had helped them many times. "**Politician**s don't understand people who do good simply because it's right. Makes 'em nervous. They've **been gunnin' for** Supers for years. Today was all they needed. . . ." His voice **trail**ed **off**. His sad eyes said it all: he **genuine**ly felt bad about the whole situation. "Anyway . . . I'm done. I'm afraid two more weeks in the motel is the best I can do for ya. It ain't much."

"You've done plenty, Rick," said Helen, **grateful**. She **lean**ed in and gave him a **hug** through the window.

"We won't forget," said Bob.

"Well, it has been a great **honor** workin' with you good people," said Dicker.

Bob and Helen thanked him for all he had done and wished him luck. Then they **wave**d and watched the van go.

Later that night, the Parr family sat down to dinner around a small, round table. It had been months since they'd moved in, and the motel room felt **clutter**ed and crowded. It wasn't nearly big enough for a family of five.

Several **carton**s of Chinese **takeout** sat in the center of the table as they prepared to eat. Helen placed Jack-Jack in his high chair★ and **click**ed the **buckle** around his

---

★high chair 유아의 식사용 의자. 다리가 길고 음식을 놓을 수 있는 작은 탁자가 딸린 의자.

waist. Dash reached for the egg rolls,[★] but Violet created a force **field** around the food and quickly asked, "Did you wash your hands?"

He **scowl**ed and **race**d from the table in a **blur**. In a **flash** he was back, reaching for the egg rolls again.

Violet protected the egg rolls with another force field and asked, "With soap?"

Dash **zip**ped off again, returning within seconds.

"Did you dry them?" she asked, **grin**ning.

Dash **narrow**ed his eyes and speed-shook his hands. Then, with a **triumphant grunt**, he finally **grab**bed an egg roll. He looked in the rest of the cartons and **frown**ed. "Is this all vegetables?" he asked. "Who ordered all vegetables?"

"I did," said Helen. Her **strict tone** said she **wasn't up for** hearing **complaint**s. "They're good, and you're going to have some," she added, **serving** him a **heap**ing **portion**.

"Are we going to talk about **the elephant in the room**?" asked Violet.

★egg roll 에그롤. 채소, 해산물, 고기 등을 잘게 다진 소를 달걀을 넣은 피(皮)에 넣고 말아서 튀긴 중국 요리.

Bob looked up at Violet with his mouth full of **stir-fried** beans. "What?" he asked.

"The elephant in the room," repeated Violet.

"What elephant?" asked Bob, **clueless**.

"I guess not, then," said Violet.

"You're **refer**ring to today," said Helen.

"Yeah, what's the **deal** with today?" asked Dash.

"We all made mistakes," said Helen calmly. "For example, you kids were supposed to watch Jack-Jack."

"Babysitting," said Violet, **annoy**ed. "While you guys did the important **stuff**."

"We talked about this," said Helen. "You're not old enough to decide about these things—"

"We are old enough to help out," Violet **interrupt**ed. Dash agreed as Violet turned to her father. "Isn't that what you tell us, Dad?"

Bob looked down at his food. "Yeah, well, 'help out' can mean many different things. . . ."

"But we're supposed to help if there's trouble . . . ," said Violet.

"Well . . . yeah, but—" Bob **stammer**ed.

"Aren't you glad we helped today?" asked Violet.

"Well, yeah. I was—AM—" said Bob, **stumbling** as he tried to find the right words.

"We wanna fight bad guys!" **exclaim**ed Dash.

Jack-Jack **babbled** in **approval** and raised his **fist**s, then **slam**med them down on the **tray** of his high chair.

"No—you don't!" said Helen, finally **weigh**ing **in**.

Violet turned to Helen. "You said things were different now."

Helen explained that they *were* different when they were on the island with Syndrome. The rules weren't the same because they were all in danger, but since they were now back at home, everything was supposed to be normal again.

"So now we've gotta go back to never using our powers?" said Violet angrily.

"It **define**s who I am," said Dash.

"We're not saying you have—" Bob looked at Dash as his son's words **register**ed. "What?"

"Someone on TV said it," replied Dash, **shrug**ging it **off**.

"Can—can we just eat? The dinner? While it's—hot?" asked Helen, wishing the conversation would just stop.

"Did we do something wrong?" asked Dash.

"Yes," said Helen.

"No," said Bob. Helen gave Bob a sharp look, but Bob refused to agree with her. *"We didn't do anything wrong,"* he **insist**ed.

"Superheroes ARE **illegal**," said Helen. "Whether it's fair or not, that's the law."

"The law should be fair," said Bob. "What are we teaching our kids?"

"To **respect** the law!" replied Helen, getting **heated**.

"Even when the law is **disrespectful**?"

"If laws are **unjust**, there are laws to change them—otherwise it's **chaos**!"

"Which is exactly what we have!" boomed Bob.

Frustrated, Helen slammed her hand on the table, causing the **plate**s to **bounce** and **rattle**. Everyone **froze**, **stun**ned by her **outburst**. The **awkward** moment of silence seemed to linger before everyone slowly **resume**d eating.

Then Violet said softly, "I just thought it was kind

of cool."

"What was?" asked Helen calmly.

"Fighting **crime**. As a family," she answered.

Everyone exchanged **glance**s, and without a word they knew: they all agreed.

"It was cool," said Helen. "But it's over. The world is what it is. We have to . . . **adapt**."

"Are things . . . bad?" asked Dash, **concern**ed.

"Things are fine," answered Helen.

Happy to hear those words, Dash cleared his mind of the whole conversation and asked to be excused. In a matter of seconds he cleared his plate, turned on the television, and **settle**d onto the **couch** to watch a giant Japanese monster attack a city.

Violet got up and turned to Bob. "How much longer in the motel?" she asked.

Bob stammered, unsure of how to answer. He looked over at Helen.

"Not much longer, honey," said Helen. She forced a smile, trying to hide the **weight** of the big question that hung in her mind: Where would they go next?

After the kids were asleep, Helen and Bob sat outside by the small motel **pool, staring** at the **rippling reflect**ion of the moonlight on the water, deep in thought.

"What are we gonna do?" asked Helen.

"I don't know," said Bob with a **shrug**. "Maybe Dicker'll find something—"

"Dicker is done, Bob," Helen said. "Any thought we had about being Supers again is **fantasy**. One of us has gotta get a job."

Helen said she knew that Bob's job at the **insurance** company had **be**en **hard on** him. She suggested that maybe it was her **turn** to get a job and he could stay home and **take care of** the kids.

"NO," said Bob. "I'm the **breadwinner**. I'll start . . . **win**ning some bread tomorrow." He **sigh**ed. "You know where my **suit** and ties are?"

"**Burn**ed up when—" Helen started.

"—the **jet** destroyed our house," Bob said along with her as he **recall**ed the **obvious** truth. The two smiled at each other, trying to remember to **appreciate** the fact that they had all **made it** through that **awful** day.

Helen gently rested her hand on top of his as she **remind**ed him that they couldn't **count on** anyone but themselves. Just then, they heard a noise as a **shadowy silhouette** approached, watching them from the other side of the pool. Helen and Bob stood up **defensive**ly. The **figure** stepped into the light—it was their good friend Lucius.

After breathing a sigh of **relief**, Bob **frown**ed at him. "Well, where'd YOU go today?" he said. "I noticed you missed all the fun," he added **sarcastic**ally.

"Don't be mad because I know when to leave a party,"

said Lucius. "I'm just as illegal as you guys. **Besides**, I knew the **cop**s would let you go."

Helen smiled. "Yeah, **in spite of** Bob's best efforts."

Bob **rolled his eyes** and **smirk**ed at her **comment**.

"I heard the program **shut down**," said Lucius. "How much longer you in this motel?"

"Two weeks," said Bob.

"Now, you know the offer still **stand**s," said Lucius.

"You're very **generous**, but there are five of us," said Helen. "We wouldn't do that to you and Honey," said Helen.

"Door's always open," said Lucius. Then he told them about a man he had met on his way home from the Underminer attack. He pulled out a **business card** and handed it to Helen. He explained that the man **represent**ed a business **tycoon** named Winston Deavor, who wanted to meet the three of them to talk about "hero **stuff**." Lucius opened his coat, **reveal**ing that he was wearing his Frozone Supersuit.

"Aw, **geez**," **groan**ed Helen. "More Superhero trouble? We just came from the police **station**, Lucius."

Bob looked up at his friend and **grin**ned. "When?" he asked.

"Tonight. I'm going there now."

"You enjoy," said Helen. "I'm **sit**tin' this one **out**."

Lucius explained that Deavor wanted to see all three of them.

Bob turned to Helen. "Let's just at least hear what he has to say."

Helen sighed. Then she **nod**ded, slowly **surrender**ing to the **pressure**. Bob **beam**ed, **thorough**ly excited at the **prospect** of discussing hero stuff.

"Go . . . in our Supersuits?" asked Helen.

"Yeah, might want to wear the old Supersuits," said Lucius. "Got a feeling he's **nostalgic**."

4

Mr. Incredible, Elastigirl, and Frozone soon arrived in a town car★ in front of DevTech **headquarters**. The modern **skyscraper** seemed to **stretch** up into the clouds. As they stepped out of the car, the driver handed each of them a **security badge**. Then he **usher**ed them through the **revolving** door and into the building.

The **sleek** glass elevator rose to the top floor, offering an **incredible** view of the city below. When the doors opened, a man took their coats and led them into the

★ town car 운전석과 뒷좌석 사이를 유리로 칸막이하고 문이 4개 있는 승용차.

enormous penthouse.★

"I LOVE SUPERHEROES!" said a **lively** voice behind them. They turned to see Winston Deavor, beaming as he **trot**ted down a **curved staircase**. "The powers, the **costume**s, the **mythic struggle**s ...," he said as he crossed over to them. He introduced himself and shook their hands, **enthusiastic**ally singing each of their **theme** songs.

"I can't tell you what a **thrill** this is," said Winston as a woman entered the room. He **gesture**d toward her. "And this is my **tardy** sister, Evelyn."

"Hello there, Superheroes," she said. "I'm late." She turned to Winston and added, "I'm **scold**ing myself so you don't have to."

Winston shot her a **disapproving** look and then turned back to the Supers, **admiring** their suits. "**Spectacular**," he said. "**Sport**ing the old suits from **yesteryear**, not the ones you wore earlier today with your kids."

Mr. Incredible and Elastigirl **swap**ped a look, **visibly shaken** by the fact that Winston Deavor knew their

★penthouse 펜트하우스. 고층 건물 맨 위층에 위치한 고급 아파트나 특별 객실.

children.

He quickly responded. "You're uncomfortable that I know your **alter egos**—that you two are married and have kids." He told them they had nothing to worry about. "You probably don't remember me," he added, "but I worked for Rick Dicker for a short period, right before you all went **underground**."

Frozone studied his face, and something suddenly **click**ed. "Yeah!" he said, **recapturing** the image in his mind. "Long hair?"

Winston **nod**ded. "Dicker made me cut it. My father was SO proud that I was even **remote**ly connected to you guys." Looking over at a **portrait** of his father hanging on the wall, Winston explained that he had **adore**d Supers. "He **donate**d to Superhero causes, he **raise**d **money** for the Dynaguy **statue** in Avery Park. . . ." Winston's thoughts **drift**ed to his parent's admiration. "He got to know Supers **personal**ly, even **install**ed a phone with direct lines to Gazerbeam and Fironic **in case** of **emergencies**. He loved that, **show**ed it **off** to everyone. . . ." Winston's voice **trail**ed **off** as he **pause**d for a moment, enjoying the

fond memory. Then he **snap**ped back to the conversation and fixed his **gaze** on the Supers. "He was **heartbroken** when you were all forced to go underground," he said.

"Father believed the world would become more dangerous without you," added Evelyn.

"He didn't know how right he was," said Winston. Then he shared a **painful** event from their **childhood**. One night, someone had **broken into** their family's home. "My mother wanted to hide, but my father **insist**ed they call Gazerbeam—on the direct line. No answer. He called Fironic; no answer. Superheroes had just been made illegal, but somehow he was sure they'd answer his call. The **rob**bers discovered him on the phone . . . and shot him."

"Must have been hard," said Elastigirl.

"Especially for Mother," said Evelyn. "She died a few months later. **Heartbreak**."

"If Superheroes had not been forced underground, it never would have happened. I'm sure of it," said Winston.

"Or . . . Dad could've taken Mom to the safe room*
as soon as he knew—" added Evelyn, a **tinge** of **irritation**

to her voice.

"I disagree *strongly,*" Winston **interrupt**ed. "But we're not going into it right now," he added, his **tone** becoming light again. He turned to the Supers. "We've had this argument forever. Pay no attention. The point is—we picked ourselves up and put our energy into building DevTech."

"A world-class **telecommunication**s company," said Frozone.

"Perfectly **position**ed to make some wrong things right. **Hence** this meeting!" said Winston.

Moments later, Mr. Incredible, Elastigirl, and Frozone were seated on a **couch** inside a screening room. Winston stood before them as Evelyn shut the **blind**s. "Let me ask you something. What is the main reason you were all forced underground?"

"**Ignorance**," Mr. Incredible answered quickly.

"**Perception**," said Winston.

Evelyn clicked a button on a remote, and **footage**

★safe room 건물이나 집에서 외부의 침투가 불가능한 안전한 장소.

from the Underminer attack appeared on a wall-sized screen. "Take today, for example, with the Underminer. Difficult situation. You were faced with a lot of hard decisions."

"Ah, **tell me about it**," said Mr. Incredible.

"I can't," said Winston. He **lean**ed in **dramatic**ally. "Because I didn't see it." The Supers exchanged **glances**. "Neither did anyone else. So when you fight bad guys— like today—people don't see the fight or what **led up to** it. They see what **politician**s tell them to see: they see **destruction**, and they see you." Winston paused before continuing. "You know what they don't see? This—"

Footage of a woman speaking to a camera appeared. "My car was headed over the **edge**, and suddenly, I felt this arm **wrap**ping around me and pulling me out of my window to safety," the woman said. "Elastigirl saved my life," she added **gratefully**.

"Yeah, you're darn⋆ straight, she did!" said Mr. Incredible.

⋆darn 말하는 내용을 강조하기 위해 덧붙이는 속어로 '끝내주게', '지독히'라는 뜻이다.

The footage paused, freezing on the image, and Winston turned to the Supers. "If we want to change people's perceptions about Superheroes, we need *you* to share *your* perceptions with the world."

"How do we do that?" asked Elastigirl.

Evelyn put three **separate** images on the screen. Two of them showed different **angle**s of Elastigirl's face, and one showed Winston. It was footage from just minutes before. On the screen, Winston said, "We need *you* to share *your* perceptions with the world."

Then Elastigirl asked her question. "How do we do that?"

Evelyn clicked the remote again, and a live **feed** appeared on the screen, showing the three Supers' faces. **Simultaneous**ly, they looked down at the security badges **clip**ped to their suits. "With cameras," said Evelyn. She explained that they would **sew tiny** cameras into the **fabric** of their Supersuits.

Elastigirl was **impress**ed. "That is so cool," she said, **inspect**ing the badge. She looked up at the screen, admiring the **crystal clear** images. "So small, and the picture is

outstanding."

Evelyn thanked her for the **compliment**. "**Design**ed 'em myself."

"Well, that's **fantastic**," said Mr. Incredible, getting more and more excited. "The public needs to **be in our shoes**."

"All we need now are the Superest Superheroes. We need you three!" said Winston enthusiastically.

"But our family just had a **run-in** with the law," said Elastigirl, bringing them all back to **reality**. "I can't risk that happening again."

"Understood—but do you change your kids to **fit** into a smaller world, or do you make the world larger *for* your kids?" asked Winston. "We've got **resource**s, lobbyists,★ **worldwide** connections, and, most important, **insurance**."

"Insurance is key," said Mr. Incredible.

Winston explained that it would be their top **priority**. "You just be Super, and we'll get the public on your side. We won't stop until you're all **legal** again," he said.

★lobbyist 로비스트. 특정 조직의 이익을 위해 의회 공작 운동을 하는 사람.

"This sounds GREAT!" said Mr. Incredible. He slapped his hands together. "Let's say we're all in—what's my first assignment?"

"That enthusiasm is golden," Winston replied. "Hold on to it. But for our first move, Elastigirl is our best play."

As Winston extended a hand to Elastigirl, Mr. Incredible stood, completely stunned, as if he had just been punched in the gut. "Better than . . . me?" he asked, finally getting out a few words. Elastigirl cleared her throat and glared at her husband, and he stammered, "I mean, she's good. She's—uh—really a credit to her—uh, but . . . I mean, you know?"

Winston smiled at Mr. Incredible. "With great respect, let's not test the whole 'insurance will pay for everything' idea on the first go-round, okay?" he said gently, trying not to offend him.

Frozone clenched his lips together, trying to hold back the laughter that wanted to blast out of his mouth.

"Wait a minute—you're saying, what, I'm . . . messy?" said Mr. Incredible, still trying to process what was happening.

Winston handed Mr. Incredible a folder. He looked at it, **bewilder**ed, as Winston explained that Evelyn had compared the costs and **benefit**s of their last five years of **crime** fighting. "Elastigirl's numbers are **self-explanatory**," he said.

Mr. Incredible **shift**ed his **weight** uncomfortably. "Well, it's not a fair **comparison** . . . ," he said, feeling the need to **defend** himself. "**Heavyweight** problems need heavyweight solutions."

Winston smiled. "Of course, we'll solve all kinds of problems together, after the perfect **launch** with Elastigirl," he said brightly, **wrap**ping **up** the meeting.

Evelyn turned to Elastigirl. "So, whaddya say?" she asked.

All eyes turned to Elastigirl, waiting for her response. "What do I say?" she said, **stall**ing and looking over at Mr. Incredible. She **chuckle**d. "I don't know."

5

Bob sat up in bed later that night, frowning as Helen **brush**ed her teeth in the bathroom. He **cringe**d with every *swoosh* of her toothbrush and finally called out the question he had been **stew**ing about since they'd left the Deavors. "Whaddya mean you *don't know?* A few hours before, you were saying it was over and being a Superhero was a **fantasy**! Now you get the offer of a **lifetime** and you *don't know!*"

"It's not that simple, Bob," Helen said. "I want to protect the kids—"

"So do I!" he **blurt**ed.

"—from **jail**, Bob!" Helen said, **spit**ting a **mouthful** of **toothpaste** into the **sink**.

"And how do you do that?" he asked. "By **turn**ing **down** a chance to change the law that **force**s them to hide what they are?"

Helen put down her toothbrush and walked into the bedroom, irritated by Bob's **refusal** to understand where she was coming from. "They haven't decided what they are!" she **yell**ed. "They're still kids—"

"Kids with powers, which makes them Supers— whether they decide to use those powers or not!" said Bob, **firm**ly **plant**ed in his opinion. "This will **benefit** them!"

"Maybe. In twenty years," Helen said, climbing into bed. "It's not a good time to be away," she said. "Dash is having trouble with homework. Vi is worried about her first date with that boy she likes—Tony. And Jack-Jack . . ." Her voice **trail**ed **off**.

Bob looked at her, waiting for her to finish the sentence. "Jack-Jack?" he said, **prompt**ing her to continue. "What's wrong with him?"

"Okay, nothing is wrong with Jack-Jack," she said. "But even a normal baby needs a lot of attention. I'm just not sure I can leave."

"Of course you can leave!" said Bob, **exasperate**d. "You've got to! So that I—we—can be Supers again! So our kids can have that choice!"

"So YOU can have that choice," Helen said with a **chuckle**.

"All right—yes," said Bob, admitting the truth. "So I can have that choice. And I would do a GREAT job, **regardless** of what Winston's pie charts★ say." He **pause**d. "But they want you." He took a deep breath as his face **twist**ed up, trying to spit out his words. "And you'll . . . do a great—job. Too."

Helen stared at him, **taking note of** his **miserable** expression and tone. "Well, that was **excruciating** to watch," she said with a smile.

Bob laughed.

"I can't lie to you—it's nice to be wanted," she

★ pie chart 원형 도표. 개별 항목을 전체에 대한 비율에 따라 원 내부의 면적을 분할한 파이(pie) 모양의 도표.

confessed. "To be taken seriously again after all this time. **Flatter**ing, you know? But . . ." She sighed as she **toss**ed the idea over in her mind.

"What's the choice?" said Bob, feeling like he was **point**ing **out** the **obvious**. "One: Do this right, get paid well, we're out of the motel, and things get better for all Supers—including our kids. Or two: I find a job in two weeks or we're **homeless**."

Helen knew what he was saying **made sense**, but she was still **uncertain** about whether it was the right thing to do. "You know it's crazy, right?" she said. "To help my family, I gotta leave it; to fix the law, I gotta break it."

"You'll be great," said Bob.

"I know I will," said Helen. "But what about you? We have kids."

"I'll watch the kids, no problem. Easy," said Bob.

Helen grinned. "Easy, huh?" she said, taking his hand. "You're **adorable**. Well, if there IS a problem, I'll drop this thing and come right back—"

"You won't need to," said Bob. "I got it. You go, do this thing." He rolled over, ready to get to sleep. "Do it so"—he paused and grinned—"I can do it better."

Helen **playful**ly hit him with her **pillow**. They said good night, knowing that in the morning she would call Winston to give him the news: Elastigirl was in.

6

A couple days later, the Parr family sat inside a **limousine** as it drove them over **lush** rolling hills and toward their new home. Helen spoke with Winston on the phone.

"We're partners now," he said. "Can't have my partners livin' in a motel."

"But who—whose house—is it a house?" Helen asked. Just then, up on a hill, an enormous modern **mansion** came into view. Dash's **jaw** dropped as he **took in** the **sight** of it. It **was a far cry from** the Safari Court Motel.

"It's my house," said Winston. "I have several; I'm not using that one. Stay as long as you need."

"I don't know what to say," said Helen, shocked.

"How about thanks!" said Bob.

They **hop**ped out of the limo and **rush**ed to the **front door**. As it **swung** open, the family stood for a moment, **staring**. With its high **ceilings**, **massive boulders**, indoor **fountains**, and **waterfalls**, it looked like the **luxurious lair** of a **high-profile spy**.

"THIS . . . is our new house?" said Dash, beyond **thrill**ed.

"Okay, easy, tiger—it's being **loan**ed to us," said Helen as they slowly **made their way** through, looking around.

"Ehhh, this is . . . **homey**," said Violet **sarcastic**ally, not nearly as taken as Dash.

"I mean, look at this place," said Bob. "Winston bought it from an **eccentric billionaire** who liked to come and go without being seen, so the house has **multiple** hidden **exit**s."

Eager to **explore**, Dash **zoom**ed away.

"Good thing we won't **stand out**," said Violet, her voice still **drip**ping with **sarcasm**. "Wouldn't want to **attract** any unnecessary attention."

"IT'S GOT A BIG **YARD**!" screamed Dash from outside.

Helen turned to Bob, a little **uncertain**. "This is . . . Isn't this a bit much?"

"NEAR A FOREST!" added Dash.

"Would you rather be at the motel?" Bob asked, knowing the answer.

"AND A **POOL**!" shouted Dash. They heard a loud *SPLASH* as Dash did a cannonball★ into the pool.

"What exactly IS Mom's new job?" asked Violet.

Instead of answering the question, Bob **remind**ed her that they were out of the motel.

Dash **zip**ped back in, **soak**ing wet, with a huge smile on his face. He shook himself dry, like a dog. Then he **notice**d a **remote control** hanging on the wall. He **grab**bed it and started **press**ing random buttons. Suddenly, a deep **hum**ming came from beneath the house as **section**s of the floor began to separate! The sections pulled apart like pieces of a **puzzle**, **reveal**ing more fountains and hidden

---

★cannonball 수영이나 다이빙 경기에서 양 무릎을 껴안고 물속으로 뛰어드는 동작을 말한다.

streams. Dash pressed another button and more secret **panel**s **part**ed, **unveil**ing a secret waterfall! The water **spill**ed from the ceiling and dropped in rolling patterns, falling into hidden pools beneath the floor.

"**WICKED** COOL!" he **exclaim**ed.

Just then, a large couch began to **tumble** into one of the streams in the floor. Dash **panic**ked and **poke**d at the button again—and the floor started closing on the couch, **crush**ing it! Bob and Helen shouted at him and he nervously pressed more buttons, but the floors continued to open and close, **bash**ing the couch. Finally, Dash **gave up**, **chuck**ing the remote and running off.

Later that day, Bob held Jack-Jack as Elastigirl **emerge**d from the bathroom wearing the new Super**suit** the Deavors had sent. It was a shiny gray, and patterned with light black **scale**s.

"This isn't me . . . ," she said, looking at herself in a full-length mirror. She turned, **assess**ing the suit from different **angle**s. "I'm not all dark and **angst**y. I'm

Elastigirl! I'm, ya know, **flexible!**"

"E **design**ed this?" asked Bob.

"No, some guy named Alexander Galbaki," she answered.

Bob **burst** out laughing at the thought of Edna seeing Elastigirl wearing another designer's suit. He knew she'd be **furious**. "Glad it's you and not me. 'Cause you're gonna hear from her." Then he handed her a card that had come with the Supersuit.

In **neat handwriting**, it read *Elastigirl, there's an accessory in the garage. –Evelyn*

Minutes later, Elastigirl and Bob entered the garage and saw a **gleam**ing, **high-tech** red motorcycle. Clearly designed **specific**ally for her, it was made of two separate unicycles,⋆ powered by a small **rocket**.

Elastigirl's eyes lit up. "A new Elasticycle . . . ," she said.

"I didn't know you had a bike," said Bob, surprised.

"Hey, I had a Mohawk,✱" she said. "There's a lot about me you don't know." Elastigirl sat on the bike

---

⋆unicycle 외발자전거. 한 개의 바퀴 위에 안장을 부착한 형태의 자전거.
✱Mohawk 머리 가운데에만 모발을 남겨두는 헤어스타일.

and felt a rush of excitement. She **activat**ed the **handles** and it **spark**ed to life, humming with power. A message appeared on the **dashboard**: HOPE YOU LIKE IT! —E.D.

She gave it a little gas and it **roar**ed, **spin**ning around in a tight **circle**. She hopped on one leg as it **swerve**d into a wall. "WHOA, WHOA—WHOA! OHHH!" she **shriek**ed. She stopped the bike. "Eh, I'll **get the hang of** it."

"You will be great," said Bob.

"I will be great," she said. "And you will, too."

"We will both be great," said Bob, smiling **confident**ly.

They said goodbye and Bob pressed a button on the wall. The garage door **slid** open and a thin waterfall rushed down, dividing the garage and the beautiful **landscape** outside. Elastigirl hit the **accelerator** and the waterfall created a hole that she zoomed through. Feeling a **mixture** of **pride** and **envy**, Bob stood holding Jack-Jack as he watched her **race** out onto the open road.

The next morning, he prepared breakfast for the kids. Jack-Jack sat in his high chair, **shoving cereal** into his mouth and dropping a lot on the floor. Dash started to fill a bowl with a **sugary** cereal called Sugar Bombs, but Bob grabbed the box out of his hands. "No Sugar Bombs **on my watch**." Dash **grumbl**ed as Bob **replace**d the sugary cereal with a more **reasonable** box of **Fiber** O's.

Dash **shrug**ged and asked where his mother was as he held up a **spoonful** of the **bland** cereal.

"She's up and out," answered Bob. "She's at her new job doing hero work."

"But I thought Superheroes were still **illegal**," said Violet.

"They are," said Bob. "For now," he added.

"So Mom is getting paid to break the law," Violet said, **amaze**d that neither of her parents saw anything wrong with this idea.

"She's an **advocate** for Superheroes," said Bob, trying to make it sound good. "It's a new job."

"So Mom is going out, illegally, to explain why she shouldn't be illegal," said Violet.

Bob **squirm**ed and looked out the window as he tried to think of how to get Violet to see it his way. He **brighten**ed when he saw the school bus arrive. "The bus is here!" he **cheer**ed.

With Super speed, Dash finished his cereal, **refill**ed a second bowl with Sugar Bombs, **wolf**ed it **down**, and grabbed his **backpack**. Violet headed for the door. Bob **stuff**ed a textbook into Dash's backpack before he raced out.

Relieved, Bob lifted Jack-Jack out of his high chair and **coo**ed, "Oh, we're gonna get along just fine, 'cause you don't ask any hard questions."

Jack-Jack **giggle**d and **babble**d happily.

7

Violet got ready that night for her date with Tony as Bob tried to put Jack-Jack to bed. He sat in an **easy chair** with Jack-Jack resting on his chest, **sleepily suck**ing on a bottle. Bob read him a bedtime story,★ and once Jack-Jack's head started to **droop**, Bob carefully closed the book, rose, and put him in his **crib**. Then he **tiptoe**d out of the room and **downstairs**.

Bob **collapse**d onto the **couch** and got ready to watch some television. As he **settle**d comfortably and **click**ed

---

★bedtime story 엄마나 아빠가 아이가 자기 전에 침대에서 들려주는 이야기.

on the remote, Dash appeared, holding up his math textbook. Bob **sigh**ed and clicked off the television. He got off the couch and **drag**ged himself over to sit with Dash at the kitchen table.

Bob **squint**ed as he read through the problems in the textbook and then reached for a pencil. He sat **sweat**ing. He **scrawl**ed some math **equation**s across a piece of **scrap** paper.

"That's not the way you're supposed to do it, Dad," said Dash, pointing to the solved problem in the book.

"I don't know that way," **snap**ped Bob. "Why would they change math? Math is math! MATH IS MATH!"

"Ehh—it's okay, Dad," said Dash, **let**ting his father **off the hook**. "I'll just wait for Mom to get back."

"What?" asked Bob, **offend**ed. "Well, she won't understand it any better than I do—" The television suddenly **blare**d from the other room. He went into the family room, **startle**d to find Jack-Jack sitting on the couch, using the remote to **flip through** the channels!

Bob took Jack-Jack back **upstairs**. He sat in the recliner*

★recliner 등받이가 뒤로 넘어가는 안락의자.

and read the bedtime story to the baby again. Bob **sank** lower and lower into the comfortable recliner until his head drooped to the side and he fell asleep. Jack-Jack **slap**ped him in the face a couple times to wake him up and start the story again.

Elastigirl sat on her cycle in New Urbem. She watched as a **crowd gather**ed in the center of the city, waiting to see the **unveil**ing of a new hovertrain.★ The **mayor** appeared at a **podium** and proudly gave a speech as he prepared to cut the ribbon and **declare** the train open to the public.

The Deavors sat **nearby** in a remote **edit**ing **suite**. They watched the live **footage** from Elastigirl's suit**cam** on monitors and communicated with her through a **headset**.

In an effort to find **crime**s to stop, the Deavors had suggested she listen to the police **scan**ner that was connected to her cycle. Even though she wasn't crazy about the idea, she turned up the volume on the scanner.

★hovertrain 자기부상열차. 자기력을 이용해 차량을 선로 위에 부상시켜 움직이는 열차. 선로와의 접촉이 없어 소음과 진동이 매우 적고 고속도를 유지할 수 있다.

"Are you sure the police are gonna be okay with this?" Elastigirl **whisper**ed into her headset.

"Sure, you're making life easy for them," replied Evelyn.

"They still haven't forgiven us for the last time we made life easy for them," said Elastigirl.

"With all due **respect**," said Evelyn, "if YOU had handled the Underminer, things would have been different."

Elastigirl chuckled.

"I'm just saying," Evelyn added.

The mayor continued his speech. "But I am happy to report that we are here today ahead of schedule, to **launch** our **magnificent** new hovertrain. It can get you where you need to go at **ridiculous** speeds. The future is open for business!"

The mayor cut the ribbon with a giant pair of **scissors**, and the crowd cheered. While a live band played **boisterous** music and a **storm** of **flashbulbs went off**, the doors to the hovertrain **slid** open. **Passenger**s **pour**ed inside and the train rose up, **hover**ing over the **track**. It began to pull out of the **station**, but then suddenly, it stopped, dropping back onto the track with a loud **thud**.

The crowd **murmur**ed, **confuse**d, as the train slowly rose above the track again. **Uncertain applause** filled the station, and the train began to move . . . but it was going backward! As the train **accelerate**d, the crowd's excitement turned to **terror**.

"It's going in the wrong direction!" Elastigirl shouted. She **took off** on her Elasticycle, and it moved with her every **stretch**, **separating** and coming together as she tried to **catch up** to the high-speed train. "This thing's really movin'!" she said. "Two hundred and climbing! How much track has been built?"

"About twenty-five miles,★" answered Evelyn.

"No one can **shut** this thing **down**?" asked Elastigirl.

"They've tried! No go!" **urge**d Evelyn.

"**Override**s?" asked Elastigirl.

"They're **lock**ed out of the system!" said Evelyn.

Elastigirl's mind raced as she tried to think of a way to stop the train. She knew the chances of her catching up to it were **slim** at best. "What about a **fail-safe**?"

★mile 거리의 단위 마일. 1마일은 약 1.6킬로미터이다.

"Not enough time!"

"Someone's calling!" said Elastigirl. "**Switch**ing over!" Elastigirl picked up her phone—it was Dash asking if she knew where his favorite sneakers were. In the **background**, she could hear Bob yelling, "DO NOT CALL YOUR MOTHER!"

"Dash, honey?" said Elastigirl. "Now's not a good time to talk!" She told him she would call him back, then switched back to Evelyn. "How much time?"

"Less than two minutes," Evelyn answered.

Elastigirl rode through **tunnel**s and onto **rooftop**s, trying to catch up to the train, until she finally managed to **land** directly on top of it. But before she could **figure out** her next move, she saw a tunnel approaching! She **hop**ped off her cycle, sending it **crash**ing into the side of the mountain as she **flatten**ed herself on top of the train. Elastigirl **clung** to it as it made its way through the tunnel. She **crawl**ed to the back of the train and she saw the **engineer** staring straight ahead. He didn't **blink** or move a **muscle** when she **bang**ed on the **windshield**, trying to get his attention.

Just as the train **was about to** race off the track, Elastigirl stretched herself into a **parachute** to slow it down. The train **bust**ed through a **construction barricade** and finally came to a stop as it **dangle**d over the end of the tracks!

Elastigirl ran through the **cabin, check**ing **on** the passengers. "Is everybody all right? Is anybody **injure**d?" she asked as she hurried through. Her eyes moved to the **opposite** end of the train, where she noticed an **odd pulsing** light coming from the engineer's cabin. She headed toward it.

Kicking down the door, she burst in and found the engineer blinking his eyes, as if coming back to **conscious**ness. "Your story better be good!" she said, helping him to his feet. Then she slapped him in the face to wake him up.

"Uh, where am I?" asked the engineer, **daze**d.

A message **flash**ed on the large monitor in the train's control panel: WELCOME BACK, ELASTIGIRL. —THE SCREENSLAVER

Then the screen went black.

8

For what felt like the hundredth time, Bob lowered Jack-Jack into his **crib** and turned off the reading lamp. The soft **glow** of the nightlight★ made the baby look **peaceful** and sweet. Bob **linger**ed, staring for a moment, then **flip**ped a table **upside down** and placed it over the crib. **Determine**d to keep Jack-Jack from climbing out, he put a **stack** of books on top of the table before heading **downstairs**.

On his way to the couch, Bob noticed Violet sitting

★ nightlight 복도, 계단, 어린이 방 등에 안전을 위해 밤중에 켜 놓는 조명.

with her head down. She had never left for her date.

"Honey, why are you—" he started.

"DON'T say anything," said Violet, **cut**ting him **off**.

Bob watched in silence as Violet **trudge**d off to her bedroom.

A moment later, he **knock**ed on her door. "Are you okay?" he asked.

"I'm fine," said Violet, her voice sounding flat and **irritate**d. "I don't want to talk about it."

"Tony didn't even call?" Bob asked gently.

"I DON'T wanna talk about it," repeated Violet. Bob tried to say something else, but Violet **interrupt**ed again. "Dad! If you want me to feel better, then leave me alone. Please?" Her voice **crack**ed.

Bob tried to think of something **comfort**ing to say but unable to, he stood silently. Finally, he headed back down to the family room. Before he reached the bottom of the stairs, he heard the television. His face dropped as he entered to find Jack-Jack, once again, sitting on the couch, holding the remote, **flick**ing through channels!

Finally **surrender**ing, Bob sat beside Jack-Jack and

soon fell asleep. Jack-Jack sucked on his bottle and watched an old **crime** movie. Bob **snore**d away as Jack-Jack took in every detail. A **mask**ed **rob**ber held a shop owner at **gunpoint** and **clean**ed **out** his **cash register**. Fully **enthrall**ed by the drama, Jack-Jack climbed down from the couch and **crawl**ed closer to the television, sitting right in front of it.

He turned to look at the sliding-glass door and saw a **raccoon rummaging** through the **garbage** can in the **backyard**. He looked at the masked robber **dig**ging through the cash register on television and then back at the raccoon. He **frown**ed. The raccoon noticed Jack-Jack staring and let out a **fierce hiss**, showing off its sharp teeth. Jack-Jack babbled at it angrily.

The raccoon turned its attention back to the half-eaten chicken leg it had taken from the garbage can. Jack-Jack **toddle**d to the door and pressed his hands against the glass . . . then passed right through it! Standing on his little feet, he grabbed the chicken leg from the raccoon and **toss**ed it back into the garbage can. *CLANG!* He used his mind to make the **lid float** into the air and back onto the can.

Jack-Jack unleashed **multiple** Super powers as he **took on** the raccoon, **wrestling**, **punch**ing, and kicking it. He giggled as laser **beam**s suddenly came out of his eyes and shot at the raccoon. Trying to escape the lasers, the raccoon jumped onto the patio* umbrella and **clung** to it. The umbrella snapped closed, **trap**ping the raccoon inside. Jack-Jack pointed his lasers at the umbrella's **pole**, **slicing** it in half! The raccoon tumbled into Jack-Jack just as the baby Superhero turned **goop**y and **sticky**. The raccoon was stuck to him, unable to move!

CRASH! Bob was **awaken**ed by the loud noises on the patio. He saw Jack-Jack and the raccoon **brawl**ing in the backyard and rushed outside to stop the fight. When he reached for Jack-Jack, the baby **display**ed another Super power—he **multiplied**! Suddenly, there were a half-**dozen** Jack-Jacks all over the **yard**!

"No, no, no! NO! NO! NO! NO!" Bob screamed as he tried to **scoop** up all the babies. Then each one

---

★patio 파티오. 집의 뒤쪽에 만드는 테라스.

vibrated and merged back into a single Jack-Jack. The raccoon paused before taking off. It fixed its gaze on Jack-Jack and let out a long hiss, crinkling its nose and baring its teeth. Jack-Jack giggled at it, waving his fist in the air.

"You . . . have . . . POWERS! Yeah, BABY!" Bob cheered. He inspected Jack-Jack. "And there's not a scratch on you!" He looked at the sliding-glass door and remembered he had unlocked it to get outside. "Did you go through the locked door?" he asked, laughing loudly. "Who can multiply like rabbits and go right through any . . . solid . . . Oh . . . my God." The consequences of Jack-Jack's powers finally settled in, and Bob realized how disastrous it could be. Before he spiraled into full panic mode, the phone rang.

He picked it up. "Hello?" he said.

It was Helen calling from her hotel room. Bob tried to hide his shock and confusion over what he had just witnessed. Jack-Jack babbled in the background and Bob set him on the floor.

"Sounds like I just woke you up," said Helen.

"No, no, it's just—Jack-Jack—"

"He had an accident!" said Helen, cutting him off. "I knew it! I'm coming home right now. I never should've—"

"No, no! No accident. Stay there and finish your **mission**," said Bob. "And you 'never should've' what? You don't think I can do this?" He was suddenly **defensive**.

"Sorry," said Helen. "I **misspoke**." She took a breath. "Do you need me to come back?" she asked.

"No, no, no," said Bob. "I've got this. Everything's GREAT."

"What happened with Jack-Jack?" Helen asked.

"Nothing. He's in excellent health," answered Bob.

Violet **march**ed into the room, **sob**bing quietly.

Helen asked Bob about Violet's date. "Uh . . ." He **stall**ed as he watched Violet head straight for the **fridge** with her head down. She **methodical**ly **remove**d a **tub** of ice cream from the **freezer**, grabbed a big spoon from the **silverware drawer**, and trudged back **upstairs**, still **weep**ing. "Good. All fine and . . . good," he said quickly.

"And Jack-Jack **went down** with no trouble?" Helen asked.

Bob turned to see Jack-Jack pressed against the sliding-glass door, **glaring** at the raccoon. It had returned and was hissing at Jack-Jack. "Fine. Yes. No trouble," he said, putting his hand over the **receiver**.

"And Dash got his homework done?" asked Helen.

Bob **glance**d toward the dining room to see Dash sitting at the table, **slump**ed over his math textbook, sleeping. "All done," he lied.

"So things didn't spiral out of control the moment I left?" asked Helen.

"**Amazing** as it may seem," said Bob, "it has been quite un**eventful**, in fact. How about you?"

"I SAVED A **RUNAWAY** TRAIN!" **shriek**ed Helen, happy to finally burst with her exciting news. "It was SO GREAT!" She told Bob every detail of her **rescue**. He picked up the remote and turned on the television, **surf**ing through the channels. He watched, frowning, as various **anchor**s reported on Elastigirl's big rescue. The story was everywhere.

"I'm on this runaway super train full of **passenger**s going backward at 200, 250, 300 miles per hour, and I pull this **sucker** into the station!" she **rambl**ed. "**BOOM**! NO **CASUALTIES**!" She **squeal**ed, **delight**ed. Bob clicked off the television. "I'm telling ya, honey, it was a **SAGA**!"

"That's **fantastic**." Bob was really proud of her, but he couldn't deny the fact that he was also very **jealous**. He missed doing hero work . . . and having all the reporters talk about *his* great rescues. "I'm so proud of you," he said as he **bang**ed his head against a wall.

"I'm proud of *you,* honey," said Helen. "I know you want to get out there, and you will—soon. And you'll be amazing. I couldn't have done this if you hadn't **taken over** so well. Thanks for handling everything."

They said good night, and Bob **hung up** the phone. He looked at Dash **slumber**ing at the table, then at Jack-Jack, who was now **fast asleep, lean**ing against the sliding-glass door. He gently picked up both boys and carried them upstairs to their bedrooms. Then Bob went to bed.

Even though he was completely **exhaust**ed, he **toss**ed **and turn**ed. *"'Eh, Dad, it's okay,'"* he **grumbl**ed, repeating Dash's words. *"'I'll just wait for Mom to get back'*—as if only she could do it. *I* know how to do math," Bob said to himself. He checked the clock. It was a little after two a.m. He sighed, sat up, and headed downstairs, determined to **tackle** the **challenge**. *"'Wait for Mom.'* What am I? A **substitute** parent?"

A few minutes later, he was in the kitchen. He poured himself a cup of coffee and sat at the kitchen table with Dash's math book in front of him. He put on his glasses and began to read.

Dash was **sound asleep** when Bob gently woke him a few hours later. "I think I understand your math **assign**ment," he **whisper**ed. Dash tossed the **sheet**s over his head and **groan**ed. "We still have some time to finish it before your test."

Moments later, Bob, with a big cup of coffee, and Dash, with a glass of juice, sat at the kitchen table **go**ing **over** the math assignment, problem by problem. As Bob explained, Dash **nod**ded, **scribbling** with his pencil, working to solve the **equation**s.

"You got it?" Bob asked after he was done.

Dash smiled.

"Yeah, baby!" cheered Bob. They **clink**ed glasses,

and Bob sent Dash to get dressed for school. With a big **grin**, he closed the math book and put it into Dash's **backpack**. *"'Wait for Mom.'"* He **chuckle**d to himself.

9

While Bob was getting Violet and Dash off for another day of school, the Deavors and Elastigirl headed to the KQRY television studio for Elastigirl's interview with news **anchor** Chad Brentley. They sat in the **greenroom** watching Chad's live interview with a foreign **ambassador**. A **makeup** artist **powder**ed Elastigirl's face, preparing her for the camera. Elastigirl admitted she was a bit nervous. It had been a long time since she was last interviewed. Deavor tried to **boost** her confidence with a few **positive** words before a **stagehand** appeared.

"Ms. Elastigirl? They're ready for you."

Winston and Evelyn wished her luck, and Elastigirl followed the stagehand into the **hallway**. As they walked toward the set, the ambassador, **flank**ed by her **security** team, approached.

"Oh!" said Elastigirl. "**Madam** Ambassador, hello!" She **was about to** introduce herself when the ambassador pushed past her **guard**s to shake Elastigirl's hand.

"You are Elastigirl!" the ambassador said. She looked **tickle**d to see her. "It was so sad when you went **underground**, and I am glad to see you are back in your shiny **outfit**!"

"That means so much coming from you," said Elastigirl. "Good luck with your speech! Bring . . . **last**ing peace!"

As the ambassador's guards started leading her away, she called, "I will—when you **defeat evil**!"

Moments later, Elastigirl was sitting next to Chad on the set. She smiled as he introduced her.

"For over fifteen years, Superheroes have been in hiding, **force**d into it by a society no longer **willing** to **support** them. That may soon be changing, **due to** a growing movement to bring the Supers back. Here, **fresh on the heels of** her own **heroic** save of a **runaway** train, and **sport**ing a new look, is the Superhero Elastigirl. Welcome!"

"Hello, Chad," said Elastigirl, trying to **settle** in.

"Well, all the **poll**s are going in your direction," said Chad.

"That's true. Things are good—"

Suddenly, Chad's eyes **glaze**d over and his **tone shift**ed as he interrupted Elastigirl. "Hello," he said.

"Uh . . . hello," said Elastigirl, a little confused.

"Do I have your attention?" asked Chad in a **robotic** voice.

Elastigirl looked at her interviewer, trying to read his face, and **notice**d a strange flashing-light pattern **reflect**ed in his eyes.

"Of course I do," said Chad **mechanical**ly. "I'm appearing on your screen. Reading the words I'm saying off another screen."

Elastigirl followed his gaze to the teleprompter,★ where she caught a **glimpse** of **hypnotic** light patterns

---

★teleprompter 텔레프롬프터. 원고 내용을 원하는 속도와 형태로 모니터에 나오게 할 수 있는 장치.

blazing across the screen. She started to fall under its **spell**, but **avert**ed her eyes just **in time, break**ing **free**.

"Screens are everywhere," Chad continued. "We are **control**led by screens."

Elastigirl hurried into the studio's control room, where she saw everyone there **frozen, transfix**ed by the **dazzling** lights flashing across all the screens.

The Screenslaver appeared on the monitors. He wore big, round **goggle**s over a large **hood** that **cover**ed his face. "And screens are controlled by me. The Screenslaver," he added.

Elastigirl **yell**ed at the **crew**, but they stayed **absolute**ly still, **mesmerize**d by their screens.

"I control this **broadcast**, and this **idiot**ic anchorman you see before you," continued Chad.

Evelyn hurried over to Elastigirl. "The **signal**'s been **hijack**ed!" she yelled. "I'll **check** it **out!**"

Elastigirl ran back to the set and **rush**ed to Chad, trying to slap him out of his **trance**.

"I could hijack the ambassador's **aerocade** while it's still **airborne**, right, Elastigirl?" Chad asked in his robotic voice.

Elastigirl **sprint**ed off the set and into the hallway. "NEAREST WINDOW! WHERE'S THE NEAREST WINDOW?" she shouted. A **frighten**ed **assistant gesture**d toward a door, and Elastigirl **dash**ed through it. **Spot**ting a window at the end of another hallway, Elastigirl **grab**bed a chair and **flung** it, **shatter**ing the glass. She stretched and **propel**led herself out the window.

Chad's trance seemed to break as he blinked and **stare**d at the camera, **bewilder**ed. In the control room, the **pulsing** lights stopped and the crew **snap**ped out of their trances, too. They looked at their screens and saw Chad looking at the empty chair where Elastigirl had been sitting, wondering where she had gone.

Elastigirl stretched upward, using the buildings to pull herself to a high **rooftop**. She **scan**ned the **horizon** and spotted three helicopters in the **distance**. Then she stretched herself across two buildings, grabbing onto each one, creating a giant **slingshot** with her body. She **aim**ed for one of the helicopters, pulled herself all the way back, and **release**d, shooting into the sky! The force of it **smash**ed her right through the window of the **chopper** and she **tumble**d inside . . . but the ambassador wasn't there.

Elastigirl hurried into the **cockpit**, and the **pilot** yelled, "This is a **restrict**ed **aircraft!**"

"Too late!" she yelled back. "They've been **compromise**d!" She told the pilot the ambassador was in danger and asked him which chopper she was in. Suddenly, a helicopter **blade slice**d through the cockpit, **barely** missing their heads! Elastigirl **figure**d the ambassador must be in that one, and told the pilot to get her close to it. "Get to safety!" she added. "I'll find the ambassador. And don't look at the screens!"

The pilot flew as close as possible and Elastigirl **leap**ed out, **swing**ing to the other helicopter's window. She pulled herself through as a **bullet** flew by, just missing her! A security guard held a gun, with the **terrified** ambassador at his side.

"**Stand down!**" **insist**ed the ambassador. "It's Elastigirl!"

The guard lowered his gun, and Elastigirl entered the **cabin**. Turning to the ambassador, she said, "Stay in your seat, ma'am!" Then she tried to open the door to the cockpit, but it was locked. She stretched to grab the security guard's gun and shot the lock off, opening it. Inside were two **hypnotized** pilots, sitting **rigid**ly at the controls. She quickly punched the screens to break them, releasing the pilots from their trance. They looked completely confused, but there was no time to explain. Elastigirl spotted the third chopper coming straight for them. "GET DOWN!" she shouted.

The helicopter crashed into them, and they **careen**ed toward a building! Elastigirl grabbed the controls and pulled up, barely missing it. "Open the door!" she yelled, **struggling** to gain control of the chopper.

"Do as she says!" the ambassador cried.

The cockpit door opened, and Elastigirl yelled to the pilots, "Can you guys swim?' They both nodded, and Elastigirl stretched a leg back, kicking them out of the helicopter and into the river below. Then she turned to the ambassador. "We're too low to **parachute**! We're gonna have to slingshot. **Hang on**! Trust me!"

"I trust you!" shouted the ambassador.

Holding on to the ambassador, Elastigirl stretched herself and snapped back to propel the two of them toward the clouds. Once they were high enough, she **flatten**ed and **expand**ed her body, **turn**ing **into** a giant parachute. They gently **drift**ed down to the ground.

"Are you all right, ma'am?" asked Elastigirl.

"I'm fine," said the ambassador. Then she **faint**ed in Elastigirl's arms.

The morning after Elastigirl's **daring rescue**, Dash and Jack-Jack were busy eating breakfast. Bob prepared a **plate** for Violet as he heard her coming down the stairs.

Violet felt **awful**. The day before at school, she had asked Tony why he had missed their date, but he acted like she was a complete stranger.

"Boys are **jerk**s, and Superheroes **suck**," she said, **collapsing** into her chair.

"Good morning!" said Bob, handing her a plate of waffles.★

"He takes one look at me in that **suit** and decides to

pretend he doesn't even know me," Violet said.

"Well, he's protecting himself," said Bob, **pour**ing her some orange juice. "If he really did see you, it's best that he forget." He headed over to the **refrigerator** and opened the door, placing the juice back inside. "I can't tell you how many memories Dicker's had to **erase** over the years, when"—Bob pulled out the milk **container** and **sniff**ed it, **assess**ing whether it was still okay to drink—"someone **figure**d **out** your mother's or my **identity**." He closed the refrigerator door and was surprised to see Violet standing right in front of him.

"It was Dicker!" she **growl**ed, **seething**. "You told him about Tony!"

"Honey—" started Bob, feeling **guilty**.

"You had me erased from Tony's mind!" she yelled.

Violet **stomp**ed off. Jack-Jack watched her go, looked at Bob, and **dump**ed his bowl of **cereal** over his head, laughing. Bob cleaned the cereal from the floor as Violet returned, holding her Supersuit.

★waffle 와플. 밀가루, 달걀, 우유, 설탕 등을 섞은 반죽을 바둑판무늬가 있는 틀에 넣어 구운 것.

"I HATE Superheroes, and I **renounce** them!" she shouted. Then she **march**ed over to the kitchen **sink** and **stuff**ed the suit into the **garbage disposal**. She turned the disposal on and the suit **spun** around and around—but stayed completely un**damage**d. **Furious**, Violet **bit** into the suit and pulled at it, trying to **rip** it apart. The suit was **indestructible**. Bob and Dash watched as Violet finally let out a **frustrate**d shriek, threw the suit against the wall, and stomped off again.

Dash looked at Bob. "Is she having **adolescence**?" he asked.

Bob **sigh**ed in the **affirmative** and **hung his head**.

Meanwhile, Elastigirl sat in the back of a **limousine**. As it **pull**ed **up** to DevTech, a **crowd** began **chant**ing outside.

"**KABOOM! KAPOW!** SUPERS SHOULD BE **LEGAL** NOW!"

Elastigirl asked the driver what was going on.

"They're here in support," he replied.

"Support of what?" she asked.

"Well, in support of you."

Elastigirl **exit**ed the car, and a **cheer erupt**ed as the **adoring** crowd reached out, trying to shake her hand. She couldn't believe she had **inspire**d so many people.

"Thanks for coming!" she said. She **crouch**ed down to shake a little girl's hand and noticed her **sign**. It read THE SCREENSLAVER IS STILL OUT THERE. Suddenly, all the joy she felt from the **outpouring** of **admiration** disappeared. She knew it was true. She still had a **villain** to catch.

Elastigirl entered Winston's office to find him busy answering calls. He handed her one of the newspapers **scatter**ed across his desk, pointing out a **headline**: SAVED AMBASSADOR GIVES PRO-SUPER★ SPEECH.

"It's working!" he said. He told Elastigirl that he was getting calls from all over the world. Then he told her about the next **phase**. "We're going to have a **summit** at sea! We'll use our **yacht**! We'll **gather** leaders and Supers from all over the world. . . ."

Elastigirl said she was happy to hear it, but she

★pro- '찬성하는'이라는 뜻을 나타내는 접두사.

sounded pretty **glum**. When Winston asked her what was wrong, she said she was **upset** that she hadn't caught the Screenslaver.

He told her she should take time to **appreciate** the victories. "What do you want on your **tombstone**? 'She worried a lot'?" he asked.

"All right, stop talking," said Evelyn. "Show her."

Winston smiled and nodded. Then he led Elastigirl into a room full of Supers. She didn't **recognize** any of them, but they were all wearing Supersuits, many of which looked **homemade**. When she entered, they erupted in excitement, **applauding** and looking at her with great **respect**.

One woman rushed up and **awkward**ly introduced herself. "I—my Superhero name is Voyd. I just want to thank you for, like, for being you, and . . . I just, like . . . Okay, what I can do, um, is this. . . ." **Blush**ing, the woman grabbed a **mug** from a table. She flung it into the air, and as it dropped, she used her Super power to create a series of portals.★ The mug fell in and out of them as

---

★portal 포털. 공상 과학 영화나 소설 등에 등장하는 가상의 통로로, 시공간을 뛰어넘는 별도의 두 공간을 연결한다.

Voyd continued to **show off** her special skill. Finally, the mug fell out of the last portal and **land**ed back on the desk where it had started. There was a moment of silence as everyone in the room **took in** what they'd just seen. Then they **broke out** in **applause**.

"That's **fantastic**," said Elastigirl.

"I felt like an **outcast**," said Voyd. "Before. But now, with you being . . . you, I feel like . . ." Too **emotional** to finish her sentence, Voyd **hug**ged Elastigirl. "**Yay**, me," she added.

Elastigirl was truly **touched**.

"I flew them in from all over," said Winston. "They've all been in hiding. They have powers, secret identities, and names they've given themselves."

The Supers were **ecstatic** to meet Elastigirl and share their stories.

"I'm Screech," said one Super, who **resemble**d an **owl**. "I've always considered you the **gold standard** for Superheroes."

"Well, thanks!" said Elastigirl, **flatter**ed. "You're too nice!"

"I am called Brick," said a large woman with a serious expression. Elastigirl asked her where she was from, and she answered, "Wisconsin.★"

Another Super named He-lectrix explained his powers. "You know, **zap**ping things **electronic**ally, **charging** things, **bolt**s of **lightning**, that kinda stuff."

An older man approached. "Name's Reflux,✲" he said. "Medical condition or Super power? You decide. . . ." He laughed, and Elastigirl chuckled along with him. "That's a little line I say just to put people at ease. Hope I don't **offend**."

"Oh, no no no, that's fantastic," Elastigirl said.

The Supers **hung out**, **chat**ting away as the time flew by. Elastigirl couldn't believe what a **positive impact** she had made on these people. She felt proud of her decision to take the job to make Supers legal again, and that felt great.

Once the party started **wind**ing **down** and Winston

★Wisconsin 위스콘신주(州). 미국 오대호 서쪽에 있는 주. 세계적인 낙농 지대이며, 목재, 가구 등의 공업도 발달하였다.
✲reflux 위산 역류라는 의학적 질병을 나타내기도 한다. 이를 활용하여 용암을 뱉는 자신의 능력에 대해 농담했다.

bid everyone a good night, Elastigirl and Evelyn sat down together for a drink.

"It must be nice for you. Being out front after all this time," said Evelyn.

"Out front?" asked Elastigirl.

"Well, it's been a while since your Superhero days. And even then, you were kind of in Mr. Incredible's shadow," said Evelyn.

Elastigirl smiled. "Oh, **I beg to differ**," she replied. Then she asked Evelyn how she felt about her brother running DevTech.

"I don't want his job. I **invent**; he sells," said Evelyn.

The two continued to chat until an idea **pop**ped into Elastigirl's mind. She knew how to **capture** the Screenslaver! "I need to lock onto a **signal** and **trace** its **origin**."

Elastigirl and Evelyn **work**ed **out** the details. Evelyn would create a **track**ing **device**. Then they would schedule a **remote** interview with Chad Brentley and set a **trap** for the Screenslaver.

The two women **bump**ed fists, more than ready to **carry out** their plan.

11

Back at home, Bob picked up the phone and **dial**ed as he un**pack**ed a few moving boxes. Dicker answered, and Bob asked him if he remembered **wiping** Tony's mind.

"Yeah," said Dicker. "Nice kid."

"Well, you also wiped out the Friday-night date my daughter had with him. In fact, you wiped out my daughter," Bob said.

"**Oops**. Not an exact science, Bob," said Dicker.

"Rick, you gotta help me here," said Bob. "Violet hates me. And you. And Superheroes. I gotta fix this. What do you know about Tony?"

Dicker had already moved to his **filing cabinet** and was **thumb**ing **through** the files. He found Tony's. He opened it and quickly scanned it. "Not much. Seems like a good kid. Popular. Plays sports. Music. Parents own the Happy Platter. Kid works there **part-time**."

"Happy . . . Platter . . . ?" said Bob, **concoct**ing an idea. He thanked Dicker for his time and **hung up** the phone, turning his attention back to unpacking.

Later that evening, Bob gathered the kids and took them out to the Happy Platter restaurant. It was a **modest** place with wood **panel**ing and linoleum* floors.

Violet looked around, a bit **confuse**d. "Why did we drive all the way across town for the Happy Platter?" asked Violet.

Bob faced the **hostess**. "We'd like a **booth** over there, near the philodendron,* " he said, **ignoring** Violet's question.

The hostess **nod**ded un**enthusiastic**ally, grabbed some menus, and led them toward the booth.

★ linoleum 리놀륨. 두꺼운 종이 모양으로 눌러 편 실내 바닥에 까는 재료. 내구성, 내열성, 탄력성 등이 뛰어나다.
✤ philodendron 필로덴드론. 브라질과 서인도제도가 원산지인 덩굴성의 관엽식물.

As they followed her, Violet added, "This **platter** doesn't look all that happy to me. It looks . . . **bored**,"

"Ha! The Bored Platter," said Dash.

"I thought Vi would want a **change of pace** from drive-in* food," said Bob.

"I like drive-in food," said Violet.

"Does this mean vegetables?" asked Dash.

"A **balance**d **diet** means vegetables, kiddo. Get used to it," said Bob.

Their **server** arrived with a **pitcher** of water and began **pour**ing it into red plastic tumblers.* Violet took a **sip** as the server said, "Good evening, everyone." She looked up and **gag**ged, water **spurt**ing out of her nose. It was Tony Rydinger!

"Whoa! Hey, Violet, are you okay?" asked Bob.

"EWWW!" **exclaim**ed Dash.

"Is she all right?" asked Tony. He handed her some napkins and tried to make her feel less **embarrass**ed by saying, "It's okay, it's fine, happens all the time."

★ drive-in 차에 탄 채로 음식을 주문하고 받을 수 있는 식당.
✻ tumbler 음료수를 마시는 데 쓰는 밑이 편평한 잔.

"I'm okay. I'm fine," said Violet, wishing she could use her **invisibility** power and disappear.

Bob asked for more napkins.

"Maybe she needs something bigger," said Dash. "Like a towel."

Tony pulled a **wad** of napkins from his pocket, and he and Bob helped **mop** up the water. Violet lowered her head, letting her hair fall around her face, trying to hide as she continued to **cough**.

"Normally she doesn't ever **drip** like this," said Bob.

Tony looked at Bob. "Would, uhh . . . would you like water, sir?"

Violet coughed and coughed as Tony filled Bob's glass to the top.

"This is my daughter," said Bob. "Who you must know, right?"

"God. Stop," said Violet **under her breath**.

"Hello," said Tony, facing Violet.

"Violet . . ."

"Hello, Violet," said Tony.

"Hey, Vi, say hi to—"

"Don't push it, Dad," Violet said, **interrupt**ing him through **grit**ted teeth.

"I'm Dash, her little brother." Dash reached over and shook Tony's hand.

"This is really good water," said Bob enthusiastically. "It's very **refresh**ing. **Spring** water, is it?"

"I don't know, sir. I think it's **tap**," said Tony.

"Well, it is very good," repeated Bob.

"Excellent tap," said Dash, raising his glass to Tony.

Unable to **handle** another **mortify**ing second, Violet excused herself, got up from the table, and walked away.

Tony smiled at Bob, Dash, and Jack-Jack. "Nice to meet you," he said. Then he walked off.

"Well, where'd SHE go?" asked Bob.

"To find a good place to be angry?" said Dash.

12

Inside the KQRY television studio, Chad Brentley introduced his special remote interview with Elastigirl.

"How you feeling, Chad?" asked Elastigirl, her voice coming through a speaker.

"I'm fine—the doctors **check**ed me **out**," he said. "I have NO memory of the event. I gotta tell you, it's pretty strange to see a **record**ing of yourself from the night before and have no **recollect**ion." Chad then told the viewers that the studio had taken **additional precaution**s to **prevent** the Screenslaver from attacking again. Continuing with the interview, he asked Elastigirl where she was.

"On a case," she said. "In a **secure** undisclosed **location**." **Unbeknownst** to Chad, Elastigirl sat directly on top of the studio, on a large **transmission** tower. She watched the news show on her **handheld device**.

Chad showed a **clip** taken from Elastigirl's suit**cam** during the hovertrain **rescue**. Viewers watched from her point of view as she **sprang** into action, jumping onto her Elasticycle and **taking off** after the train. Then the **footage** suddenly became **fuzzy** as the **newscast** turned to **static** and the Screenslaver appeared!

"The Screenslaver interrupts this program for an important **announce**ment," he said. His voice sounded deep and **warp**ed, as if it had been **electronic**ally **alter**ed.

Elastigirl studied the screen of her handheld tracker as it worked to locate the source of the Screenslaver's transmission. Once it was **lock**ed in, Elastigirl looked in the direction of the signal and **whisper**ed, "Gotcha."

Inside DevTech, the Deavors both watched with **anticipation**. "I'll be—" said Evelyn. "She knew. . . ."

"Let's see if your **gadget** works," said Winston.

Elastigirl continued to check the tracker as she followed it toward the Screenslaver's location. She **stretch**ed across **rooftop**s and **vault**ed herself from one building to the next as she followed the signal.

"Don't **bother** watching the rest," said the Screenslaver, still on the screen. "Elastigirl doesn't **save the day**; she only **postpone**s her **defeat**." He **went on** to **rant** about how people use screens because they're lazy. And how they want Superheroes to **take care of** them so they don't have to take care of themselves. "Go ahead, send your Supers to stop me. **Grab** your **snack**s, watch your screen, and see what happens. You are no longer in **control**. I am."

Elastigirl **fire**d herself like a **slingshot** to the top of a building in a dark part of the city. Thousands of **antennae** **jut**ted out of the rooftops, **mess**ing with her signal, but luckily, she was close to her **destination**. She followed the tracker to the side of an apartment building and faced a window **cover**ed in thick wrought iron* bars.

★wrought iron 연철. 탄소를 0.2% 이하로 함유하며, 철선이나 못을 만드는 데에 쓴다.

Flattening herself, she **slip**ped through the bars and got into the building. She hurried along a **hallway** and approached the apartment where the Screenslaver's transmission was coming from.

Stretching out her arm, she **snake**d it beneath the door and unlocked it. The apartment looked like a **messy laboratory** with **tools**, **lens**es, and **masks strew**n about. Elastigirl walked through it, **inspect**ing all the stuff **scatter**ed around: plans for the hovertrain, **sketch**es of helicopters, **scientific** textbooks, and **tatter**ed notebooks. Then she **notice**d a piece of **fabric** covering something on a table. She walked toward it and lifted it to **reveal** a pair of **goggles strap**ped to a **mannequin** head.

"Find anything interesting?" a voice asked. The Screenslaver appeared behind her with an electronic tool. He **slam**med the door, locking them both in a large **wire cage**, and **zap**ped her with his Taser!★ Then he **flick**ed on **hypnotic** lights that were scattered on the cage walls. The bright lights **blink**ed and **swirl**ed in a **mesmerizing**

★Taser 전기 충격기. 작은 쇠화살을 쏘아 전기 충격을 가하는 무기로, Taser사에서 판매한다.

pattern. Elastigirl tried to **shield** her eyes, but he zapped her again. She fought back hard and managed to push him out of the cage.

They continued **battling** inside the apartment, **crash**ing into bookshelves and furniture, until finally, the Screenslaver escaped through the door, **activating** a timer on his way out.

As Elastigirl took off after him, the Screenslaver **yank**ed on one of the building's fire **alarm**s and it let out a **blaring** sound. **Ceiling sprinkler**s rained down as people ran out of their apartments, creating **chaos** around the **chase**. Just as she **was about to** reach the Screenslaver, he **slid** down an elevator **shaft** and onto a **roof**. Then he **leap**ed off the building! But Elastigirl was right behind him. She stretched herself into a **parachute**, grabbed the Screenslaver in **midair**, and **float**ed down with him. As she did, the timer **went off** and the apartment building **explode**d behind them! They landed and Elastigirl **rip**ped off his mask.

"Elastigirl?" he said, confused. "Wh-what happened?"

"What happened is you destroyed my **evidence**," she

said, **irritate**d, looking over at the **level**ed apartment building.

Moments later, Elastigirl watched as the **cop**s took the Screenslaver away in **handcuff**s. "What's going on?" he asked, sounding **puzzle**d.

"That's right, **punk**. **Blame** the system," said the cop.

Elastigirl pulled her **emblem** away from her chest, looking down at the suitcam. "Your tracker **work**ed **like a charm**," she said, knowing Evelyn was watching. "You're a **genius**."

"Aw, **shucks**," said Evelyn, **chuckling**. "I'm just the genius behind the genius."

They both smiled, feeling great—their plan had worked!

In the Parr house, Bob looked **daze**d as he watched TV with Jack-Jack. Suddenly, Dash **burst** in.

"Hey, Dad," he said, holding up his math textbook. "We're doing **fraction**s and demicels and **percentage**s, and I don't get 'em."

Bob **rub**bed his eyes. "Didn't we get all **caught up**?"

"Yeah, we WERE caught up, and now we're doing fractions and percentages and demicels."

"**Decimal**s," Bob said.

A news story **flash**ed on the television, catching Bob's attention. A reporter **announce**d, "Superheroes are back in the news again, and so is their **gear**. The car collection of **billionaire** Victor Cachet grew a little bit more SUPER today with the addition of the INCREDIBILE, the Super car once driven by Superhero Mr. Incredible."

"It's the kind of thing you buy when you have everything else," said the **smug** billionaire, standing beside the **gleam**ing Incredibile.

"They said it was beyond repair," said Bob, **staring** at the television.

"And hey, it was in perfect condition," added the billionaire, **tap**ping the **hood** of the **amazing vehicle**.

"You used to drive THAT?" asked Dash.

"They said it was destroyed," said Bob, his anger growing by the second.

"Long thought lost or destroyed, the famous car **turn**ed **up** at a **private auction**," said the reporter.

"They said it was—THAT'S MY CAR!" **yell**ed Bob, finally **releasing** his **fury**. He **bolt**ed from the room.

SPLASH! Bob fell into one of the hidden rivers in the floor of the house. **Grumbling**, he pulled himself out of the water and **march**ed into the **den**. **Soak**ing wet, he began **rummaging** through some boxes until he finally found what he was looking for: the **remote** control to the Incredibile!

Bob ran back to the television with Dash **on his heels**.

The reporter turned to the Incredibile's new owner. "This car's just *loaded* with amazing **gadget**s. Care to **demonstrate**?"

Victor Cachet smiled. "I'd love to, but we haven't **figure**d **out** how to make them work yet."

Bob **press**ed the remote and the Incredibile **roar**ed to life! The reporter and Victor looked at the car, both **stun**ned as it **spun** around and around.

"WOW!" said Dash. "IT WORKS?"

Dash **snatch**ed the remote from Bob and pressed a button. On the screen, people **dove** out of the way as **dual rocket launch**ers **emerge**d from the car's grill.★

"WHAT ARE YOU DOING?" said Bob, **retrieving** the remote. He pressed another button and the rocket launchers **retract**ed.

★ grill 그릴. 라디에이터의 앞에 격자 모양으로 설치되어 통풍구 역할을 하는 장치.

"THIS IS NOT A TOY!" yelled Bob. "That's a rocket launcher!"

"Sweeeet!" said Dash, snatching back the remote. "Which one launches the rockets?"

"HEY! This is not your car!"

"It's not your car either!" said Dash, **gesturing** to the television.

"It is SO! It's the Incredibile!"

"Well, why's that guy have it?" asked Dash.

"Well, he SHOULDN'T!" Bob said. He grabbed the remote back and pressed another button. The rocket launchers reappeared. Dash tried to grab the remote, but Bob kept it from him.

"Launch the rockets!" **chant**ed Dash.

"I'm not launching anything!" said Bob. "Do you think I want an angry rich guy coming after me right now? When I'm trying not to . . . **distract** . . . your . . . mother?"

Everyone on the news show had taken cover from the suddenly dangerous car. Bob **grunt**ed as he pressed the remote again, **power**ing **down** the Incredibile.

"So . . . you're not gonna **blow** up the rich guy's wall?" asked Dash.

Bob **sank** into the sofa next to Jack-Jack. *ACHOO!* Jack-Jack **sneeze**d and suddenly flew across the room and up the stairs with a **jet** of smoke coming out of his nose and mouth! **Intangible** as a ghost, he disappeared through the wall, leaving a **smolder**ing ring of fire.

"AHHHH!" **Upstairs** in her room, Violet screamed. Jack-Jack sneezed again and Violet appeared, running from Jack-Jack, who was now a little red monster!

"What the heck★ is that?" **shriek**ed Violet.

Jack-Jack smiled, **show**ing **off** his **fang**s. Then he **transform**ed back into his normal baby self.

"Jack-Jack has . . . powers?" asked Dash, completely shocked.

"Well—yeah—but, um," Bob **stammer**ed as he nodded his head.

"You knew about this?" asked Violet. She couldn't believe he hadn't told them. She asked him if he had told

---

★heck '젠장', '제기랄'이라는 뜻으로 당혹스럽거나 짜증스러운 감정을 강조하는 속어.

their mother.

Bob put Jack-Jack into his playpen★ and answered nervously, "Yeah. I dunno—NO. Your mother is not— because I didn't want—because it's not the time— because—"

"Why not?" asked Violet, shocked. "Why would you not tell Mom?"

Dash, finally **process**ing the information, added, "We're your kids! We need to know these things! You'd want us to tell YOU, wouldn't you!" Then he quietly added, "Come on, man. So **uncool**."

Violet still wanted him to answer her question: Why hadn't he told their mother? "What! Why?"

"Because I'm **FORMULATING**, OKAY!" Bob yelled. His **intensity force**d Violet and Dash to jump back. The kids watched as Bob **explode**d into a **rant**, **vent**ing all his feelings. "I'M **TAKING IN** INFORMATION! I'M PROCESSING! I'M DOING THE MATH, I'M FIXING THE BOYFRIEND AND KEEPING THE BABY

★playpen 유아용 놀이장. 유아나 어린 아이가 안전하게 놀 수 있도록 작은 구역에 빙 둘러 치는 틀을 말한다.

FROM **TURN**ING **INTO** A **FLAMING** MONSTER! HOW DO I DO IT? BY **ROLL**ING **WITH PUNCHES**, BABY! I EAT **THUNDER** AND **CRAP LIGHTNING,**★ OKAY? BECAUSE I'M MR. INCREDIBLE! NOT 'MR. SO-SO' OR 'MR. **MEDIOCRE** GUY'! MR. INCREDIBLE!"

There was a short moment of silence as Violet and Dash waited, to be sure he was finished. They looked at each other, and Violet said, "We should call Lucius."

"NO," said Bob. "I can handle it! There's **no way** I'm gonna—" Bob screamed as Jack-Jack **hiccup**ped and burst into flames. Then Jack-Jack sneezed, turned into a smoking ball of fire, and flew right up through the **roof** of the house!

Bob let out a **primal** scream as he ran outside and into the **backyard**. He **scramble**d as he looked up, trying to get under the baby. He dove to catch him, and they both splashed down into a **pool**!

Dash and Violet watched Bob emerge from the water

★I eat thunder and crap lightning 영화 '록키(Rocky)'에 나온 대사인 'you eat lightning and crap thunder'를 살짝 바꾼 것으로, '나는 위대한 사람이다'라고 의역할 수 있다.

holding Jack-Jack, who was now back to his usual self, **giggling** and **coo**ing.

"I'm calling Lucius," said Violet.

14

A little later, Lucius came to the house. He stood with Bob as they watched Jack-Jack play with his teddy bear* in the middle of the family room.

"Looks normal to me," said Lucius. "When did this start happening?"

"Since Helen got the job," said Bob.

"I **assume** she knows," said Lucius.

"Are you **kid**ding?" said Bob. "I can't tell her about this, not while she's doing hero work!"

★teddy bear 테디 베어. 미국의 26대 대통령, 테어도어 루스벨트(Theodore Roosevelt)의 애칭을 따서 만든 곰 인형.

Jack-Jack walked over to the television, pointing and calling out, "Mama! Mama!"

Bob saw Elastigirl on the screen. He changed the channel as he and Lucius continued to talk.

"When was the last time you slept?" asked Lucius.

"Who **keeps track of** that?" said Bob, sounding a little **insane**. "**Besides**, he's a baby. I can **handle** it, I got this handled—"

"So . . . you good, then?" said Lucius, **sarcastic**ally. "You got everything under control, right?"

Just then, Jack-Jack **vanished**!

Bob **rush**ed to the kitchen and grabbed the cookie **jar**. "Cha-cha wanna cookie? **Num**-Num cookie. Cha-cha wanna Num-Num?" said Bob.

Lucius started **freak**ing out because Jack-Jack was gone, but Bob continued to try to **tempt** the baby back with cookies. **Out of nowhere**, Jack-Jack reappeared. He took a cookie, **gobble**d it down, and reached toward Bob for more.

"Whoa," said Lucius. "Okay. So, he can still hear you from—"

"From the other **dimension**. Yeah," replied Bob, his voice **flat**.

Lucius had never seen anything like it. "That is freaky. I mean, that's not like—"

"Not like our other kids. No, it is not. Full powers. Totally random," said Bob.

Jack-Jack reached for the cookie jar and said, "Num-Num? Num-Num?"

"So now . . . he's what? Is he good?" asked Lucius.

Bob smiled. "Well, you'd think so, right?" Then his smile dropped as he looked at Lucius with wild eyes. "**Obvious**ly, I can't keep giving him cookies!" Bob sounded more and more un**stable** as Jack-Jack continued to **request** cookies. "But if I stop—" Bob closed the cookie jar to **demonstrate**.

Jack-Jack started getting angry. "NUM-NUM!" he **demand**ed.

With a quick *POP*, Jack-Jack **transform**ed into the red monster and **gnaw**ed up and down Bob's arm.

"HE IS FREAKIN'!" said Lucius, in a **panic**.

"No!" said Bob, trying to get the monster baby off

his arm. "No **biting** the daddy! No biting!"

Later, Bob and Lucius were **slump**ed on the **couch**, staring off into space. Jack-Jack sat between them **snack**ing on something. Once it was gone, he looked down at his empty hands and then over at Lucius, **frown**ing and **babbling** angrily. Lucius **conjure**d a **smooth** ball of ice and gave it to him. Jack-Jack happily **gum**med it.

"I think I just need a little bit of 'me' time," said Bob, his voice **crack**ing. "Then I'll be good to go."

"Oh, you need more than 'me' time, Bob," said Lucius. "You need **major** life **realign**ment on a number of levels. Starting with baby super freak here. You need some **solid**, **outside-the-box** thinking."

Bob thought about what Lucius had said, and later that day, he headed out with Jack-Jack. He soon **pull**ed the car **up** to an **ornate** front gate, and Edna Mode's eyes appeared on the **security** monitor.

"Galbaki?" shouted Edna. Her face filled the screen. "Elastigirl's Super**suit** is by Galbaki! Explain yourself!"

Bob stared into the monitor, too **worn out** to speak.

"Oh my God, you're worse than I thought," said Edna, **narrow**ing her eyes at him **disapproving**ly.

"It's the baby," Bob said. "I brought the baby." He **lean**ed back, revealing Jack-Jack in his car seat★ making loud **screech**ing sounds.

"Highly **unusual**," said Edna.

The laser gate opened and Bob drove through.

Moments later, Bob carried Jack-Jack as he walked beside Edna toward her **entrance** hall.

"You look **ghastly**, Robert," said Edna, leading him into her **gigantic** living room.

"I haven't been sleeping. . . . I broke my daughter. . . . They keep changing math . . . ," he **rambled**. "We needed double-A batteries, but I got triple-As, and now we still need double-A batteries; I put one red thing in with a **load** of whites and now everything's pink. And I think

---

★ car seat 자동차의 좌석에 설치하는 유아용 의자.

we need eggs."

Edna shook her head. "Done **properly**, **parenting** is a **heroic** act. Done properly," she repeated. "I am **fortunate** that it has never **afflict**ed me. But you do not come to me for eggs and batteries, Robert. I **design** herowear . . . and Elastigirl must have a new suit."

Bob **collapse**d into a chair and placed Jack-Jack on the floor. "Actually, it's Jack-Jack," he said.

Jack-Jack **toddle**d toward Edna.

"You also wish for a new suit for the baby?" she asked, backing away from him. "I would **hardly classify** this as an **emergency**. . . ."

"Well, he's a special case," said Bob. "Worth studying. If I could just leave him with you for a while, I—"

"Leave him? HERE?" said Edna, **cut**ting him **off**. She looked down at Jack-Jack, **irritate**d as he grabbed the **edge** of her **robe** and **stuff**ed it into his mouth. She quickly **snatch**ed it from him. "I am not a baby person, Robert! I have no baby **facilities**! I am an artist; I do not **involve** myself in the **prosaic day-to-day**."

Jack-Jack **gaze**d at Edna **intense**ly. Suddenly, his

nose **inflate**d and looked **identical** to hers. Edna's voice **drift**ed off as she became **absorb**ed in Jack-Jack's slow transformation. **Feature** by feature, he began to turn into Edna—right down to the short black hair.

"**Fascinating**," said Edna. "Are you seeing this, Robert?" She **glance**d over at Bob, who seemed to be sleeping with his eyes still open. Edna turned back to Jack-Jack, who **sneeze**d, **rocket**ing up toward the high ceiling. As he **plummet**ed down, Edna dove to catch him. But he sneezed again and stopped, **midair**, and returned to his original Jack-Jack form. He **hover**ed above Edna's **outstretched** hands and giggled.

"Oh my God . . . YES," said Edna.

Edna carried Jack-Jack in one arm while **shoo**ing Bob out with the other. "Of course you can leave the baby **overnight**," she said, **rapid**ly firing out the words. "I'm sure **filling in** for Helen is **challenging** and you are very tired, and the other children need you and miss you and you must go to them. Auntie Edna will **take care of** everything." She **coo**ed at Jack-Jack and **impatient**ly **usher**ed Bob out the door. "So drive safely and goodbye.

I enjoy our visits."

Bob stood at the **doorstep**, a little **confuse**d. "Auntie Edna?" he said to himself.

A little later, Violet looked up as Bob entered the house without the baby. "Where's Jack-Jack?" she asked.

"E's taking him for a little bit," he said.

"Edna is . . . *babysitting?*" she asked, shocked.

"Yeah."

"And you're okay with this?" asked Violet, wondering what she was missing.

Bob looked more tired than ever, but he **grin**ned widely as he crossed to the couch and collapsed onto it. "Yeah," he said with a heavy **sigh**. "I don't know why, but yeah." He took a deep breath. "I wanted to say something to you." He stared out at the wall. "I'm sorry about Tony. I didn't think about Dicker **erasing** his memory, or about you having to **pay the price** for a choice you never made. It's not fair, I know. And then I made it worse at the restaurant by trying to—" He stopped himself, **realizing** he was rambling. He sighed before continuing. "Anyway, I'm sorry. I'm used to knowing what the right thing to do is, but now I'm not sure anymore. I just want to be a good dad."

Violet smiled. "You're not good"—she **wrap**ped her arms around him and gave him a **hug**—"you're Super."

Bob began to **snore**, and Violet realized that even though he was sitting straight up, he was **fast asleep**.

15

The Deavors' penthouse was **lavish**ly **decorate**d, as a party was **in full swing**. Live music played, and both Supers and non-Supers enjoyed **chat**ting, eating, and drinking. Giant video screens on the walls **display**ed a **slow-motion loop** of Elastigirl's suit**cam footage** that showed her **capture** of the Screenslaver. **Crowd**s of people **circle**d around Elastigirl as they **celebrate**d her success.

Winston Deavor called everyone's attention as he raised his champagne★ glass. "I want to thank everyone

★ champagne 샴페인. 프랑스의 샹파뉴 지방에서 만든 스파클링 와인으로, 거품이 많고 상쾌한 맛이 있다.

who came out tonight in **support** of Superheroes and bringing them back to society." The crowd **applaud**ed. "You all made it happen! The need for this has been made **crystal clear** in recent days, with bad actors like the self-**proclaim**ed Screenslaver **threaten**ing our peace. His **reign** was short, huh?" He held up the Screenslaver's **mask** and **hood**, and the crowd **roar**ed with **approval**. "And **thanks to** this woman . . . a great Super, you love her, you missed her . . . WELCOME BACK, ELASTIGIRL! Come on up here—don't be **bashful**!"

The crowd applauded as Elastigirl **reluctant**ly **made her way** to the microphone. Winston hugged her and handed her the Screenslaver **headgear**. "I want you to have this. A **memento**," he **whisper**ed.

"Thanks, Winston, Evelyn, and everyone at DevTech," said Elastigirl. "I am forever in your **debt**. And thanks to *all* of you. Your **pressure** changed the right minds!"

She handed the microphone back to Winston and he made another announcement. "Just now at a **worldwide summit**, leaders from more than a hundred of the world's top countries have agreed to make Superheroes **legal** again!" **Enthusiastic cheers** filled the room. "We'll **gather** Superheroes and leaders from all over the planet on our ship, the *EVERJUST,* for a **televised signing ceremony** at sea!"

The live music started up again, and everyone continued to enjoy the celebration. As a **swarm** of Supers ran up to **congratulate** Elastigirl, her eyes **drifted** to one of the monitors playing the Screenslaver loop. She **fixated** on his face and just knew, deep in her **gut**, that something was not right.

Later that evening, as the party started **winding down**, Elastigirl **slipped** away to the **editing suite**. She began to **review** some of the **raw** footage of the Screenslaver captured by her suitcam.

Just then, Evelyn entered, carrying drinks. "Are Superheroes allowed?" she asked, offering Elastigirl one.

"I am **definitely** not on **duty**," said Elastigirl. "**Ignore** the **costume**."

She smiled as Evelyn handed her a drink. They **clinked** glasses.

"Had to step away from the **grips** 'n' grins, you know?"

said Elastigirl.

"Gotta get away to keep it pure," said Evelyn. "I know I do."

"Get away . . . from what?"

"Eh, you know, company **stuff**. My brother, mostly."

"But you love him. You two *are* this company—Yin and Yang.★"

"Yeah, I **invent** the stuff; he's good with people— **pleasing** them, **engaging** them, giving out what they want. I never know what people want."

"What do you think they want?" asked Elastigirl.

"Ease. People will **trade quality** for ease every time. It may be **crap**, but it's so **convenient**."

Elastigirl thought about her words and said, "Yeah. Kinda like this case." She explained that something was **not sit**ting **right** with her. "It was too easy," she added.

"THAT was too easy? Wow . . . ," said Evelyn.

Elastigirl's eyes drifted back to the screen on the editing machine and she **notice**d something. "Look at that,"

★Yin and Yang 음양(陰陽). 우주 만물의 서로 반대되는 두 가지 기운으로서 이원적 대립 관계를 나타내는 것.

she said, pointing to an image. "One of the Screenslaver's monitors is **tune**d into my suitcam."

"What?" Evelyn looked closer as Elastigirl used the **control**s to **rock** the image **back and forth**.

"Isn't the suitcam a closed **circuit**?" asked Elastigirl.

"It is," replied Evelyn.

"Then how come the Screenslaver has it?"

"Maybe he—**hack**ed it?"

"So he's **sophisticated** enough to do that, but he has simple **lock**s on his doors?" said Elastigirl, trying to **work out** the **mystery** in her mind.

"Maybe he wanted you to find him," suggested Evelyn.

"He wanted to get caught?" Elastigirl asked, **doubtful**.

"He wanted you to win," said Evelyn.

Elastigirl frowned. "That **make**s no **sense**. He's a **brilliant** guy. If he's smart enough to **conceive** of **technology** like this, he's smart enough to think of something to DO with it. The guy we put in **jail** delivered pizzas—"

"So? Einstein★ was a **patent clerk**. Look. You won.

★Einstein 알버트 아인슈타인. 독일 태생의 미국 이론 물리학자. '특수 상대성 원리', '일반 상대성 원리', '광양자 가설', '통일장 이론' 등을 발표하였고, 1921년에 노벨 물리학상을 받았다.

You got the guy who—"

"WAIT," said Elastigirl. Her mind was **racing** with thoughts. "All the Screenslaver needs to do to **hypnotize** someone is get a screen in front of their eyes. But what if the screen doesn't look like a screen?" She lifted up the Screenslaver hood and **goggle**s fell out. She picked them up and **inspect**ed them closely. "What if the pizza guy is really a pizza guy, but he was controlled by the screens built into his glasses?"

Evelyn's hands flew out and she forced the goggles over Elastigirl's eyes. In an **instant**, their **lens**es **blaze**d with light, sending Elastigirl into a **hypnotic state**.

"You are good," said Evelyn.

16

Bob opened his eyes, in a **fog**, and looked around the family room. It only took a few seconds for it to **dawn** on him: he had spent the whole night on the **couch**. Violet had **removed** his shoes and given him a **blanket** and a **pillow**. Dash sat at the end of the couch, eating a bowl of **cereal** and watching television.

"I thought it was best to just let you sleep," said Violet. "Seventeen hours. How do you feel?"

Bob **grin**ned. "Super."

Later, at Edna's house, Bob was walking with Edna and Jack-Jack toward her **lab**. Jack-Jack **imitate**d her step for step.

"I can't tell you how much I **appreciate** you watching Jack-Jack for me, E," said Bob.

"Yes, I'm sure your **gratitude** is quite **inexpressible**," said Edna. "Don't ask me to do it again, *dahling;* my **rate**s are far too high." Bob **stutter**ed in his response, and Edna said, "I'm **joking**, Robert. I enjoyed the **assign**ment. He is bright and I am **stimulating**—we **deserve** each other."

Jack-Jack continued to imitate Edna as they approached the lab.

"Your child is a polymorph,*" she said. "Like all babies, he has **enormous potential**. It is not unknown for Supers to have more than one power when young, but this little one has many." She turned to Jack-Jack. "Yes?" she said **adoring**ly. "You have many powers?"

Jack-Jack **babble**d back to her. When they arrived at the door to the lab, Edna **punch**ed a **code** on the **keypad**,

---

★polymorph 다형체. 동일 개체가 시기에 따라 다른 형태가 되는 것.

then picked him up for the security **protocol**. Like an old **pro**, Jack-Jack placed his hand on the **scan**ner, opened his eyes wide for the **retinal** scan, and said into the microphone, "Ba-ba-bow."

Edna grinned at Bob as the doors opened and they entered the lab. "I understand you **lack** sleep and **coherency**, Robert," said Edna, directing him to sit in one of the chairs **affix**ed to a moving **platform**. "Babies can be anything, and your child is no **exception**! He is pure un**limit**ed potential, Robert! He slept while I worked in a **creative fever**!" She **shift**ed her voice to **address** Jack-Jack. "Auntie Edna **stay**ed **up** all night making sure you look **fabulous** in your many forms." She placed Jack-Jack in the testing **chamber** and closed the door.

Bob's eyes went wide. "What're you . . . ? You're putting him in the—?"

"In the chamber, Robert. He is part of the demonstration and will be fine," she said. "Your challenge is to manage a baby who has **multiple** powers and no control over them, yes?"

"That **sums** it **up**," said Bob.

"I often work to music, and I noticed the baby responds well to it, **specific**ally Mozart,★" said Edna. She **press**ed a button, and music began to play over the speaker system. Jack-Jack **snap**ped to attention, completely **engage**d. "I **blend**ed Kevlar✳ with carbine✱ for **durability** under **duress** and cotton✲ for **comfort**," she continued. Then she handed him a **sleek** monitor, its screen full of information. "**Interwoven** with these **fabric**s is a **mesh** of **tiny sensor**s that monitor the baby's **physical properties**—"

Suddenly, the monitor lit up and read REPLICATION IMMINENT IN 3, 2, 1—

Jack-Jack stood up and fell to the floor. As soon as he hit it, he **multiplied** into five Jack-Jacks, and they all happily danced around the chamber to the music.

"Oh, **lord**," Bob said. "What's he doing?"

★ Mozart 모차르트. 오스트리아의 작곡가. 18세기의 빈 고전파를 대표하는 한 사람으로, 고전파의 양식을 확립하였다.

✳ Kevlar 케블라. 미국의 듀폰에서 개발한 폴리아라미드 섬유. 강도, 탄성, 진동 흡수력이 높으며, 특히 방탄성능이 우수해 방탄복이나 방탄모 등에 사용한다.

✱ carbine 카르빈. 탄소 원자가 체인 형태로 연결된 물질. 세상에서 가장 강한 물질로 알려져 있으며 유연성을 갖추고 있다.

✲ cotton 면. 무명이나 목화솜 등을 원료로 한 실. 또는 그 실로 짠 천.

"Well, it's Mozart, Robert!" said Edna. "Can you **blame** him? The important thing is that the suit and **track**er **anticipate**d the change and **alert**ed you."

She pressed a button, and a cookie appeared in the chamber, **mount**ed to a moving **pole**. All the Jack-Jacks focused on the cookie and began to **chase** after it as it moved across the chamber. Just before the Jack-Jacks reached the cookie, it disappeared, vanishing through a door in the chamber. One by one, the Jack-Jacks **slap**ped into the wall and **merge**d back into a single Jack-Jack.

Bob started to **panic**. "Oh, no," he said. "Cookies! I gotta get cookies!"

"You do not need cookies," said Edna. "As I learned quite **painful**ly last night, any solution **involving** cookies will **inevitably** result in the **demon** baby."

Bob and Edna looked down at the tracker. It read PHASE SHIFT DETECTED. Jack-Jack tried to **penetrate** the wall but was unable to, and quickly became very angry, **turn**ing **into** the red monster. Then the tracking **pad** lit up: **COMBUSTION** IMMINENT.

"What does THAT mean?" asked Bob. Just then,

Jack-Jack **burst** into **flame**s and Bob screamed.

"It means 'fire,' Robert," said Edna. "For which the suit has **countermeasure**s. I suggest you **extinguish** the baby's flames before he **trip**s the **sprinkler** system."

Bob hit the tracker, and **foam erupt**ed from Jack-Jack's suit, quickly **put**ting **out** the fire. Jack-Jack **giggle**d, **lick**ing the **substance** from his face.

"The flame **retardant** is blackberry* lavender,* *dahling*," said Edna. "**Effective, edible**, and delicious."

"Well, whaddya know,*" said Bob with a **relieve**d **chuckle**. "That is useful."

A little later, Bob **clutch**ed Jack-Jack in one arm and an Edna Mode bag in the other while he stood on Edna's **doorstep**, thanking her for everything. When he asked her how much he owed her, she cut him off.

"Eh, **pish-posh**, *dahling.* Your **bill** will be **deduct**ed from my **fee** for being Mr. Incredible's, Elastigirl's, and Frozone's **EXCLUSIVE design**er throughout the known

---

★blackberry 블랙베리. 장미과 나무딸기의 하나로 검은색의 열매를 먹을 수 있다.
✳lavender 라벤더. 여름에 보라색의 꽃이 피며, 향유는 향수와 향료로 사용하며 약용으로도 이용한다.
✳whaddya know 'what do you know'의 줄임말. '이런!', '설마!'라는 뜻으로 놀라움을 나타낸다.

universe and until the end of time." Edna watched as Bob **buckle**d Jack-Jack into his car seat and added, "But **babysit**ting this one . . . I do for free, *dahling*." She **caress**ed Jack-Jack's **cheek** and said goodbye.

Elastigirl **blink**ed as the **flicker**ing lights in the goggles **went out**. Breaking from the **trance**, she looked around and found herself in a chair with her arms and legs **bound**. When she tried to move, she screamed in pain.

Evelyn pressed a button on an **intercom** and her voice came through speakers in the room. "I would **resist** the **tempt**ation to **stretch**," she said, **staring** at Elastigirl through a glass wall that divided them. "The **temperature** around you is well below **freezing**. Try to stretch, and— you'll break."

"So you're the Screenslaver," Elastigirl said, **shiver**ing.

"Yes and no," said Evelyn, crossing over to get a closer look at Elastigirl through the glass. "Let's say I created the character, and I own the **franchise**s."

"Does Winston know?" Elastigirl asked.

"That I'm the Screenslaver? Of course not. Can you imagine what Mr. **Free Enterprise** would do with my **hypnosis technology**?" she said **sarcastic**ally.

"Worse than what you're doing?" said Elastigirl.

"I'm using the technology to destroy people's trust in it. Like I'm using Superheroes."

"Who did I put in **jail**?" asked Elastigirl.

"Pizza-delivery guy," Evelyn said. "Seemed the right **height**, **build**. He gave you a pretty good fight. I should say I gave you a good fight through him."

Elastigirl said Evelyn was smart for hypnotizing someone to play the hypnotizer. "But," she asked, "it doesn't **bother** you that an **innocent** man is in jail?"

"Ehh, he was **surly**. And the pizza was cold," she replied.

"I **count**ed **on** you," said Elastigirl.

Evelyn smiled. "That's why you failed."

Elastigirl wanted an explanation.

"Why would you count on me?" said Evelyn. "Because I built you a bike? Because my brother knows the words to your **theme** song? We don't know each other."

"But you can count on me anyway," said Elastigirl.

"I'm supposed to, aren't I? Because you have some strange abilities and a shiny **costume**, the rest of us are supposed to put our lives into your **glove**d hands. We're **helpless**, and Superheroes are the **grand** answer."

"But why would you—Your brother—"

"—is a child," Evelyn finished. "He remembers a time when we had parents and Superheroes. So, like a child, Winston **conflate**s the two. Mommy and Daddy went away BECAUSE Supers went away. Our sweet parents were **fool**s to put their lives in anybody else's hands. Superheroes keep us weak."

"Are you going to kill me?' asked Elastigirl.

"Nah," said Evelyn. "Using you is better. You're going to help me make Supers **illegal** forever." She pressed a button, **igniting** the lights on the goggles, and Elastigirl's eyes **glaze**d over as she fell back under Evelyn's **wicked spell**.

18

Out in the Parr **backyard**, Violet and Dash watched as Bob brought out Jack-Jack wearing his new **suit**.

"Ready . . . laser eyes!" said Bob, **demonstrating**.

Jack-Jack appeared to **concentrate**, and **ray**s came out of his eyes. They **land**ed on a **target wrap**ped around a patio umbrella, and the umbrella snapped in half.

"Stop!" said Bob. Jack-Jack stopped.

"Wow!" said Dash.

"That's not all—watch this," said Bob. "Jack- Jack . . . blaster.* Ready?" Bob picked up Jack-Jack and held him with his **belly** down. Then he said, *"Pew! Pew! Pew!"*

Giggling, Jack-Jack **fired** lasers as Bob **aim**ed.

"Whoa!" said Dash. "**No way!**"

"That is CRAZY COOL!" said Violet. "Let me try him! I want him!"

"I'm just demonstrating. No firing the baby around the house, you understand?" said Bob, chuckling. "We're trying to teach him to **control** his powers."

Jack-Jack **squeal**ed in excitement, loving every second of the special attention. The tracker sounded an **alert**, and Bob picked it up. It read **MORPH IMMINENT.**

"See the screen?' said Bob, showing Dash and Violet.

Jack-Jack let out a **playful** squeal and disappeared into a blue **vortex.**

Bob pointed to the screen. "That's the **current readout**," he said.

Violet held the tracker and **swept** it around until it **beep**ed. Dash and Bob followed her as she moved into the house with the tracker, trying to find Jack-Jack.

"**Click** it!" said Bob. "See the readout? **Dimension**

★blaster 스타워즈와 같은 SF 장르에 나오는 총을 말한다.

3. See the shape? That's the room. See where he is in **relation**? So where is he?"

Dash looked over Violet's shoulder as she **pan**ned the **device** across the family room, finally landing in the corner.

"He's THERE!" Dash **exclaim**ed, pointing. He held out a cookie and Jack-Jack appeared, **gobbling** it down. Everyone **cheer**ed!

Suddenly, the Incrediphone rang, and Bob **rush**ed to pick it up. "Elastigirl is in trouble," said Evelyn.

"What happened to her?" asked Bob.

Evelyn said she didn't want to tell him over the phone. "Meet me on our ship at DevTech," she told him.

"The ship at DevTech. I'll be there in fifteen minutes," Bob replied, and **hung up** the phone.

"What's at the ship at DevTech?" asked Violet.

Bob didn't answer her. He **immediate**ly called Lucius. He asked him to come watch the kids and added, "**Suit up**. It might get **weird**."

"I'll be there ASAP,★" said Lucius. "Fifteen tops."

★ASAP 'as soon as possible(가능한 빨리)'의 약어.

Lucius hung up and pointed a **remote** control at the wall. It **hiss**ed as it opened, **reveal**ing his **mount**ed Frozone Supersuit.

"Where you going ASAP?" shouted Honey from the other room. "You better be back ASAP! And leaving that suit!"

Bob hurried through the family room wearing his Supersuit. "I gotta go," he said to the kids. He told them Lucius would be there soon, and headed out the door.

"WHAT'S AT THE SHIP AT DEVTECH? AND WHY ARE YOU IN YOUR SUPERSUIT?" shouted Violet. But Bob was already in his car, **rip**ping down the road toward the **pier**.

Dash headed straight to his parents' bedroom and found the Incredibile remote in the **nightstand drawer**. He quickly hid it behind his back when Violet burst into the room. She **blew** right by him and went over to the **dresser**, pulling open the bottom drawer.

"What's going on?" Dash asked **nonchalant**ly, still hiding the remote behind his back.

"I dunno," answered Violet. "But Dad called Lucius

AFTER getting a call about Mom. Then left in his Supersuit." Violet pulled everyone's Supersuits out of the drawer and **toss**ed Dash's to him.

"I thought you **renounce**d Superheroes," said Dash.

"Yeah. Well, I renounce my renunciation. Put that on," she said.

Dash didn't need to be asked twice. He **zip**ped into the bathroom with his suit, and in the blink of an eye appeared again, standing in front of Violet with it on.

The doorbell rang, and Dash rushed **downstairs** to open it. Voyd, Brick, Reflux, He-lectrix, Screech, and Krushauer stood there, wearing **glow**ing **goggle**s. They were all being controlled by Evelyn.

"You kids aren't safe," said Voyd. "The Deavors sent us—"

Voyd looked over her shoulder, **noticing** that . . . it was suddenly snowing.

"Well, isn't that **redundant!**" said Frozone. Voyd and the other Supers turned to see Frozone calmly crossing the **driveway**. "The Deavors just sent ME here to **guard** the house." He **protective**ly moved between the kids and the other Supers. "Because the kids aren't safe."

Dash, still **clutch**ing the Incredibile remote behind his back, slowly found the button to **summon** the car.

"I get it—**managerial screw-up**," said Frozone. "Tell Winston I **handle**d it. You understand, Miss—"

"Voyd," she replied.

"Miss Voyd. Drive safely." Frozone moved to close the door, but Brick stopped the door with her foot.

Dash pressed the summoning button on the remote, and inside Victor Cachet's **mansion** the Incredibile **power**ed **up** and **took off, blast**ing a hole through a wall!

"The thing is," said Voyd, "he wants us to bring you, too."

Frozone **crack**ed **a smile** and started to speak, then— *WHOOM!*—he **knock**ed Voyd back with a wall of snow. He **cover**ed it with a blast of ice before **slam**ming the **front door**. He turned to the kids. "That isn't gonna hold them long. Where's the baby? Dash, **grab** the baby!"

Dash ran up to get Jack-Jack from his **crib** as a **shower** of ice hit the front windows. In a **flash**, the **hypnotize**d Supers were inside the house, **battling** the kids and

Frozone!

Dash carried Jack-Jack as he tried to run outside, but kept finding himself back in the house. He finally **realize**d he was running through Voyd's portals.

As Frozone tried to fight off Screech, Violet created a **force field** around herself and her brothers to protect them from He-lectrix's **electrical** blasts. Then, just as Krushauer began to **crush** Violet's force field, the Incredibile ripped through the house, stopping right in front of Dash.

"Incredibile! WINDOWS DOWN!" shouted Frozone, the ice-powered hero, as he tried to keep the hypnotized Supers away from the kids. The car windows opened and Frozone turned to the kids and ordered them to **dive** in. Once the kids were **secure** in the car, Frozone **command**ed, "Incredibile! Set voice **identification**! Loudly—say your names!"

"Violet Parr!" said Violet.

"Dashiell Robert Parr!"

Dash and Violet watched in **horror** as the hypnotized Supers **restrain**ed Frozone long enough for Screech to put hypno-goggles over his eyes!

"Oh, no—LUCIUS!" said Dash.

Frozone stopped **struggling** as his eyes glowed. Then he **lunge**d toward the kids.

"NO!" screamed Dash.

"Incredibile! ESCAPE!" shouted Violet.

Just before Frozone could reach them, the Incredibile took off!

19

Mr. Incredible ran onto the hydroliner* and quickly found Evelyn.

"Good news and bad news," she said as she led him toward the **ballroom**. "We've found her, she seems **physical**ly fine, but she's had an **encounter** with the Screenslaver and she's acting kind of strange. In here—" She opened the doors and Mr. Incredible went in.

"Strange how?" he asked. He looked up to see Elastigirl **crouch**ed between the wall and **ceiling**, but

---

★hydroliner 수중익선(水中翼船). 수면 아래의 날개에 부력을 받아 선체를 띄워 물의 저항을 덜 받게 하여 고속으로 활주가 가능한 선박을 말한다.

before he even **noticed** her glowing eyes, her **fist**s were in his face. She **punch**ed him four times before he could **react**.

After he **block**ed the fifth punch, he said, "Helen?"

But she was already gone—stretching in a **blur** behind him. When he turned back, he saw two **spin**ning kicks coming at his **jaw**. His head **snap**ped back with the force. He **duck**ed to miss the next one and **lunge**d for her, but she **flip**ped him and punched him twice more.

Mr. Incredible and Elastigirl battled it out. Evelyn watched from the **doorway**, enjoying watching Elastigirl's **agility** and speed **pit**ted **against** Mr. Incredible's strength and size. But there was another difference. Elastigirl was using all her skills against him, while Mr. Incredible clearly didn't feel right battling his wife. Finally, when he managed to get his hands on her and keep her still for a moment, he **whisper**ed, "Helen . . . it's me!"

Elastigirl kissed him. **Throw**n **off guard**, he kissed back. At that moment, Elastigirl stretched an arm across the room and grabbed a pair of hypno-goggles from Evelyn. She **slap**ped them over Mr. Incredible's eyes.

He screamed for only a moment, then fell silent . . . hypnotized.

Winston stood on the **deck** of the hydroliner, waiting for Mr. Incredible, Elastigirl, and Frozone. He had expected them for the big **sign**ing **ceremony**, but they hadn't arrived. Evelyn walked up to the deck, and he asked if she had heard from them.

"They're all **on board**. They're resting," she said.

"**Weird** that I missed them," Winston replied. "Well, good. Let's **shove** off!"

The Incredibile **sped** away from the Parr house like **lightning**, taking the kids on a wild ride. Violet ordered it to **pull over** so they could **figure out** what they were doing.

Violet and Dash thought about what their father always said to do when facing **challenge**s: **analyze** their strengths.

"Okay. Bad guys are after us. No Mom, no Dad, no Lucius. But we have our powers. This car. And . . . what?" said Dash, thinking out loud.

In the backseat, Jack-Jack **transform**ed **rapid**ly through his many forms before going back to his normal self. Dash and Violet look at each other, **confident** that they could **take on** any problem.

"Incredibile, take us to DevTech," said Violet.

The car shot off toward the **pier**. But as soon as they arrived, the ship **pull**ed **away** from the **dock**!

"I wish the Incredibile could follow that boat," said Dash, **disappoint**ed. The car suddenly backed up—and drove up onto the dock!

"What did you do?" asked Violet.

"I dunno," said Dash.

"WHAT DID YOU DO?" repeated Violet.

"I DIDN'T DO ANYTHING!" said Dash.

The Incredibile **launch**ed off the **edge** of the dock! The kids screamed as it **jet**ted along the water after the ship. The car quickly **caught up** and **pull**ed **up alongside** it.

Violet wondered how they were going to get onto the boat.

"Hey," said Dash, "what if the Incredibile has **eject**or seats?"

The car responded with a message flashing across the **dashboard**: EJECTOR SEATS **ACTIVATED**.

"Wait, what? No—" said Violet.

"Yeah, baby!" said Dash, preparing for the ride.

"NO! Don't say any more—" **urge**d Violet.

"**MAX** POWER!" said Dash.

The message changed to read EJECTOR SEATS: MAXIMUM POWER. Violet tried to get Dash to stop, but he refused to listen. He ordered the car to launch the seats, and the kids shot into the air!

Violet created a force field around them, and they safely landed on the deck of the ship. Then they started searching for their parents.

Winston Deavor stood at the front of the hydroliner, welcoming the guests as they arrived. "You're **in for a treat**! This ship is the largest hydrofoil⋆ on the planet, so hold on to something, because we're going to open her up!"

At that moment, the hydroliner began to **accelerate** as its **gigantic** hydrofoils **emerge**d from the **hull** and lifted the entire ship above the ocean's **surface**.

Violet, Dash, and Jack-Jack had managed to **slip** down to a quiet **corridor** below the deck. Violet whispered to Dash, "We need to find Mom and Dad. Stay here; I'm gonna search for them." She **vanish**ed.

Dash whispered, "Wait—who's gonna watch Jack-Jack?"

Violet reappeared from the shoulders up. "**Suck it up**. I won't be long," she said. Then she vanished again.

"But—"

"It**'s up to** *us,* understand?" said Violet. "Keep him **amuse**d but quiet."

She disappeared, and the door opened and closed as she headed off. Dash **scowl**ed. He turned to Jack-Jack, **sarcastic**ally repeating his sister's **command**s, which made Jack-Jack laugh loudly. Dash slapped a hand over

---

★ hydrofoil 수중익선 아래쪽에 달린 이수(離水) 장치.

his brother's mouth to quiet him.

Violet moved through the ship until she **spot**ted her parents and Frozone heading into the **conference** room. She hurried back to her brothers and discovered that Jack-Jack was gone! Dash didn't have any excuses, and there was no time to argue. They started using the **track**er to search for him.

The **delegate**s and their Supers **gather**ed around a meeting table in the hydroliner's **massive** conference room. **Oversized** windows gave a **spectacular** view both above and below the **waterline**. The delegates all sat with their **respective** Supers behind them. Elastigirl, Frozone, and Mr. Incredible entered wearing hypno-goggles. Winston noticed and whispered into the microphone on his **lapel**, "Hey, did you make them new **mask**s?"

Evelyn sat in the **master** control room—a transformed **security** center where she had placed several monitors to provide **multiple** views of the meeting. She answered Winston by speaking into her microphone, explaining that the masks had night **vision** and other **capabilities**. Then she **cue**d him—it was **go time**. "Aaand . . . we're live in three, two, one . . . go," said Evelyn. They were **broadcast**ing the event across the **globe**.

"This is a **momentous occasion**," Winston began. "We've all managed to **accomplish** something **rare** in today's world: we agree on something!" The **crowd** **chuckle**d and cheered before he continued. "We agree to **undo** a bad decision, to make sure a few **extraordinarily** **gift**ed members of the world's many countries are **treat**ed fairly. To invite them, once again, to use their gifts to **benefit** the world." He **went on** to thank everyone and made a special point to thank the **ambassador** who had been one of the first to express **support** for the Supers. She shook Winston's hand and then signed the **accord**.

Violet and Dash were not having any luck finding Jack-Jack, but when they saw his image moving upward on the tracker that Edna had given Bob, Violet **gasp**ed. "He's in an elevator!"

"Let's go!" said Dash, disappearing in a blur.

Violet turned to follow Dash when Voyd approached. The hypnotized Super **corner**ed Violet, and they began to battle. Violet threw force fields at her, but Voyd managed to **deflect** them all by opening portals!

As Dash reached the elevator where Jack-Jack was, he **realize**d Violet wasn't behind him. He **dart**ed back and speed-punched Voyd just as she **was about to** put hypno-goggles on his sister. In a flash, Dash grabbed Violet and **took off**, escaping before Voyd even knew what happened!

Suddenly, Dash and Violet heard the **growl**ing of monster Jack-Jack.

"That way!" said Dash, pointing down a hall. They soon found Jack-Jack, who had transformed into his **fireball state**. He had **set off** the **sprinkler**s.

"MAMA! MAMA!" cried a **blazing** Jack-Jack.

Violet looked down at the tracker, **frustrate**d. "I know he's on fire—just **put** him **out**!" she said, punching buttons. Lavender **foam ooze**d out of Jack-Jack's Supersuit, quickly **extinguish**ing the **flame**s. He **giggle**d as he **lick**ed up the sweet **retardant**.

"They're coming!" Violet said, spotting the hypnotized Supers. She grabbed Jack-Jack and they climbed up into the ceiling **vent** to hide.

Jack-Jack played with the tracker. "Is it okay to give him that?" whispered Dash.

"I wasn't hearing any better ideas," said Violet. She was just happy it was keeping Jack-Jack happy and **relative**ly quiet.

But the hypnotized Supers heard them, and Krushauer used his crushing power to **smash** and **squeeze** the metal vent from a **distance**. The kids were **trap**ped inside!

Violet tried her best to quiet Jack-Jack, but he began to **whine** and cry.

"I've got you now!" **yell**ed Krushauer, aiming for the exact spot in the vent where they were hiding. Before he made his move, Jack-Jack transformed into a giant baby, **burst**ing through the vent! He knocked Krushauer out— and destroyed the baby tracker!

Violet and Dash had to get giant Jack-Jack to follow them to the conference room. "Cookie **Num**-Num," Violet said, attempting to **coax** him with a treat. The massive baby took the cookie, then **crash**ed through a wall and kept going!

Violet and Dash **chase**d him as he ran out of **sight**,

yelling, "MOM-MOM-MOM-MOM-MOM!"

Soon they came to a wall with a hole in it that was the size of a regular baby. It was too small for them to **crawl** through. Dash **peek**ed his head in and saw Jack-Jack, now back to his normal size, **toddling** down a **hallway**.

"I see him," said Dash. "He's **get**ting **away**!"

"Stand back," said Violet. She created a force field within the hole and began **expand**ing it until the hole had grown big enough for them to fit through. They hurried in to see Jack-Jack **penetrating** another wall!

"Darn it!" said Dash.

"He's heading for Mom!" said Violet.

They **separate**d and went in different directions, searching for another way to catch him.

In the conference room, Winston **announce**d, "It is done! The world is Super again!" Everyone **applaud**ed as people all over the world watched on their television screens, cheering. Winston had everyone **pose** for a group photo. "**Historic** occasion!" he said. "Everyone smile!"

The group faced the camera and smiled just as the giant monitors in the room lit up with **hypnotic** light patterns. Every person was **instant**ly **lock**ed into Evelyn's trance.

Evelyn **press**ed a button, and a monitor in the center of the room **switch**ed over to a **shot** of Elastigirl, Mr. Incredible, and Frozone. The hypnotized Supers picked up the microphone and began to speak. Evelyn controlled their every word.

"Years of **mandate**d hiding and silence have made us **bitter**!" said Elastigirl.

"Your promises are empty!" said Mr. Incredible.

"We no longer **serve** you! We serve only us! May the **fit**test **survive**!" said Frozone.

They reached for the camera. Everyone watching the live broadcast saw **static** on their screens . . . and then the **signal** went dead.

20

Chad Brentley **shift**ed uncomfortably in his chair at the TV studio as he tried to **cover** for the **interrupt**ed **broadcast**. "Well, uh . . . some very **alarm**ing moments there before the, uh, **technical** difficulties. Please **bear** with us."

Evelyn watched from her control room as Mr. Incredible, Frozone, and Elastigirl **exit**ed the **conference** room and **lock**ed the **delegate**s and their **hypnotize**d Supers inside. They **robotic**ally **march**ed to the top **deck** and toward the **command** center, quickly **disarm**ing the **officer**s on **guard**. When one of the officers went for his

radio, Evelyn ordered the Supers to **hold off** and let him use it.

"Superheroes have **forcibly** taken the **bridge!**" the officer said into his radio.

Then Evelyn commanded, "Now." Mr. Incredible **flung** the officer into a wall and **rip**ped out the radio **equipment**. Elastigirl grabbed the **steer**ing **wheel**, directing the ship to head straight for the city. Mr. Incredible **crush**ed the steering wheel, locking it into its **current trajectory**. The ship was going to crash!

Violet and Dash caught up with Jack-Jack just as he **barge**d into the ship's bridge. Elastigirl, Mr. Incredible, and Frozone didn't **think twice** when they saw the kids—they **instant**ly attacked! Violet quickly threw a force **field** around them, **deflect**ing the **blow**s. The three hypnotized Supers **stare**d **curious**ly at the kids through the **transparent** force field for a moment, almost as if they **recognize**d them. Just then, Jack-Jack **penetrate**d the force field and slowly **float**ed toward Elastigirl!

"What the—?" said Evelyn, watching from the control room, "No, no, no! Put him down!" she ordered.

Elastigirl looked **confused** as Jack-Jack landed in her arms, **upside down**. She turned the baby right-side up. Jack-Jack **gazed** at Elastigirl and **frowned** at the **glow**ing hypno-**goggle**s. Then he **yank**ed them right off! She **blink**ed as she came out of her **trance** and smiled at Jack-Jack.

Furious, Evelyn punched at Frozone's and Mr. Incredible's controls. "GRAB HER!" she ordered.

Mr. Incredible and Frozone **lunge**d for Elastigirl, but she handed Jack-Jack off to Violet and ripped off their hypno-goggles, freeing them from Evelyn's **spell**!

Evelyn screamed with **rage** from the control room, "NOOOOO!"

Mr. Incredible and Frozone took a moment to **get their bearings**. When Mr. Incredible saw Elastigirl, he faced her **defensive**ly.

"Hey!" she said. "It's me!"

"Yeah, that's what I thought last time," he said.

Elastigirl quickly tried to explain everything, and told the kids she was very proud of them.

Then Violet **toss**ed her mother's original Super**suit**

to her.

In the **master** control room, Evelyn turned on her monitors and **activate**d the remaining hypnotized Supers, commanding them to **spring** into action. "**Phase** three!" she **announced**.

Moments later, the hypnotized Supers burst through the wall, taking Mr. Incredible and Frozone by surprise.

Jack-Jack transformed into a raging monster.

Elastigirl was shocked. "What the—Jack-Jack has powers?" she exclaimed.

"We know!" yelled Mr. Incredible. "Fight now, talk later!"

Mr. Incredible **battle**d Brick as Voyd threw portal after portal at Elastigirl. Elastigirl managed to punch her arm through them and **remove** Voyd's hypno-goggles!

He-lectrix tried to **electrocute** Violet, but she protected herself inside a force field. Monster Jack-Jack lunged at He-lectrix and removed his goggles.

Evelyn watched everything **unfold** from the control room. She was becoming more **frustrate**d by the minute as she lost control of the Supers one by one.

Then Reflux faced Violet and began to **spew molten lava** toward her. She threw up a force field and **block**ed it. Frozone blasted the lava with ice, **putting out** some of the **flames**. Suddenly, Screech **swoop**ed down and grabbed Dash. Thinking fast, Violet picked up Jack-Jack and **aim**ed him at Screech. "Jack-Jack? Laser eyes! *Pew-pew-pew!*"

Screech fell to the deck of the ship and Dash speed-kicked him.

All the hypno-goggles were finally off and the Supers stopped fighting. However, danger was still **imminent**, as the ship was getting closer to the city.

Then Elastigirl looked up and saw that the **roof** of the hydroliner was **turn**ing **into** a jet! "Evelyn! She's escaping!" she exclaimed.

"Go after her. Finish your **mission**," replied Mr. Incredible.

"I can't just go! What about the kids? Jack-Jack? Who's gonna—"

"Mom!" Violet **cut** her **off**. "Go. We've got this."

Elastigirl smiled, gave Violet a **nod**, and then told

Voyd to come with her.

"I'll **shut down** the engine!" said Mr. Incredible.

"I'll try to slow the ship from the **bow**!" said Frozone.

As he approached the engine room, Mr. Incredible was **confront**ed by Krushauer, who still had his goggles on. The hypnotized Super **compact**ed a wall around Mr. Incredible. But the Superhero was too quick. He **leap**ed out of the way and threw a large piece of **debris** at Krushauer, knocking off his goggles.

Krushauer was finally free from his trance, but now **rubble** was blocking the **hallway**. Mr. Incredible couldn't get to the engine room.

"You did this. Can you **undo** it?" Mr. Incredible asked Krushauer.

"No," the Super replied. "To uncrush is **silly**. Why uncrush?"

"To get into the engine roo—Oh, **forget it**. We don't have enough time," said Mr. Incredible as he **race**d off.

Meanwhile, Evelyn grabbed Winston and **drag**ged him toward her secret jet. He slowly came out of **hypnosis** and was confused.

"Where are the delegates and the Supers?" he asked.

"Still hypnotized," replied Evelyn.

Winston started to **freak** out. "Oh, no, no, no—you're the Screenslaver!" he cried.

Evelyn pressed a **launch** button, **releasing** the jet from the hydroliner. "**Strap** in NOW!" she yelled.

Winston **glare**d at her, then **shove**d her out of his way as he went for the stairs. Evelyn leaped to the controls and hit the thruster.* The jet rose from the deck of the hydroliner as she yelled, "IT'S **FOR YOUR** OWN **GOOD!**"

"NO!" Deavor yelled back. He opened the door to the jet. "THIS IS!" He jumped out and landed hard on the deck of the ship. Evelyn let out a frustrated **groan**, then hit a button, **seal**ing the door of the jet.

Winston headed back to the conference room and quickly turned off the hypnosis screen. As the **diplomat**s and their international Supers **snap**ped out of Evelyn's spell, he called to everyone, "We need to get to the back

---

★thruster 반동 추진 엔진. 비행체의 자세를 변경하는 데 사용되는 소형 로켓 엔진.

of the ship! All Supers, protect your **ambassador**s!"

They followed his lead, **rush**ing to the **rear** of the ship, **bracing** for the crash.

Elastigirl and Voyd **sprint**ed up the stairs to the top of the hydroliner just **in time** to see Evelyn's jet lift off into the sky.

21

"Get me up to the **jet**!" screamed Elastigirl.

Voyd opened a portal, and Elastigirl jumped in, **exit**ing it in the middle of the sky! With nothing to hold on to, Elastigirl began to **spiral** downward. But then Voyd opened another portal that Elastigirl **slip**ped through. This time, she exited the other end on top of the jet. The winds were so **powerful** that they sent Elastigirl flying off, so Voyd continued opening portals, catching her until she finally climbed out of one right beneath the jet. Elastigirl **stretch**ed her body, reaching inside the portal, and shot herself into the **belly** of the jet.

When Elastigirl opened the floor **hatch**, Evelyn saw warning **flash** on her **control panel**. She **immediate**ly knew who it was.

"Welcome **aboard**, Elastigirl," she said as she flew the jet wildly, throwing Elastigirl around. Evelyn sent the jet straight up and then straight down, **spin**ning and **diving** all over the place. "Although we haven't reached our **cruising altitude**, feel free to **roam** about the **cabin**."

Elastigirl pulled herself toward the controls and finally reached Evelyn. She went to deliver a **punch**, but Evelyn quickly placed an **oxygen** mask over her own face. As she **force**d the jet directly up into the clouds, climbing higher and higher into the sky, Elastigirl became weaker and weaker.

Down below, the hydroliner was close to **crash**ing into the city.

"I can't get to the engine room!" said Mr. Incredible.

"We gotta do something, because trying to slow it down isn't working," said Frozone.

"Hey, what about turning the ship?" asked Dash.

Both Mr. Incredible and Frozone **remind**ed him that

the **steer**ing had been destroyed.

"Dash means from the outside!" **exclaim**ed Violet. "If we break off one of the foils and turn the **rudder**, we can **veer** the ship away from the city."

Frozone and Mr. Incredible agreed that it was their only option. "I'll turn the front; you turn the rear," said Frozone. He began to **freeze** the water to **knock** off the front right foil.

"Using the rudder?" asked Mr. Incredible. "But that's **underwater**! How am I supposed to get—All right. C'mon, kids!"

As Mr. Incredible and Dash headed **belowdeck**s, Violet stopped them. "Dad! I know this is going to work, but if it doesn't and we crash, my **shield**s are probably better protection than the boat. I should stay here with Jack-Jack."

Mr. Incredible smiled at Violet. "That's my girl."

"Remember, Bob, we're both turning right!" **yell**ed Frozone.

Mr. Incredible found the ship's **anchor**, broke it off, and **strap**ped himself to the **massive** chain. He looked at

Dash and pointed at the anchor's controls. "Once I turn the ship, you hit the pull-up button."

"Okay, Dad!" said Dash.

He told Dash to lower him slowly, but Dash quickly **press**ed the button and Mr. Incredible **yelp**ed as he immediately **plunge**d into the water. He **struggle**d to **dodge** the boat's **propeller**s while trying to push the rudder.

After several minutes went by, Violet grew **concern**ed. "Dad's been underwater too long!" she said. "We gotta pull him up!"

"Wait—it's too soon!" said Frozone.

"Just press the button, Dash!" said Violet.

"Not yet!" said Dash.

Violet looked over the side of the boat and saw that it was starting to turn. It was working! "Dash, now!" she said.

Dash pushed the button, pulling Mr. Incredible up.

Meanwhile, in Evelyn's jet, Elastigirl was struggling to stay **coherent**, **disorient**ed by the **lack** of oxygen. Evelyn kicked Elastigirl in the face, sending her flying backward. When Elastigirl **land**ed, she **spot**ted a **flare** gun that had fallen in the **chaos** of the fight. She picked it up and **fire**d it at Evelyn's oxygen tank. The force of the **impact** sent Evelyn crashing through the **windshield** of the **cockpit**. She began to **plummet** toward the ocean! Elastigirl set the jet on **autopilot** and shot herself out the broken window toward Evelyn. She quickly **caught up** to her in **midair**, **grab**bed her, and **expand**ed into a **parachute**.

But Evelyn refused to be saved by a Super. She kicked Elastigirl to free herself and continued her **descent** toward the ocean. Elastigirl again **propel**led herself toward Evelyn and **wrap**ped her arms around her. Without a second to **spare**, Voyd opened a portal on the water's **surface**. Elastigirl and Evelyn fell through the portal and landed safely on the **deck** of the ship.

Frozone continued to create **iceberg**s in the water until the hydrofoil finally **collapse**d. As the ship turned away from the city, a giant **wave** formed. Frozone used his powers to transform the wave into a **snowbank**, which acted as a soft **barrier** for the ship to **run into**. At last, the hydroliner came to a stop in front of a large building. The Incredibles and Frozone had saved everyone!

Elastigirl turned to her family. "I missed Jack-Jack's first power?" she said.

"Actually, you missed the first seventeen," replied Mr. Incredible.

Right on **cue**, Jack-Jack **multiplied** himself, and the whole family **burst** out laughing.

22

Evelyn Deavor was **handcuff**ed and **escort**ed into a police car. She turned to Elastigirl before getting **cart**ed **off**. "The fact that you saved me doesn't make you right."

"But it does make you alive," said Elastigirl.

"And I'm **grateful** for that," said Winston.

Mr. Incredible walked over to Violet. He had something on his mind. He **clear**ed **his throat**. "I've been thinking. Tony forgetting you isn't the worst thing. Just . . . take **control**. Reintroduce yourself. Go up to him and say, 'You don't know me, but I'm Violet Parr.' That'll be enough."

Violet thanked him and gave him a **hug**.

The Incredibile **pull**ed **up**, and Dash handed his dad the **remote**.

Over the next few days, life took a **turn** for the better. Inside a **courtroom**, a **judge rule**d to **restore** the **legal status** of the Supers. Elastigirl, Mr. Incredible, and Frozone were in the **crowd**, **cheer**ing and **applaud**ing.

In Western View Junior High School* one afternoon, Tony Rydinger sat reading. Violet walked up and **tap**ped his book with her pencil. "You don't know me, do you?" she asked.

"No, I don't. . . . Wait," he said, **chuckling**. "Are you the girl with the water?"

"Violet Parr!" she said quickly.

Tony smiled and shook her hand. "I'm Tony."

The two continued **chat**ting as they got to know each other . . . again.

★junior high school 미국에서 12~14세 학생들이 다니는 중학교.

Early one evening, Tony closed his **front door** and **trot**ted out to the station wagon★ waiting at the **curb**. Violet sat in the back along with the rest of the Parr family. Tony got in and sat beside her.

Violet introduced everyone, then said, "I tried to **limit** it to *one* parent."

"We're all going to a movie, too," said Helen. "Tony, don't mind us."

"We'll be sitting on the other side of the theater. Not watching you," Bob said. He **wink**ed at Tony in the **rear**view mirror.

"He's **kid**ding," said Violet. "They're only **drop**ping us **off** at the theater. They have other things to do."

"So . . . you guys are close, I guess," said Tony.

"We can get closer!" said Bob.

"Bob!" said Helen, laughing.

But when they **pull**ed **up** to the theater, **sirens blare**d

---

★station wagon 스테이션왜건. 뒷좌석 뒤에 화물실을 만들어 사람과 화물을 동시에 운반할 수 있게 제작된 자동차.

as police cars **race**d past in **pursuit** of a **suspect**. The Parrs exchanged **glance**s, and Violet **usher**ed Tony out of the car.

"Here," she said, handing him some money. "Large popcorn, small soda.* Save me a seat, center, about eight **row**s back." Violet **hop**ped back into the car and stuck her head out the window. "Oh, and butter only **halfway** up, unless you like it all the way through!"

Tony watched as the car drove off, wondering what had just happened.

The Parrs put on their **mask**s, and the station wagon **transform**ed around them into a family-sized Incredi-Wagon. Bob hit the **booster** and they **blast**ed off after the bad guys—and into a new **adventure**.

★soda 탄산음료. 이산화탄소를 물에 녹여 만든, 맛이 산뜻하고 시원한 음료.

DISNEY · PIXAR

인크레더블 2

CONTENTS

주부가 된 미스터 인크레더블?! 돌아온 슈퍼히어로 가족!

디즈니·픽사의 〈인크레더블 2〉은 2004년 〈인크레더블〉 개봉 이후 무려 14년 만에 돌아온 속편입니다. 개봉과 동시에 박스오피스 1위에 올랐고, 전 세계적으로 흥행한 〈겨울왕국〉은 물론, 역대 애니메이션 흥행 1위였던 〈도리를 찾아서〉의 성적을 제치고 흥행 역사를 새로 쓰고 있습니다.

전작에 이어 슈퍼히어로는 여전히 법으로 금지되어 있습니다. 그리고 가족들은 이제 집조차 없이 모텔을 떠도는 신세가 됩니다. 당장 살길이 막막한 가족 앞에 글로벌 기업 CEO 윈스턴과 에블린 남매가 나타납니다. 이들은 다시 슈퍼히어로가 부활할 수 있도록 홍보 프로젝트를 제안합니다. 미스터 인크레더블은 다시 자신이 활약할 수 있을 것으로 생각하고 대환영합니다. 그런데 윈스턴과 에블린은 미스터 인크레더블이 아닌 엘라스티 걸이 프로젝트에 더 적합하다고 말합니다.

엘라스티 걸은 슈퍼히어로로서 많은 사람을 위기에서 구하며 승승장구합니다. 반면 미스터 인크레더블은 이제 엘라스티 걸을 대신해서 삼남매를 돌보며 집안일을 책임져야 합니다. 하지만 그가 감당하기에 사춘기 딸 바이올렛과 철없는 아들 대쉬는 버겁기만 합니다. 그 와중에 막내 잭잭이 엄청난 초능력을 가지고 있다는 사실이 밝혀집니다.

과연 우리의 슈퍼히어로 가족은 이 위기를 극복하고 정체불명의 악당을 물리칠 수 있을까요? 돌아온 가족의 이야기 〈인크레더블 2〉를 지금 영어 원서로 읽어 보세요!

한국인을 위한 맞춤형 영어원서!

원서 읽기는 모두가 인정하는 최고의 영어 공부법입니다. 하지만 영어 구사력이 뛰어나지 않은 보통 영어 학습자들에게는 원서 읽기를 선뜻 시작하기가 부담되는 것도 사실이지요.

이 책은 영어 초보자들도 쉽게 원서 읽기를 시작하고, 꾸준한 읽기를 통해 '영어원서 읽기 습관'을 형성할 수 있도록 만들어진 책입니다. 남녀노소 누구나 좋아할 만한 내용의 원서를 기반으로 내용 이해와 영어 실력 향상을 위한 다양한 콘텐츠를 덧붙였고, 리스닝과 낭독 훈련에 활용할 수 있는 오디오북까지 함께 제공하여, 원서를 부담 없이 읽으면서 자연스럽게 영어 실력이 향상되도록 도와줍니다.

특히 원서와 워크북을 분권하여 휴대와 학습이 효과적으로 이루어지도록 배려했습니다. 일반 원서에서 찾아볼 수 없는 특장점으로, 워크북과 오디오북을 적절히 활용하면 더욱 쉽고 재미있게 영어 실력을 향상시킬 수 있습니다. ('원서'와 '워크북' 및 '오디오북 MP3 CD'의 3가지 패키지가 이상 없이 갖추어져 있는지 다시 한 번 확인해보세요!)

이런 분들께 강력 추천합니다!

- 영어원서 읽기를 처음 시작하는 독자
- 쉽고 재미있는 원서를 찾고 있는 영어 학습자
- 영화 『인크레더블 2』를 재미있게 보신 분
- 특목고 입시를 준비하는 초·중학생
- 토익 600~750점, 고등학교 상위권 수준의 영어 학습자
- 엄마표 영어를 위한 교재를 찾고 있는 부모님

본문 텍스트

내용이 담긴 본문입니다.

원어민이 읽는 일반 원서와 같은 텍스트지만, 암기해야 할 중요 어휘들은 볼드체로 표시되어 있습니다. 이 어휘들은 지금 들고 계신 워크북에 챕터별로 정리되어 있습니다.

학습 심리학 연구 결과에 따르면, 한 단어씩 따로 외우는 단어 암기는 거의 효과가 없다고 합니다. 대신 단어를 제대로 외우기 위해서는 문맥(Context) 속에서 단어를 암기해야 하며, 한 단어 당 문맥 속에서 15번 이상 마주칠 때 완벽하게 암기할 수 있다고 합니다.

이 책의 본문은 중요 어휘를 볼드로 강조하여, 문맥 속의 단어들을 더 확실히 인지(Word Cognition in Context)하도록 돕고 있습니다. 또한 대부분의 중요한 단어들은 다른 챕터에서도 반복해서 등장하기 때문에 이 책을 읽는 것만으로도 자연스럽게 어휘력을 향상시킬 수 있습니다.

또한 본문에는 내용 이해를 돕기 위해 '각주'가 첨가되어 있습니다. 각주는 굳이 암기할 필요는 없지만, 알아두면 내용을 더 깊이 있게 이해할 수 있어 원서를 읽는 재미가 배가됩니다.

워크북(Workbook)의 구성

Check Your Reading Speed
해당 챕터의 단어 수가 기록되어 있어, 리딩 속도를 측정할 수 있습니다. 특히 리딩 속도를 중시하는 독자들이 유용하게 사용할 수 있습니다.

Build Your Vocabulary
본문에 볼드 표시되어 있는 단어들이 정리되어 있습니다. 리딩 전, 후에 반복해서 보면 원서를 더욱 쉽게 읽을 수 있고, 어휘력도 빠르게 향상됩니다.

단어는 〈빈도 – 스펠링 – 발음기호 – 품사 – 한글 뜻 – 영문 뜻〉 순서로 표기되어 있으며 빈도 표시(★)가 많을수록 필수 어휘입니다. 반복 등장하는 단어는 빈도 대신 '복습'으로 표기되어 있습니다. 품사는 아래와 같이 표기했습니다.

n. 명사 │ a. 형용사 │ ad. 부사 │ v. 동사

conj. 접속사 │ prep. 전치사 │ int. 감탄사 │idiom 숙어 및 관용구

Comprehension Quiz
간단한 퀴즈를 통해 읽은 내용에 대한 이해력을 점검해 볼 수 있습니다.

영어원서 읽기, 이렇게 시작해보세요!!

아래와 같이 프리뷰(Preview) → 리딩(Reading) → 리뷰(Review) 세 단계를 거치면서 원서를 읽으면, 더욱 효과적으로 영어실력을 향상할 수 있습니다!

1. 프리뷰(Preview) : 오늘 읽을 내용을 먼저 점검한다!

* 워크북을 통해 오늘 읽을 Chapter에 나와 있는 단어들을 쭉 훑어봅니다. 어떤 단어들이 나오는지, 내가 아는 단어와 모르는 단어가 어떤 것들이 있는지 가벼운 마음으로 살펴봅니다.

* 평소처럼 하나하나 쓰면서 암기하려고 하지는 마세요! 그렇게 해서는 원서를 읽기도 전에 지쳐 쓰러져버릴 것입니다. 익숙하지 않은 단어들을 주의 깊게 보되, 어차피 리딩을 하면서 점차 익숙해질 단어라는 것을 잊지 말고 빠르게 훑어봅니다.

* 뒤 Chapter로 갈수록 '복습'이라고 표시된 단어들이 늘어나는 것을 알 수 있습니다. '복습' 단어인데도 여전히 익숙하지 않다면 더욱 신경을 써서 봐야겠죠? 매일매일 꾸준히 읽는다면, 익숙한 단어들이 점점 많아진다는 것을 몸으로 느낄 수 있습니다.

2. 리딩(Reading) : 내용에 집중하며 빠르게 읽어가자!

* 프리뷰를 마친 후 바로 리딩을 시작합니다. 방금 살펴봤던 어휘들을 문장 속에서 다시 만나게 되는데 이 과정에서 단어의 쓰임새와 어감을 자연스럽게 익히게 됩니다.

* 모르는 단어, 이해 가지 않는 문장이 나오더라도 멈추지 말고 전체적인 맥락을 잡아가면서 스피디하게 읽어가세요. 특히 영화를 먼저 보고 책을 읽으면 맥락을 통해 읽을 수 있어 훨씬 수월합니다.

* 이해 가지 않는 문장들은 따로 표시를 하되, 일단 넘어가서 계속 읽는 것이 좋습니다. 뒷부분을 읽다 보면 자연히 이해가 되는 경우도 있고, 정 이해가 되지 않는 부분은 리딩을 마친 이후에 따로 리뷰하는 시간을 가지면 됩니다. 문제집을 풀듯이 모든 문장을 분석하면서 원서를 읽는 것이 아니라, 리딩할 때는 리딩에만, 리뷰할 때는 리뷰에만 집중하는 것이 필요합니다.

* 볼드 처리된 단어의 의미가 궁금하더라도, 워크북을 바로 펼치지 마세요. 정 궁금하다면 한 번씩 참고하는 것도 나쁘진 않지만, 워크북과 원서를 번갈아

보면서 읽는 것은 리딩의 흐름을 끊고 단어 하나하나에 집착하는 좋지 않은
리딩 습관을 만들 수 있습니다.

- 초보자라면 분당 150단어의 리딩 속도를 목표로 잡아서 리딩을 합니다. 분당
150단어는 원어민이 말하는 속도로, 영어 학습자들이 리스닝과 스피킹으로
넘어가기 위해 가장 기초적으로 달성해야 하는 단계입니다. 분당 50~80단어
정도의 낮은 리딩 속도를 가지고 있는 경우는 대부분 영어 실력이 부족해서라
기보다 '잘못된 리딩 습관'을 가지고 있어서 그렇습니다. 이해력이 조금 떨어진
다고 하더라도 분당 150단어까지는 속도에 대한 긴장감을 놓치지 말고 스피디
하게 읽어나가도록 하세요.

- 이미 150단어 이상의 리딩 속도에 도달한 상태라면, 각자의 상황에 맞게 원
서를 보다 다양한 방식으로 활용해보세요. 이에 대한 자세한 조언이 워크북
말미에 실려 있습니다.

3. 리뷰(Review) : 이해력을 점검하고 꼼꼼하게 다시 살펴보자!

- 해당 Chapter의 Comprehension Quiz를 통해 이해력을 점검해봅니다.
- 오늘 만난 어휘도 다시 한 번 복습합니다. 읽으면서 중요하다고 생각했던 단
어를 연습장에 써보면서 꼼꼼하게 외우는 것도 좋습니다.
- 이해가 되지 않는다고 표시해뒀던 부분도 주의 깊게 분석해봅니다. 다시 한
번 문장을 꼼꼼히 읽고, 어떤 이유에서 이해가 되질 않았는지 생각해봅니다.
따로 메모를 남기거나 노트를 작성하는 것도 좋은 방법입니다.
- 사실 꼼꼼히 리뷰하는 것은 매우 고된 과정입니다. 원서를 읽고 리뷰하는 시
간을 가지는 것은 영어 실력 향상에 많은 도움이 되긴 하나, 이 과정을 철저
히 지키려다가 원서 읽기의 재미를 반감시키는 것은 바람직하지 않습니다. 그
럴 때는 차라리 리뷰를 가볍게 하는 것이 좋을 수 있습니다. '내용에 빠져서
재미있게', 문제집에서는 상상도 못할 '많은 양'을 읽으면서, 매일매일 조금씩
꾸준히 실력을 향상하는 것이 원서를 활용하는 기본적인 방법이며, 영어 공
부의 왕도입니다. 문제집 풀듯이 원서 읽기를 시도하고 접근해서는 실패할 수
밖에 없습니다.

Prologue &
Chapter 1

1. What did Tony do when he saw the tunneler?

   A. He rushed toward it.

   B. He followed it with his friends.

   C. He hid behind a car.

   D. He looked for a Superhero.

2. How did Tony react when he saw Violet?

   A. He said hi to her shyly.

   B. He ran away from her.

   C. He demanded an explanation from her.

   D. He pretended that he did not know her.

3. What did the Underminer do in the bank?

A. He locked up his own money in the vaults.

B. He replaced the real money with fake money.

C. He sucked up the money through a tube.

D. He dug a hole and buried all the money there.

4. Why did the tunneler get out of control?

A. Its control panel no longer worked.

B. Its treads got badly damaged.

C. The Underminer put it on maximum power.

D. The Underminer removed its steering wheel.

5. How did Elastigirl and Mr. Incredible stop the tunneler?

A. They put an explosive on it.

B. They hit it with poles.

C. They drove it into city hall.

D. They made it overheat.

Check Your Reading Speed

1분에 몇 단어를 읽는지 리딩 속도를 측정해보세요.

$$\frac{850 \text{ words}}{\text{reading time (} \quad \text{) sec}} \times 60 = (\qquad) \text{ WPM}$$

Build Your Vocabulary

stark [stɑːrk] a. 삭막한; (차이가) 극명한; 냉혹한
Something that is stark is very plain in appearance.

‡ **flood** [flʌd] v. (빛·색채가) 가득 들어오다; 물에 잠기다; n. 홍수; 쇄도, 폭주
If light floods a place or floods into it, it suddenly fills it.

‡ **agent** [éidʒənt] n. 요원, 첩보원; 대리인, 중개상
An agent is a person who is employed by a government to find out the secrets of other governments.

interrogate [intérəgèit] v. 심문하다, 추궁하다
If someone, especially a police officer, interrogates someone, they question them thoroughly for a long time in order to get some information from them.

straight-faced [streit-féist] a. 무표정한 얼굴을 한
A straight-faced person appears not to be amused in a funny situation.

‡ **awkward** [ɔ́ːkwərd] a. 어색한; (처리하기) 곤란한; 불편한
Someone who feels awkward behaves in a shy or embarrassed way.

teenage [tíːnèidʒ] a. 십대의
Teenage children are aged between thirteen and nineteen years old.

‡‡ **state** [steit] v. 말하다, 진술하다; n. 상태; 국가, 나라; 주(州)
If you state something, you say or write it in a formal or definite way.

squirm [skwəːrm] v. (몸을) 꼼지락대다; 몹시 당혹해 하다
If you squirm, you move your body from side to side, usually because you are nervous or uncomfortable.

wince [wins] v. (통증·당혹감으로) 움찔하고 놀라다
If you wince, the muscles of your face tighten suddenly because you have felt a pain or because you have just seen, heard, or remembered something unpleasant.

squint [skwint] v. 눈을 가늘게 뜨고 보다; 사시이다; n. 사시; 잠깐 봄
If you squint at something, you look at it with your eyes partly closed.

⁑ **blind** [blaind] v. (잠시) 안 보이게 하다; a. 눈이 먼; 눈치 채지 못하는; n. (창문에 치는) 블라인드
(blinding a. 눈이 부신)
A blinding light is extremely bright.

⁑ **incident** [ínsədənt] n. 일, 사건
An incident is something that happens, often something that is unpleasant.

* **recount** [rikáunt] v. 자세히 말하다, 이야기하다; 다시 세다
If you recount a story or event, you tell or describe it to people.

track meet [trǽk miːt] n. 육상 경기 대회
A track meet is a sports competition between two or more teams, involving
various different running races and jumping and throwing events.

⁑ **confident** [kánfədənt] a. 자신감 있는; 확신하는 (confidently ad. 자신 있게)
If a person or their manner is confident, they feel sure about their own abilities,
qualities, or ideas.

* **blush** [blʌʃ] v. 얼굴을 붉히다; ~에 부끄러워하다; n. 얼굴이 붉어짐
When you blush, your face becomes redder than usual because you are ashamed
or embarrassed.

clear one's throat idiom 목을 가다듬다; 헛기침하다
If you clear your throat, you cough once in order to make it easier to speak or to
attract people's attention.

* **relay** [ríːlei] v. 전달하다; (텔레비전·라디오로) 중계하다; n. 계주
If you relay something that has been said to you, you repeat it to another person.

parking lot [páːrkiŋ lat] n. 주차장
A parking lot is an area of ground where people can leave their cars.

rumble [rʌmbl] v. 웅웅거리는 소리를 내다; 덜커덩거리며 나아가다; n. 우르렁거리는 소리
If something rumbles, it makes a low, continuous noise.

quake [kweik] v. (땅·건물이) 마구 흔들리다; (공포·긴장감으로) 몸을 떨다
If a building or land quakes, it shakes or vibrates, usually from shock or instability.

⁑ **violent** [váiələnt] a. 격렬한, 맹렬한; 폭력적인; 지독한
A violent event happens suddenly and with great force.

* **enormous** [inɔ́:rməs] a. 막대한, 거대한
Something that is enormous is extremely large in size or amount.

* **armor** [á:rmər] v. ~에게 갑옷을 입히다; n. 갑옷; 철갑; 무기 (armored a. 장갑을 두른)
Armored vehicles are fitted with a hard metal covering in order to protect them from gunfire and other missiles.

‡ **vehicle** [ví:ikl] n. 차량, 운송 수단; 수단, 매개체
A vehicle is a machine such as a car, bus, or truck which has an engine and is used to carry people from place to place.

‡ **powerful** [páuərfəl] a. 강력한; 영향력 있는, 유력한
A powerful machine or substance is effective because it is very strong.

earthmover [ɔ́:rθmù:vər] n. 흙 파는 기계
An earthmover is a large road vehicle for digging large holes and moving large quantities of earth.

* **drill** [dril] n. 드릴; 송곳; 반복 연습; v. (드릴로) 구멍을 뚫다; 훈련시키다
A drill is a tool or machine that you use for making holes.

* **attach** [ətǽtʃ] v. 붙이다, 첨부하다; 연관되다
If you attach something to an object, you join it or fasten it to the object.

* **explode** [iksplóud] v. 갑자기 ~하다; 폭발하다; (갑자기 강한 감정을) 터뜨리다
To explode means to move very quickly.

* **flip** [flip] v. 홱 뒤집다, 휙 젖히다; 톡 던지다; n. 회전; 톡 던지기
If something flips over, or if you flip it over or into a different position, it moves or is moved into a different position.

* **squat** [skwat] v. 웅크리다, 쪼그리고 앉다; a. 땅딸막한; 쪼그리고 앉은
If you squat, you lower yourself toward the ground, balancing on your feet with your legs bent.

* **peer** [piər] v. 유심히 보다, 눈여겨보다; n. 또래
If you peer at something, you look at it very hard, usually because it is difficult to see clearly.

* **chaos** [kéias] n. 혼돈; 혼란
Chaos is a state of complete disorder and confusion.

envelop [invéləp] v. 감싸다, 뒤덮다
If one thing envelops another, it covers or surrounds it completely.

* **thicket** [θíkit] n. 복잡하게 뒤얽힌 것; 덤불, 잡목 숲
A thicket is a large number of things that are not easy to understand or separate.

* **panic** [pǽnik] v. 어쩔 줄 모르다, 공황 상태에 빠지다; n. 극심한 공포, 공황; 허둥지둥함
If you panic or if someone panics you, you suddenly feel anxious or afraid, and act quickly and without thinking carefully.

‡ **crowd** [kraud] n. 사람들, 군중; v. 가득 메우다; 바싹 붙어 서다
A crowd is a large group of people who have gathered together, for example to watch or listen to something interesting, or to protest about something.

* **platform** [plǽtfɔːrm] n. (장비 등을 올려놓는) 대(臺); 연단, 강단
A platform is a flat raised structure or area, usually one which something can stand on or land on.

‡ **extend** [iksténd] v. 늘리다, 펼치다; (팔·다리를) 뻗다; 연장하다
If an object extends from a surface or place, it sticks out from it.

hulking [hʌ́lkiŋ] a. 몸집이 큰, 부피가 큰
You use hulking to describe a person or object that is extremely large, heavy, or slow-moving, especially when they seem threatening in some way.

villain [vílən] n. 악인, 악한; (이야기·연극 등의) 악당
A villain is someone who deliberately harms other people or breaks the law in order to get what they want.

‡ **cover** [kʌ́vər] v. 덮다; 적당히 둘러대다; 씌우다, 가리다; n. 위장, 속임수; 몸을 숨길 곳; 덮개
If one thing covers another, it has been placed over it in order to protect it, hide it, or close it.

* **clamp** [klæmp] n. 죔쇠; v. 꽉 잡다; 죔쇠로 고정시키다 (clamplike a. 죔쇠 같은)
A clamp is a device that holds two things firmly together.

oversized [óuvərsàizd] a. 너무 큰; 특대의
Oversize or oversized things are too big, or much bigger than usual.

‡ **mine** [main] v. (광물질을) 캐다, 채굴하다; 지뢰를 매설하다; n. 광산; 지뢰
When a mineral such as coal, diamonds, or gold is mined, it is obtained from the ground by digging deep holes and tunnels.

* **boom** [buːm] v. 굵은 목소리로 말하다; 쾅 하는 소리를 내다; n. 쾅 (하는 소리)
When something such as someone's voice, a cannon, or a big drum booms, it makes a loud, deep sound that lasts for several seconds.

‡ **evil** [íːvəl] a. 사악한, 악랄한; 유해한; 악마의; n. 악
If you describe someone as evil, you mean that they are very wicked by nature and take pleasure in doing things that harm other people.

cackle [kækl] n. 낄낄거림; v. (불쾌하게) 낄낄 웃다, 키득거리다
A cackle is a loud unpleasant laugh.

behold [bihóuld] v. 보다
If you behold someone or something, you see them.

hereby [hirbái] ad. 이에 의하여, 이로써
You use hereby when officially or formally saying what you are doing.

‡ **declare** [diklέər] v. 선언하다, 공표하다; 분명히 말하다
If you declare something, you state officially and formally that it exists or is the case.

‡ **route** [ruːt] n. 길, 경로; 방법; v. 보내다, 전송하다
A route is a way from one place to another.

* **scramble** [skræmbl] v. 재빨리 움직이다; 허둥지둥 해내다; n. (힘들게) 기어가기; 서로 밀치기
If you scramble to a different place or position, you move there in a hurried, awkward way.

‡ **notice** [nóutis] v. 알아채다, 인지하다; 주의하다; n. 신경 씀, 알아챔; 통지, 예고
If you notice something or someone, you become aware of them.

* **illegal** [ilíːgəl] a. 불법적인; 비합법적인
If something is illegal, the law says that it is not allowed.

back and forth idiom 여기저기에, 왔다갔다; 좌우로; 앞뒤로
If someone moves back and forth, they repeatedly move in one direction and then in the opposite direction.

* **tunnel** [tʌnl] v. 굴을 뚫다; n. 터널, 굴
To tunnel somewhere means to make a tunnel there.

* **patrol** [pətróul] v. 순찰을 돌다; (특히 위협적으로) 돌아다니다; n. 순찰; 순찰대
When soldiers, police, or guards patrol an area or building, they move around it in order to make sure that there is no trouble there.

‡ **earth** [əːrθ] n. 땅, 지면; 지구; 세상; 흙
The earth is the land surface on which we live and move about.

* **perimeter** [pərímitər] n. (어떤 구역의) 주위, 주변; 방어선
The perimeter of an area of land is the whole of its outer edge or boundary.

* **recall** [rikɔ́:l] v. 기억해 내다, 상기하다; 다시 불러들이다; n. 회상; (제품의) 회수
When you recall something, you remember it and tell others about it.

take off idiom (서둘러) 떠나다; 날아오르다
To take off means to leave a place suddenly.

‡ **call** [kɔ:l] v. (원하는 것을) 외치다; ~라고 부르다; 전화하다; n. 전화
To call means to claim a specified privilege for yourself, typically by shouting out a particular word or set phrase.

maggoty [mǽgəti] a. 변덕스러운; 구더기가 우글대는
If you describe someone as maggoty, you mean that they are despicable.

* **creep** [kri:p] n. 너무 싫은 사람; v. 살금살금 움직이다; 기다
If you describe someone as a creep, you mean that you dislike them a great deal, especially because they are insincere and flatter people.

‡ **recognize** [rékəgnàiz] v. 알아보다; 인식하다; 공인하다
If you recognize someone or something, you know who that person is or what that thing is.

babysit [béibisìt] v. (부모가 외출한 동안) 아이를 봐 주다
If you babysit for someone or babysit their children, you look after their children while they are out.

idiot [ídiət] n. 바보, 멍청이
If you call someone an idiot, you are showing that you think they are very stupid or have done something very stupid.

* **mask** [mæsk] n. 마스크; 가면; v. 가면을 쓰다; (감정·냄새·사실 등을) 가리다
A mask is a piece of cloth or other material, which you wear over your face so that people cannot see who you are, or so that you look like someone or something else.

* **stare** [stɛər] v. 빤히 쳐다보다, 응시하다; n. 빤히 쳐다보기, 응시
If you stare at someone or something, you look at them for a long time.

take in idiom ~을 눈여겨보다; 이해하다
If you take in something, you spend time looking at it.

‡ **sight** [sait] n. 광경, 모습; 보기; 시력; v. 갑자기 보다
A sight is something that you see.

‡ **suit** [suːt] n. (특정한 활동 때 입는) 옷; 정장; 소송; v. ~에게 편리하다; 어울리다
A particular type of suit is a piece of clothing that you wear for a particular
activity.

* **weird** [wiərd] a. 기이한, 기묘한; 기괴한, 섬뜩한
If you describe something or someone as weird, you mean that they are strange.

‡ **handle** [hændl] v. (사람·작업 등을) 처리하다; 들다, 옮기다; n. 손잡이
If you say that someone can handle a problem or situation, you mean that they
have the ability to deal with it successfully.

* **react** [riǽkt] v. 반응하다; 반응을 보이다
When you react to something that has happened to you, you behave in a particular
way because of it.

run away idiom (~에서) 달아나다
If you run away, you move quickly away from someone or a place.

switch on idiom (전등 등의) 스위치를 켜다
If you switch on something like an electrical device, a machine, or an engine, you
start it working by pressing a switch or a button.

* **mount** [maunt] v. 끼우다, 고정시키다; (자전거·말 등에) 올라타다; n. (전시품을 세우는) 판; 산
If you mount an object on something, you fix it there firmly.

‡ **ceiling** [síːliŋ] n. 천장
A ceiling is the horizontal surface that forms the top part or roof inside a room.

* **beam** [biːm] n. 빛줄기; 기둥; v. 활짝 웃다; 비추다
A beam is a line of energy, radiation, or particles sent in a particular direction.

* **eyebrow** [áibràu] n. 눈썹
Your eyebrows are the lines of hair which grow above your eyes.

‡ **fault** [fɔːlt] n. 잘못, 책임; 결점
If a bad or undesirable situation is your fault, you caused it or are responsible
for it.

* **secure** [sikjúər] a. 안심하는; 안전한; v. 얻어 내다; (단단히) 고정시키다
If you feel secure, you feel safe and happy and are not worried about life.

manhood [mǽnhùd] n. 남자다움, 남성성; (남자) 성인
Manhood is typical or traditional male qualities, especially those that men are
proud of.

gadget [gǽdʒit] n. (작은) 기계 장치; 도구
A gadget is a small machine or device which does something useful.

ignore [ignɔ́ːr] v. 무시하다; (사람을) 못 본 척하다
If you ignore someone or something, you pay no attention to them.

suction [sʌ́kʃən] n. 빨아들이기, 흡입
Suction is the process by which two surfaces stick together when the air between them is removed.

fire [faiər] v. 발사하다; (엔진이) 점화되다; 해고하다; n. 화재, 불; 발사, 총격
If you fire an arrow, you send it from a bow.

forehead [fɔ́ːrhèd] n. 이마
Your forehead is the area at the front of your head between your eyebrows and your hair.

flutter [flʌ́tər] v. (가볍게) 흔들다; 훨훨 날아가다; n. 흔들림; 소동, 혼란
If something thin or light flutters, or if you flutter it, it moves up and down or from side to side with a lot of quick, light movements.

Check Your Reading Speed

1분에 몇 단어를 읽는지 리딩 속도를 측정해보세요.

$$\frac{1,240 \text{ words}}{\text{reading time ( ) sec}} \times 60 = (\quad) \text{ WPM}$$

Build Your Vocabulary

* **cling** [kliŋ] v. (clung-clung) 꼭 붙잡다, 매달리다; 들러붙다; 애착을 갖다
If you cling to someone or something, you hold onto them tightly.

* **massive** [mǽsiv] a. (육중하면서) 거대한; 엄청나게 심각한
Something that is massive is very large in size, quantity, or extent.

* **tunnel** [tʌnl] v. 굴을 뚫다; n. 터널, 굴
To tunnel somewhere means to make a tunnel there.

* **chew** [ʧuː] v. 물어뜯다, 깨물다; (음식을) 씹다; n. 씹기, 깨물기
If a person or animal chews an object, they bite it with their teeth.

* **earth** [əːrθ] n. 땅, 지면; 지구; 세상; 흙
The earth is the land surface on which we live and move about.

* **fling** [fliŋ] v. (힘껏) 던지다; (머리·팔 등을) 휘두르다; n. (한바탕) 실컷 즐기기
If you fling something somewhere, you throw it there using a lot of force.

gag [gæg] v. 토할 것 같다; (입에) 재갈을 물리다; 말문을 막다; n. 재갈; 장난
If you gag, you cannot swallow and nearly vomit.

debris [dəbríː] n. 파편, 잔해; 쓰레기
Debris is pieces from something that has been destroyed or pieces of rubbish or unwanted material that are spread around.

* **drill** [dril] n. 드릴; 송곳; 반복 연습; v. (드릴로) 구멍을 뚫다; 훈련시키다
A drill is a tool or machine that you use for making holes.

* **enormous** [inɔ́ːrməs] a. 막대한, 거대한
Something that is enormous is extremely large in size or amount.

cavern [kǽvərn] n. (특히 큰) 동굴
A cavern is a large deep cave.

INCREDIBLES 2

financial [finǽnʃəl] a. 금융의, 재정의
Financial means relating to or involving money.

district [dístrikt] n. 지구, 지역, 구역
A district is an area of a town or country which has been given official boundaries for the purpose of administration.

hatch [hæʧ] n. (배·항공기의) 출입구; v. 부화하다; (계획 등을) 만들어 내다
A hatch is an opening in the deck of a ship, through which people or cargo can go. You can also refer to the door of this opening as a hatch.

emerge [imə́:rdʒ] v. 나오다, 모습을 드러내다; (어려움 등을) 헤쳐 나오다
To emerge means to come out from an enclosed or dark space such as a room or a vehicle, or from a position where you could not be seen.

detonate [détəneit] v. 폭발하다; 폭발시키다 (detonator n. 기폭 장치)
A detonator is a small amount of explosive or a piece of electrical or electronic equipment which is used to explode a bomb or other explosive device.

carve [ka:rv] v. 깎아서 만들다; (글씨를) 새기다
If you carve an object, you make it by cutting it out of a substance such as wood or stone.

undermine [ʌndərmáin] v. (자신감·권위 등을) 약화시키다; 기반을 약화시키다
If you undermine something such as a feeling or a system, you make it less strong or less secure than it was before, often by a gradual process or by repeated efforts.

press [pres] v. 누르다; (무엇에) 바짝 대다; 꾹 밀어 넣다; n. 언론
If you press a button or switch, you push it with your finger in order to make a machine or device work.

tremendous [triméndəs] a. 엄청난; 굉장한, 대단한
You use tremendous to emphasize how strong a feeling or quality is, or how large an amount is.

explode [iksplóud] v. 폭발하다; 갑자기 ~하다; (갑자기 강한 감정을) 터뜨리다
(explosion n. 폭발)
An explosion is a sudden, violent burst of energy, for example one caused by a bomb.

vault [vɔ:lt] n. 금고, 보관실; 뛰기, 도약; v. 뛰어넘다
A vault is a secure room where money and other valuable things can be kept safely.

deafening [défəniŋ] a. 귀청이 터질 듯한, 귀가 먹먹한
A deafening noise is a very loud noise.

✱ **alarm** [əláːrm] n. 경보 장치; 불안, 공포; v. 불안하게 하다; 경보장치를 달다
An alarm is an automatic device that warns you of danger, for example by ringing a bell.

✱ **emergency** [imə́ːrdʒənsi] n. 비상
An emergency is an unexpected and difficult or dangerous situation, especially an accident, which happens suddenly and which requires quick action to deal with it.

flicker [flíkər] v. (불·빛 등이) 깜박거리다; 움직거리다; n. (빛의) 깜박거림; 움직거림
If a light or flame flickers, it shines unsteadily.

✱ **urgent** [ə́ːrdʒənt] a. 다급한; 긴급한, 시급한 (urgently ad. 급히)
If something is urgent, it needs to be dealt with as soon as possible.

✱ **tube** [tjuːb] n. 관; 튜브; 통
A tube is a long hollow object that is usually round, like a pipe.

✱ **drag** [dræg] v. 끌다, 끌고 가다; 힘들게 움직이다; n. 끌기, 당기기; 장애물
If you drag something, you pull it along the ground, often with difficulty.

✱ **plant** [plænt] v. 자리를 잡다; 심다; n. 시설; 식물, 초목
If you plant someone, something, or yourself, you firmly put them or yourself in a particular place or position.

복습 **powerful** [páuərfəl] a. 강력한; 영향력 있는, 유력한
A powerful machine or substance is effective because it is very strong.

복습 **suction** [sʌ́kʃən] n. 빨아들이기, 흡입
Suction is the process by which liquids, gases, or other substances are drawn out of somewhere.

✱ **bond** [band] n. 채권; 유대; 접착, 접합; v. 결합시키다; 유대감을 형성하다
When a government or company issues a bond, it borrows money from investors. The certificate which is issued to investors who lend money is also called a bond.

✱ **deed** [diːd] n. (소유권을 증명하는) 증서; 행위, 행동
A deed is a document containing the terms of an agreement, especially an agreement concerning the ownership of land or a building.

‡ **suck** [sʌk] v. (특정한 방향으로) 빨아들이다; 빨아 먹다; 엉망이다, 형편없다; n. 빨기, 빨아 먹기
If something sucks a liquid, gas, or object in a particular direction, it draws it there with a powerful force.

⁎ **hip** [hip] n. 둔부, 엉덩이
Your hips are the two areas at the sides of your body between the tops of your legs and your waist.

⁎ **startle** [staːrtl] v. 깜짝 놀라게 하다; 움찔하다; n. 깜짝 놀람
If something sudden and unexpected startles you, it surprises and frightens you slightly.

⁎ **vacuum** [vǽkjuəm] n. 진공 청소기; 진공; v. 진공청소기로 청소하다
A vacuum cleaner or a vacuum is an electric machine which sucks up dust and dirt from carpets.

‡ **flash** [flæʃ] n. 순간; (잠깐) 반짝임; v. 휙 내보이다; 휙 나타나다; (잠깐) 번쩍이다
If you say that something happens in a flash, you mean that it happens suddenly and lasts only a very short time.

bulge [bʌldʒ] v. 툭 불거져 나오다; 가득 차다; n. 툭 튀어 나온 것, 불룩한 것
If you say that something is bulging with things, you are emphasizing that it is full of them.

‡ **twist** [twist] v. 휘다, 구부리다; 일그러뜨리다; (고개·몸 등을) 돌리다;
n. (손으로) 돌리기; (고개·몸 등을) 돌리기
If you twist something, you turn it to make a spiral shape, for example by turning the two ends of it in opposite directions.

‡ **snake** [sneik] v. 구불구불 가다, 꿈틀꿈틀 움직이다; n. 뱀
Something that snakes in a particular direction goes in that direction in a line with a lot of bends.

⁎ **bark** [baːrk] v. (명령·질문 등을) 빽 내지르다; (개가) 짖다; n. 나무껍질; (개 등이) 짖는 소리
If you bark at someone, you shout at them aggressively in a loud, rough voice.

⁎ **irritate** [írətèit] v. 짜증나게 하다, 거슬리다; 자극하다 (irritated a. 짜증이 난)
If something irritates you, it keeps annoying you.

⁎ **agenda** [ədʒéndə] n. 의제, 안건
An agenda is a list of the items that have to be discussed at a meeting.

‡ **pressure** [préʃər] n. 압력; 압박, 스트레스; v. 강요하다; 압력을 가하다
The pressure in a place or container is the force produced by the quantity of gas or liquid in that place or container.

clog [klag] v. 막다
When something clogs a hole or place, it blocks it so that nothing can pass through.

force [fɔːrs] v. 억지로 ~하다; ~를 강요하다; n. 작용력; 힘; 영향력
If a situation or event forces you to do something, it makes it necessary for you to do something that you would not otherwise have done.

tumble [tʌmbl] v. 굴러 떨어지다; 폭삭 무너지다; n. (갑자기) 굴러 떨어짐; 폭락
If someone or something tumbles somewhere, they fall there with a rolling or bouncing movement.

blizzard [blízərd] n. (위압적일 정도로) 많은 양; 눈보라
A blizzard is a sudden large amount of something that must be dealt with.

pile [pail] n. 무더기; 쌓아 놓은 것, 더미; v. 쌓다; 집어 넣다; 우르르 가다
A pile of things is a mass of them that is high in the middle and has sloping sides.

scowl [skaul] v. 노려보다, 쏘아보다; n. 노려봄, 쏘아봄
When someone scowls, an angry or hostile expression appears on their face.

bang [bæŋ] v. 쾅 하고 치다; 쾅 하고 닫다; 쿵 하고 찧다; n. 쾅 (하는 소리)
If you bang on something or if you bang it, you hit it hard, making a loud noise.

dent [dent] n. 움푹 들어간 곳; v. 찌그러뜨리다; (자신감·명성 등을) 훼손하다
A dent is a hollow in the surface of something which has been caused by hitting or pressing it.

control [kəntróul] n. (기계·차량의) 제어 장치; 통제, 제어; v. 지배하다; 조정하다
A control is a device such as a switch or lever which you use in order to operate a machine or other piece of equipment.

autopilot [ɔ́ːtoupàilət] n. (항공기·배의) 자동 조종 장치
An automatic pilot or an autopilot is a device in an aircraft that automatically keeps it on a particular course.

burst [bəːrst] v. (burst-burst) 불쑥 움직이다; 갑자기 ~하다; n. (갑자기) ~을 함; 파열, 폭발
To burst into or out of a place means to enter or leave it suddenly with a lot of energy or force.

whack [wæk] v. 세게 치다, 후려치다; n. 퍽, 철썩; 강타
If you whack someone or something, you hit them hard.

* **claw** [klɔ:] n. 갈고리 모양의 기계; (동물·새의) 발톱; v. (손톱·발톱으로) 할퀴다
(clawlike a. 갈고리 같은)
A claw is a curved end on a tool or machine, used for pulling or picking things up.

* **punch** [pʌnʧ] v. 주먹으로 치다; (자판·번호판 등을) 치다; n. 주먹으로 한 대 침
If you punch someone or something, you hit them hard with your fist.

* **panel** [pænl] n. (자동차 등의) 계기판; 판; 자문단; v. 판으로 덮다
A control panel or instrument panel is a board or surface which contains switches
and controls to operate a machine or piece of equipment.

* **surface** [sə́:rfis] n. 수면, 표면, 지면; 외관; v. 수면으로 올라오다; (갑자기) 나타나다
The surface of something is the flat top part of it or the outside of it.

duck [dʌk] v. 급히 움직이다; (머리나 몸을) 휙 수그리다; n. [동물] 오리
To duck means to move somewhere very quickly, especially to avoid being seen
or to get away from someone.

* **separate** [sépərèit] v. 분리하다, 나누다; 갈라지다; a. 별개의; 분리된
If you separate people or things that are together, or if they separate, they move
apart.

pod [pad] n. (우주선·선박의 본체에서) 분리 가능한 부분; (콩이 들어 있는) 꼬투리
A pod is a detachable or self-contained unit on an aircraft, spacecraft, vehicle, or
vessel, having a particular function.

miniature [míniəʧər] a. 아주 작은, 축소된; n. 축소 모형, 미니어처
Miniature is used to describe something which is very small, especially a smaller
version of something which is normally much bigger.

* **burrow** [bə́:rou] v. 굴을 파다; (속으로) 파고들다; n. 굴, 은신처
If an animal burrows into the ground or into a surface, it moves through it by
making a tunnel or hole.

* **vanish** [vǽniʃ] v. 사라지다, 없어지다; 모습을 감추다
If someone or something vanishes, they disappear suddenly or in a way that
cannot be explained.

zigzag [zígzæg] v. 지그재그로 나아가다; n. 지그재그, 갈지자형
If you zigzag, you move forward by going at an angle first to one side then to the
other.

haphazard [hæphǽzərd] a. 무계획적인, 되는 대로의 (haphazardly ad. 아무렇게나)
If you describe something as haphazard, you are critical of it because it is not at
all organized or is not arranged according to a plan.

* **pound** [paund] v. (여러 차례) 두드리다; 쿵쾅거리며 걷다
If you pound something or pound on it, you hit it with great force, usually loudly and repeatedly.

복습 **flip** [flip] v. 홱 뒤집다, 휙 젖히다; 툭 던지다; n. 회전; 톡 던지기
If something flips over, or if you flip it over or into a different position, it moves or is moved into a different position.

* **switch** [switʃ] n. 스위치; 전환; v. 전환하다, 바꾸다
A switch is a small control for an electrical device which you use to turn the device on or off.

* **lever** [lévər] n. (기계·차량 조작용) 레버; 지레; 수단; v. 지렛대로 움직이다
A lever is a handle or bar that is attached to a piece of machinery and which you push or pull in order to operate the machinery.

* **blink** [bliŋk] v. (불빛이) 깜박거리다; 눈을 깜박이다; n. 눈을 깜박거림
When a light blinks, it flashes on and off.

* **breach** [briːʃ] v. (방어벽 등에) 구멍을 뚫다; (합의나 약속을) 위반하다; n. 위반; ~의 파괴
If someone or something breaches a barrier, they make an opening in it, usually leaving it weakened or destroyed.

* **yell** [jel] v. 고함치다, 소리 지르다; n. 고함, 외침
If you yell, you shout loudly, usually because you are excited, angry, or in pain.

* **fist** [fist] n. 주먹
Your hand is referred to as your fist when you have bent your fingers in toward the palm in order to hit someone, to make an angry gesture, or to hold something.

‡ **crash** [kræʃ] n. 요란한 소리; (자동차·항공기) 사고; v. 부딪치다; 충돌하다; 굉음을 내다
A crash is a sudden, loud noise.

* **stadium** [stéidiəm] n. 경기장, 스타디움
A stadium is a large sports ground with rows of seats all round it.

복습 **parking lot** [páːrkiŋ lat] n. 주차장
A parking lot is an area of ground where people can leave their cars.

‡ **block** [blak] n. 구역, 블록; 사각형 덩어리; v. 막다, 차단하다; 방해하다
A block in a town is an area of land with streets on all its sides.

복습 **crowd** [kraud] n. 사람들, 군중; v. 가득 메우다; 바싹 붙어 서다
A crowd is a large group of people who have gathered together, for example to watch or listen to something interesting, or to protest about something.

notice [nóutis] v. 알아채다, 인지하다; 주의하다; n. 신경 씀, 알아챔; 통지, 예고
If you notice something or someone, you become aware of them.

plume [plu:m] n. (연기·수증기) 기둥; (커다란) 깃털
A plume of smoke, dust, fire, or water is a large quantity of it that rises into the air in a column.

distance [dístəns] n. 먼 곳; 거리; v. (~에) 관여하지 않다 (in the distance idiom 저 멀리)
If you can see something in the distance, you can see it, far away from you.

zoom [zu:m] v. 쌩 하고 가다; 급등하다; n. (빠르게) 쌩 하고 지나가는 소리
If you zoom somewhere, you go there very quickly.

spot [spat] v. 발견하다, 찾다, 알아채다; n. (특정한) 곳; (작은) 점
If you spot something or someone, you notice them.

whip [hwip] v. 격렬하게 움직이다; 휙 빼내다; n. 채찍
If you whip in a particular direction, you move fast or suddenly in that direction.

blur [blə:r] n. 흐릿한 형체; v. 흐릿해지다; 모호해지다
A blur is a shape or area which you cannot see clearly because it has no distinct outline or because it is moving very fast.

babysit [béibisit] v. (부모가 외출한 동안) 아이를 봐 주다
If you babysit for someone or babysit their children, you look after their children while they are out.

stroller [stróulər] n. 유모차; 산책하는 사람
A stroller is a small chair on wheels, in which a baby or small child can sit and be wheeled around.

challenge [ʧælindʒ] n. 도전; 저항; v. 도전하다; 도전 의식을 북돋우다
A challenge is something new and difficult which requires great effort and determination.

villain [vílən] n. 악인, 악한; (이야기·연극 등의) 악당
A villain is someone who deliberately harms other people or breaks the law in order to get what they want.

strike [straik] v. (struck-struck/stricken) 공격하다; (세게) 치다, 부딪치다; n. 공격; 때리기
To strike means to attack someone or something quickly and violently.

stretch [streʧ] v. (길이·폭 등을) 늘이다; 뻗어 있다; n. 뻗기, 펴기; (길게) 뻗은 구간
When something soft or elastic stretches or is stretched, it becomes longer or bigger as well as thinner, usually because it is pulled.

‡ **swing** [swiŋ] v. 휙 움직이다; (전후·좌우로) 흔들다; n. 흔들기; 휘두르기
If something swings in a particular direction or if you swing it in that direction, it moves in that direction with a smooth, curving movement.

make one's way idiom 나아가다, 가다
When you make your way somewhere, you walk or travel there.

* **steer** [stiər] v. (보트·자동차 등을) 조종하다; (특정 방향으로) 움직이다
When you steer a car, boat, or plane, you control it so that it goes in the direction that you want.

* **widen** [waidn] v. 넓어지다; (정도·범위 등이) 커지다
If your eyes widen, they open more.

* **slam** [slæm] v. 세게 치다, 놓다; 쾅 닫다; n. 쾅 하고 닫기; 탕 하는 소리
If one thing slams into or against another, it crashes into it with great force.

* **column** [káləm] n. 기둥; 줄
A column is something that has a tall narrow shape.

‡ **track** [træk] n. (기차) 선로; 경주로, 트랙; 자국; v. 추적하다, 뒤쫓다
Railway tracks are the rails that a train travels along.

crumble [krʌmbl] v. (건물이나 땅이) 허물어지다; 바스러지다; (힘·조직 등이) 흔들리다
If an old building or piece of land is crumbling, parts of it keep breaking off.

‡ **dive** [daiv] v. 급강하다; 급히 움직이다; (물 속으로) 뛰어들다; n. 급강하; (물 속으로) 뛰어들기
If an airplane dives, it flies or drops down quickly and suddenly.

* **breeze** [briːz] n. 산들바람, 미풍; v. 경쾌하게 움직이다
A breeze is a gentle wind.

‡ **sweep** [swiːp] v. (swept-swept) 휩쓸고 가다; (빗자루로) 쓸다; 훑다; n. 쓸기, 비질하기
If wind, a stormy sea, or another strong force sweeps someone or something along, it moves them quickly along.

‡ **guide** [gaid] v. (특정한 방향으로) 인도하다; (길·장소로) 안내하다; n. 안내
If you guide a vehicle somewhere, you control it carefully to make sure that it goes in the right direction.

‡ **smooth** [smuːð] a. 순조로운; (소리가) 감미로운; 매끈한; v. 매끈하게 하다
(smoothly ad. 순조롭게)
You use smooth to describe something that is going well and is free of problems or trouble.

✽ **harm** [haːrm] n. 해, 피해, 손해; v. 해치다; 해를 끼치다, 손상시키다
(out of harm's way idiom 아무런 피해 없이)
If someone or something is out of harm's way, they are in a safe place away from danger or from the possibility of being damaged.

✽ **destruction** [distrʌ́kʃən] n. 파괴, 파멸; 말살
Destruction is the action or process of causing so much damage to something that it no longer exists or cannot be repaired.

overpass [óuvərpæs] n. (입체 교차의) 고가 도로
An overpass is a structure which carries one road over the top of another one.

✽ **jam** [dʒæm] v. 밀어 넣다; 움직이지 못하게 되다; n. 교통 체증; 혼잡; 잼
If you jam something somewhere, you push or put it there roughly.

lamppost [lǽmppòust] n. 가로등의 기둥
A lamppost is a tall post with a light at the side of roads and in other public places.

＊ **tread** [tred] n. (타이어의) 접지면; 걸음걸이; v. (발을) 디디다; 밟아서 뭉개다
The tread of a tire or shoe is the pattern of thin lines cut into its surface that stops it slipping.

＊ **scrape** [skreip] v. (상처가 나도록) 긁다; (무엇을) 긁어내다; n. 긁기; 긁힌 상처
If something scrapes against something else or if someone or something scrapes something else, it rubs against it, making a noise or causing slight damage.

✽ **crush** [krʌʃ] v. 으스러뜨리다; 밀어 넣다; 좌절시키다; n. 홀딱 반함
To crush something means to press it very hard so that its shape is destroyed or so that it breaks into pieces.

✽ **race** [reis] v. 쏜살같이 가다; (머리·심장 등이) 바쁘게 돌아가다; 경주하다; n. 경주; 인종, 종족
If you race somewhere, you go there as quickly as possible.

✽ **scatter** [skǽtər] v. 흩뿌리다; 황급히 흩어지다; n. 흩뿌리기; 소수, 소량
If you scatter things over an area, you throw or drop them so that they spread all over the area.

＊ **swift** [swift] a. 빠른, 날랜; 신속한, 재빠른 (swiftly ad. 신속히, 빨리)
Something that is swift moves very quickly.

＊ **giggle** [gigl] v. 피식 웃다, 킥킥거리다; n. 피식 웃음, 킥킥거림
If someone giggles, they laugh in a childlike way, because they are amused, nervous, or embarrassed.

babble [bǽbl] v. 지껄이다, 횡설수설하다; n. 횡설수설; 와글와글, 왁자지껄
If someone babbles, they talk in a confused or excited way.

* **grunt** [grʌnt] v. 끙 앓는 소리를 내다; (돼지가) 꿀꿀거리다; n. (사람이) 끙 하는 소리
If you grunt, you make a low sound, especially because you are annoyed or not
interested in something.

* **realize** [ríːəlàiz] v. 깨닫다, 알아차리다; 실현하다, 달성하다
If you realize that something is true, you become aware of that fact or understand
it.

* **responsible** [rispánsəbl] a. 책임감 있는; (~을) 책임지고 있는 (responsibility n. 책임)
If you have responsibility for something or someone, or if they are your
responsibility, it is your job or duty to deal with them and to take decisions
relating to them.

복습 **evil** [íːvəl] n. 악; a. 사악한, 악랄한; 유해한; 악마의
Evil is used to refer to all the wicked and bad things that happen in the world.

* **nearby** [nìərbái] a. 인근의, 가까운 곳의; ad. 가까운 곳에
If something is nearby, it is only a short distance away.

* **invisible** [invízəbl] a. 보이지 않는, 볼 수 없는 (invisibility n. 눈에 보이지 않음)
If you describe something as invisible, you mean that it cannot be seen, for
example because it is transparent, hidden, or very small.

be up for idiom 기꺼이 ~하려고 하다
If you are up for something, you are willing to take part in a particular activity.

* **shield** [ʃiːld] v. 보호하다, 가리다; (기계 등에) 보호 장치를 두르다; n. 보호 장치; 방패
If something or someone shields you from a danger or risk, they protect you from
it.

복습 **field** [fiːld] n. ~장; 경기장; 들판, 밭
A magnetic, gravitational, or electric field is the area in which that particular
force is strong enough to have an effect.

복습 **chase** [ʧeis] v. 뒤쫓다, 추적하다; 추구하다; n. 추적, 추격; 추구함
If you chase someone, or chase after them, you run after them or follow them
quickly in order to catch or reach them.

복습 **struggle** [strʌgl] v. 애쓰다; 몸부림치다, 허우적거리다; 힘겹게 나아가다; n. 투쟁, 분투; 몸부림
If you struggle to do something, you try hard to do it, even though other people
or things may be making it difficult for you to succeed.

take down idiom (구조물을 해체하여) 치우다
If you take something down, you remove it by separating it into pieces.

⠶ **support** [səpɔ́:rt] n. 버팀대; 지지, 지원; v. 지지하다; (넘어지지 않도록) 떠받치다
A support is something that holds the weight of an object, building, or structure so that it does not move or fall.

⁎ **collapse** [kəlǽps] v. 붕괴되다, 무너지다; 주저앉다; 쓰러지다; n. 실패; (건물의) 붕괴
If a building or other structure collapses, it falls down very suddenly.

⁎ **grab** [græb] v. (와락·단단히) 붙잡다; 급히 ~하다; n. 와락 잡아채려고 함
If you grab something, you take it or pick it up suddenly and roughly.

streetlight [strí:tlàit] n. 가로등
A streetlight is a tall post with a light at the top, which stands by the side of a road to light it up, usually in a town.

⠶ **pole** [poul] n. 막대, 기둥; 장대; 극
A pole is a long thin piece of wood or metal, used especially for supporting things.

⁎ **snap** [snæp] v. 툭 부러지다; 급히 움직이다; 날카롭게 말하다; n. 탁 하는 소리
If something snaps or if you snap it, it breaks suddenly, usually with a sharp cracking noise.

heads up idiom 조심해라!
Yoy use 'Heads up!' to warn someone about something dangerous or call for their attention.

bystander [báistændər] n. 구경꾼, 행인
A bystander is a person who is present when something happens and who sees it but does not take part in it.

sprint [sprint] v. (짧은 거리를) 전력 질주하다; n. 전력 질주; 단거리 경기
If you sprint, you run or ride as fast as you can over a short distance.

⁎ **leap** [li:p] v. 뛰다, 뛰어오르다; (서둘러) ~하다; n. 높이뛰기, 도약; 급증
If you leap, you jump high in the air or jump a long distance.

city hall [siti hɔ́:l] n. 시청
The city hall is the building which a city council uses as its main offices.

⠶ **machinery** [məʃí:nəri] n. 기계(류); 조직, 기구
You can use machinery to refer to machines in general, or machines that are used in a factory or on a farm.

‡ **limit** [límit] n. 한계, 한도; 제한, 허용치; v. 제한하다; 한정하다
A limit is the greatest amount, extent, or degree of something that is possible.

* **spill** [spil] v. (액체를) 흘리다, 쏟다; 쏟아져 나오다; n. 흘린 액체, 유출물
If a liquid spills or if you spill it, it accidentally flows over the edge of a container.

overheat [òuvərhíːt] v. 과열되다
If something overheats or if you overheat it, it becomes hotter than is necessary
or desirable.

* **urge** [əːrdʒ] v. 재촉하다; 충고하다, 설득하려 하다; n. (강한) 욕구, 충동
If you urge someone somewhere, you make them go there by touching them or
talking to them.

‡ **rush** [rʌʃ] v. 급히 움직이다; 서두르다; n. (감정이 갑자기) 치밀어 오름; 혼잡; 기쁨, 흥분
If you rush somewhere, you go there quickly.

pry [prai] v. ~을 비틀어 열다; 엿보다; n. 지레; 엿보기; 탐색
If you pry something open or pry it away from a surface, you force it open or away
from a surface.

topple [tapl] v. 넘어지다; 넘어뜨리다; 실각시키다
If someone or something topples somewhere or if you topple them, they become
unsteady or unstable and fall over.

복습 **panic** [pǽnik] v. 어쩔 줄 모르다, 공황 상태에 빠지다; n. 극심한 공포, 공황; 허둥지둥함
If you panic or if someone panics you, you suddenly feel anxious or afraid, and
act quickly and without thinking carefully.

‡ **blow** [blou] v. 폭파하다; (휙하니) 떠나다; (바람·입김에) 날리다; n. 강타
To blow something out, off, or away means to remove or destroy it violently with
an explosion.

복습 **boom** [buːm] n. 쾅 (하는 소리); v. 굵은 목소리로 말하다; 쾅 하는 소리를 내다
A boom is a deep loud sound that continues for some time, for example the noise
of thunder or an explosion.

* **ripple** [ripl] v. 잔물결을 이루다; (감정 등이) 파문처럼 번지다; n. 잔물결, 파문 (모양의 것)
When the surface of an area of water ripples or when something ripples it, a
number of little waves appear on it.

* **stall** [stɔːl] v. (차량·엔진이) 멎다, 시동이 꺼지다; 시간을 끌다; n. 가판대, 좌판
If a vehicle stalls or if you accidentally stall it, the engine stops suddenly.

* **huddle** [hʌdl] v. 모이다; 몸을 움츠리다; n. 모여 서 있는 것; 혼잡
If people huddle together or huddle round something, they stand, sit, or lie close to each other, usually because they all feel cold or frightened.

* **relieve** [rilíːv] v. 안도하다; (불쾌감·고통 등을) 없애 주다; 완화하다 (relief n. 안도, 안심)
If you feel a sense of relief, you feel happy because something unpleasant has not happened or is no longer happening.

‡ **cheer** [ʧíər] v. 환호성을 지르다, 환호하다; n. 환호(성), 응원
When people cheer, they shout loudly to show their approval or to encourage someone who is doing something such as taking part in a game.

‡ **freeze** [friːz] v. (두려움 등으로 몸이) 얼어붙다; 얼다; n. 동결; 한파
If someone who is moving freezes, they suddenly stop and become completely still and quiet.

* **cop** [kap] n. 경찰관
A cop is a policeman or policewoman.

‡ **weapon** [wépən] n. 무기, 흉기
A weapon is an object such as a gun, a knife, or a missile, which is used to kill or hurt people in a fight or a war.

‡ **draw** [drɔː] v. (drew-drawn) (총·칼 등을 꺼내서) 겨누다; 그리다; 끌어당기다; n. 추첨, 제비뽑기
If someone draws a gun, knife, or other weapon, they pull it out of its container and threaten you with it.

‡ **aim** [eim] v. 겨누다; 목표하다; n. 겨냥, 조준; 목적
If you aim a weapon or object at something or someone, you point it toward them before firing or throwing it.

Chapters 2 & 3

1. Why couldn't Dicker help the Parr family anymore?

   A. He was moving far away from the city.

   B. He quit his job at the National Supers Agency.

   C. The Super Relocation Program was over.

   D. The Parr family was assigned a new agent.

2. What was the motel like?

   A. It was just like a real home.

   B. It was cluttered but new.

   C. It was empty but comfortable.

   D. It was too small for the Parr family.

3. How did Helen generally feel about the kids fighting bad guys?

A. She felt like it was worth the risk.

B. She felt like it was essential.

C. She felt like it was their choice.

D. She felt like it was not a good idea.

4. What were Bob and Helen considering before Lucius appeared?

A. Moving to a motel across the country

B. Finding a job to support the family

C. Buying a new house in the neighborhood

D. Doing Super work without the kids

5. What did Lucius tell Bob and Helen?

A. A businessman wanted to meet them in person.

B. A businessman was concerned about their safety.

C. A businessman knew where the Underminer was.

D. A businessman desperately needed their assistance.

CHAPTER 2

Check Your Reading Speed

1분에 몇 단어를 읽는지 리딩 속도를 측정해보세요.

$$\frac{1{,}238 \text{ words}}{\text{reading time (} \quad \text{) sec}} \times 60 = (\quad) \text{ WPM}$$

Build Your Vocabulary

agent [éidʒənt] n. 요원, 첩보원; 대리인, 중개상
An agent is a person who is employed by a government to find out the secrets of other governments.

agency [éidʒənsi] n. (특정 서비스를 제공하는) 정부 기관; 대리점, 대행사
An agency is a government organization responsible for a certain area of administration.

hum [hʌm] n. 윙윙거리는 소리; v. 윙윙거리다; 왁자지껄하다
Hum is a low continuous noise made by a machine or a lot of people talking.

armor [áːrmər] v. ~에게 갑옷을 입히다; n. 갑옷; 철갑; 무기 (armored a. 장갑을 두른)
Armored vehicles are fitted with a hard metal covering in order to protect them from gunfire and other missiles.

van [væn] n. 승합차; 밴
A van is a small or medium-sized road vehicle with one row of seats at the front and a space for carrying goods behind.

mask [mæsk] n. 마스크; 가면; v. 가면을 쓰다; (감정·냄새·사실 등을) 가리다
A mask is a piece of cloth or other material, which you wear over your face so that people cannot see who you are, or so that you look like someone or something else.

pull into idiom ~에 도착하다, ~에 들어오다
If a vehicle or a driver pulls into, they move to the side of the road and stop.

parking lot [páːrkiŋ lat] n. 주차장
A parking lot is an area of ground where people can leave their cars.

current [kɔ́ːrənt] a. 현재의, 지금의; n. (물·공기의) 흐름, 해류; 전류
Current means happening, being used, or being done at the present time.

‡ **sign** [sain] n. 표지판; 몸짓; 기색, 흔적; v. 서명하다; 신호를 보내다
A sign is a piece of wood, metal, or plastic with words or pictures on it. Signs give you information about something, or give you a warning or an instruction.

복습 **flicker** [flíkər] v. (불·빛 등이) 깜박거리다; 움직거리다; n. (빛의) 깜박거림; 움직거림
If a light or flame flickers, it shines unsteadily.

* **rear** [riər] a. 뒤쪽의; n. 뒤쪽; v. 앞다리를 들어올리며 서다
The rear of something such as a building or vehicle is the back part of it.

‡ **pour** [pɔːr] v. 쏟아져 나오다; 마구 쏟아지다; 붓다, 따르다
If people pour into or out of a place, they go there quickly and in large numbers.

* **linger** [líŋgər] v. 더 오래 머물다; 계속되다
If you linger somewhere, you stay there for a longer time than is necessary, for example because you are enjoying yourself.

복습 **incident** [ínsədənt] n. 일, 사건
An incident is something that happens, often something that is unpleasant.

talkative [tɔ́ːkətiv] a. 말이 많은, 수다스러운
Someone who is talkative talks a lot.

복습 **whip** [hwip] v. 휙 빼내다; 격렬하게 움직이다; n. 채찍
If someone whips something out or whips it off, they take it out or take it off very quickly and suddenly.

* **pad** [pæd] n. (메모지 등의) 묶음; 패드; v. 소리 안 나게 걷다; 완충재를 대다
A pad of paper is a number of pieces of paper which are fixed together along the top or the side, so that each piece can be torn off when it has been used.

scribble [skribl] v. 갈겨쓰다, 휘갈기다; 낙서하다; n. 낙서
If you scribble something, you write it quickly and roughly.

check out idiom ~을 확인하다; (흥미로운 것을) 살펴보다
If you check out someone or something, you examine them in order to be certain that everything is correct, true, or satisfactory.

one's face falls idiom 실망한 표정을 짓다; 낙담한 얼굴이 되다
If someone's face falls, they suddenly look very disappointed or upset.

shut down idiom 종료하다; (기계가) 멈추다
If a shop, school, factory, or business shuts down, or if someone shuts it down, it closes, usually permanently.

* **sigh** [sai] n. 한숨; v. 한숨을 쉬다, 한숨짓다; 탄식하듯 말하다
A sigh is a slow breath out that makes a long soft sound, especially because you are disappointed, tired, annoyed, or relaxed.

relocate [ri:lóukeit] v. 이전하다, 이동하다 (relocation n. 재배치)
If people or businesses relocate or if someone relocates them, they move to a different place.

force [fɔ:rs] v. 억지로 ~하다; ~를 강요하다; n. 작용력; 힘; 영향력
If a situation or event forces you to do something, it makes it necessary for you to do something that you would not otherwise have done.

* **underground** [Ándərgráund] a. 비밀의; 지하의; ad. 지하에
If you go underground, you hide from the authorities or the police because your political ideas or activities are illegal.

politician [pàlitíʃən] n. 정치인
A politician is a person whose job is in politics, especially a member of parliament or congress.

be gunning for idiom ~를 비난할 기회를 찾다
To be gunning for someone means to often criticize them or be trying to cause trouble for them.

trail off idiom (목소리가) 차츰 잦아들다
If someone's speech trails off, it gradually becomes quieter and then stops.

* **genuine** [dʒénjuin] a. 진실한, 진심 어린; 진짜의, 진품의 (genuinely ad. 진정으로)
Genuine refers to things such as emotions that are real and not pretended.

grateful [gréitfəl] a. 고마워하는, 감사하는
If you are grateful for something that someone has given you or done for you, you have warm, friendly feelings toward them and wish to thank them.

lean [li:n] v. 기울이다, (몸을) 숙이다; ~에 기대다; a. 군살이 없는, 호리호리한
When you lean in a particular direction, you bend your body in that direction.

hug [hʌg] n. 포옹; v. 껴안다, 포옹하다
A hug is the act of holding someone or something close to your body with your arms.

honor [ánər] n. 영광(스러운 것); 존경, 공경; v. 존경하다, 공경하다; ~에게 영광을 베풀다
If you describe doing or experiencing something as an honor, you mean you think it is something special and desirable.

∴ wave [weiv] v. (손·팔을) 흔들다; 손짓하다; n. 물결; (손·팔을) 흔들기

If you wave or wave your hand, you move your hand from side to side in the air, usually in order to say hello or goodbye to someone.

clutter [klʌ́tər] v. (어수선하게) 채우다; n. 잡동사니; 어수선함 (cluttered a. 어수선한)

If things or people clutter a place, they fill it in an untidy way.

carton [ká:rtn] n. (음식이나 음료를 담는) 갑, 통; 상자

A carton is a plastic or cardboard container in which food or drink is sold.

takeout [téikaut] n. (식당에서 먹지 않고) 가지고 가는 음식

A takeout or takeout food is hot cooked food which you buy from a store or restaurant and eat somewhere else.

· click [klik] v. 딸깍 하는 소리를 내다; 분명해지다; n. 딸깍 (하는 소리)

If something clicks or if you click it, it makes a short, sharp sound.

· buckle [bʌ́kl] n. 버클, 잠금장치; v. 버클로 잠그다; 찌그러지다

A buckle is a piece of metal or plastic attached to one end of a belt or strap, which is used to fasten it.

∴ waist [weist] n. 허리

Your waist is the middle part of your body where it narrows slightly above your hips.

field [fi:ld] n. ~장; 경기장; 들판, 밭

A magnetic, gravitational, or electric field is the area in which that particular force is strong enough to have an effect.

scowl [skaul] v. 노려보다, 쏘아보다; n. 노려봄, 쏘아봄

When someone scowls, an angry or hostile expression appears on their face.

race [reis] v. 쏜살같이 가다; (머리·심장 등이) 바쁘게 돌아가다; 경주하다; n. 경주; 인종, 종족

If you race somewhere, you go there as quickly as possible.

blur [blə:r] n. 흐릿한 형체; v. 흐릿해지다; 모호해지다

A blur is a shape or area which you cannot see clearly because it has no distinct outline or because it is moving very fast.

flash [flæʃ] n. 순간; (잠깐) 반짝임; v. 휙 내보이다; 휙 나타나다; (잠깐) 번쩍이다

If you say that something happens in a flash, you mean that it happens suddenly and lasts only a very short time.

* **zip** [zip] v. (어떤 방향으로) 쌩 하고 가다; 지퍼를 잠그다; n. 지퍼
If you say that something or someone zips somewhere, you mean that they move very fast.

⁑ **grin** [grin] v. 활짝 웃다; n. 활짝 웃음
When you grin, you smile broadly.

⁂ **narrow** [nǽrou] v. (눈을) 찌푸리다; 좁히다; a. 좁은
If your eyes narrow or if you narrow your eyes, you almost close them, for example because you are angry or because you are trying to concentrate on something.

triumphant [traiʌ́mfənt] a. 의기양양한; 크게 성공한, 큰 승리를 거둔
Someone who is triumphant has gained a victory or succeeded in something and feels very happy about it.

복습 **grunt** [grʌnt] n. (사람이) 끙 하는 소리; v. 끙 앓는 소리를 내다; (돼지가) 꿀꿀거리다
A grunt is a short low sound made by a person or an animal.

복습 **grab** [græb] v. (와락·단단히) 붙잡다; 급히 ~하다; n. 와락 잡아채려고 함
If you grab something, you take it or pick it up suddenly and roughly.

* **frown** [fraun] v. 얼굴을 찡그리다; 눈살을 찌푸리다; n. 찡그림, 찌푸림
When someone frowns, their eyebrows become drawn together, because they are annoyed, worried, or puzzled, or because they are concentrating.

⁑ **strict** [strikt] a. 엄격한; 엄밀한
If a parent or other person in authority is strict, they regard many actions as unacceptable and do not allow them.

* **tone** [toun] n. 어조, 말투; (글 등의) 분위기; 음색
Someone's tone is a quality in their voice which shows what they are feeling or thinking.

복습 **be up for** idiom 기꺼이 ~하려고 하다
If you are up for something, you are willing to take part in a particular activity.

* **complaint** [kəmpléint] n. 불평
A complaint is a statement in which you express your dissatisfaction with a particular situation.

⁑ **serve** [səːrv] v. (음식을) 제공하다; (상품·서비스를) 제공하다; (어떤 조직·국가 등을 위해) 일하다
When you serve food and drink, you give people food and drink.

* **heap** [hiːp] v. 수북이 담다; (아무렇게나) 쌓다; n. 더미, 무더기; 많음 (heaping a. 수북한)
If you heap things somewhere, you arrange them in a large pile.

* **portion** [pɔ́ːrʃən] n. 1인분; 부분, 일부; 몫; v. 나누다
A portion is the amount of food that is given to one person at a meal.

the elephant in the room idiom 모두 알지만 말하지 않고 있는 문제
The elephant in the room means a serious problem that everyone is aware of but no one wants to talk about.

stir-fry [stɔ́ːr-frai] v. (재빨리) 볶다
If you stir-fry vegetables, meat, or fish, you cook small pieces of them quickly by stirring them in a small quantity of very hot oil.

clueless [klúːlis] a. 아주 멍청한; ~을 할 줄 모르는
If you describe someone as clueless, you are showing your disapproval of the fact that they do not know anything about a particular subject or that they are incapable of doing a particular thing properly.

‡ **refer** [rifɔ́ːr] v. 언급하다; 인용하다; 지시하다, 나타내다
If you refer to a particular subject or person, you talk about them or mention them.

‡ **deal** [diːl] n. 일, 사항; 거래; 처리; v. 처리하다
You can say 'what's the deal?' to someone to ask them what is happening or going to happen.

‡ **annoy** [ənɔ́i] v. 짜증나게 하다; 귀찮게 하다 (annoyed a. 짜증이 난, 약이 오른)
If you are annoyed, you are fairly angry about something.

* **stuff** [stʌf] n. 일, 것, 물건; v. 쑤셔 넣다; 채워 넣다
You can use stuff to refer to things such as a substance, a collection of things, events, or ideas, or the contents of something in a general way without mentioning the thing itself by name.

‡ **interrupt** [intərʌ́pt] v. (말·행동을) 방해하다; 중단시키다; 차단하다
If you interrupt someone who is speaking, you say or do something that causes them to stop.

* **stammer** [stǽmər] v. 말을 더듬다; n. 말 더듬기
If you stammer, you speak with difficulty, hesitating and repeating words or sounds.

* **stumble** [stʌ́mbl] v. (말·글 읽기를 하다가) 더듬거리다; 비틀거리다; 발을 헛디디다
If you stumble while you are reading aloud or speaking, you make a mistake, and have to pause before saying the words properly.

exclaim [ikskléim] v. 소리치다, 외치다
If you exclaim, you cry out suddenly in surprise, strong emotion, or pain.

babble [bæbl] v. 지껄이다, 횡설수설하다; n. 횡설수설; 와글와글, 왁자지껄
If someone babbles, they talk in a confused or excited way.

approve [əprúːv] v. 찬성하다; 승인하다 (approval n. 찬성)
If someone or something has your approval, you like and admire them.

fist [fist] n. 주먹
Your hand is referred to as your fist when you have bent your fingers in toward the palm in order to hit someone, to make an angry gesture, or to hold something.

slam [slæm] v. 세게 치다, 놓다; 쾅 닫다; n. 쾅 하고 닫기; 탕 하는 소리
If you slam something down, you put it there quickly and with great force.

tray [trei] n. 쟁반; (납작한 플라스틱) 상자
A tray is a flat piece of wood, plastic, or metal, which usually has raised edges and which is used for carrying things, especially food and drinks.

weigh in idiom (논의·활동 등에) 끼어들다
If you weigh in with something such as a discussion or argument, you become involved in it.

define [difáin] v. 규정하다, 분명히 밝히다; 정의하다
If you define something, you show, describe, or state clearly what it is and what its limits are, or what it is like.

register [rédʒistər] v. 인식되다; 기록하다, 나타내다; 기억하다; n. 기록부, 명부
If a piece of information does not register or if you do not register it, you do not really pay attention to it, and so you do not remember it or react to it.

shrug off idiom ~을 대수롭지 않게 취급하다
If you shrug something off, you treat it as if it is not important or not a problem.

insist [insíst] v. 고집하다, 주장하다, 우기다
If you insist that something should be done, you say so very firmly and refuse to give in about it.

illegal [ilíːgəl] a. 불법적인; 비합법적인
If something is illegal, the law says that it is not allowed.

respect [rispékt] v. (법률·원칙 등을) 준수하다; 존경하다; 존중하다; n. 존경(심); 존중
If you respect a law or moral principle, you agree not to break it.

heated [híːtid] a. 흥분한; 뜨거워진, 가열된
If someone gets heated about something, they get angry and excited about it.

disrespectful [dìsrispéktfəl] a. 무례한, 실례되는
If you are disrespectful, you show no respect in the way that you speak or behave to someone.

‡ **unjust** [ʌndʒʌ́st] a. 부당한, 불공평한
If you describe an action, system, or law as unjust, you think that it treats a person or group badly in a way that they do not deserve.

복습 **chaos** [kéias] n. 혼돈; 혼란
Chaos is a state of complete disorder and confusion.

* **frustrate** [frʌ́streit] v. 좌절감을 주다, 불만스럽게 하다; 방해하다
(frustrated a. 좌절감을 느끼는)
If something frustrates you, it upsets or angers you because you are unable to do anything about the problems it creates.

‡ **plate** [pleit] n. 접시, 그릇; (자동차) 번호판; 판
A plate is a round or oval flat dish that is used to hold food.

* **bounce** [bauns] v. (공 등이) 튀다; 깡충깡충 뛰다; n. 탄력
If something bounces or if something bounces it, it swings or moves up and down.

* **rattle** [rætl] v. 덜거덕거리다; 당황하게 하다; n. 덜컹거리는 소리
When something rattles or when you rattle it, it makes short sharp knocking sounds because it is being shaken or it keeps hitting against something hard.

복습 **freeze** [friːz] v. (froze-frozen) (두려움 등으로 몸이) 얼어붙다; 얼다; n. 동결; 한파
If someone who is moving freezes, they suddenly stop and become completely still and quiet.

* **stun** [stʌn] v. 깜짝 놀라게 하다; 어리벙벙하게 하다; 기절시키다
If you are stunned by something, you are extremely shocked or surprised by it and are therefore unable to speak or do anything.

outburst [áutbəːrst] n. (감정의) 폭발; (특정 활동·태도의) 급격한 증가
An outburst of an emotion, especially anger, is a sudden strong expression of that emotion.

복습 **awkward** [ɔ́ːkwərd] a. 어색한; (처리하기) 곤란한; 불편한
An awkward situation is embarrassing and difficult to deal with.

* **resume** [rizúːm] v. 재개하다; 자기 위치로 돌아가다
If you resume an activity or if it resumes, it begins again.

* **crime** [kraim] n. 범죄, 죄
A crime is an illegal action or activity for which a person can be punished by law.

* **glance** [glæns] n. 흘낏 봄; v. 흘낏 보다; 대충 훑어보다
A glance is a quick look at someone or something.

* **adapt** [ədǽpt] v. 적응하다; 조정하다
If you adapt to a new situation or adapt yourself to it, you change your ideas or behavior in order to deal with it successfully.

* **concern** [kənsɔ́ːrn] v. 걱정스럽게 하다; 관련되다; n. 우려, 걱정; 관심사
(concerned a. 걱정하는, 염려하는)
If something concerns you, it worries you.

* **settle** [setl] v. 자리를 잡다; (서서히) 가라앉다; 결정하다
If you settle yourself somewhere or settle somewhere, you sit down or make yourself comfortable.

* **couch** [kauʧ] n. 긴 의자, 소파
A couch is a long, comfortable seat for two or three people.

* **weight** [weit] n. 중요성, 영향력; 무게, 체중; 무거운 것; 추
If something is given a particular weight, it is given a particular value according to how important or significant it is.

CHAPTER 3

Check Your Reading Speed
1분에 몇 단어를 읽는지 리딩 속도를 측정해보세요.

$$\frac{546 \text{ words}}{\text{reading time (} \quad \text{) sec}} \times 60 = (\qquad) \text{ WPM}$$

Build Your Vocabulary

‡ **pool** [puːl] n. 수영장; 웅덩이; v. (자금·정보 등을) 모으다; 고이다
A pool is the same as a swimming pool which is a large hole in the ground that has been made and filled with water so that people can swim in it.

복습 **stare** [stɛər] v. 빤히 쳐다보다, 응시하다; n. 빤히 쳐다보기, 응시
If you stare at someone or something, you look at them for a long time.

복습 **ripple** [ripl] v. 잔물결을 이루다; (감정 등이) 파문처럼 번지다; n. 잔물결, 파문 (모양의 것)
When the surface of an area of water ripples or when something ripples it, a number of little waves appear on it.

‡ **reflect** [riflékt] v. (상을) 비추다; 반사하다; 깊이 생각하다 (reflection n. (거울 등에 비친) 상)
A reflection is an image that you can see in a mirror or in glass or water.

⁎ **shrug** [ʃrʌg] n. 어깨를 으쓱하기; v. (어깨를) 으쓱하다
A shrug is the action of raising and lowering your shoulders to express something.

⁎ **fantasy** [fǽntəsi] n. 공상, 환상
A fantasy is a pleasant situation or event that you think about and that you want to happen, especially one that is unlikely to happen.

‡ **insurance** [inʃúərəns] n. 보험, 보증; 보호 수단
Insurance is an arrangement in which you pay money to a company, and they pay money to you if something unpleasant happens to you, for example if your property is stolen or damaged, or if you get a serious illness.

be hard on idiom ~에게 힘들다
If something is hard on someone, it is difficult for or unfair to them.

‡ **turn** [təːrn] n. 차례, 순번; 전환; 돌기; v. 돌다; 변하다
If it is your turn to do something, you now have the duty, chance, or right to do it, when other people have done it before you or will do it after you.

take care of idiom ~을 돌보다; ~을 처리하다
If you take care of someone or something, you look after them and prevent them from being harmed or damaged.

breadwinner [brédwinər] n. (집안의) 생계비를 버는 사람, 가장
The breadwinner in a family is the person in it who earns the money that the family needs for essential things.

win [win] v. (노력을 통해 무엇을) 얻다; 이기다; (경기 등에서 이겨 무엇을) 따다; n. 승리
If you win something that you want or need, you succeed in getting it.

sigh [sai] v. 한숨을 쉬다, 한숨짓다; 탄식하듯 말하다; n. 한숨
When you sigh, you let out a deep breath, as a way of expressing feelings such as disappointment, tiredness, or pleasure.

suit [suːt] n. 정장; (특정한 활동 때 입는) 옷; 소송; v. ~에게 편리하다; 어울리다
A man's suit consists of a jacket, trousers, and sometimes a waistcoat, all made from the same fabric.

burn [bəːrn] v. 불에 타다; 태우다; 상기되다; n. 화상
If you burn something, you destroy or damage it with fire.

jet [dʒet] n. 제트기; 분출; v. 급속히 움직이다; 분출하다
A jet is an aircraft that is powered by jet engines.

recall [rikɔ́ːl] v. 기억해 내다, 상기하다; 다시 불러들이다; n. 회상; (제품의) 회수
When you recall something, you remember it and tell others about it.

obvious [ábviəs] a. 분명한, 확실한; 명백한
If something is obvious, it is easy to see or understand.

appreciate [əpríːʃièit] v. 고마워하다; 진가를 알아보다
If you appreciate something that someone has done for you or is going to do for you, you are grateful for it.

make it idiom (힘든 경험 등을) 버텨 내다; 가다; 해내다
If you make it, you are successful in achieving something difficult, or in surviving through a very difficult period.

awful [ɔ́ːfəl] a. 끔찍한, 지독한; (정도가) 대단한, 아주 심한
If you say that something is awful, you mean that it is extremely unpleasant, shocking, or bad.

remind [rimáind] v. 상기시키다, 다시 한 번 알려 주다
If someone reminds you of a fact or event that you already know about, they say something which makes you think about it.

count on idiom 기대하다, 의지하다
If you count on someone, you depend on them to do what you want or expect them to do for you.

shadowy [ʃǽdoui] a. (어둑해서) 잘 보이지 않는, 어슴푸레한; 그늘이 진, 어둑어둑한
A shadowy figure or shape is someone or something that you can hardly see because they are in a dark place.

silhouette [siluét] n. 외형, 윤곽, 실루엣; v. 실루엣으로 나타내다
The silhouette of something is the outline that it has, which often helps you to recognize it.

defensive [difénsiv] a. 방어적인; 방어의 (defensively ad. 방어적으로)
Someone who is defensive is behaving in a way that shows they feel unsure or threatened.

figure [fígjər] n. (멀리서 흐릿하게 보이는) 사람; 수치; (중요한) 인물; v. 생각하다; 중요하다
You refer to someone that you can see as a figure when you cannot see them clearly or when you are describing them.

relieve [rilíːv] v. 안도하다; (불쾌감·고통 등을) 없애 주다; 완화하다 (relief n. 안도, 안심)
If you feel a sense of relief, you feel happy because something unpleasant has not happened or is no longer happening.

frown [fraun] v. 얼굴을 찡그리다; 눈살을 찌푸리다; n. 찡그림, 찌푸림
When someone frowns, their eyebrows become drawn together, because they are annoyed, worried, or puzzled, or because they are concentrating.

sarcastic [saːrkǽstik] a. 빈정대는, 비꼬는; 풍자적인 (sarcastically ad. 비꼬는 투로)
Someone who is sarcastic says or does the opposite of what they really mean in order to mock or insult someone.

besides [bisáidz] ad. 게다가, 뿐만 아니라; prep. ~외에
Besides is used to emphasize an additional point that you are making, especially one that you consider to be important.

cop [kap] n. 경찰관
A cop is a policeman or policewoman.

in spite of idiom ~에도 불구하고
You use in spite of to introduce a fact which makes the rest of the statement you are making seem surprising.

roll one's eyes idiom 눈을 굴리다
If you roll your eyes or if your eyes roll, they move round and upward to show you are bored or annoyed.

smirk [sməːrk] v. 히죽히죽 웃다; n. 능글맞은 웃음
If you smirk, you smile in an unpleasant way, often because you believe that you have gained an advantage over someone else or know something that they do not know.

⁑ **comment** [kάment] n. 논평, 언급; v. 논평하다, 견해를 밝히다
A comment is something that you say which expresses your opinion of something or which gives an explanation of it.

⁑ **shut down** idiom 종료하다; (기계가) 멈추다
If a shop, school, factory, or business shuts down, or if someone shuts it down, it closes, usually permanently.

⁑ **stand** [stænd] v. (제의·결정 등이 아직도) 유효하다; 서다; n. (경기장의) 관중석; 가판대, 좌판
If a decision, law, or offer stands, it still exists and has not been changed or canceled.

⁑ **generous** [dʒénərəs] a. 관대한; 후한; 넉넉한
A generous person is friendly, helpful, and willing to see the good qualities in someone or something.

business card [bíznis kaːrd] n. 명함
A person's business card or their card is a small card which they give to other people, and which has their name and details of their job and company printed on it.

⁑ **represent** [rèprizént] v. 대표하다; 보여주다, 제시하다; 상징하다
If you represent a person or group at an official event, you go there on their behalf.

tycoon [taikúːn] n. (재계의) 거물
A tycoon is a person who is successful in business and so has become rich and powerful.

⁑ **stuff** [stʌf] n. 일, 것, 물건; v. 쑤셔 넣다; 채워 넣다
You can use stuff to refer to things such as a substance, a collection of things, events, or ideas, or the contents of something in a general way without mentioning the thing itself by name.

* **reveal** [riví:l] v. (보이지 않던 것을) 드러내 보이다; (비밀 등을) 밝히다
If you reveal something that has been out of sight, you uncover it so that people can see it.

geez [dʒi:z] int. 이런, 맙소사
Some people say geez when they are shocked or surprised about something, or to introduce a remark or response.

* **groan** [groun] v. (고통·짜증으로) 신음 소리를 내다; 끙끙거리다; n. 신음, 끙 하는 소리
If you groan, you make a long, low sound because you are in pain, or because you are upset or unhappy about something.

‡ **station** [stéiʃən] n. 구역, 부서; 위치, 장소; 역; v. 배치하다 (police station n. 경찰서)
A police station is the local office of a police force in a particular area.

복습 **grin** [grin] v. 활짝 웃다; n. 활짝 웃음
When you grin, you smile broadly.

sit out idiom 빠지다, 참여하지 않다
If you sit something out, you are not involved in it.

‡ **nod** [nad] v. (고개를) 끄덕이다, 까딱하다; n. (고개를) 끄덕임
If you nod, you move your head downward and upward to show that you are answering 'yes' to a question, or to show agreement, understanding, or approval.

* **surrender** [səréndər] v. 항복하다, 투항하다; (권리 등을) 포기하다; n. 항복, 굴복
If you surrender, you stop fighting or resisting someone and agree that you have been beaten.

복습 **pressure** [préʃər] n. 압박, 스트레스; 압력; v. 강요하다; 압력을 가하다
If there is pressure on a person, someone is trying to persuade or force them to do something.

복습 **beam** [bi:m] v. 활짝 웃다; 비추다; n. 빛줄기; 기둥
If you say that someone is beaming, you mean that they have a big smile on their face because they are happy, pleased, or proud about something.

* **thorough** [θə́:rou] a. 완전한; 철저한; 빈틈없는, 철두철미한 (thoroughly ad. 완전히)
Thorough is used to emphasize the great degree or extent of something.

‡ **prospect** [práspekt] n. (어떤 일이 있을) 가망, 기대, 전망
If there is some prospect of something happening, there is a possibility that it will happen.

nostalgic [nastǽldʒik] a. 향수의, 향수를 불러 일으키는
If you feel nostalgic, you think affectionately about experiences you had in the past.

Chapters
4 & 5

1. How did Winston know about Mr. Incredible and Elastigirl's personal life?

A. He had worked for the agent Rick Dicker.

B. He had been spying on them for several years.

C. He had seen them take off their masks after fighting crime.

D. He had heard about their real identities from other Supers.

2. What did Winston's father do right before he died?

A. He told his wife and kids that he loved them.

B. He donated all his money to Superhero causes.

C. He tried to contact a few Supers.

D. He hid his wife in a safe room.

3. How did Winston and Evelyn plan to make Superheroes legal again?

A. By showing the world how normal they were

B. By having them go out and meet ordinary people

C. By making Superhero movies with them

D. By sharing video footage of them in action

4. Why did Winston choose Elastigirl for the first assignment?

A. She was smarter and stronger than Mr. Incredible.

B. She caused less damage than Mr. Incredible.

C. She had caught more criminals than Mr. Incredible.

D. She had been a Super longer than Mr. Incredible.

5. Why did Helen hesitate to accept Winston's offer?

A. She did not think she could succeed on her own.

B. She did not think Winston could be trusted.

C. She did not want to make Bob jealous.

D. She did not want to leave her kids.

CHAPTER 4

Check Your Reading Speed
1분에 몇 단어를 읽는지 리딩 속도를 측정해보세요.

$$\frac{1,498 \text{ words}}{\text{reading time ( ) sec}} \times 60 = (\qquad) \text{ WPM}$$

Build Your Vocabulary

headquarter [hédkwɔ̀ːrtər] n. (pl.) 본사, 본부; v. ~에 본부를 두다
The headquarters of an organization are its main offices.

* **skyscraper** [skáiskrèipər] n. 고층 건물
A skyscraper is a very tall building in a city.

복습 **stretch** [streʧ] v. 뻗어 있다; (길이·폭 등을) 늘이다; n. 뻗기, 펴기; (길게) 뻗은 구간
Something that stretches over an area or distance covers or exists in the whole of
that area or distance.

* **security** [sikjúərəti] n. 보안, 경비; 경비 담당 부서; 안도감, 안심
Security refers to all the measures that are taken to protect a place, or to ensure
that only people with permission enter it or leave it.

* **badge** [bædʒ] n. (경찰 등의) 신분증; 표, 배지
A badge is a piece of metal or cloth which you wear to show that you belong to an
organization or support a cause.

usher [ʌ́ʃər] v. 안내하다; n. (교회·극장 등의) 좌석 안내원
If you usher someone somewhere, you show them where they should go, often by
going with them.

* **revolve** [riválv] v. 회전하다; 공전(公轉)하다 (revolving door n. 회전문)
If one object revolves around another object, the first object turns in a circle
around the second object.

sleek [sliːk] a. (모양이) 매끈한; 윤이 나는
Sleek vehicles, furniture, or other objects look smooth, shiny, and expensive.

* **incredible** [inkrédəbl] a. 믿을 수 없는, 믿기 힘든
If you describe something or someone as incredible, you like them very much or
are impressed by them, because they are extremely or unusually good.

^복_습 **enormous** [inɔ́ːrməs] a. 막대한, 거대한
Something that is enormous is extremely large in size or amount.

* **lively** [láivli] a. 활기 넘치는, 활발한; 적극적인, 의욕적인; 선명한
You can describe someone as lively when they behave in an enthusiastic and cheerful way.

* **trot** [trat] v. 빨리 걷다; 총총걸음을 걷다; n. 속보, 빠른 걸음
If you trot somewhere, you move fairly fast at a speed between walking and running, taking small quick steps.

* **curve** [kəːrv] v. 곡선으로 나아가다, 곡선을 이루다; n. 커브, 곡선 (curved a. 곡선의)
A curved object has the shape of a curve or has a smoothly bending surface.

* **staircase** [stɛ́ərkèis] n. (건물 내부에 죽 이어져 있는) 계단
A staircase is a set of stairs inside a building.

* **costume** [kástjuːm] n. 의상, 복장; 분장
An actor's or performer's costume is the set of clothes they wear while they are performing.

mythic [míθik] a. (대단히 유명해서) 신화적인
If you describe someone or something as mythic, you mean that they have become very famous or important.

^복_습 **struggle** [strʌgl] n. 투쟁, 분투; 몸부림; v. 애쓰다; 몸부림치다, 허우적거리다; 힘겹게 나아가다
A struggle is a long and difficult attempt to achieve something such as freedom or political rights.

* **enthusiastic** [inθùːziǽstik] a. 열렬한, 열광적인 (enthusiastically ad. 열광적으로)
If you are enthusiastic about something, you show how much you like or enjoy it by the way that you behave and talk.

* **theme** [θiːm] n. 주제, 테마
Theme music or a theme song is a piece of music that is played at the beginning and end of a film or of a television or radio program.

* **thrill** [θril] n. 흥분, 설렘; 전율; v. 열광시키다, 정말 신나게 하다
If something gives you a thrill, it gives you a sudden feeling of great excitement, pleasure, or fear.

* **gesture** [dʒésʧər] v. (손·머리 등으로) 가리키다; 몸짓을 하다; n. 몸짓; (감정·의도의) 표시
If you gesture, you use movements of your hands or head in order to tell someone something or draw their attention to something.

tardy [tá:rdi] a. (도착 등이) 늦은; 더딘, 느린; n. 지각
If you describe something or someone as tardy, you think that they are later than they should be or later than expected.

* **scold** [skould] v. 야단치다, 꾸짖다
If you scold someone, you speak angrily to them because they have done something wrong.

* **disapprove** [dìsəprú:v] v. 탐탁찮아 하다, 못마땅해 하다 (disapproving a. 못마땅해 하는)
A disapproving action or expression shows that you do not approve of something or someone.

* **admire** [ædmáiər] v. 감탄하며 바라보다; 존경하다, 칭찬하다 (admiration n. 감탄, 존경)
If you admire someone or something, you look at them with pleasure.

* **spectacular** [spektǽkjulər] a. 장관을 이루는; 극적인; n. 화려한 쇼
Something that is spectacular is very impressive or dramatic.

* **sport** [spɔ:rt] v. 자랑스럽게 보이다; n. 스포츠, 운동
If you sport something, you wear or be decorated with it.

yesteryear [jéstərjíər] n. 지난날, 왕년
You use yesteryear to refer to the past, often a period in the past with a set of values or a way of life that no longer exists.

swap [swap] v. 교환하다; (다른 것으로) 바꾸다; n. 바꾸기, 교환
If you swap something with someone, you give it to them and receive a different thing in exchange.

* **visible** [vízəbl] a. (눈에) 보이는, 알아볼 수 있는; 뚜렷한 (visibly ad. 눈에 띄게)
If something is visible, it can be seen.

* **shaken** [ʃéikən] a. 충격을 받은; 화가 난; 겁먹은
If you are shaken, you are feeling nervous or frightened because of something that has happened.

alter ego [ɔ:ltər í:gou] n. 또 다른 자아
Your alter ego is the other side of your personality from the one which people normally see.

underground [ʌndərgráund] a. 비밀의; 지하의; ad. 지하에
If you go underground, you hide from the authorities or the police because your political ideas or activities are illegal.

^{복습} **click** [klik] v. 분명해지다; 딸깍 하는 소리를 내다; n. 딸깍 (하는 소리)
When you suddenly understand something, you can say that it clicks.

recapture [rìːkǽptʃər] v. (과거의 느낌·경험을) 되찾다; 탈환하다; 다시 체포하다
When you recapture something such as an experience, emotion, or a quality that
you had in the past, you experience it again.

^{복습} **nod** [nad] v. (고개를) 끄덕이다, 까딱하다; n. (고개를) 끄덕임
If you nod, you move your head downward and upward to show that you are
answering 'yes' to a question, or to show agreement, understanding, or approval.

remote [rimóut] a. 먼; 외진, 외딴; 원격의; n. (= remote control) 리모컨; 원격 조종
(remotely ad. 아주 약간)
You use remotely with a negative statement to emphasize the statement.

portrait [póːrtrit] n. 초상, 초상화
A portrait is a painting, drawing, or photograph of a particular person.

adore [ədóːr] v. 아주 좋아하다; 흠모하다
If you adore someone, you feel great love and admiration for them.

donate [dóuneit] v. 기부하다, 기증하다; 헌혈하다
If you donate something to a charity or other organization, you give it to them.

raise money idiom 모금하다
If you raise money, you collect money for a particular purpose.

statue [stǽtʃuː] n. 조각상
A statue is a large sculpture of a person or an animal, made of stone or metal.

drift [drift] v. (자신도 모르게) ~하게 되다; (물·공기에) 떠가다; (서서히) 이동하다; n. 표류; 흐름
If someone or something drifts into a situation, they get into that situation in a
way that is not planned or controlled.

personal [pɚ́rsənl] a. 개인적인, 개인의 (personally ad. 직접, 개인적으로)
If you meet or know someone personally, you meet or know them in real life,
rather than knowing about them or knowing their work.

install [instóːl] v. (장비·가구를) 설치하다
If you install a piece of equipment, you fit it or put it somewhere so that it is ready
to be used.

in case idiom (~할) 경우에 대비해서
If you do something in case or just in case a particular thing happens, you do it
because that thing might happen.

emergency [imə́:rdʒənsi] n. 비상
An emergency is an unexpected and difficult or dangerous situation, especially an accident, which happens suddenly and which requires quick action to deal with it.

show off idiom ~을 자랑하다; 돋보이게 하다
To show off someone or something means to try to make people pay attention to them because you are proud of them.

trail off idiom (목소리가) 차츰 잦아들다
If someone's speech trails off, it gradually becomes quieter and then stops.

pause [pɔːz] v. (말·일을) 잠시 멈추다; (테이프·시디 등을) 정지시키다; n. (말·행동 등의) 멈춤
If you pause while you are doing something, you stop for a short period and then continue.

fond [fand] a. 다정한, 애정 어린; 좋아하는
If you have fond memories of someone or something, you remember them with pleasure.

snap [snæp] v. 급히 움직이다; 툭 부러지다; 날카롭게 말하다; n. 탁 하는 소리
(snap back idiom 회복하다)
To snap back means to quickly return to a previous condition.

gaze [geiz] n. 응시, (눈여겨보는) 시선; v. (가만히) 응시하다, 바라보다
You can talk about someone's gaze as a way of describing how they are looking at something, especially when they are looking steadily at it.

heartbroken [há:rtbròukən] a. 비통해하는
Someone who is heartbroken is very sad and emotionally upset.

painful [péinfəl] a. (마음이) 괴로운; 고통스러운
Situations, memories, or experiences that are painful are difficult and unpleasant to deal with, and often make you feel sad and upset.

childhood [ʧáildhùd] n. 어린 시절
A person's childhood is the period of their life when they are a child.

break into idiom (건물에) 침입하다
If you break into something such as a building or a car, you enter the building or open the car illegally and by force.

insist [insíst] v. 고집하다, 주장하다, 우기다
If you insist that something should be done, you say so very firmly and refuse to give in about it.

‡ **rob** [rab] v. (사람·장소를) 도둑질하다 (robber n. 강도)
A robber is someone who steals money or property from a bank, a shop, or a vehicle, often by using force or threats.

heartbreak [háːrtbreik] n. 비통
Heartbreak is very great sadness and emotional suffering, especially after the end of a love affair or close relationship.

tinge [tindʒ] n. 기미, 기운; v. (색채를) 더하다; (어떤 느낌·기운 등을) 가미하다
A tinge of a color, feeling, or quality is a small amount of it.

복습 **irritate** [írətèit] v. 짜증나게 하다, 거슬리다; 자극하다 (irritation n. 짜증)
Irritation is a feeling of annoyance, especially when something is happening that you cannot easily stop or control.

복습 **interrupt** [intərʌ́pt] v. (말·행동을) 방해하다; 중단시키다; 차단하다
If you interrupt someone who is speaking, you say or do something that causes them to stop.

복습 **tone** [toun] n. 어조, 말투; (글 등의) 분위기; 음색
Someone's tone is a quality in their voice which shows what they are feeling or thinking.

telecommunication [tèləkəmjùːnəkéiʃən] n. (라디오·전화 등의) 통신
Telecommunications is the technology of sending signals and messages over long distances using electronic equipment, for example by radio and telephone.

‡ **position** [pəzíʃən] v. ~의 자리를 잡다; n. 자세; 위치; 자리
If you position someone or something, you put or arrange them in a particular place or way.

* **hence** [hens] ad. 이런 이유로, 그러므로, 따라서
You use hence to indicate that the statement you are about to make is a consequence of what you have just said.

복습 **couch** [kauʧ] n. 긴 의자, 소파
A couch is a long, comfortable seat for two or three people.

복습 **blind** [blaind] n. (창문에 치는) 블라인드; v. (잠시) 안 보이게 하다; a. 눈이 먼; 눈치 채지 못하는
A blind is a roll of cloth or paper which you can pull down over a window as a covering.

복습 **ignore** [ignɔ́ːr] v. 무시하다; (사람을) 못 본 척하다 (ignorance n. 무지, 무식)
Ignorance of something is lack of knowledge about it.

perception [pərsépʃən] n. 지각, 인식, 인지
Your perception of something is the way that you think about it or the impression you have of it.

footage [fútidʒ] n. (특정한 사건을 담은) 장면
Footage of a particular event is a film of it or the part of a film which shows this event.

tell me about it idiom 무슨 말인지 잘 안다
If you say 'tell me about it' to someone, you mean that you already know about something unpleasant that they have just described because you have experienced it yourself.

lean [li:n] v. 기울이다, (몸을) 숙이다; ~에 기대다; a. 군살이 없는, 호리호리한
When you lean in a particular direction, you bend your body in that direction.

dramatic [drəmǽtik] a. 과장된; 극적인; 감격적인, 인상적인 (dramatically ad. 호들갑스럽게)
A dramatic action, event, or situation is exciting and impressive.

glance [glæns] n. 흘낏 봄; v. 흘낏 보다; 대충 훑어보다
A glance is a quick look at someone or something.

lead up to idiom ~에 이르다; ~로 통하다
If events, problems, or actions lead up to an important event, they happen one after another in a way that makes it possible for the event to happen.

politician [pàlitíʃən] n. 정치인
A politician is a person whose job is in politics, especially a member of parliament or congress.

destruction [distrʌ́kʃən] n. 파괴, 파멸; 말살
Destruction is the action or process of causing so much damage to something that it no longer exists or cannot be repaired.

edge [edʒ] n. 끝, 가장자리; 우위; v. 조금씩 움직이다; 테두리를 두르다
The edge of something is the place or line where it stops, or the part of it that is furthest from the middle.

wrap [ræp] v. (무엇의 둘레를) 두르다; 포장하다; 둘러싸다; n. 포장지; 랩
If someone wraps their arms, fingers, or legs around something, they put them firmly around it.

grateful [gréitfəl] a. 고마워하는, 감사하는 (gratefully ad. 감사하여)
If you are grateful for something that someone has given you or done for you, you have warm, friendly feelings toward them and wish to thank them.

separate [sépərèit] a. 별개의; 분리된; v. 분리하다, 나누다; 갈라지다
If you refer to separate things, you mean several different things, rather than just one thing.

angle [æŋgl] n. 각도, 각; 기울기; 관점; v. 비스듬히 움직이다
An angle is the direction from which you look at something.

feed [fi:d] n. 텔레비전 방송 프로그램; (동물의) 먹이; v. 먹이를 주다; 먹여 살리다
A feed is a broadcast distributed by a satellite or network from a central source to a large number of radio or television stations.

simultaneous [sàiməltéiniəs] a. 동시에 일어나는, 동시의 (simultaneously ad. 동시에)
Things which are simultaneous happen or exist at the same time.

clip [klip] v. 핀으로 고정하다; 깎다, 자르다; n. 짧은 영상; 핀, 클립
When you clip things together or when things clip together, you fasten them together using a clip or clips.

sew [sou] v. 바느질하다, 깁다
When you sew something such as clothes, you make them or repair them by joining pieces of cloth together by passing thread through them with a needle.

tiny [táini] a. 아주 작은
Something or someone that is tiny is extremely small.

fabric [fǽbrik] n. 직물, 천
Fabric is cloth or other material produced by weaving together cotton, nylon, wool, silk, or other threads. Fabrics are used for making things such as clothes, curtains, and sheets.

impress [imprés] v. 깊은 인상을 주다, 감동을 주다 (impressed a. 감명을 받은)
If something impresses you, you feel great admiration for it.

inspect [inspékt] v. 면밀하게 살피다, 점검하다; 시찰하다
If you inspect something, you look at every part of it carefully in order to find out about it or check that it is all right.

crystal clear [kristl klíər] a. 수정같이 맑은; 명명백백한, 아주 분명한
If you describe a thing or image as crystal clear, you mean that it is strikingly clear or clean.

outstanding [àutstǽndiŋ] a. 뛰어난; 두드러진
If you describe someone or something as outstanding, you think that they are very remarkable and impressive.

* **compliment** [kámpləmənt] n. 칭찬(의 말), 찬사; v. 칭찬하다
A compliment is a polite remark that you say to someone to show that you like
their appearance, appreciate their qualities, or approve of what they have done.

‡ **design** [dizáin] v. 설계하다; 고안하다; n. 설계; 계획, 의도
When someone designs a garment, building, machine, or other object, they plan
it and make a detailed drawing of it from which it can be built or made.

* **fantastic** [fæntǽstik] a. 기막히게 좋은, 환상적인; 기상천외한; 엄청난, 굉장한
If you say that something is fantastic, you are emphasizing that you think it is very
good or that you like it a lot.

be in one's shoes idiom ~의 입장에 처하다
If you talk about being in someone's shoes, you talk about what you would do or
how you would feel if you were in their situation.

run-in [rʌ́n-in] n. 언쟁, 싸움
A run-in is an argument or quarrel with someone.

‡ **reality** [riǽləti] n. 현실; 실제로 존재하는 것
The reality of a situation is the truth about it, especially when it is unpleasant or
difficult to deal with.

‡ **fit** [fit] v. 어울리게 하다; (모양·크기가) 맞다; 적절하다; a. 건강한; 적합한, 알맞은
If something fits something else or fits into it, it goes together well with that thing
or is able to be part of it.

‡ **resource** [rí:sɔ:rs] n. 자원, 재원; 자산; v. 자원을 제공하다
The resources of an organization or person are the materials, money, and other
things that they have and can use in order to function properly.

* **worldwide** [wə́:rldwaid] a. 전 세계적인
If something exists or happens worldwide, it exists or happens throughout the
world.

복습 **insurance** [inʃúərəns] n. 보호 수단; 보험, 보증
If you do something as insurance against something unpleasant happening, you
do it to protect yourself in case the unpleasant thing happens.

* **priority** [praió:rəti] n. 우선 사항; 우선, 우선권
If something is a priority, it is the most important thing you have to do or deal
with, or must be done or dealt with before everything else you have to do.

‡ **legal** [lí:gəl] a. 법이 허용하는, 합법적인; 법률과 관련된
An action or situation that is legal is allowed or required by law.

* **slap** [slæp] v. (손바닥으로) 철썩 때리다; 털썩 놓다; n. 철썩 때리기, 치기
  If you slap someone, you hit them with the palm of your hand.

* **assign** [əsáin] v. (일·책임 등을) 맡기다; (사람을) 배치하다 (assignment n. 임무, 과제)
  An assignment is a task or piece of work that you are given to do, especially as part of your job or studies.

* **golden** [góuldən] a. 특별한, 소중한; 금으로 만든
  If you describe something as golden, you mean it is wonderful because it is likely to be successful and rewarding, or because it is the best of its kind.

hold on idiom (유리한 것을) 고수하다; 기다려, 멈춰
To hold on to something means to not lose it, or to not let someone else have it.

복습 **extend** [iksténd] v. (팔·다리를) 뻗다; 늘리다, 펼치다; 연장하다
If someone extends their hand, they stretch out their arm and hand to shake hands with someone.

복습 **stun** [stʌn] v. 깜짝 놀라게 하다; 어리벙벙하게 하다; 기절시키다
If you are stunned by something, you are extremely shocked or surprised by it and are therefore unable to speak or do anything.

복습 **punch** [pʌnʧ] v. 주먹으로 치다; (자판·번호판 등을) 치다; n. 주먹으로 한 대 침
If you punch someone or something, you hit them hard with your fist.

gut [gʌt] n. 배; (pl.) 배짱; 직감; v. 내부를 파괴하다
You can refer to someone's stomach as their gut, especially when it is very large and sticks out.

복습 **clear one's throat** idiom 목을 가다듬다; 헛기침하다
If you clear your throat, you cough once in order to make it easier to speak or to attract people's attention.

* **glare** [glɛər] v. 노려보다; 환하다, 눈부시다; n. 노려봄; 환한 빛, 눈부심
  If you glare at someone, you look at them with an angry expression on your face.

복습 **stammer** [stǽmər] v. 말을 더듬다; n. 말 더듬기
If you stammer, you speak with difficulty, hesitating and repeating words or sounds.

* **credit** [krédit] n. 자랑스러운 사람; 칭찬; 신뢰; 입금; v. 입금하다; ~의 공으로 믿다
  If you say that someone is a credit to someone or something, you mean that their qualities or achievements will make people have a good opinion of the person or thing mentioned.

respect [rispékt] n. 존경(심); 존중; v. (법률·원칙 등을) 준수하다; 존경하다; 존중하다
You can say with respect when you are politely disagreeing with someone or criticizing them.

go-round [góu-ràund] n. 한 차례의 승부; 언쟁, 격론
A go-round is one of a series of recurring actions or events.

offend [əfénd] v. 기분 상하게 하다; 불쾌하게 여겨지다; 범죄를 저지르다
If you offend someone, you say or do something rude which upsets or embarrasses them.

clench [klenʧ] v. (이를) 악물다; (주먹을) 꽉 쥐다; ~을 단단히 고정시키다
When you clench your teeth or they clench, you squeeze your teeth together firmly, usually because you are angry or upset.

hold back idiom ~을 저지하다; (진전·발전을) 저해하다
To hold back means to stop yourself from expressing or showing how you feel.

blast [blæst] v. 쾅쾅 울리다; 폭발시키다; 빠르게 가다; n. 폭발; (한 줄기의) 강한 바람
If you blast something such as a car horn, or if it blasts, it makes a sudden, loud sound.

messy [mési] a. 지저분한, 엉망인; (상황이) 엉망인, 골치 아픈
A messy person or activity makes things dirty or untidy.

process [práses] v. (공식적으로) 처리하다; 가공하다; n. 과정, 절차; 공정
To process means to think about a difficult or sad situation so that you can gradually accept it.

bewilder [biwíldər] v. 어리둥절하게 하다, 혼란스럽게 하다 (bewildered a. 당혹한)
If you are bewildered, you are very confused and cannot understand something or decide what you should do.

benefit [bénəfit] n. 혜택, 이득; v. 유익하다; (~에서) 득을 보다
The benefit of something is the help that you get from it or the advantage that results from it.

crime [kraim] n. 범죄, 죄
A crime is an illegal action or activity for which a person can be punished by law.

self-explanatory [sèlf-iksplǽnətɔ̀:ri] a. 자명한, 따로 설명이 필요 없는
Something that is self-explanatory is clear and easy to understand without needing any extra information or explanation.

* **shift** [ʃift] v. 바꾸다; (장소를) 옮기다; n. 교대 근무 (시간); 변화
If you shift, you move your body or a part of your body slightly, for example because you are bored.

복습 **weight** [weit] n. 무게, 체중; 무거운 것; 추; 중요성, 영향력
If you move your weight, you change position so that most of the pressure of your body is on a particular part of your body.

* **comparison** [kəmpǽrisn] n. 비교, 대조
When you make a comparison, you consider two or more things and discover the differences between them.

* **defend** [difénd] v. 옹호하다, 변호하다; 방어하다, 수비하다
If you defend someone or something when they have been criticized, you argue in support of them.

heavyweight [héviweit] a. 중요한, 심각한; n. 무게가 보통 이상인 것; 유력자
If you describe something as heavyweight, you mean that it is serious, important, or influential.

* **launch** [lɔːnʧ] n. 시작; 발사; 개시, 진수; v. 시작하다; 발사하다
A launch is the start of a major activity such as a military attack, a public investigation, or a new career or project.

wrap up idiom 마무리짓다; 옷을 따뜻하게 챙겨 입다
If you wrap up something, you complete it in an acceptable way.

복습 **stall** [stɔːl] v. 시간을 끌다; (차량·엔진이) 멎다, 시동이 꺼지다; n. 가판대, 좌판
If you stall, you try to avoid doing something until later.

* **chuckle** [ʧʌkl] v. 킬킬 웃다; 빙그레 웃다; n. 킬킬거림; 속으로 웃기
When you chuckle, you laugh quietly.

Check Your Reading Speed

1분에 몇 단어를 읽는지 리딩 속도를 측정해보세요.

$$\frac{655 \text{ words}}{\text{reading time (} \quad \text{) sec}} \times 60 = (\quad) \text{ WPM}$$

Build Your Vocabulary

brush [brʌʃ] v. 솔질을 하다; (솔이나 손으로) 털다; n. 붓; 솔; 비 (toothbrush n. 칫솔)
If you brush something or brush something such as dirt off it, you clean it or tidy it using a brush.

cringe [krindʒ] v. (겁이 나서) 움츠리다, 움찔하다; 민망하다
If you cringe at something, you feel embarrassed or disgusted, and perhaps show this feeling in your expression or by making a slight movement.

swoosh [swuʃ] n. 바스락거리는 소리; v. 휙 하는 소리를 내며 움직이다
A swoosh is the sound produced by a sudden rush of air or liquid.

stew [stjuː] v. 생각하다; 마음 졸이다; 약한 불로 끓이다; n. 스튜
If you stew about something, you are angry or worried about it.

fantasy [fǽntəsi] n. 공상, 환상
A fantasy is a pleasant situation or event that you think about and that you want to happen, especially one that is unlikely to happen.

lifetime [láiftàim] n. 평생, 일생, 생애
If you describe something as the chance or experience of a lifetime, you are emphasizing that it is the best or most important chance or experience that you are ever likely to have.

blurt [bləːrt] v. 불쑥 내뱉다, 말하다
If someone blurts something, they say it suddenly, after trying hard to keep quiet or to keep it secret.

jail [dʒeil] n. 교도소, 감옥; v. 수감하다
A jail is a place where criminals are kept in order to punish them, or where people waiting to be tried are kept.

INCREDIBLES 2

* **spit** [spit] v. (~을) 뱉다; ~에서 나오다; n. 침; (침 등을) 뱉기
If you spit liquid or food somewhere, you force a small amount of it out of your mouth.

* **mouthful** [máuθfùl] n. (음식) 한 입, 한 모금; 길고 복잡한 말
A mouthful of drink or food is the amount that you put or have in your mouth.

toothpaste [túːθpèist] n. 치약
Toothpaste is a thick substance which you put on your toothbrush and use to clean your teeth.

sink [siŋk] n. 개수대; v. 가라앉다, 빠지다; 박다; 주저앉다
A sink is a large bowl, usually with taps for hot and cold water, for washing your hands and face.

turn down idiom ~을 거절하다
If you turn someone or something down, you reject or refuse an offer or request.

force [fɔːrs] v. 억지로 ~하다; ~를 강요하다; n. 작용력; 힘; 영향력
If a situation or event forces you to do something, it makes it necessary for you to do something that you would not otherwise have done.

refusal [rifjúːzəl] n. 거절, 거부
Someone's refusal to do something is the fact of them showing or saying that they will not do it, allow it, or accept it.

yell [jel] v. 고함치다, 소리 지르다; n. 고함, 외침
If you yell, you shout loudly, usually because you are excited, angry, or in pain.

firm [fəːrm] a. 단호한, 확고한; 단단한 (firmly ad. 단호히)
If you describe someone as firm, you mean they behave in a way that shows that they are not going to change their mind, or that they are the person who is in control.

plant [plænt] v. 자리를 잡다; 심다; n. 시설; 식물, 초목
If you plant someone, something, or yourself, you firmly put them or yourself in a particular place or position.

benefit [bénəfit] v. (~에서) 득을 보다; 유익하다; n. 혜택, 이득
If you benefit from something or if it benefits you, it helps you or improves your life.

trail off idiom (목소리가) 차츰 잦아들다
If someone's speech trails off, it gradually becomes quieter and then stops.

* **prompt** [prampt] v. 유도하다; (어떤 일이 일어나도록) 하다; a. 즉각적인, 지체 없는
If you prompt someone when they stop speaking, you encourage or help them to continue.

exasperate [igzǽspərèit] v. 몹시 화나게 하다, 짜증나게 하다 (exasperated a. 몹시 화가 난)
If you describe a person as exasperated, you mean that they are frustrated or angry because of something that is happening or something that another person is doing.

^{복습} **chuckle** [ʧʌkl] n. 킬킬거림; 속으로 웃기; v. 킬킬 웃다; 빙그레 웃다
A chuckle is a quiet or suppressed laugh.

* **regardless** [rigá:rdlis] ad. 상관하지 않고
If something happens regardless of something else, it is not affected or influenced at all by that other thing.

^{복습} **pause** [pɔ:z] v. (말·일을) 잠시 멈추다; (테이프·시디 등을) 정지시키다; n. (말·행동 등의) 멈춤
If you pause while you are doing something, you stop for a short period and then continue.

^{복습} **twist** [twist] v. 일그러뜨리다; 휘다, 구부리다; (고개·몸 등을) 돌리다;
n. (손으로) 돌리기; (고개·몸 등을) 돌리기
If you twist something, especially a part of your body, or if it twists, it moves into an unusual, uncomfortable, or bent position, for example because of being hit or pushed, or because you are upset.

take note of idiom 주목하다, 알아채다
If you take note of something, you notice and think about or remember it.

* **miserable** [mízərəbl] a. 비참한; 우울하게 하는; 보잘것없는
If you are miserable, you are very unhappy.

excruciating [ikskrú:ʃièitiŋ] a. 극심한 고통을 주는; 맹렬한, 극심한
If you describe something as excruciating, you are emphasizing that it is extremely painful, either physically or emotionally.

‡ **confess** [kənfés] v. 고백하다, 인정하다; 자백하다
If someone confesses to doing something wrong, they admit that they did it.

* **flatter** [flǽtər] v. 아첨하다; (실제보다) 돋보이게 하다 (flattering a. 으쓱하게 하는)
If someone's remarks are flattering, they praise you and say nice things about you.

* **toss** [tɔ:s] v. (문제 등을) 가볍게 논하다; (가볍게) 던지다; (고개를) 홱 쳐들다; n. 던지기
To toss means to discuss or put forward for discussion in an informal way.

point out idiom 지적하다, 언급하다; 알려주다
If you point out a fact or circumstance, you mention it in order to give someone information about it or make them notice it.

obvious [ábviəs] a. 분명한, 확실한; 명백한
If something is obvious, it is easy to see or understand.

homeless [hóumlis] a. 집 없는, 노숙자의; n. (pl.) 노숙자들
Homeless people have nowhere to live.

make sense idiom 타당하다; 이해가 되다
If something makes sense, it is a sensible or practical thing to do.

uncertain [ʌnsə́:rtn] a. 확신이 없는, 잘 모르는; 자신 없는; 불확실한
If you are uncertain about something, you do not know what you should do, what is going to happen, or what the truth is about something.

adorable [ədɔ́:rəbl] a. 사랑스러운
If you say that someone or something is adorable, you are emphasizing that they are very attractive and you feel great affection for them.

playful [pleifl] a. 장난으로 한; 장난기 많은 (playfully ad. 장난삼아)
A playful gesture or person is friendly or humorous.

pillow [pílou] n. 베개
A pillow is a rectangular cushion which you rest your head on when you are in bed.

Chapters
6 & 7

1. **How did the Parr family feel about Winston's house?**
   A. Bob was quite disappointed.
   B. Helen was extremely excited.
   C. Dash was a bit skeptical.
   D. Violet was not fully satisfied.

2. **What was true about Elastigirl's new suit?**
   A. It had lots of bright colors.
   B. It looked different from Elastigirl's old suit.
   C. It was designed by E.
   D. It reflected Elastigirl's personality well.

3. What did Violet think of her mom's new job?

A. She thought it was strange that her mom was breaking the law.

B. She thought her mom should be paid more to break the law.

C. She thought it was nice that her mom was standing up for Superheroes.

D. She thought it would be better to keep Superheroes illegal.

4. What was wrong with the hovertrain?

A. Its doors would not open.

B. It fell completely off the track.

C. It was going the wrong way.

D. It was moving slower than expected.

5. What did the engineer do while Elastigirl tried to stop the train?

A. He did not do anything.

B. He stared at her with confusion.

C. He locked the cabin door.

D. He panicked and fainted.

Check Your Reading Speed
1분에 몇 단어를 읽는지 리딩 속도를 측정해보세요.

$$\frac{1{,}178 \text{ words}}{\text{reading time (} \quad \text{) sec}} \times 60 = (\qquad) \text{ WPM}$$

Build Your Vocabulary

limousine [límǝziːn] n. (= limo) 리무진(대형 승용차)
A limousine is a large and very comfortable car. Limousines are usually driven by a chauffeur and are used by very rich or important people.

lush [lʌʃ] a. (식물·정원 등이) 무성한, 우거진; 멋진
Lush fields or gardens have a lot of very healthy grass or plants.

mansion [mǽnʃǝn] n. 대저택, 저택
A mansion is a very large house.

jaw [dʒɔː] n. 턱
Your jaw is the lower part of your face below your mouth.

take in idiom ~을 눈여겨보다; 이해하다
If you take in something, you spend time looking at it.

sight [sait] n. 광경, 모습; 보기; 시력; v. 갑자기 보다
A sight is something that you see.

be a far cry from idiom ~와는 상당히 다르다
Something that is a far cry from something else is very different from it.

hop [hap] v. 급히 움직이다; 깡충깡충 뛰다; n. 깡충깡충 뛰기
If you hop somewhere, you move there quickly or suddenly.

rush [rʌʃ] v. 급히 움직이다; 서두르다; n. (감정이 갑자기) 치밀어 오름; 혼잡; 기쁨, 흥분
If you rush somewhere, you go there quickly.

front door [frʌnt dɔ́ːr] n. (주택의) 현관
The front door of a house or other building is the main door, which is usually in the wall that faces a street.

^복_습 **swing** [swiŋ] v. (swung-swung) 휙 움직이다; (전후·좌우로) 흔들다; n. 흔들기; 휘두르기
If something swings in a particular direction or if you swing it in that direction, it moves in that direction with a smooth, curving movement.

^복_습 **stare** [stɛər] v. 빤히 쳐다보다, 응시하다; n. 빤히 쳐다보기, 응시
If you stare at someone or something, you look at them for a long time.

^복_습 **ceiling** [sí:liŋ] n. 천장
A ceiling is the horizontal surface that forms the top part or roof inside a room.

^복_습 **massive** [mǽsiv] a. (육중하면서) 거대한; 엄청나게 심각한
Something that is massive is very large in size, quantity, or extent.

boulder [bóuldər] n. 바위
A boulder is a large rounded rock.

* **fountain** [fáuntən] n. 분수; 원천, 근원; v. 분출하다
A fountain is an ornamental feature in a pool or lake which consists of a long narrow stream of water that is forced up into the air by a pump.

* **waterfall** [wɔ́:tərfɔ:l] n. 폭포
A waterfall is a place where water flows over the edge of a steep, high cliff in hills or mountains, and falls into a pool below.

* **luxurious** [lʌgʒúəriəs] a. 호화로운, 아주 편안한
If you describe something as luxurious, you mean that it is very comfortable and expensive.

lair [lɛər] n. 은신처; (야생 동물의) 집, 굴
Someone's lair is the particular room or hiding place that they go to, especially when they want to get away from other people.

high-profile [hai-próufail] a. 세간의 이목을 끄는
A high-profile person or a high-profile event attracts a lot of attention or publicity.

* **spy** [spai] n. 스파이, 정보원; v. (갑자기) 보다, 알아채다
A spy is a person whose job is to find out secret information about another country or organization.

^복_습 **thrill** [θril] v. 열광시키다, 정말 신나게 하다; n. 흥분, 설렘; 전율 (thrilled a. 아주 흥분한)
If someone is thrilled, they are extremely pleased about something.

^복_습 **loan** [loun] v. 빌려주다; n. 대출; 대여
If you loan something to someone, you lend it to them.

make one's way idiom 나아가다, 가다
When you make your way somewhere, you walk or travel there.

homey [hóumi] a. 제집 같은, 편안한
If you describe a room or house as homey, you like it because you feel comfortable and relaxed there.

sarcastic [sa:rkǽstik] a. 빈정대는, 비꼬는; 풍자적인 (sarcastically ad. 비꼬는 투로)
Someone who is sarcastic says or does the opposite of what they really mean in order to mock or insult someone.

eccentric [ikséntrik] a. 괴짜인, 별난, 기이한
If you say that someone is eccentric, you mean that they behave in a strange way, and have habits or opinions that are different from those of most people.

billionaire [biljənέər] n. 억만장자, 갑부
A billionaire is an extremely rich person who has money or property worth at least a thousand million pounds or dollars.

multiple [mʌ́ltəpl] a. 많은, 다수의; 복합적인; n. 배수
You use multiple to describe things that consist of many parts, involve many people, or have many uses.

exit [égzit] n. (공공건물의) 출구; (고속도로의) 출구; 퇴장; v. 나가다, 떠나다; 퇴장하다
The exit is the door through which you can leave a public building.

explore [iksplɔ́:r] v. 탐험하다, 탐사하다; 분석하다
If you explore a place, you travel around it to find out what it is like.

zoom [zu:m] v. 쌩 하고 가다; 급등하다; n. (빠르게) 쌩 하고 지나가는 소리
If you zoom somewhere, you go there very quickly.

stand out idiom 두드러지다
If someone or something stands out, they are easy to see or notice because of being different.

drip [drip] v. 가득 담고 있다; (액체가) 뚝뚝 흐르다; n. (액체가) 뚝뚝 떨어짐
If you say that something is dripping with a particular thing, you mean that it contains a lot of that thing.

sarcasm [sá:rkæzm] n. 빈정댐, 비꼼
Sarcasm is speech or writing which actually means the opposite of what it seems to say. Sarcasm is usually intended to mock or insult someone.

attract [ətrǽkt] v. (어떤 반응을) 불러일으키다; 마음을 끌다
If something attracts support, publicity, or money, it receives support, publicity, or money.

yard [jɑ:rd] n. 마당, 뜰; (학교의) 운동장; 정원
A yard is a piece of land next to someone's house, with grass and plants growing in it.

uncertain [ʌnsə́:rtn] a. 확신이 없는, 잘 모르는; 자신 없는; 불확실한
If you are uncertain about something, you do not know what you should do, what is going to happen, or what the truth is about something.

pool [pu:l] n. 수영장; 웅덩이; v. (자금·정보 등을) 모으다; 고이다
A pool is the same as a swimming pool which is a large hole in the ground that has been made and filled with water so that people can swim in it.

splash [splæʃ] n. 첨벙 하는 소리; (어디에 떨어지는) 방울; v. 첨벙거리다; (물 등을) 끼얹다
A splash is the sound made when something hits water or falls into it.

remind [rimáind] v. 상기시키다, 다시 한 번 알려 주다
If someone reminds you of a fact or event that you already know about, they say something which makes you think about it.

zip [zip] v. (어떤 방향으로) 쌩 하고 가다; 지퍼를 잠그다; n. 지퍼
If you say that something or someone zips somewhere, you mean that they move very fast.

soak [souk] v. 흠뻑 적시다; (지식 등을) 흡수하다; n. (액체 속에) 담그기
(soaking wet a. 완전히 다 젖은, 흠뻑 젖은)
If something is soaking or soaking wet, it is very wet.

notice [nóutis] v. 알아채다, 인지하다; 주의하다; n. 신경 씀, 알아챔; 통지, 예고
If you notice something or someone, you become aware of them.

remote [rimóut] n. (= remote control) 리모컨; 원격 조종; a. 먼; 외진, 외딴; 원격의
The remote control for a television or video recorder is the device that you use to control the machine from a distance, by pressing the buttons on it.

control [kəntróul] n. (기계·차량의) 제어 장치; 통제, 제어; v. 지배하다; 조정하다
A control is a device such as a switch or lever which you use in order to operate a machine or other piece of equipment.

grab [græb] v. (와락·단단히) 붙잡다; 급히 ~하다; n. 와락 잡아채려고 함
If you grab something, you take it or pick it up suddenly and roughly.

press [pres] v. 누르다; (무엇에) 바짝 대다; 꾹 밀어 넣다; n. 언론
If you press a button or switch, you push it with your finger in order to make a machine or device work.

hum [hʌm] v. 윙윙거리다; 왁자지껄하다; n. 윙윙거리는 소리
If something hums, it makes a low continuous noise.

section [sékʃən] n. 구역; 부분; (조직의) 부서; v. 구분하다, 구획하다
A section of something is one of the parts into which it is divided or from which it is formed.

puzzle [pʌzl] n. 퍼즐; 수수께끼; v. 어리둥절하게 하다
A puzzle is a question, game, or toy which you have to think about carefully in order to answer it correctly or put it together properly.

reveal [riví:l] v. (보이지 않던 것을) 드러내 보이다; (비밀 등을) 밝히다
If you reveal something that has been out of sight, you uncover it so that people can see it.

stream [stri:m] n. 개울, 시내; (계속 이어진) 줄; v. (액체·기체가) 줄줄 흐르다; 계속 이어지다
A stream is a small narrow river.

panel [pænl] n. 판; (자동차 등의) 계기판; 자문단; v. 판으로 덮다
A panel is a flat rectangular piece of wood or other material that forms part of a larger object such as a door.

part [pa:rt] v. (두 사물·부분이) 갈라지다; (~와) 헤어지다; n. 일부, 약간; 부분
If things that are next to each other part or if you part them, they move in opposite directions, so that there is a space between them.

unveil [ʌnvéil] v. 밝히다, 드러나다; 발표하다
If you unveil a plan, new product, or some other thing that has been kept secret, you introduce it to the public.

spill [spil] v. (액체를) 흘리다, 쏟다; 쏟아져 나오다; n. 흘린 액체, 유출물
If a liquid spills or if you spill it, it accidentally flows over the edge of a container.

wicked [wíkid] a. 아주 좋은; 못된, 사악한; 짓궂은
If you describe someone or something as wicked, you means that they are excellent.

exclaim [ikskléim] v. 소리치다, 외치다
If you exclaim, you cry out suddenly in surprise, strong emotion, or pain.

^복^습 **tumble** [tʌmbl] v. 굴러 떨어지다; 폭삭 무너지다; n. (갑자기) 굴러 떨어짐; 폭락
If someone or something tumbles somewhere, they fall there with a rolling or bouncing movement.

^복^습 **panic** [pǽnik] v. (panicked-panicked) 어쩔 줄 모르다, 공황 상태에 빠지다;
n. 극심한 공포, 공황; 허둥지둥함
If you panic or if someone panics you, you suddenly feel anxious or afraid, and act quickly and without thinking carefully.

⁎ **poke** [pouk] v. (손가락 등으로) 쿡 찌르다; 쑥 내밀다; n. (손가락 등으로) 찌르기
If you poke someone or something, you quickly push them with your finger or with a sharp object.

^복^습 **crush** [krʌʃ] v. 으스러뜨리다; 밀어 넣다; 좌절시키다; n. 홀딱 반함
To crush something means to press it very hard so that its shape is destroyed or so that it breaks into pieces.

bash [bæʃ] v. 후려치다, 세게 치다; 맹비난하다; n. 강타
If you bash something, you hit it hard in a rough or careless way.

give up idiom 포기하다; 그만두다; 단념하다
If you give up, you stop trying to do something, usually because it is too difficult.

⁎ **chuck** [ʧʌk] v. (아무렇게나) 던지다; ~을 그만두다
When you chuck something somewhere, you throw it there in a casual or careless way.

^복^습 **emerge** [imɔ́ːrdʒ] v. 나오다, 모습을 드러내다; (어려움 등을) 헤쳐 나오다
To emerge means to come out from an enclosed or dark space such as a room or a vehicle, or from a position where you could not be seen.

^복^습 **suit** [suːt] n. (특정한 활동 때 입는) 옷; 정장; 소송; v. ~에게 편리하다; 어울리다
A particular type of suit is a piece of clothing that you wear for a particular activity.

⁑ **scale** [skeil] n. 비늘; 규모; 눈금; v. (아주 높고 가파른 곳을) 오르다
The scales of a fish or reptile are the small, flat pieces of hard skin that cover its body.

⁎ **assess** [əsés] v. (특성·자질 등을) 재다; 평가하다, 가늠하다
When you assess a person, thing, or situation, you consider them in order to make a judgment about them.

^복^습 **angle** [ǽŋgl] n. 각도, 각; 기울기; 관점; v. 비스듬히 움직이다
An angle is the direction from which you look at something.

angst [æŋkst] n. 불안, 고뇌 (angsty a. 고뇌하는)
If you are angsty, you are full of anxiety and unhappiness because you are worried about your life, your future, or what you should do in a particular situation.

‡ **flexible** [fléksəbl] a. 잘 구부러지는, 유연한; 용통성 있는
A flexible object or material can be bent easily without breaking.

복습 **design** [dizáin] v. 설계하다; 고안하다; n. 설계; 계획, 의도
When someone designs a garment, building, machine, or other object, they plan it and make a detailed drawing of it from which it can be built or made.

복습 **burst** [bə:rst] v. (burst-burst) 갑자기 ~하다; 불쑥 움직이다; n. (갑자기) ~을 함; 파열, 폭발
To burst into something means to suddenly start doing it.

＊ **furious** [fjúəriəs] a. 몹시 화가 난; 맹렬한
Someone who is furious is extremely angry.

‡ **neat** [ni:t] a. 뛰어난; 정돈된, 단정한; 깔끔한
If you say that something is neat, you mean that it is very good.

＊ **handwriting** [hǽndraitiŋ] n. (개인의) 필적
Your handwriting is your style of writing with a pen or pencil.

＊ **accessory** [æksésəri] n. 부대용품, 액세서리
Accessories are items of equipment that are not usually essential, but which can be used with or added to something else in order to make it more efficient, useful, or decorative.

＊ **garage** [gərá:dʒ] n. 차고; v. (자동차를) 차고에 넣다
A garage is a building in which you keep a car. A garage is often built next to or as part of a house.

＊ **gleam** [gli:m] v. 희미하게 빛나다; 환하다; n. 어슴푸레한 빛 (gleaming a. 빛나는)
If an object or a surface gleams, it reflects light because it is shiny and clean.

＊ **high-tech** [hai-ték] a. 최첨단의; 첨단 기술의
High-tech activities or equipment involve or result from the use of the most advanced and developed machines and methods.

‡ **specific** [spisífik] a. 특정한; 구체적인, 명확한 (specifically ad. 특별히; 분명히)
You use specifically to emphasize that something is given special attention and considered separately from other things of the same kind.

rocket [rákit] n. 로켓; 로켓 추진 미사일; v. 로켓처럼 가다, 돌진하다; 급증하다
A rocket is an engine that operates by the combustion of its contents, providing thrust as in a jet engine but without depending on the intake of air for combustion.

activate [ǽktəvèit] v. 작동시키다; 활성화시키다
If a device or process is activated, something causes it to start working.

handle [hǽndl] n. 손잡이; v. (사람·작업 등을) 처리하다; 들다, 옮기다
A handle is a small round object or a lever that is attached to a door and is used for opening and closing it.

spark [spɑːrk] v. 불꽃을 일으키다; 촉발시키다; n. 불꽃, 불똥; (전류의) 스파크
If something sparks, sparks of fire or light come from it.

dashboard [dǽʃbɔːrd] n. (승용차의) 계기판
The dashboard in a car is the panel facing the driver's seat where most of the instruments and switches are.

roar [rɔːr] v. 웅웅거리다; 굉음을 내며 질주하다; 고함치다; n. 함성; 울부짖는 듯한 소리
If something roars, it makes a very loud noise.

spin [spin] v. (빙빙) 돌다; 돌아서다; n. 회전
If something spins or if you spin it, it turns quickly around a central point.

circle [sə́ːrkl] n. 원형; v. 에워싸다, 둘러싸다; 빙빙 돌다
A circle is a shape consisting of a curved line completely surrounding an area. Every part of the line is the same distance from the center of the area.

swerve [swəːrv] v. (갑자기) 방향을 바꾸다
If a vehicle or other moving thing swerves or if you swerve it, it suddenly changes direction, often in order to avoid hitting something.

shriek [ʃriːk] v. (날카롭게) 비명을 지르다; 악을 쓰며 말하다; n. (날카로운) 비명
When someone shrieks, they make a short, very loud cry, for example because they are suddenly surprised, are in pain, or are laughing.

get the hang of idiom ~을 할 줄 알게 되다; 요령을 알다
If you get the hang of something such as a skill or activity, you begin to understand or realize how to do it.

confident [kánfədənt] a. 자신감 있는; 확신하는 (confidently ad. 자신 있게)
If a person or their manner is confident, they feel sure about their own abilities, qualities, or ideas.

* **slide** [slaid] v. (slid-slid/slidden) 미끄러지듯이 움직이다; 슬며시 넣다; n. 떨어짐; 미끄러짐
When something slides somewhere or when you slide it there, it moves there smoothly over or against something.

* **landscape** [lǽndskèip] n. 풍경; v. 조경을 하다
The landscape is everything you can see when you look across an area of land, including hills, rivers, buildings, trees, and plants.

accelerator [æksélərèitər] n. 가속 장치, 액셀러레이터
The accelerator in a car or other vehicle is the pedal which you press with your foot in order to make the vehicle go faster.

* **mixture** [míksʧər] n. 혼합; 뒤섞인 것
A mixture of things consists of several different things together.

* **pride** [praid] n. 자랑스러움, 자부심; 자존심
Pride is a feeling of satisfaction which you have because you or people close to you have done something good or possess something good.

* **envy** [énvi] n. 부러움, 선망; v. 부러워하다, 선망하다
Envy is the feeling you have when you wish you could have the same thing or quality that someone else has.

* **race** [reis] v. 쏜살같이 가다; (머리·심장 등이) 바쁘게 돌아가다; 경주하다; n. 경주; 인종, 종족
If you race somewhere, you go there as quickly as possible.

* **shove** [ʃʌv] v. (거칠게) 밀치다; 아무렇게나 놓다; n. 힘껏 떠밂
If you shove someone or something, you push them with a quick, violent movement.

* **cereal** [síəriəl] n. 시리얼; 곡물, 곡류
Cereal or breakfast cereal is a food made from grain. It is mixed with milk and eaten for breakfast.

sugary [ʃúgəri] a. 설탕 맛이 나는; 단
Sugary food or drink contains a lot of sugar.

on one's watch idiom ~의 책임일 때, ~가 지켜보고 있을 때
If something happens on your watch, it is done while you are in charge.

* **grumble** [grʌmbl] v. 투덜거리다, 불평하다; n. 투덜댐; 불평
If someone grumbles, they complain about something in a bad-tempered way.

replace [ripléis] v. 대신하다, 대체하다; 교체하다
If you replace one thing or person with another, you put something or someone else in their place to do their job.

reasonable [rí:zənəbl] a. 합당한; 사리를 아는, 합리적인
If you say that a decision or action is reasonable, you mean that it is fair and sensible.

fiber [fáibər] n. (식품의) 섬유소; 섬유
Fiber consists of the parts of plants or seeds that your body cannot digest. Fiber is useful because it makes food pass quickly through your body.

shrug [ʃrʌg] v. (어깨를) 으쓱하다; n. 어깨를 으쓱하기
If you shrug, you raise your shoulders to show that you are not interested in something or that you do not know or care about something.

spoonful [spú:nfùl] n. 한 숟가락 (가득한 양)
You can refer to an amount of food resting on a spoon as a spoonful of food.

bland [blænd] a. (맛이) 자극적이지 않은; 특징 없는, 단조로운
Food that is bland has very little flavor.

illegal [ilí:gəl] a. 불법적인; 비합법적인
If something is illegal, the law says that it is not allowed.

amaze [əméiz] v. (대단히) 놀라게 하다; 경악하게 하다 (amazed a. 놀란)
If something amazes you, it surprises you very much.

advocate [ǽdvəkèit] n. 옹호자, 지지자; v. 지지하다
An advocate of a particular action or plan is someone who recommends it publicly.

squirm [skwə:rm] v. (몸을) 꼼지락대다; 몹시 당혹해 하다
If you squirm, you move your body from side to side, usually because you are nervous or uncomfortable.

brighten [braitn] v. (얼굴 등이) 환해지다; (기쁨·희망으로) 밝아지다; 반짝이다
If someone brightens or their face brightens, they suddenly look happier.

cheer [ʧiər] v. 환호성을 지르다, 환호하다; n. 환호(성), 응원
When people cheer, they shout loudly to show their approval or to encourage someone who is doing something such as taking part in a game.

refill [ri:fíl] v. 다시 채우다, 리필하다
If you refill something, you fill it again after it has been emptied.

wolf down idiom 게걸스럽게 먹다
If you wolf down something, you eat it very quickly.

backpack [bǽkpæk] n. 책가방, 배낭
A backpack is a bag with straps that go over your shoulders, so that you can carry things on your back when you are walking or climbing.

^복_습 **stuff** [stʌf] v. 쑤셔 넣다; 채워 넣다; n. 일, 것, 물건
If you stuff something somewhere, you push it there quickly and roughly.

^복_습 **relieve** [rilíːv] v. 안도하다; (불쾌감·고통 등을) 없애 주다; 완화하다 (relieved a. 안도하는)
If you are relieved, you feel happy because something unpleasant has not happened or is no longer happening.

coo [kuː] v. 정답게 소곤거리다; 구구 울다; n. 구구 (하고 새가 우는 소리)
When someone coos, they speak in a very soft, quiet voice which is intended to sound attractive.

^복_습 **giggle** [gigl] v. 피식 웃다, 킥킥거리다; n. 피식 웃음, 킥킥거림
If someone giggles, they laugh in a childlike way, because they are amused, nervous, or embarrassed.

^복_습 **babble** [bæbl] v. 지껄이다, 횡설수설하다; n. 횡설수설; 와글와글, 왁자지껄
If someone babbles, they talk in a confused or excited way.

Check Your Reading Speed
1분에 몇 단어를 읽는지 리딩 속도를 측정해보세요.

$$\frac{1,113 \text{ words}}{\text{reading time (} \quad \text{) sec}} \times 60 = (\quad) \text{ WPM}$$

Build Your Vocabulary

easy chair [íːzi ʧéər] n. 큰 안락의자
An easy chair is a large, comfortable padded chair.

* **sleepy** [slíːpi] a. 졸린, 졸음이 오는; 나른한 (sleepily ad. 졸리는 듯이)
If you are sleepy, you are very tired and are almost asleep.

복습 **suck** [sʌk] v. 빨아 먹다; (특정한 방향으로) 빨아들이다; 엉망이다, 형편없다; n. 빨기, 빨아 먹기
If you suck something, you hold it in your mouth and pull at it with the muscles in
your cheeks and tongue, for example in order to get liquid out of it.

* **droop** [druːp] v. 아래로 처지다; 풀이 죽다, (기가) 꺾이다
If something droops, it hangs or leans downward with no strength or firmness.

crib [krib] n. 아기 침대; 구유, 여물통
A crib is a bed for a small baby.

tiptoe [típtòu] v. (발끝으로) 살금살금 걷다
If you tiptoe somewhere, you walk there very quietly without putting your heels
on the floor when you walk.

복습 **downstairs** [daunstéərz] ad. 아래층으로; n. 아래층
If you go downstairs in a building, you go down a staircase toward the ground
floor.

복습 **collapse** [kəlǽps] v. 주저앉다; 붕괴되다, 무너지다; 쓰러지다; n. 실패; (건물의) 붕괴
If you collapse onto something, you sit or lie down suddenly because you are
very tired.

복습 **couch** [kauʧ] n. 긴 의자, 소파
A couch is a long, comfortable seat for two or three people.

^{복습} **settle** [setl] v. 자리를 잡다; (서서히) 가라앉다; 결정하다
If you settle yourself somewhere or settle somewhere, you sit down or make yourself comfortable.

^{복습} **click** [klik] v. 딸깍 하는 소리를 내다; 분명해지다; n. 딸깍 (하는 소리)
If something clicks or if you click it, it makes a short, sharp sound.

^{복습} **sigh** [sai] v. 한숨을 쉬다, 한숨짓다; 탄식하듯 말하다; n. 한숨
When you sigh, you let out a deep breath, as a way of expressing feelings such as disappointment, tiredness, or pleasure.

^{복습} **drag** [dræg] v. 힘들게 움직이다; 끌다, 끌고 가다; n. 끌기, 당기기; 장애물
If you say that you drag yourself somewhere, you are emphasizing that you have to make a very great effort to go there.

^{복습} **squint** [skwint] v. 눈을 가늘게 뜨고 보다; 사시이다; n. 사시; 잠깐 봄
If you squint at something, you look at it with your eyes partly closed.

[*] **sweat** [swet] v. 땀을 흘리다; 식은땀을 흘리다, 불안해하다; n. 땀; 노력, 수고
When you sweat, sweat comes through your skin.

scrawl [skrɔːl] v. 휘갈겨 쓰다, 낙서를 하다; n. 휘갈겨 쓰기
If you scrawl something, you write it in a careless and untidy way.

[*] **equation** [ikwéiʒən] n. 등식, 방정식
An equation is a mathematical statement saying that two amounts or values are the same, for example 6x4=12x2.

[*] **scrap** [skræp] n. (종이·옷감 등의) 조각; 폐품; v. 폐기하다, 버리다
A scrap of something is a very small piece or amount of it.

^{복습} **snap** [snæp] v. 날카롭게 말하다; 급히 움직이다; 툭 부러지다; n. 탁 하는 소리
If someone snaps at you, they speak to you in a sharp, unfriendly way.

let off the hook idiom ~을 곤경에서 모면케 하다, 자유롭게 해주다
If you let someone off the hook, you allow them to escape from a difficult situation or to avoid doing something that they do not want to do.

^{복습} **offend** [əfénd] v. 기분 상하게 하다; 불쾌하게 여겨지다; 범죄를 저지르다
If you offend someone, you say or do something rude which upsets or embarrasses them.

blare [blɛər] v. (소리를) 요란하게 울리다; n. 요란한 소리
If something such as a siren or radio blares or if you blare it, it makes a loud, unpleasant noise.

startle [stɑ́:rtl] v. 깜짝 놀라게 하다; 움찔하다; n. 깜짝 놀람
If something sudden and unexpected startles you, it surprises and frightens you slightly.

flip through idiom ~을 휙휙 넘기다
If you flip through something, you quickly look through a magazine or book, or you quickly look at several different television programs.

upstairs [ʌpstέərz] ad. 위층으로; 위층에; n. 위층
If you go upstairs in a building, you go up a staircase toward a higher floor.

sink [siŋk] v. (sank-sunk) 주저앉다; 가라앉다, 빠지다; 박다; n. 개수대
If you sink, you lower yourself or drop down gently.

slap [slæp] v. (손바닥으로) 철썩 때리다; 털썩 놓다; n. 철썩 때리기, 치기
If you slap someone, you hit them with the palm of your hand.

crowd [kraud] n. 사람들, 군중; v. 가득 메우다; 바싹 붙어 서다
A crowd is a large group of people who have gathered together, for example to watch or listen to something interesting, or to protest about something.

gather [gǽðər] v. (사람들이) 모이다; (여기저기 있는 것을) 모으다
If people gather somewhere or if someone gathers people somewhere, they come together in a group.

unveil [ʌnvéil] v. 발표하다; 밝히다, 드러나다
If you unveil a plan, new product, or some other thing that has been kept secret, you introduce it to the public.

mayor [méiər] n. (시·군 등의) 시장
The mayor of a town or city is the person who has been elected to represent it for a fixed period of time or, in some places, to run its government.

podium [póudiəm] n. 단(壇), 지휘대
A podium is a small platform on which someone stands in order to give a lecture or conduct an orchestra.

declare [dikléər] v. 선언하다, 공표하다; 분명히 말하다
If you declare something, you state officially and formally that it exists or is the case.

nearby [nìərbái] ad. 가까운 곳에; a. 인근의, 가까운 곳의
If something is nearby, it is only a short distance away.

edit [édit] v. 편집하다; 수정하다
If you edit a film or a television or radio program, you choose some of what has been filmed or recorded and arrange it in a particular order.

suite [swi:t] n. 잇달아 붙은 방; (호텔 등의) 스위트 룸; 한 벌
A suite is a set of rooms in a hotel or other building.

footage [fútidʒ] n. (특정한 사건을 담은) 장면
Footage of a particular event is a film of it or the part of a film which shows this event.

cam [kæm] n. (= camera) 카메라
A cam is short for camera.

headset [hédsèt] n. (마이크가 붙은) 헤드폰
A headset is a small pair of headphones that you can use for listening to a radio or recorded music, or for using a telephone.

crime [kraim] n. 범죄, 죄
A crime is an illegal action or activity for which a person can be punished by law.

scan [skæn] v. 정밀 촬영하다; (유심히) 살피다; 훑어보다; n. 정밀 검사
(scanner n. 경찰·소방의 무선기)
A police scanner is a device that is used for listening to the police as they talk to each other over the radio.

whisper [hwíspər] v. 속삭이다, 소곤거리다; n. 속삭임, 소곤거리는 소리
When you whisper, you say something very quietly, using your breath rather than your throat, so that only one person can hear you.

respect [rispékt] n. 존경(심); 존중; v. (법률·원칙 등을) 준수하다; 존경하다; 존중하다
You can say with respect when you are politely disagreeing with someone or criticizing them.

launch [lɔ:nʧ] v. 발사하다; 시작하다; n. 시작; 발사; 개시, 진수
To launch a ship or a boat means to put it into water, often for the first time after it has been built.

magnificent [mægnífəsnt] a. 웅장한, 장엄한; 훌륭한, 굉장히 좋은
If you say that something or someone is magnificent, you mean that you think they are extremely good, beautiful, or impressive.

ridiculous [ridíkjuləs] a. 웃기는, 말도 안 되는, 터무니없는
If you say that something or someone is ridiculous, you mean that they are very foolish.

scissors [sízərz] n. 가위
Scissors are a small cutting tool with two sharp blades that are screwed together. You use scissors for cutting things such as paper and cloth.

boisterous [bɔ́istərəs] a. 활기가 넘치는, 잠시도 가만히 있지 못하는
Someone who is boisterous is noisy, lively, and full of energy.

storm [stɔ:rm] n. 쇄도; 폭풍, 폭풍우; v. 쿵쾅대며 가다, 뛰쳐나가다; 기습하다
A storm of applause or other noise is a sudden loud amount of it made by an audience or other group of people in reaction to something.

flashbulb [flǽʃbʌlb] n. (카메라의) 플래시 전구
A flashbulb is a small bulb that can be fixed to a camera. It makes a bright flash of light so that you can take photographs indoors.

go off idiom 터지다; (경보기 등이) 울리다
To go off means to make a sudden loud noise or flash.

slide [slaid] v. (slid-slid/slidden) 미끄러지듯이 움직이다; 슬며시 넣다; n. 떨어짐; 미끄러짐
When something slides somewhere or when you slide it there, it moves there smoothly over or against something.

passenger [pǽsəndʒər] n. 승객
A passenger in a vehicle such as a bus, boat, or plane is a person who is traveling in it, but who is not driving it or working on it.

pour [pɔ:r] v. 쏟아져 나오다; 마구 쏟아지다; 붓다, 따르다
If people pour into or out of a place, they go there quickly and in large numbers.

hover [hʌ́vər] v. (허공을) 맴돌다; 서성이다; 주저하다; n. 공중에 떠다님
To hover means to stay in the same position in the air without moving forward or backward.

track [træk] n. (기차) 선로; 경주로, 트랙; 자국; v. 추적하다, 뒤쫓다
Railway tracks are the rails that a train travels along.

station [stéiʃən] n. 역; 구역, 부서; 위치, 장소; v. 배치하다
A station is a building by a railway line where trains stop so that people can get on or off.

thud [θʌd] n. 쿵 (하는 소리); v. 쿵 치다; (심장이) 쿵쿵거리다
A thud is a dull sound, such as that which a heavy object makes when it hits something soft.

* **murmur** [mə́:rmə] v. 속삭이다, 소곤거리다, 중얼거리다; n. 속삭임, 소곤거림
If you murmur something, you say it very quietly, so that not many people can hear what you are saying.

‡ **confuse** [kənfjúːz] v. (사람을) 혼란시키다; 혼동하다 (confused a. 혼란스러워하는)
If you are confused, you do not know exactly what is happening or what to do.

복습 **uncertain** [ʌnsə́:rtn] a. 확신이 없는, 잘 모르는; 자신 없는; 불확실한
If you are uncertain about something, you do not know what you should do, what is going to happen, or what the truth is about something.

* **applause** [əplɔ́:z] n. 박수 (갈채)
Applause is the noise made by a group of people clapping their hands to show approval.

* **accelerate** [æksélərèit] v. 속도를 높이다, 가속화되다
When a moving vehicle accelerates, it goes faster and faster.

* **terror** [térər] n. 두려움, 공포; 공포의 대상
Terror is very great fear.

복습 **take off** idiom (서둘러) 떠나다; 날아오르다
To take off means to leave a place suddenly.

복습 **stretch** [stretʃ] n. 뻗기, 펴기; (길게) 뻗은 구간; v. (길이·폭 등을) 늘이다; 뻗어 있다
Stretch is the ability of a material or piece of clothing to become wider or longer when you pull it, and return to its original shape and size when you stop pulling it.

복습 **separate** [sépərèit] v. 분리하다, 나누다; 갈라지다; a. 별개의; 분리된
If you separate people or things that are together, or if they separate, they move apart.

catch up idiom 따라잡다, 따라가다; (소식 등을) 듣다
If you catch someone or something up, you go faster so that you reach them in front of you.

복습 **shut down** idiom (기계가) 멈추다; 종료하다
If a machine shuts down, or someone shuts it down, it stops working.

복습 **urge** [ə:rdʒ] v. 재촉하다; 충고하다, 설득하려 하다; n. (강한) 욕구, 충동
If you urge someone somewhere, you make them go there by touching them or talking to them.

override [óuvərraid] n. (자동 제어 장치의) 보조 수동 장치; v. 중단시키다; 무시하다
An override is a device for suspending an automatic function on a machine.

lock [lak] v. (자물쇠로) 잠그다; 고정시키다; n. 잠금장치
To lock means to prevent information on a computer from being changed or looked at by someone who does not have permission.

slim [slim] a. 아주 적은, 보잘것없는; 날씬한, 호리호리한
A slim chance or possibility is a very small one.

fail-safe [féil-sèif] n. 안전장치; a. 안전장치가 되어 있는
Something that is fail-safe is designed or made in such a way that nothing dangerous can happen if a part of it goes wrong.

switch [switʃ] v. 전환하다, 바꾸다; n. 스위치; 전환
If you switch to something different, for example to a different system, task, or subject of conversation, you change to it from what you were doing or saying before.

background [bǽkgraund] n. 배경
The background is sounds, such as music, which you can hear but which you are not listening to with your full attention.

tunnel [tʌnl] n. 터널, 굴; v. 굴을 뚫다
A tunnel is a long passage which has been made under the ground, usually through a hill or under the sea.

rooftop [rúːftap] n. (건물의) 옥상
A rooftop is the outside part of the roof of a building.

land [lænd] v. (땅·표면에) 내려앉다, 착륙하다; 놓다, 두다; n. 육지; 땅; 지역
When someone or something lands, they come down to the ground after moving through the air or falling.

figure out idiom ~을 이해하다, 알아내다; 계산하다, 산출하다
If you figure out someone or something, you come to understand them by thinking carefully.

hop [hap] v. 급히 움직이다; 깡충깡충 뛰다; n. 깡충깡충 뛰기
If you hop somewhere, you move there quickly or suddenly.

crash [kræʃ] v. 부딪치다; 충돌하다; 굉음을 내다; n. (자동차·항공기) 사고; 요란한 소리
If something crashes somewhere, it moves and hits something else violently, making a loud noise.

flatten [flætn] v. 납작하게 엎드리다; 납작하게 하다; 때려눕히다
If you flatten yourself against something, you press yourself flat against it, for example to avoid getting in the way or being seen.

^{복습} **cling** [kliŋ] v. (clung-clung) 꼭 붙잡다, 매달리다; 들러붙다; 애착을 갖다
If you cling to someone or something, you hold onto them tightly.

^{복습} **crawl** [krɔːl] v. 기어가다; 우글거리다; n. 기어가기
When you crawl, you move forward on your hands and knees.

^{복습} **engineer** [èndʒiníər] n. (선박·항공기의) 기관사; 엔지니어; 기술자; v. 수작을 부리다
An engineer is a person who is responsible for maintaining the engine of a ship while it is at sea.

^{복습} **blink** [bliŋk] v. 눈을 깜박이다; (불빛이) 깜박거리다; n. 눈을 깜박거림
When you blink or when you blink your eyes, you shut your eyes and very quickly open them again.

^{복습} **muscle** [mʌsl] n. 근육 (do not move a muscle idiom 꿈쩍도 하지 않다)
If you say that someone did not move a muscle, you mean that they stayed absolutely still.

^{복습} **bang** [bæŋ] v. 쾅 하고 치다; 쾅 하고 닫다; 쿵 하고 찧다; n. 쾅 (하는 소리)
If you bang on something or if you bang it, you hit it hard, making a loud noise.

windshield [wíndʃìːld] n. (자동차 등의) 앞 유리
The windshield of a car or other vehicle is the glass window at the front through which the driver looks.

be about to idiom 막 ~하려는 참이다
If you are about to do something, you are going to do it immediately.

parachute [pǽrəʃùːt] n. 낙하산; v. 낙하산을 타고 뛰어내리다
A parachute is a device which enables a person to jump from an aircraft and float safely to the ground.

bust [bʌst] v. 부수다; 파열하다; 급습하다; n. 흉상, 반신상
If you bust something, you break it or damage it so badly that it cannot be used.

construct [kənstrʌ́kt] v. 건설하다; 구성하다; n. 건축물; 생각 (construction n. 건설, 공사)
Construction is the building of things such as houses, factories, roads, and bridges.

barricade [bǽrəkèid] n. 바리케이드, 장애물; v. 방어벽을 치다
A barricade is a line of vehicles or other objects placed across a road or open space to stop people getting past, for example during street fighting or as a protest.

dangle [dǽŋgl] v. 매달리다; (무엇을 들고) 달랑거리다
If something dangles from somewhere or if you dangle it somewhere, it hangs or swings loosely.

cabin [kǽbin] n. (항공기·배의) 선실; (나무로 된) 오두막집
A cabin is one of the areas inside a plane.

check on idiom (이상이 없는지를) 확인하다
If you check on someone or something, you make sure they are in a safe or satisfactory condition.

injure [índʒər] v. 부상을 입히다; (평판·자존심 등을) 해치다 (injured a. 부상을 입은)
An injured person or animal has physical damage to part of their body, usually as a result of an accident or fighting.

opposite [ápəzit] a. (정)반대의; 건너편의; 맞은편의; prep. 맞은편에
Opposite is used to describe things of the same kind which are completely different in a particular way.

odd [ad] a. 이상한, 특이한; 홀수의
If you describe someone or something as odd, you think that they are strange or unusual.

pulse [pʌls] v. 맥박 치다, 고동치다; 활기가 넘치다; n. 맥박; (강한) 리듬
If something pulses, it moves, appears, or makes a sound with a strong regular rhythm.

conscious [kánʃəs] a. 의식이 있는; 자각하는; 의도적인 (consciousness n. 의식)
Consciousness is the state of being awake rather than being asleep or unconscious.

daze [deiz] v. 멍하게 하다; 눈부시게 하다; n. 멍한 상태; 눈이 부심 (dazed a. 멍한)
If someone is dazed, they are confused and unable to think clearly, often because of shock or a blow to the head.

flash [flæʃ] v. 휙 나타나다; 휙 내보이다; (잠깐) 번쩍이다; n. 순간; (잠깐) 반짝임
If a picture or message flashes up on a screen, or if you flash it onto a screen, it is displayed there briefly or suddenly, and often repeatedly.

Chapters 8 & 9

1. **What was one of Jack-Jack's powers?**

   A. He could move at high speed from one place to another.

   B. He could unlock doors from a distance.

   C. He could make things move with his mind.

   D. He could block laser beams with his hands.

2. **Why was Bob so determined to help Dash with his homework?**

   A. He wanted to show Dash how fun math could be.

   B. He wanted to show Dash how important math was in life.

   C. He wanted to prove that anyone could do math.

   D. He wanted to prove that he was a useful parent.

3. How did the ambassador react when she first saw Elastigirl?

A. She was enthusiastic to meet the Super.

B. She was unsure of who the Super was.

C. She was unimpressed by the Super.

D. She was nervous about talking to the Super.

4. How did the Screenslaver hypnotize Chad?

A. He put scary pictures on a teleprompter.

B. He showed patterns of light on a screen.

C. He spoke with a robotic voice into a microphone.

D. He played strange music through speakers.

5. What did NOT happen when Elastigirl got into the ambassador's helicopter?

A. She noticed that the ambassador had been hypnotized.

B. She took a gun from the ambassador's security guard.

C. She shot the lock off the cockpit door.

D. She used her hands to break the control screens.

Check Your Reading Speed

1분에 몇 단어를 읽는지 리딩 속도를 측정해보세요.

$$\frac{1,574 \text{ words}}{\text{reading time (} \quad \text{) sec}} \times 60 = (\quad) \text{ WPM}$$

Build Your Vocabulary

crib [krib] n. 아기 침대; 구유, 여물통
A crib is a bed for a small baby.

glow [glou] n. (은은한) 불빛; 홍조; v. 빛나다, 타다; (얼굴이) 상기되다
A glow is a dull, steady light, for example the light produced by a fire when there are no flames.

peaceful [píːsfəl] a. 평화로운; 평화적인
A peaceful place or time is quiet, calm, and free from disturbance.

linger [língər] v. 더 오래 머물다; 계속되다
If you linger somewhere, you stay there for a longer time than is necessary, for example because you are enjoying yourself.

flip [flip] v. 휙 뒤집다, 휙 젖히다; 툭 던지다; n. 회전; 툭 던지기
If something flips over, or if you flip it over or into a different position, it moves or is moved into a different position.

upside down [ápsàid dáun] ad. (아래위가) 거꾸로
If something has been moved upside down, it has been turned round so that the part that is usually lowest is above the part that is usually highest.

determine [ditə́ːrmin] v. ~을 하기로 결정하다; 알아내다, 밝히다
(determined a. 단단히 결심한)
If you are determined to do something, you have made a firm decision to do it and will not let anything stop you.

stack [stæk] n. 무더기, 더미; v. (깔끔하게 정돈하여) 쌓다
A stack of things is a pile of them.

downstairs [daunstéərz] ad. 아래층으로; n. 아래층
If you go downstairs in a building, you go down a staircase toward the ground floor.

cut off idiom (말을) 중단시키다; 단절시키다
To cut off means to prevent someone from continuing what they are saying.

trudge [trʌdʒ] v. 터덜터덜 걷다; 느릿느릿 걷다; n. 터덜터덜 걷기
If you trudge somewhere, you walk there slowly and with heavy steps, especially because you are tired or unhappy.

knock [nak] v. (문 등을) 두드리다; 치다, 부딪치다; n. 문 두드리는 소리; 부딪침
If you knock on something such as a door or window, you hit it, usually several times, to attract someone's attention.

flat [flæt] a. 생기가 없는; 평평한, 편평한; 납작한; ad. 평평하게, 반듯이
You use flat to describe someone's voice when they are saying something without expressing any emotion.

irritate [írətèit] v. 짜증나게 하다, 거슬리다; 자극하다 (irritated a. 짜증이 난)
If something irritates you, it keeps annoying you.

interrupt [intərʌ́pt] v. (말·행동을) 방해하다; 중단시키다; 차단하다
If you interrupt someone who is speaking, you say or do something that causes them to stop.

crack [kræk] v. (목소리가) 갈라지다; 깨지다, 부서지다; n. 날카로운 소리; 금; (좁은) 틈
If your voice cracks when you are speaking or singing, it changes in pitch because you are feeling a strong emotion.

comfort [kʌ́mfərt] v. 위로하다, 위안하다; n. 안락, 편안; 위로, 위안
If you comfort someone, you make them feel less worried, unhappy, or upset, for example by saying kind things to them.

flick [flik] v. (버튼·스위치를) 탁 누르다; 튀기다; 털다; n. 재빨리 움직임
If you flick through television channels, you continually change channels very quickly, for example using a remote control.

surrender [səréndər] v. 항복하다, 투항하다; (권리 등을) 포기하다; n. 항복, 굴복
If you surrender, you stop fighting or resisting someone and agree that you have been beaten.

crime [kraim] n. 범죄, 죄
A crime is an illegal action or activity for which a person can be punished by law.

snore [snɔːr] v. 코를 골다; n. 코 고는 소리
When someone who is asleep snores, they make a loud noise each time they breathe.

^복^습 **mask** [mæsk] v. 가면을 쓰다; (감정·냄새·사실 등을) 가리다; n. 마스크; 가면
(masked a. 가면을 쓴)
If someone is masked, they are wearing a mask.

^복^습 **rob** [rab] v. (사람·장소를) 도둑질하다 (robber n. 강도)
A robber is someone who steals money or property from a bank, a shop, or a
vehicle, often by using force or threats.

gunpoint [gʌ́npɔint] n. 총부리, 총구 (hold at gunpoint idiom ~에게 총구를 들이대다)
If you are held at gunpoint, someone is threatening to shoot and kill you if you
do not obey them.

clean out idiom ~에서 다 훔치다
To clean out means to empty a place of objects or goods, especially by stealing or
buying them in large quantities.

cash register [kǽʃ redʒistər] n. 금전 등록기
A cash register is a machine in a shop, pub, or restaurant that is used to add up
and record how much money people pay, and in which the money is kept.

enthrall [inθrɔ́ːl] v. 마음을 사로잡다
If you are enthralled by something, you enjoy it and give it your complete
attention and interest.

^복^습 **crawl** [krɔːl] v. 기어가다; 우글거리다; n. 기어가기
When you crawl, you move forward on your hands and knees.

* **raccoon** [rækúːn] n. [동물] 미국너구리
A raccoon is a small animal that has dark-colored fur with white stripes on its
face and on its long tail.

rummage [rʌ́midʒ] v. 뒤지다; n. 뒤지기
If you rummage through something, you search for something you want by
moving things around in a careless or hurried way.

* **garbage** [gáːrbidʒ] n. 쓰레기 (garbage can n. 쓰레기통)
Garbage is rubbish, especially waste from a kitchen.

* **backyard** [bækjáːrd] n. 뒷마당; 뒤뜰
A backyard is an area of land at the back of a house.

^복^습 **dig** [dig] v. (무엇을 찾기 위해) 뒤지다; (구멍 등을) 파다; n. 쿡 찌르기
If you dig into something such as a deep container, you put your hand in it to
search for something.

frown [fraun] v. 얼굴을 찡그리다; 눈살을 찌푸리다; n. 찡그림, 찌푸림
When someone frowns, their eyebrows become drawn together, because they are annoyed, worried, or puzzled, or because they are concentrating.

fierce [fiərs] a. 사나운, 험악한; 격렬한, 맹렬한
A fierce animal or person is very aggressive or angry.

hiss [his] n. 쉭쉭거리는 소리; v. 쉿 하는 소리를 내다; (화난 어조로) 낮게 말하다
A hiss is a long 's' sound like the sound that a snake makes.

toddle [tadl] v. (어린 아이가) 아장아장 걷다
When a child toddles, it walks unsteadily with short quick steps.

toss [tɔːs] v. (가볍게) 던지다; (문제 등을) 가볍게 논하다; (고개를) 홱 쳐들다; n. 던지기
If you toss something somewhere, you throw it there lightly, often in a rather careless way.

clang [klæŋ] n. 쨍그랑 (하는 소리); v. (서로 부딪쳐) 쨍그랑 하는 소리를 내다
A clang is a loud, resonant metallic sound or series of sounds.

lid [lid] n. 뚜껑
A lid is the top of a box or other container which can be removed or raised when you want to open the container.

float [flout] v. (물 위나 공중에서) 떠가다; (물에) 뜨다; n. 부표
Something that floats in or through the air hangs in it or moves slowly and gently through it.

leash [liːʃ] v. 속박하다, 억제하다; 가죽끈으로 매다; n. 가죽 끈; 통제
(unleash v. 풀어놓다; 해방하다)
If you say that someone or something unleashes a powerful force, feeling, activity, or group, you mean that they suddenly start it or send it somewhere.

multiple [mʌltəpl] a. 많은, 다수의; 복합적인; n. 배수
You use multiple to describe things that consist of many parts, involve many people, or have many uses.

take on idiom ~와 싸우다; (일 등을) 맡다; (책임을) 지다
If you take on someone, you fight or compete against them.

wrestle [resl] v. 몸싸움을 벌이다, 맞붙어 싸우다; (힘든 문제와) 씨름하다
If you wrestle with someone, you fight them by forcing them into painful positions or throwing them to the ground, rather than by hitting them.

^복_습 **punch** [pʌntʃ] v. 주먹으로 치다; (자판·번호판 등을) 치다; n. 주먹으로 한 대 침
If you punch someone or something, you hit them hard with your fist.

^복_습 **beam** [biːm] n. 빛줄기; 기둥; v. 활짝 웃다; 비추다
A beam is a line of energy, radiation, or particles sent in a particular direction.

^복_습 **cling** [kliŋ] v. (clung-clung) 꼭 붙잡다, 매달리다; 들러붙다; 애착을 갖다
If you cling to someone or something, you hold onto them tightly.

* **trap** [træp] v. (위험한 장소에) 가두다; (함정으로) 몰아넣다; n. 함정; 덫
If you are trapped somewhere, something falls onto you or blocks your way and
prevents you from moving or escaping.

^복_습 **pole** [poul] n. 막대, 기둥; 장대; 극
A pole is a long thin piece of wood or metal, used especially for supporting things.

* **slice** [slais] v. 베다; (하늘·물 등을) 가르듯이 달리다; n. (얇게 썬) 조각; 부분, 몫
If you slice bread, meat, fruit, or other food, you cut it into thin pieces.

goop [guːp] n. 끈적거리는 것 (goopy a. 끈적거리는, 끈적끈적한)
Goop is a thick, slimy substance.

* **sticky** [stíki] a. 끈적거리는, 끈적끈적한; 힘든, 불쾌한
A sticky substance is soft, or thick and liquid, and can stick to other things.

* **awaken** [əwéikən] v. (잠에서) 깨다; (감정을) 불러일으키다
When you awaken, or when something or someone awakens you, you wake up.

brawl [brɔːl] v. 싸움을 벌이다; n. (공공장소에서의) 싸움, 소동
If someone brawls, they fight in a very rough or violent way.

* **display** [displéi] v. (자질·느낌을) 드러내다; 전시하다; (정보를) 보여주다; n. 진열; 디스플레이
If you display a characteristic, quality, or emotion, you behave in a way which
shows that you have it.

^복_습 **multiply** [mʌ́ltəplài] v. 증식하다; 크게 증가하다; 곱하다
When something multiplies or when you multiply it, it increases greatly in
number or amount.

^복_습 **dozen** [dʌzn] n. 12개; 십여 개; (pl.) 다수, 여러 개
If you have a dozen things, you have twelve of them.

^복_습 **yard** [jaːrd] n. 마당, 뜰; (학교의) 운동장; 정원
A yard is a piece of land next to someone's house, with grass and plants growing
in it.

scoop [sku:p] v. 재빨리 들어올리다; (큰 숟갈 같은 것으로) 뜨다; n. 한 숟갈(의 양)
If you scoop a person or thing somewhere, you put your hands or arms under or round them and quickly move them there.

vibrate [váibreit] v. (가늘게) 떨다, 진동하다
If something vibrates or if you vibrate it, it shakes with repeated small, quick movements.

merge [mə:rdʒ] v. 합치다; 어우러지다
If one thing merges with another, or is merged with another, they combine or come together to make one whole thing.

pause [pɔ:z] v. (말·일을) 잠시 멈추다; (테이프·시디 등을) 정지시키다; n. (말·행동 등의) 멈춤
If you pause while you are doing something, you stop for a short period and then continue.

gaze [geiz] n. 응시, (눈여겨보는) 시선; v. (가만히) 응시하다, 바라보다
You can talk about someone's gaze as a way of describing how they are looking at something, especially when they are looking steadily at it.

crinkle [kríŋkl] v. 많은 잔주름이 생기다; 버스럭거리다; n. 주름
If something crinkles or if you crinkle it, it becomes slightly creased or folded.

bare [bɛər] v. (신체의 일부를) 드러내다; a. 벌거벗은; 아무것도 안 덮인; 텅 빈
If you bare something, you uncover it and show it.

wave [weiv] v. (손·팔을) 흔들다; 손짓하다; n. 물결; (손·팔을) 흔들기
If you wave something, you hold it up and move it rapidly from side to side.

fist [fist] n. 주먹
Your hand is referred to as your fist when you have bent your fingers in toward the palm in order to hit someone, to make an angry gesture, or to hold something.

inspect [inspékt] v. 면밀하게 살피다, 점검하다; 시찰하다
If you inspect something, you look at every part of it carefully in order to find out about it or check that it is all right.

scratch [skrætʃ] n. 긁힌 자국; 긁는 소리; v. 긁힌 자국을 내다; (가려운 데를) 긁다
Scratches on someone or something are small shallow cuts.

lock [lak] v. (자물쇠로) 잠그다; 고정시키다; n. 잠금장치 (unlock v. (열쇠로) 열다)
If you unlock something such as a door, a room, or a container that has a lock, you open it using a key.

solid [sálid] n. 고체, 고형물; a. 단단한; 확실한; 고체의
A solid is a substance that stays the same shape whether it is in a container or not.

consequence [kánsəkwèns] n. (발생한 일의) 결과; 중요함
The consequences of something are the results or effects of it.

realize [ríːəlàiz] v. 깨닫다, 알아차리다; 실현하다, 달성하다
If you realize that something is true, you become aware of that fact or understand it.

disastrous [dizǽstrəs] a. 처참한, 형편없는
If you describe something as disastrous, you mean that it was very unsuccessful.

spiral [spáiərəl] v. 급증하다; 나선형으로 움직이다, 나선형을 그리다; n. 나선, 나선형
If a situation spirals, it quickly gets worse in a way that becomes more and more difficult to control.

confuse [kənfjúːz] v. (사람을) 혼란시키다; 혼동하다 (confusion n. 혼란)
If there is confusion about something, it is not clear what the true situation is, especially because people believe different things.

witness [wítnis] v. (사건·사고를) 목격하다; 증명하다; n. 목격자; 증인
If you witness something, you see it happen.

background [bǽkgraund] n. 배경
The background is sounds, such as music, which you can hear but which you are not listening to with your full attention.

mission [míʃən] n. 임무; 사명; v. 길고 험난한 여정에 나서다
A mission is an important task that people are given to do, especially one that involves traveling to another country.

defensive [difénsiv] a. 방어적인; 방어의
Someone who is defensive is behaving in a way that shows they feel unsure or threatened.

misspeak [misspíːk] v. (misspoke-misspoken) 잘못 말하다
If you misspeak, you say something that is not correct, by mistake.

march [maːrʧ] v. (단호한 태도로 급히) 걸어가다; 행진하다; n. 행군, 행진; 3월
If you say that someone marches somewhere, you mean that they walk there quickly and in a determined way, for example because they are angry.

sob [sab] v. (흑흑) 흐느끼다, 흐느껴 울다; n. 흐느껴 울기, 흐느낌
When someone sobs, they cry in a noisy way, breathing in short breaths.

stall [stɔːl] v. 시간을 끌다; (차량·엔진이) 멎다, 시동이 꺼지다; n. 가판대, 좌판
If you stall, you try to avoid doing something until later.

fridge [fridʒ] n. (= refrigerator) 냉장고
A fridge is a large metal container which is kept cool, usually by electricity, so that food that is put in it stays fresh.

methodical [məθádikəl] a. 체계적인 (methodically ad. 체계적으로, 찬찬히)
If you describe someone as methodical, you mean that they do things carefully, thoroughly, and in order.

remove [rimúːv] v. 치우다, 내보내다; 없애다, 제거하다; (옷 등을) 벗다
If you remove something from a place, you take it away.

tub [tʌb] n. 통; 목욕통, 욕조
A tub is a deep container of any size.

freezer [fríːzər] n. 냉동고
A freezer is a large container like a fridge in which the temperature is kept below freezing point so that you can store food inside it for long periods.

silverware [sílvərwɛ̀ər] n. 은제품, 은식기류
You can use silverware to refer to all the things in a house that are made of silver, especially the cutlery and dishes.

drawer [drɔːr] n. 서랍
A drawer is part of a desk, chest, or other piece of furniture that is shaped like a box and is designed for putting things in.

upstairs [ʌpstɛ́ərz] ad. 위층으로; 위층에; n. 위층
If you go upstairs in a building, you go up a staircase toward a higher floor.

weep [wiːp] v. 울다, 눈물을 흘리다; 물기를 내뿜다; n. 울기
If someone weeps, they cry.

go down idiom (아기를) 재우다
If you make a baby go down, you put it in a bed so that it can go to sleep.

glare [glɛər] v. 노려보다; 환하다, 눈부시다; n. 노려봄; 환한 빛, 눈부심
If you glare at someone, you look at them with an angry expression on your face.

receiver [risíːvər] n. 수화기, 수신기; 받는 사람, 수취인
A telephone's receiver is the part that you hold near to your ear and speak into.

glance [glæns] v. 흘낏 보다; 대충 훑어보다; n. 흘낏 봄
If you glance at something or someone, you look at them very quickly and then look away again immediately.

slump [slʌmp] v. 털썩 앉다; (가치·수량 등이) 급감하다; n. 부진, 슬럼프; 급감; 불황
If you slump somewhere, you fall or sit down there heavily, for example because you are very tired or you feel ill.

amaze [əméiz] v. (대단히) 놀라게 하다; 경악하게 하다 (amazing a. 놀라운)
You say that something is amazing when it is very surprising and makes you feel pleasure, approval, or wonder.

eventful [ivéntfəl] a. 다사다난한, 파란만장한 (uneventful a. 특별한 일이 없는)
If you describe a period of time as uneventful, you mean that nothing interesting, exciting, or important happened during it.

runaway [rʌ́nəwei] a. 제멋대로 가는, 제어가 안 되는; 달아난
A runaway vehicle or animal is moving forward quickly, and its driver or rider has lost control of it.

shriek [ʃriːk] v. (날카롭게) 비명을 지르다; 악을 쓰며 말하다; n. (날카로운) 비명
When someone shrieks, they make a short, very loud cry, for example because they are suddenly surprised, are in pain, or are laughing.

* **rescue** [réskjuː] n. 구출, 구조, 구제; v. 구하다, 구출하다
Rescue is help which gets someone out of a dangerous or unpleasant situation.

surf [səːrf] v. (텔레비전·인터넷 등에서) 여기저기 찾다; 파도타기를 하다; n. (큰) 파도
If you surf through the internet or television channels, you look at a variety of things casually, especially while browsing the internet or television channels.

* **anchor** [ǽŋkər] n. (뉴스 등의) 진행자; 닻; v. 닻을 내리다, 고정시키다
The anchorman or anchorwoman on a television or radio program, especially a news program, is the person who presents it.

passenger [pǽsəndʒər] n. 승객
A passenger in a vehicle such as a bus, boat, or plane is a person who is traveling in it, but who is not driving it or working on it.

sucker [sʌ́kər] n. (강조하는 말에서) 사람, 것; 잘 속는 사람
You can use sucker to refer to a thing or person not specified by name.

station [stéiʃən] n. 역; 구역, 부서; 위치, 장소; v. 배치하다
A station is a building by a railway line where trains stop so that people can get on or off.

ramble [ræmbl] v. 횡설수설하다; 걷다, 거닐다; n. 걷기; 횡설수설(하는 말·글)
If you say that a person rambles in their speech or writing, you mean they do not make much sense because they keep going off the subject in a confused way.

boom [bu:m] n. 쾅 (하는 소리); v. 굵은 목소리로 말하다; 쾅 하는 소리를 내다
A boom is a deep loud sound that continues for some time, for example the noise of thunder or an explosion.

casualty [kǽʒuəlti] n. 사상자; 피해자; 재해
A casualty is a person who is injured or killed in a war or in an accident.

squeal [skwi:l] v. 꽤액 소리를 지르다; 끼익 하는 소리를 내다; n. 끼익 하는 소리
If someone or something squeals, they make a long, high-pitched sound.

delight [diláit] v. 많은 기쁨을 주다, 아주 즐겁게 하다; n. (큰) 기쁨; 즐거움을 주는 것
(delighted a. 아주 기뻐하는)
If you are delighted, you are extremely pleased and excited about something.

saga [sáːgə] n. 일련의 사건; 영웅 전설
A saga is a long story, account, or sequence of events.

fantastic [fæntǽstik] a. 기막히게 좋은, 환상적인; 기상천외한; 엄청난, 굉장한
If you say that something is fantastic, you are emphasizing that you think it is very good or that you like it a lot.

jealous [dʒéləs] a. 시샘하는, 질투가 많은
If you are jealous of another person's possessions or qualities, you feel angry or bitter because you do not have them.

bang [bæŋ] v. 쾅 하고 치다; 쾅 하고 닫다; 쿵 하고 찧다; n. 쾅 (하는 소리)
If you bang on something or if you bang it, you hit it hard, making a loud noise.

take over idiom (~을) 인계받다; 장악하다, 탈취하다
If you take over something, you begin to do something that someone else was doing.

hang up idiom 전화를 끊다; ~을 중지하다
To hang up means to end a telephone conversation, often very suddenly.

slumber [slʌ́mbər] v. 잠을 자다; n. 잠, 수면
If you slumber, you sleep.

fast asleep idiom 깊이 잠들다
Someone who is fast asleep is completely asleep.

lean [liːn] v. ~에 기대다; 기울이다, (몸을) 숙이다; a. 군살이 없는, 호리호리한
If you lean on or against someone or something, you rest against them so that they partly support your weight.

exhaust [igzɔ́ːst] v. 기진맥진하게 하다; 다 써 버리다; n. (자동차 등의) 배기가스
(exhausted a. 기진맥진한)
If something exhausts you, it makes you so tired, either physically or mentally, that you have no energy left.

toss and turn idiom (자면서) 계속 몸을 뒤척이다
If you toss and turn, you keep moving around in bed and cannot sleep properly, for example because you are ill or worried.

grumble [grʌmbl] v. 투덜거리다, 불평하다; n. 투덜댐; 불평
If someone grumbles, they complain about something in a bad-tempered way.

tackle [tækl] v. (힘든 문제·상황과) 씨름하다; 달려들다; n. 태클
If you tackle a difficult problem or task, you deal with it in a very determined or efficient way.

challenge [tʃǽlindʒ] n. 도전; 저항; v. 도전하다; 도전 의식을 북돋우다
A challenge is something new and difficult which requires great effort and determination.

substitute [sʌ́bstətjùːt] n. 대신하는 사람; 대체물; v. 대신하다, 교체되다
A substitute is something that you have or use instead of something else.

sound asleep idiom 푹 잠들다
If someone is in a sound sleep, they are sleeping very deeply.

assign [əsáin] v. (일·책임 등을) 맡기다; (사람을) 배치하다 (assignment n. 임무; 과제)
An assignment is a task or piece of work that you are given to do, especially as part of your job or studies.

whisper [hwíspər] v. 속삭이다, 소곤거리다; n. 속삭임, 소곤거리는 소리
When you whisper, you say something very quietly, using your breath rather than your throat, so that only one person can hear you.

sheet [ʃiːt] n. 얇은 천; (종이) 한 장
A sheet is a large rectangular piece of cotton or other cloth that you sleep on or cover yourself with in a bed.

groan [groun] v. (고통·짜증으로) 신음 소리를 내다; 끙끙거리다; n. 신음, 끙 하는 소리
If you groan, you make a long, low sound because you are in pain, or because you are upset or unhappy about something.

go over idiom ~을 점검하다
If you go over something, you check it carefully.

nod [nad] v. (고개를) 끄덕이다, 까딱하다; n. (고개를) 끄덕임
If you nod, you move your head downward and upward to show that you are answering 'yes' to a question, or to show agreement, understanding, or approval.

scribble [skribl] v. 갈겨쓰다, 휘갈기다; 낙서하다; n. 낙서
If you scribble something, you write it quickly and roughly.

equation [ikwéiʒən] n. 등식, 방정식
An equation is a mathematical statement saying that two amounts or values are the same, for example 6x4=12x2.

clink [kliŋk] v. 쨍그랑 하는 소리를 내다; n. 쨍그랑 (하는 소리)
If objects clink or if you clink them, they touch each other and make a short, light sound.

grin [grin] n. 활짝 웃음; v. 활짝 웃다
A grin is a broad smile.

backpack [bǽkpæk] n. 책가방, 배낭
A backpack is a bag with straps that go over your shoulders, so that you can carry things on your back when you are walking or climbing.

chuckle [ʧʌkl] v. 킬킬 웃다; 빙그레 웃다; n. 킬킬거림; 속으로 웃기
When you chuckle, you laugh quietly.

Check Your Reading Speed

1분에 몇 단어를 읽는지 리딩 속도를 측정해보세요.

$$\frac{1{,}159 \text{ words}}{\text{reading time (} \quad \text{) sec}} \times 60 = (\qquad) \text{ WPM}$$

Build Your Vocabulary

anchor [ǽŋkər] n. (뉴스 등의) 진행자; 닻; v. 닻을 내리다, 고정시키다
The anchorman or anchorwoman on a television or radio program, especially a news program, is the person who presents it.

greenroom [gríːnruːm] n. (공연장·스튜디오 등의) 공연자 휴게실
A greenroom is a room in a theater or television studio where performers can rest.

ambassador [æmbǽsədər] n. 대사
An ambassador is an important official who lives in a foreign country and represents his or her own country's interests there.

makeup [méikʌp] n. 분장, 메이크업; 조립, 구성
Makeup is substances that people put on their faces, including their eyes and lips, in order to look attractive or to change their appearance.

powder [páudər] v. 파우더를 바르다; n. 가루, 분말; (화장품) 파우더
If a woman powders her face or some other part of her body, she puts face powder on it.

boost [buːst] v. 신장시키다, 북돋우다; n. 격려; 증가
If something boosts your confidence or morale, it improves it.

positive [pázətiv] a. 긍정적인; 확신하는; 분명한
If you are positive about things, you are hopeful and confident, and think of the good aspects of a situation rather than the bad ones.

stagehand [stéidʒhænd] n. 무대 담당자
A stagehand is a person whose job is to move the scenery and equipment on the stage in a theater.

hallway [hɔ́ːlwèi] n. 복도; 통로; 현관
A hallway in a building is a long passage with doors into rooms on both sides of it.

INCREDIBLES 2

flank [flæŋk] v. ~이 옆에 있다; n. 측면; 옆구리
If something is flanked by things, it has them on both sides of it, or sometimes on one side of it.

security [sikjúərəti] n. 보안, 경비; 경비 담당 부서; 안도감, 안심
Security refers to all the measures that are taken to protect a place, or to ensure that only people with permission enter it or leave it.

madam [mǽdəm] n. 부인
People sometimes say Madam as a very formal and polite way of addressing a woman whose name they do not know or a woman of superior rank.

be about to idiom 막 ~하려는 참이다
If you are about to do something, you are going to do it immediately.

guard [ɡɑːrd] n. 경비 요원; 경비, 감시; 보호물; v. 지키다, 보호하다
A guard is a specially organized group of people, such as soldiers or policemen, who protect or watch someone or something.

tickle [tikl] v. 재미있게 하다; 간지럽히다; n. (장난으로) 간지럽히기
If a fact or a situation tickles you, it amuses you or gives you pleasure.

underground [ʌ̀ndərɡráund] a. 비밀의; 지하의; ad. 지하에
If you go underground, you hide from the authorities or the police because your political ideas or activities are illegal.

outfit [áutfit] n. 한 벌의 옷, 복장; 장비; v. (복장·장비를) 갖추어 주다
An outfit is a set of clothes.

last [læst] v. 오래가다; (특정한 시간 동안) 계속되다; ad. 맨 끝에, 마지막에 (lasting a. 지속적인)
You can use lasting to describe a situation, result, or agreement that continues to exist or have an effect for a very long time.

defeat [difíːt] v. 물리치다; 좌절시키다; 이해가 안 되다; n. 패배
If you defeat someone, you win a victory over them in a battle, game, or contest.

evil [íːvəl] n. 악; a. 사악한, 악랄한; 유해한; 악마의
Evil is used to refer to all the wicked and bad things that happen in the world.

force [fɔːrs] v. 억지로 ~하다; ~를 강요하다; n. 작용력; 힘; 영향력
If a situation or event forces you to do something, it makes it necessary for you to do something that you would not otherwise have done.

⁂ willing [wíliŋ] a. 기꺼이 ~하는; 자발적인
If someone is willing to do something, they are fairly happy about doing it and will do it if they are asked or required to do it.

복습 support [səpɔ́ːrt] v. 지지하다; (넘어지지 않도록) 떠받치다; n. 버팀대; 지지, 지원
If you support someone or their ideas or aims, you agree with them, and perhaps help them because you want them to succeed.

due to idiom ~때문에; ~에 기인하는
If an event is due to something, it happens or exists as a direct result of that thing.

⁂ fresh [freʃ] a. 막 ~한; 신선한; 생생한
If you are fresh from a particular place or experience, you have just come from that place or you have just had that experience.

on the heels of idiom ~후 바로
On the heels of means soon after something.

⁎ heroic [hiróuik] a. 영웅적인, 용감무쌍한; 영웅의; n. (pl.) 영웅적 행동
If you describe a person or their actions as heroic, you admire them because they show extreme bravery.

복습 runaway [rʌ́nəwei] a. 제멋대로 가는, 제어가 안 되는; 달아난
A runaway vehicle or animal is moving forward quickly, and its driver or rider has lost control of it.

복습 sport [spɔːrt] v. 자랑스럽게 보이다; n. 스포츠, 운동
If you sport something, you wear or be decorated with it.

복습 settle [setl] v. 자리를 잡다; (서서히) 가라앉다; 결정하다
If you settle yourself somewhere or settle somewhere, you sit down or make yourself comfortable.

⁎ poll [poul] n. 여론 조사; 투표; 개표; v. 득표하다; 여론 조사를 하다
A poll is a survey in which people are asked their opinions about something, usually in order to find out how popular something is or what people intend to do in the future.

glaze [gleiz] v. (눈이) 게슴츠레해지다; 유리를 끼우다; n. 유약
If you or your eyes glaze over, you start to look bored or tired and it is obvious to other people that you have stopped listening.

복습 tone [toun] n. 어조, 말투; (글 등의) 분위기; 음색
Someone's tone is a quality in their voice which shows what they are feeling or thinking.

shift [ʃift] v. 바꾸다; (장소를) 옮기다; n. 교대 근무 (시간); 변화
If you shift something or if it shifts, it moves slightly.

robotic [roubátik] a. 로봇 같은; 로봇식의
Robotic is used about someone's way of speaking or looking when it seems to show no human feeling.

notice [nóutis] v. 알아채다, 인지하다; 주의하다; n. 신경 씀, 알아챔; 통지, 예고
If you notice something or someone, you become aware of them.

reflect [riflékt] v. (상을) 비추다; 반사하다; 깊이 생각하다
When something is reflected in a mirror or in water, you can see its image in the mirror or in the water.

mechanical [məkǽnikəl] a. (행동이) 기계적인; 기계와 관련된
(mechanically ad. 기계적으로)
If you describe someone's action as mechanical, you mean that they do it automatically, without thinking about it.

glimpse [glimps] n. 잠깐 봄; 짧은 경험; v. 언뜻 보다; 깨닫다, 이해하다
If you get a glimpse of someone or something, you see them very briefly and not very well.

hypnotic [hipnátik] a. 최면을 일으키는, 최면성의
Something that is hypnotic holds your attention or makes you feel sleepy, often because it involves repeated sounds, pictures, or movements.

blaze [bleiz] v. 눈부시게 빛나다; 활활 타다; n. 불길; 휘황찬란한 빛
If something blazes with light or color, it is extremely bright.

spell [spel] n. 주문; 마법; v. (어떤 단어의) 철자를 쓰다; 철자를 맞게 쓰다
(fall under one's spell idiom ~의 통제를 받다)
If you fall under someone's spell, you are strongly influenced by someone, so that you do what you think they want, or you copy them in some way.

avert [əvə́ːrt] v. (눈·얼굴 등을) 돌리다, 외면하다; 피하다
If you avert your eyes or gaze from someone or something, you look away from them.

in time idiom 제때에, 시간 맞춰, 늦지 않게
If you are in time for a particular event, you are not too late for it.

break free idiom 떨쳐 풀다; 도망치다
If you break free from someone or something, you escape from someone or something that is trying to hold you.

control [kəntróul] v. 지배하다; 조정하다; n. (기계·차량의) 제어 장치; 통제, 제어
To control a piece of equipment, process, or system means to make it work in the way that you want it to work.

freeze [fri:z] v. (froze-frozen) (두려움 등으로 몸이) 얼어붙다; 얼다; n. 동결; 한파
If someone who is moving freezes, they suddenly stop and become completely still and quiet.

transfix [trænsfíks] v. (두려움·경악 등으로) 얼어붙게 하다
If you are transfixed by something, it captures all of your interest or attention, so that you are unable to think of anything else or unable to act.

dazzle [dǽzl] v. 눈부시게 하다; 황홀하게 하다; n. 눈부심 (dazzling a. 눈부신)
A dazzling light is very bright and makes you unable to see properly for a short time.

goggle [gagl] n. (pl.) 보호 안경, 고글
Goggles are large glasses that fit closely to your face around your eyes to protect them from such things as water, wind, or dust.

* **hood** [hud] n. (외투 등에 달린) 모자; (자동차 등의) 덮개
A hood is a part of a coat which you can pull up to cover your head. It is in the shape of a triangular bag attached to the neck of the coat at the back.

cover [kʌ́vər] v. 덮다; 적당히 둘러대다; 씌우다, 가리다; n. 위장, 속임수; 몸을 숨길 곳; 덮개
If one thing covers another, it has been placed over it in order to protect it, hide it, or close it.

yell [jel] v. 고함치다, 소리 지르다; n. 고함, 외침
If you yell, you shout loudly, usually because you are excited, angry, or in pain.

* **crew** [kru:] n. (함께 일을 하는) 팀, 조; 승무원; v. (배의) 승무원을 하다
A crew is a group of people with special technical skills who work together on a task or project.

* **absolute** [ǽbsəlùːt] a. 완전, 순; 완전한, 완벽한 (absolutely ad. 극도로, 굉장히)
Absolutely means totally and completely.

mesmerize [mézməràiz] v. 마음을 사로잡다, 완전 넋을 빼놓다
If you are mesmerized by something, you are so interested in it or so attracted to it that you cannot think about anything else.

broadcast [brɔ́ːdkæst] n. 방송; v. 방송하다; 널리 알리다, 광고하다
A broadcast is a program, performance, or speech on the radio or on television.

idiot [ídiət] n. 바보, 멍청이 (idiotic a. 바보 같은, 멍청한)
If you call someone or something idiotic, you mean that they are very stupid or silly.

signal [sígnəl] n. 신호; 징조; v. (동작·소리로) 신호를 보내다; 암시하다
A signal is a series of radio waves, light waves, or changes in electrical current which may carry information.

hijack [háidʒæk] v. 장악하다, 이용하다; (차량·비행기를) 납치하다
If you say that someone has hijacked something, you disapprove of the way in which they have taken control of it when they had no right to do so.

check out idiom ~을 확인하다; (흥미로운 것을) 살펴보다
If you check out someone or something, you examine them in order to be certain that everything is correct, true, or satisfactory.

rush [rʌʃ] v. 급히 움직이다; 서두르다; n. (감정이 갑자기) 치밀어 오름; 혼잡; 기쁨, 흥분
If you rush somewhere, you go there quickly.

trance [træns] n. 최면 상태; 실신; 무아지경
A trance is a state of mind in which someone seems to be asleep and to have no conscious control over their thoughts or actions, but in which they can see and hear things and respond to commands given by other people.

aerocade [ɛəroukéid] n. 비행기 편대
An aerocade is a line of airplanes.

airborne [ɛ́ərbɔːrn] a. 하늘에 떠 있는; 공기로 운반되는
If an aircraft is airborne, it is in the air and flying.

sprint [sprint] v. (짧은 거리를) 전력 질주하다; n. 전력 질주; 단거리 경기
If you sprint, you run or ride as fast as you can over a short distance.

frighten [fraitn] v. 겁먹게 하다, 놀라게 하다 (frightened a. 겁먹은, 무서워하는)
If you are frightened, you are anxious or afraid, often because of something that has just happened or that you think may happen.

assistant [əsístənt] n. 조수, 보조원
Someone's assistant is a person who helps them in their work.

gesture [dʒésʧər] v. (손·머리 등으로) 가리키다; 몸짓을 하다; n. 몸짓; (감정·의도의) 표시
If you gesture, you use movements of your hands or head in order to tell someone something or draw their attention to something.

* **dash** [dæʃ] v. (급히) 서둘러 가다; 내동댕이치다; n. (= dashboard) (승용차의) 계기판; 돌진, 질주
If you dash somewhere, you run or go there quickly and suddenly.

복습 **spot** [spat] v. 발견하다, 찾다, 알아채다; n. (특정한) 곳; (작은) 점
If you spot something or someone, you notice them.

복습 **grab** [græb] v. (와락·단단히) 붙잡다; 급히 ~하다; n. 와락 잡아채려고 함
If you grab something, you take it or pick it up suddenly and roughly.

복습 **fling** [fliŋ] v. (flung-flung) (힘껏) 던지다; (머리·팔 등을) 휘두르다; n. (한바탕) 실컷 즐기기
If you fling something somewhere, you throw it there using a lot of force.

* **shatter** [ʃǽtər] v. 산산이 부수다, 산산조각 내다; 엄청난 충격을 주다
If something shatters or is shattered, it breaks into a lot of small pieces.

propel [prəpél] v. 나아가게 하다; 몰고 가다
To propel something in a particular direction means to cause it to move in that direction.

복습 **stare** [stɛər] v. 빤히 쳐다보다, 응시하다; n. 빤히 쳐다보기, 응시
If you stare at someone or something, you look at them for a long time.

복습 **bewilder** [biwíldər] v. 어리둥절하게 하다, 혼란스럽게 하다 (bewildered a. 당혹한)
If you are bewildered, you are very confused and cannot understand something or decide what you should do.

복습 **pulse** [pʌls] v. 맥박 치다, 고동치다; 활기가 넘치다; n. 맥박; (강한) 리듬
If something pulses, it moves, appears, or makes a sound with a strong regular rhythm.

복습 **snap** [snæp] v. 급히 움직이다; 툭 부러지다; 날카롭게 말하다; n. 탁 하는 소리
(snap out of idiom (기분·습관에서) 재빨리 벗어나다)
To snap out of something means to become suddenly freed from a condition.

복습 **rooftop** [rúːftap] n. (건물의) 옥상
A rooftop is the outside part of the roof of a building.

복습 **scan** [skæn] v. (유심히) 살피다; 정밀 촬영하다; 훑어보다; n. 정밀 검사
When you scan a place or group of people, you look at it carefully, usually because you are looking for something or someone.

복습 **horizon** [həráizn] n. 지평선, 수평선
The horizon is the line in the far distance where the sky seems to meet the land or the sea.

distance [dístəns] n. 먼 곳; 거리; v. (~에) 관여하지 않다 (in the distance idiom 저 멀리)
If you can see something in the distance, you can see it, far away from you.

slingshot [slíŋʃət] n. 새총
A slingshot is a Y-shaped stick or piece of metal with a piece of elastic attached to
the top parts, used especially by children for shooting small stones.

aim [eim] v. 겨누다; 목표하다; n. 겨냥, 조준; 목적
If you aim a weapon or object at something or someone, you point it toward them
before firing or throwing it.

release [rilíːs] v. 놓아 주다; 풀어 주다; (감정을) 발산하다; n. 풀어 줌; 발표, 공개
If you release someone or something, you stop holding them.

smash [smæʃ] v. (세게) 부딪치다; 박살내다; 부서지다; n. 박살내기; 요란한 소리
If you smash through a wall, gate, or door, you get through it by hitting and
breaking it.

chopper [ʧápər] n. 헬리콥터; 큰 칼, 작은 도끼
A chopper is a helicopter.

tumble [tʌmbl] v. 굴러 떨어지다; 폭삭 무너지다; n. (갑자기) 굴러 떨어짐; 폭락
If someone or something tumbles somewhere, they fall there with a rolling or
bouncing movement.

cockpit [kákpit] n. (비행기·우주선 등의) 조종석, 조종실
In an airplane or racing car, the cockpit is the part where the pilot or driver sits.

pilot [páilət] n. 조종사, 비행사
A pilot is a person who is trained to fly an aircraft.

restrict [ristríkt] v. 제한하다, 통제하다; 방해하다 (restricted a. 출입이 제한되는)
A restricted area is one that only people with special permission can enter.

aircraft [érkræft] n. 항공기
An aircraft is a vehicle which can fly, for example an airplane or a helicopter.

compromise [kámprəmaiz] v. ~을 위태롭게 하다; 타협하다; 양보하다; n. 타협, 절충
If someone or something is compromised, they are brought into disrepute or
danger by indiscreet, foolish, or reckless behavior.

blade [bleid] n. (엔진·헬리콥터 등의) 날개깃; (칼·도구 등의) 날
The blades of a propeller are the long, flat parts that turn round.

^복_습 **slice** [slais] v. 베다; (하늘·물 등을) 가르듯이 달리다; n. (얇게 썬) 조각; 부분, 몫
If you slice bread, meat, fruit, or other food, you cut it into thin pieces.

* **barely** [béərli] ad. 간신히, 가까스로; 거의 ~아니게
You use barely to say that something is only just true or only just the case.

^복_습 **figure** [fígjər] v. 생각하다; 중요하다; n. (멀리서 흐릿하게 보이는) 사람; 수치; (중요한) 인물
If you figure that something is the case, you think or guess that it is the case.

^복_습 **leap** [liːp] v. (서둘러) ~하다; 뛰다, 뛰어오르다; n. 높이뛰기, 도약; 급증
If you leap somewhere, you move there suddenly and quickly.

^복_습 **swing** [swiŋ] v. 휙 움직이다; (전후·좌우로) 흔들다; n. 흔들기; 휘두르기
If something swings in a particular direction or if you swing it in that direction, it moves in that direction with a smooth, curving movement.

^책_책 **bullet** [búlit] n. 총알
A bullet is a small piece of metal with a pointed or rounded end, which is fired out of a gun.

* **terrify** [térəfài] v. (몹시) 무섭게 하다 (terrified a. (몹시) 무서워하는, 겁이 난)
If something terrifies you, it makes you feel extremely frightened.

stand down idiom 경계 태세를 해제하다; (직장·직책에서) 물러나다
If soldiers are told to stand down, they are asked to end a state of readiness or alert.

^복_습 **insist** [insíst] v. 고집하다, 주장하다, 우기다
If you insist that something should be done, you say so very firmly and refuse to give in about it.

^복_습 **cabin** [kǽbin] n. (항공기·배의) 선실; (나무로 된) 오두막집
A cabin is one of the areas inside a plane.

hypnotize [hípnətàiz] v. 최면을 걸다; 혼을 빼놓다, 홀리다
If someone hypnotizes you, they put you into a state in which you seem to be asleep but can still see, hear, or respond to things said to you.

* **rigid** [rídʒid] a. 뻣뻣한, 단단한; 엄격한, 융통성 없는 (rigidly ad. 뻣뻣하게)
If you are rigid, you are unable to move because of a strong emotion such as fear or anger.

careen [kəríːn] v. 위태롭게 달리다, 흔들리면서 질주하다
To careen somewhere means to rush forward in an uncontrollable way.

^복_습 **struggle** [strʌgl] v. 애쓰다; 몸부림치다, 허우적거리다; 힘겹게 나아가다; n. 투쟁, 분투; 몸부림
If you struggle to do something, you try hard to do it, even though other people
or things may be making it difficult for you to succeed.

^복_습 **parachute** [pǽrəʃùːt] v. 낙하산을 타고 뛰어내리다; n. 낙하산
If a person parachutes or someone parachutes them somewhere, they jump from
an aircraft using a parachute.

hang on idiom 꽉 붙잡다; 잠깐 기다려, 멈춰 봐
If you hang on to something, you hold tightly to it.

^복_습 **flatten** [flǽtn] v. 납작하게 하다; 납작하게 엎드리다; 때려눕히다
If you flatten something or if it flattens, it becomes flat or flatter.

_＊ **expand** [ikspǽnd] v. 확대시키다, 팽창시키다; 더 상세히 하다
If something expands or is expanded, it becomes larger.

turn into idiom ~이 되다, ~으로 변하다
To turn or be turned into something means to change, or to make a thing change,
into something different.

^복_습 **drift** [drift] v. (물·공기에) 떠가다; (자신도 모르게) ~하게 되다; (서서히) 이동하다; n. 표류; 흐름
When something drifts somewhere, it is carried there by the movement of wind
or water.

_＊ **faint** [feint] v. 실신하다, 기절하다; n. 실신, 기절; a. 희미한, 약한
If you faint, you lose consciousness for a short time, especially because you are
hungry, or because of pain, heat, or shock.

Chapters
10 & 11

1. Why was Violet upset with Bob?

A. He had told Tony to stay away from her.

B. He had caused Dicker to erase Tony's memory of her.

C. He had asked Dicker to lock up Tony in prison.

D. He had made Tony afraid of Superheroes.

2. Why did Elastigirl feel bad when she arrived at DevTech?

A. She remembered that she had not caught the Screenslaver yet.

B. She wished that she could be with her family.

C. She realized that many people still hated Superheroes.

D. She was uncomfortable with getting so much public attention.

3. Who did Elastigirl meet inside DevTech?

A. Supers who were jealous of her fame

B. Supers who had come up with their own Super names

C. Supers who were well known around the world

D. Supers who had just discovered their powers recently

4. How did Elastigirl and Evelyn plan to catch the Screenslaver?

A. They would schedule a meeting with him.

B. They would invite him to a remote location.

C. They would use a tracking device to find him.

D. They would set up a huge screen to trap him.

5. What did Bob claim was the reason for going to the Happy Platter?

A. So that he could finally meet Tony in person

B. So that he could apologize to Tony for his memory loss

C. So that Vi would not have to eat drive-in food

D. So that Vi would have a chance to ask Tony out

Check Your Reading Speed
1분에 몇 단어를 읽는지 리딩 속도를 측정해보세요.

$$\frac{1,212 \text{ words}}{\text{reading time ( ) sec}} \times 60 = (\qquad) \text{ WPM}$$

Build Your Vocabulary

* **daring** [déəriŋ] a. 대담한; 위험한
A daring person is willing to do things that might be dangerous.

복습 **rescue** [réskjuː] n. 구출, 구조, 구제; v. 구하다, 구출하다
Rescue is help which gets someone out of a dangerous or unpleasant situation.

복습 **plate** [pleit] n. 접시, 그릇; (자동차) 번호판; 판
A plate is a round or oval flat dish that is used to hold food.

복습 **awful** [ɔ́ːfəl] a. 끔찍한, 지독한; (정도가) 대단한, 아주 심한
If you look or feel awful, you look or feel ill.

* **jerk** [dʒəːrk] n. 얼간이; 홱 움직임; v. 홱 움직이다
If you call someone a jerk, you are insulting them because you think they are stupid or you do not like them.

복습 **suck** [sʌk] v. 엉망이다, 형편없다; (특정한 방향으로) 빨아들이다; 빨아 먹다; n. 빨기, 빨아 먹기
If someone says that something sucks, they are indicating that they think it is very bad.

복습 **collapse** [kəlǽps] v. 주저앉다; 붕괴되다, 무너지다; 쓰러지다; n. 실패; (건물의) 붕괴
If you collapse onto something, you sit or lie down suddenly because you are very tired.

복습 **suit** [suːt] n. (특정한 활동 때 입는) 옷; 정장; 소송; v. ~에게 편리하다; 어울리다
A particular type of suit is a piece of clothing that you wear for a particular activity.

복습 **pour** [pɔːr] v. 붓다, 따르다; 쏟아져 나오다; 마구 쏟아지다
If you pour a liquid or other substance, you make it flow steadily out of a container by holding the container at an angle.

* **refrigerator** [rifrídʒərèitər] n. 냉장고
A refrigerator is a large container which is kept cool inside, usually by electricity, so that the food and drink in it stays fresh.

* **erase** [iréis] v. (완전히) 지우다; (지우개 등으로) 지우다
If you erase a thought or feeling, you destroy it completely so that you can no longer remember something or no longer feel a particular emotion.

* **container** [kəntéinər] n. 용기, 그릇; (화물 수송용) 컨테이너
A container is something such as a box or bottle that is used to hold or store things in.

* **sniff** [snif] v. 냄새를 맡다; 코를 훌쩍이다; 콧방귀를 뀌다; n. 냄새 맡기; 콧방귀 뀌기
If you sniff something or sniff at it, you smell it by taking air in through your nose.

복
습 **assess** [əsés] v. (특성·자질 등을) 재다; 평가하다, 가늠하다
When you assess a person, thing, or situation, you consider them in order to make a judgment about them.

복
습 **figure out** idiom ~을 이해하다, 알아내다; 계산하다, 산출하다
If you figure out someone or something, you come to understand them by thinking carefully.

복 **identity** [aidéntəti] n. 신원, 신분, 정체; 독자성
Your identity is who you are.

* **growl** [graul] v. 으르렁거리듯 말하다; 으르렁거리다; n. 으르렁거리는 소리
If someone growls something, they say something in a low, rough, and angry voice.

seethe [siːð] v. (분노 등이) 부글거리다, 속을 끓이다; 법석을 떨다
When you are seething, you are very angry about something but do not express your feelings about it.

복 **guilty** [gílti] a. 죄책감이 드는; 책임이 있는; 유죄의
If you feel guilty, you feel unhappy because you think that you have done something wrong or have failed to do something which you should have done.

stomp [stamp] v. 쿵쿵거리며 걷다, 발을 구르다; n. (발을) 쿵쾅거리기
If you stomp somewhere, you walk there with very heavy steps, often because you are angry.

* **dump** [dʌmp] v. (아무렇게나) 내려놓다; 버리다; n. (쓰레기) 폐기장
If you dump something somewhere, you put it or unload it there quickly and carelessly.

cereal [síəriəl] n. 시리얼; 곡물, 곡류
Cereal or breakfast cereal is a food made from grain. It is mixed with milk and eaten for breakfast.

renounce [rináuns] v. 포기하다; 그만두다, 끊다
If you renounce a claim, rank, or title, you officially give it up.

march [ma:rʧ] v. (단호한 태도로 급히) 걸어가다; 행진하다; n. 행군, 행진; 3월
If you say that someone marches somewhere, you mean that they walk there quickly and in a determined way, for example because they are angry.

sink [siŋk] n. 개수대; v. 가라앉다, 빠지다; 박다; 주저앉다
A sink is a large fixed container in a kitchen, with taps to supply water. It is mainly used for washing dishes.

stuff [stʌf] v. 쑤셔 넣다; 채워 넣다; n. 일, 것, 물건
If you stuff something somewhere, you push it there quickly and roughly.

garbage [gá:rbidʒ] n. 쓰레기
Garbage is rubbish, especially waste from a kitchen.

disposal [dispóuzəl] n. 음식물 쓰레기 분쇄기; 처리; 처분
A disposal is a device fitted to the waste pipe of a kitchen sink for grinding up food waste.

spin [spin] v. (spun-spun) (빙빙) 돌다; 돌아서다; n. 회전
If something spins or if you spin it, it turns quickly around a central point.

damage [dǽmidʒ] v. 손상을 주다, 피해를 입히다, 훼손하다; n. 손상, 피해; 훼손
(undamaged a. 손상되지 않은)
Something that is undamaged has not been damaged or spoilt in any way.

furious [fjúəriəs] a. 몹시 화가 난; 맹렬한
Someone who is furious is extremely angry.

bite [bait] v. (bit-bitten) (이빨로) 물다; 베어 물다; n. 한 입; 물기; 소량
If you bite something, you use your teeth to cut into it, for example in order to eat it or break it.

rip [rip] v. (갑자기) 찢다; (거칠게) 떼어 내다, 뜯어 내다; 빠른 속도로 돌진하다; n. (길게) 찢어진 곳
When something rips or when you rip it, you tear it forcefully with your hands or with a tool such as a knife.

indestructible [ìndistrʌ́ktəbl] a. (쉽게) 파괴할 수 없는
If something is indestructible, it is very strong and cannot be destroyed.

복습 **frustrate** [frʌ́streit] v. 좌절감을 주다, 불만스럽게 하다; 방해하다
(frustrated a. 좌절감을 느끼는)
If something frustrates you, it upsets or angers you because you are unable to do
anything about the problems it creates.

★ **adolescence** [ædəlésns] n. 청소년기
Adolescence is the period of your life in which you develop from being a child
into being an adult.

복습 **sigh** [sai] v. 한숨을 쉬다, 한숨짓다; 탄식하듯 말하다; n. 한숨
When you sigh, you let out a deep breath, as a way of expressing feelings such as
disappointment, tiredness, or pleasure.

affirmative [əfə́:rmətiv] n. 긍정, 동의; 긍정의 말; a. 긍정의, 동의하는
If you reply to a question in the affirmative, you say 'yes' or make a gesture that
means 'yes.'

hang one's head idiom 낙담하다; 부끄러워 고개를 숙이다
If you hang your head, you are ashamed and discouraged.

★ **meanwhile** [mí:nwàil] ad. (다른 일이 일어나고 있는) 그동안에
Meanwhile means while a particular thing is happening.

복습 **limousine** [líməzì:n] n. (= limo) 리무진(대형 승용차)
A limousine is a large and very comfortable car. Limousines are usually driven by
a chauffeur and are used by very rich or important people.

pull up idiom (차량·운전자가) 멈추다, 서다
If a vehicle or driver pulls up, they stop.

복습 **crowd** [kraud] n. 사람들, 군중; v. 가득 메우다; 바싹 붙어 서다
A crowd is a large group of people who have gathered together, for example to
watch or listen to something interesting, or to protest about something.

★ **chant** [ʧænt] v. 되풀이하여 말하다; 구호를 외치다, 연호하다; n. (연이어 외치는) 구호
If you chant something or if you chant, you repeat the same words over and over
again.

kaboom [kəbú:m] int. 우르르 쾅
Kaboom is the sound of an explosion.

kapow [kəpáu] int. 펑 하는 소리
Kapow is a powerful sound of impact or transformation.

legal [líːgəl] a. 법이 허용하는, 합법적인; 법률과 관련된
An action or situation that is legal is allowed or required by law.

exit [égzit] v. 나가다, 떠나다; 퇴장하다; n. (고속도로의) 출구; (공공건물의) 출구; 퇴장
If you exit from a room or building, you leave it.

cheer [tʃiər] n. 환호(성), 응원; v. 환호성을 지르다, 환호하다
A cheer is a loud shout of happiness or approval.

erupt [irʌ́pt] v. (강한 감정을) 터뜨리다; 분출되다
You say that someone erupts when they suddenly have a change in mood, usually becoming quite noisy.

adore [ədɔ́ːr] v. 흠모하다; 아주 좋아하다 (adoring a. 흠모하는)
An adoring person is someone who loves and admires another person very much.

inspire [inspáiər] v. 고무하다; 영감을 주다; (감정 등을) 불어넣다
If someone or something inspires you to do something new or unusual, they make you want to do it.

crouch [krautʃ] v. (몸을) 쭈그리다, 쭈그리고 앉다; n. 쭈그리고 앉기
If you are crouching, your legs are bent under you so that you are close to the ground and leaning forward slightly.

sign [sain] n. 표지판; 몸짓; 기색, 흔적; v. 서명하다; 신호를 보내다
A sign is a piece of wood, metal, or plastic with words or pictures on it. Signs give you information about something, or give you a warning or an instruction.

outpouring [autpɔ́ːriŋ] n. (감정의) 분출, 터져 나옴; (많은 양이) 쏟아져 나옴
An outpouring of something such as an emotion or a reaction is the expression of it in an uncontrolled way.

admire [ædmáiər] v. 감탄하며 바라보다; 존경하다, 칭찬하다 (admiration n. 감탄, 존경)
Admiration is a feeling of great liking and respect for a person or thing.

villain [vílən] n. 악인, 악한; (이야기·연극 등의) 악당
A villain is someone who deliberately harms other people or breaks the law in order to get what they want.

scatter [skǽtər] v. 흩뿌리다; 황급히 흩어지다; n. 흩뿌리기; 소수, 소량
If you scatter things over an area, you throw or drop them so that they spread all over the area.

headline [hédlain] n. (신문 기사의) 표제; v. (기사에) 표제를 달다
A headline is the title of a newspaper story, printed in large letters at the top of the story, especially on the front page.

ambassador [æmbǽsədər] n. 대사
An ambassador is an important official who lives in a foreign country and represents his or her own country's interests there.

phase [feiz] n. (변화·발달의) 단계; v. 단계적으로 하다
A phase is a particular stage in a process or in the gradual development of something.

summit [sʌ́mit] n. 정상 회담; (산의) 정상
A summit is a meeting at which the leaders of two or more countries discuss important matters.

yacht [jat] n. 요트
A yacht is a large boat with sails or a motor, used for racing or pleasure trips.

gather [gǽðər] v. (사람들이) 모이다; (여기저기 있는 것을) 모으다
If people gather somewhere or if someone gathers people somewhere, they come together in a group.

glum [glʌm] a. 침울한
Someone who is glum is sad and quiet because they are disappointed or unhappy about something.

upset [ʌpsét] a. 속상한, 마음이 상한; v. 속상하게 하다; (계획·상황 등이) 잘못되게 하다
If you are upset, you are unhappy or disappointed because something unpleasant has happened to you.

appreciate [əpríːʃièit] v. 고마워하다; 진가를 알아보다
If you appreciate something that someone has done for you or is going to do for you, you are grateful for it.

tombstone [túːmstòun] n. 묘석, 묘비
A tombstone is a large stone with words carved into it, which is placed on a grave.

recognize [rékəgnàiz] v. 알아보다; 인식하다; 공인하다
If you recognize someone or something, you know who that person is or what that thing is.

homemade [houmméid] a. 집에서 만든, 손수 만든
Something that is homemade has been made in someone's home, rather than in a shop or factory.

applaud [əplɔ́ːd] v. 박수를 치다; 갈채를 보내다
When a group of people applaud, they clap their hands in order to show approval, for example when they have enjoyed a play or concert.

respect [rispékt] n. 존경(심); 존중; v. (법률·원칙 등을) 준수하다; 존경하다; 존중하다
If you have respect for someone, you have a good opinion of them.

awkward [ɔ́ːkwərd] a. 어색한; (처리하기) 곤란한; 불편한 (awkwardly ad. 어색하게)
Someone who feels awkward behaves in a shy or embarrassed way.

blush [blʌʃ] v. 얼굴을 붉히다; ~에 부끄러워하다; n. 얼굴이 붉어짐
When you blush, your face becomes redder than usual because you are ashamed or embarrassed.

mug [mʌg] n. (큰) 잔, 머그잔; v. 강도짓을 하다
A mug is a large deep cup with straight sides and a handle, used for hot drinks.

show off idiom ~을 자랑하다; 돋보이게 하다
To show off someone or something means to try to make people pay attention to them because you are proud of them.

land [lænd] v. (땅·표면에) 내려앉다, 착륙하다; 놓다, 두다; n. 육지, 땅; 지역
When someone or something lands, they come down to the ground after moving through the air or falling.

take in idiom 이해하다; ~을 눈여겨보다
If you take in something, you understand and remember something that you hear or read.

break out idiom 발생하다
To break out means to start suddenly.

applause [əplɔ́ːz] n. 박수 (갈채)
Applause is the noise made by a group of people clapping their hands to show approval.

fantastic [fæntǽstik] a. 기막히게 좋은, 환상적인; 기상천외한; 엄청난, 굉장한
If you say that something is fantastic, you are emphasizing that you think it is very good or that you like it a lot.

outcast [áutkæst] n. 따돌림받는 사람
An outcast is someone who is not accepted by a group of people or by society.

emotional [imóuʃənl] a. 감정적인; 정서의, 감정의
If someone is or becomes emotional, they show their feelings very openly, especially because they are upset.

hug [hʌg] v. 껴안다, 포옹하다; n. 포옹
When you hug someone, you put your arms around them and hold them tightly, for example because you like them or are pleased to see them.

yay [jei] int. 야호, 와!
You can use yay for expressing triumph, approval, or encouragement.

touched [tʌʃt] a. 감동한
If you are touched, you are feeling happy or emotional, for example because someone has been very kind or because a situation is sad.

ecstatic [ekstǽtik] a. 황홀해하는, 열광하는
If you are ecstatic, you feel very happy and full of excitement.

resemble [rizémbl] v. 닮다, 비슷하다
If one thing or person resembles another, they are similar to each other.

owl [aul] n. [동물] 올빼미
An owl is a bird with a flat face, large eyes, and a small sharp beak. Most owls obtain their food by hunting small animals at night.

gold standard [góuld stǽndərd] n. 최고 기준
The gold standard is something that is very good and is used for measuring how good other similar things are.

flatter [flǽtər] v. 아첨하다; (실제보다) 돋보이게 하다
If you are flattered by something that has happened, you are pleased about it because it makes you feel important or special.

zap [zæp] v. 제압하다, 해치우다; 재빠르게 하다
To zap someone or something means to kill, destroy, or hit them, for example with a gun or in a computer game.

electronic [ilektránik] a. 전자의, 전자 장비와 관련된 (electronically ad. 전자적으로)
An electronic device has transistors or silicon chips which control and change the electric current passing through the device.

charge [ʧɑːrdʒ] v. 충전하다; 급히 가다; (요금·값을) 청구하다; n. 책임, 담당; 요금
To charge a battery means to pass an electrical current through it in order to make it more powerful or to make it last longer.

* **bolt** [boult] n. 번쩍하는 번개; 볼트; v. 달아나다; 빗장을 지르다
A bolt of lightning is a flash of lightning that is seen as a white line in the sky.

* **lightning** [láitniŋ] n. 번개, 번갯불; a. 아주 빨리; 급작스럽게
Lightning is the very bright flashes of light in the sky that happen during thunderstorms.

복습 **offend** [əfénd] v. 기분 상하게 하다; 불쾌하게 여겨지다; 범죄를 저지르다
If you offend someone, you say or do something rude which upsets or embarrasses them.

hang out idiom 많은 시간을 보내다
If you hang out in a place or with a person or a group of people, you spend a lot of time in there or with them.

* **chat** [ʧæt] v. 이야기를 나누다, 수다를 떨다; n. 이야기, 대화
When people chat, they talk to each other in an informal and friendly way.

복습 **positive** [pázətiv] a. 긍정적인; 확신하는; 분명한
If you are positive about things, you are hopeful and confident, and think of the good aspects of a situation rather than the bad ones.

* **impact** [ímpækt] n. (강력한) 영향; 충돌, 충격; v. 영향을 주다; 충돌하다
The impact that something has on a situation, process, or person is a sudden and powerful effect that it has on them.

wind down idiom (서서히) 종료되다; 긴장을 풀다
If something winds down, it ends gradually or in stages.

* **bid** [bid] v. (bid-bid) (인사를) 하다; (작별을) 고하다; 값을 부르다; n. 가격 제시; 응찰
If you bid someone farewell, you say goodbye to them.

I beg to differ idiom 내 생각은 좀 다르다
You say 'I beg to differ' when you are politely emphasizing that you disagree with someone.

복습 **invent** [invént] v. 발명하다; (사실이 아닌 것을) 지어내다
If you invent something such as a machine or process, you are the first person to think of it or make it.

* **pop** [pap] v. 불쑥 나타나다; 펑 하는 소리가 나다; n. 펑 (하는 소리)
If something pops up, it appears or happens when you do not expect it.

* **capture** [kǽpʧər] v. 붙잡다; 포로로 잡다, 억류하다; n. 생포; 구금, 억류
If you capture someone or something, you catch them, especially in a war.

^복_습 **signal** [sígnəl] n. 신호; 징조; v. (동작·소리로) 신호를 보내다; 암시하다
A signal is a series of radio waves, light waves, or changes in electrical current which may carry information.

_* **trace** [treis] v. 추적하다; (형체·윤곽을) 따라가다; n. 자취, 흔적; 조금
If you trace the origin or development of something, you find out or describe how it started or developed.

_‡ **origin** [ɔ́:rədʒin] n. 기원, 근원; 출신, 태생
You can refer to the beginning, cause, or source of something as its origin or origins.

work out idiom ~을 계획해 내다; 해결하다; (일이) 잘 풀리다
If you work out something, you plan and think of it.

^복_습 **track** [træk] v. 추적하다, 뒤쫓다; n. (기차) 선로; 경주로, 트랙; 자국
To track someone or something means to follow their movements by means of a special device, such as a satellite or radar.

_* **device** [diváis] n. 장치, 기구; 폭발물; 방법
A device is an object that has been invented for a particular purpose, for example for recording or measuring something.

^복_습 **remote** [rimóut] a. 원격의; 먼; 외진, 외딴; n. (= remote control) 리모컨; 원격 조종
If you describe an electronic device as remote, it is operating or operated at a distance by means of radio or infrared signals.

^복_습 **trap** [træp] n. 함정; 덫; v. (위험한 장소에) 가두다; (함정으로) 몰아넣다
A trap is a trick that is intended to catch or deceive someone.

_* **bump** [bʌmp] v. (~에) 부딪치다; 덜컹거리며 가다; n. 쿵, 탁 (하는 소리)
If you bump into something or someone, you accidentally hit them while you are moving.

carry out idiom 수행하다, 실행하다, 집행하다; 완수하다
If you carry out something, you do something that you said you would do or that you have been asked to do.

Check Your Reading Speed

1분에 몇 단어를 읽는지 리딩 속도를 측정해보세요.

$$\frac{643 \text{ words}}{\text{reading time (\quad) sec}} \times 60 = (\qquad) \text{ WPM}$$

Build Your Vocabulary

* **dial** [dáiəl] v. 다이얼을 돌리다, 전화를 걸다; n. (시계·계기 등의) 문자반
If you dial or if you dial a number, you turn the dial or press the buttons on a telephone in order to phone someone.

* **pack** [pæk] v. (짐을) 싸다; 가득 채우다; n. 무리, 집단; 묶음 (unpack v. (짐을) 풀다)
When you unpack a suitcase, box, or similar container, or you unpack the things inside it, you take the things out of the container.

* **wipe** [waip] v. 지우다; (먼지·물기 등을) 닦다; n. 닦기
If you wipe something, you remove or eliminate it completely.

oops [uːps] int. 아이고, 이런 (놀람·당황을 나타내는 소리)
You say 'oops' to indicate that there has been a slight accident or mistake, or to apologize to someone for it.

* **file** [fail] v. (문서 등을) 보관하다; (소송 등을) 제기하다; n. 파일, 서류철; 정보
If you file a document, you put it in the correct file.

* **cabinet** [kǽbənit] n. 캐비닛, 보관장; (정부의) 내각
A cabinet is a cupboard used for storing things such as medicine or alcoholic drinks or for displaying decorative things in.

thumb through idiom (책 등을) 휙휙 넘겨보다
If you thumb through something such as a book, magazine, or a document, you turn the pages of it quickly and only read small parts of it.

* **part-time** [páːrt-táim] ad. 시간제 근무로; a. (근무가) 시간제인
If someone is a part-time worker or has a part-time job, they work for only part of each day or week.

concoct [kankákt] v. (계획·음모 등을) 꾸미다; (이것저것 섞어) 만들다
If you concoct an excuse or explanation, you invent one that is not true.

hang up idiom 전화를 끊다; ~을 중지하다
To hang up means to end a telephone conversation, often very suddenly.

modest [mádist] a. 그다지 대단하지는 않은, 보통의; 겸손한
A modest house or other building is not large or expensive.

panel [pǽnl] v. 판으로 덮다; n. (자동차 등의) 계기판; 판; 자문단 (paneling n. 판자)
Panelling consists of boards or strips of wood covering a wall inside a building.

confuse [kənfjúːz] v. (사람을) 혼란시키다; 혼동하다 (confused a. 혼란스러워하는)
If you are confused, you do not know exactly what is happening or what to do.

hostess [hóustis] n. 여종업원; 여주인; (TV·라디오 프로의) 여성 진행자
A hostess is a woman whose job is to welcome customers in a restaurant and take them to their table.

booth [buːθ] n. (칸막이를 한) 작은 공간; (임시로 만든) 점포
A booth in a restaurant or café consists of a table with long fixed seats on two or sometimes three sides of it.

ignore [ignɔ́ːr] v. 무시하다; (사람을) 못 본 척하다
If you ignore someone or something, you pay no attention to them.

nod [nad] v. (고개를) 끄덕이다, 까딱하다; n. (고개를) 끄덕임
If you nod, you move your head downward and upward to show that you are answering 'yes' to a question, or to show agreement, understanding, or approval.

enthusiastic [inθùːziǽstik] a. 열렬한, 열광적인 (unenthusiastically ad. 냉담하게)
If you are unenthusiatic about something, you are not excited about it.

platter [plǽtər] n. (큰 접시에 담긴) 모듬 요리; (큰 서빙용) 접시
A platter can refer to a meal with a particular type of food, served on a large plate in a restaurant.

bored [bɔːrd] a. 지루해하는
If you are bored, you feel tired and impatient because you have lost interest in something or because you have nothing to do.

change of pace idiom 기분전환; 활동의 변경
A change of pace is a change from what someone is used to.

balance [bǽləns] v. 균형을 이루다; n. (몸의) 균형; 균형 (상태) (balanced a. 균형 잡힌)
Something that is balanced is pleasing or useful because its different parts or elements are in the correct proportions.

* **diet** [dáiət] n. 식사; 식습관; 다이어트
Your diet is the type and range of food that you regularly eat.

해당 **serve** [sə:rv] v. (음식을) 제공하다; (상품·서비스를) 제공하다; (어떤 조직·국가 등을 위해) 일하다
(server n. (식당의) 종업원)
When you serve food and drink, you give people food and drink.

* **pitcher** [pítʃər] n. 물주전자
A pitcher is a jug which is a cylindrical container with a handle and is used for
holding and pouring liquids.

해당 **pour** [pɔ:r] v. 붓다, 따르다; 쏟아져 나오다; 마구 쏟아지다
If you pour a liquid or other substance, you make it flow steadily out of a container
by holding the container at an angle.

* **sip** [sip] n. 한 모금; v. (음료를) 홀짝거리다, 조금씩 마시다
A sip is a small amount of drink that you take into your mouth.

해당 **gag** [gæg] v. 토할 것 같다; (입에) 재갈을 물리다; 말문을 막다; n. 재갈; 장난
If you gag, you cannot swallow and nearly vomit.

spurt [spə:rt] v. 뿜어내다, 분출하다; 갑자기 속도를 더 내다; n. 분출
When liquid or fire spurts from somewhere, or when something spurts liquid or
fire, it comes out quickly in a thin, powerful stream.

해당 **exclaim** [ikskléim] v. 소리치다, 외치다
If you exclaim, you cry out suddenly in surprise, strong emotion, or pain.

해당 **embarrass** [imbǽrəs] v. 당황스럽게 하다, 어색하게 하다; 곤란하게 하다
(embarrassed a. 어색한, 당황스러운)
A person who is embarrassed feels shy, ashamed, or guilty about something.

해당 **invisible** [invízəbl] a. 보이지 않는, 볼 수 없는 (invisibility n. 눈에 보이지 않음)
If you describe something as invisible, you mean that it cannot be seen, for
example because it is transparent, hidden, or very small.

wad [wad] n. (종이·돈 등의) 뭉치; 덩이; v. 뭉치다
A wad of something such as paper or cloth is a tight bundle or ball of it.

mop [map] v. (액체를) 닦아 내다; 대걸레로 닦다; n. 대걸레
If you mop up a surface, you clean liquid or dirt from the surface using a mop,
cloth, or something soft.

해당 **cough** [kɔ:f] v. 기침하다; (기침을 하여 무엇을) 토하다; n. 기침
When you cough, you force air out of your throat with a sudden, harsh noise.

^복_습 **drip** [drip] v. (액체가) 뚝뚝 흐르다; 가득 담고 있다; n. (액체가) 뚝뚝 떨어짐
When liquid drips somewhere, or you drip it somewhere, it falls in individual small drops.

under one's breath idiom 작은 소리로; 소곤 소곤, 낮은 목소리로
If you say something under your breath, you say it in a very quiet voice, often because you do not want other people to hear what you are saying.

^복_습 **interrupt** [intərʌ́pt] v. (말·행동을) 방해하다; 중단시키다; 차단하다
If you interrupt someone who is speaking, you say or do something that causes them to stop.

grit [grit] v. 이를 갈다; 잔모래를 뿌리다; n. 투지, 기개; 모래
If you grit your teeth, you press your upper and lower teeth tightly together, usually because you are angry about something.

* **refresh** [rifréʃ] v. 생기를 되찾게 하다; ~의 기억을 되살리다 (refreshing a. 상쾌하게 하는)
A refreshing bath or drink makes you feel energetic or cool again after you have been tired or hot.

^복_습 **spring** [spriŋ] n. 샘; 봄; 생기, 활기; v. 휙 움직이다; 튀다
A spring is a place where water comes up through the ground. It is also the water that comes from that place.

* **tap** [tæp] n. 수도꼭지; (가볍게) 두드리기; v. 박자를 맞추다; (가볍게) 톡톡 두드리다
A tap is a device that controls the flow of a liquid or gas from a pipe or container, for example on a sink.

^복_습 **handle** [hǽndl] v. (사람·작업 등을) 처리하다; 들다, 옮기다; n. 손잡이
If you say that someone can handle a problem or situation, you mean that they have the ability to deal with it successfully.

mortify [mɔ́:rtəfài] v. 몹시 당황하게 하다; 굴욕감을 주다 (mortifying a. 굴욕스러운)
If you say that something is mortifying, you mean that it makes you feel extremely ashamed or embarrassed.

Chapters
12 & 13

1. **Where was Elastigirl during her interview with Chad?**
   A. Right above the television studio
   B. Down the hall from the broadcasting room
   C. In a recording room far away
   D. At an apartment in the middle of the city

2. **What was part of the Screenslaver's message to TV viewers?**
   A. People should use screens more often.
   B. People are dependent on screens and Superheroes.
   C. People like to watch Superheroes only on screens.
   D. People do not appreciate screens that much.

3. **How did the Screenslaver react when the police took him away?**

   A. He promised to get revenge on Elastigirl.

   B. He appeared sorry to have blown up an apartment building.

   C. He was pleased to have destroyed all the evidence of his crime.

   D. He seemed unaware of why he was being arrested.

4. **Why was Bob angry when he saw his Super car on TV?**

   A. It was a painful reminder of his old Superhero days.

   B. He had tried to buy it at a recent auction but lost.

   C. He had no idea that the car still existed.

   D. A billionaire had stolen it from him years ago.

5. **How did Dash and Violet react when they found out Jack-Jack had powers?**

   A. They were surprised that Bob had not told them about it earlier.

   B. They worried that it would be hard to keep Jack-Jack under control.

   C. They wondered if Helen would be excited to hear the news.

   D. They wished that Jack-Jack could just be a normal baby.

Check Your Reading Speed
1분에 몇 단어를 읽는지 리딩 속도를 측정해보세요.

$$\frac{858 \text{ words}}{\text{reading time ( ) sec}} \times 60 = (\quad) \text{ WPM}$$

Build Your Vocabulary

check out idiom ~을 확인하다; (흥미로운 것을) 살펴보다
If you check out someone or something, you examine them in order to be certain that everything is correct, true, or satisfactory.

record [rékərd] v. 녹화하다, 녹음하다; 기록하다; n. 음반; 기록 (recording n. 녹화)
A recording of something is a record, CD, tape, or video of it.

recollect [rekəlékt] v. 기억해 내다, 생각해 내다 (recollection n. 기억)
If you have a recollection of something, you remember it.

additional [ədíʃənl] a. 추가의
Additional things are extra things apart from the ones already present.

precaution [prikɔ́ːʃən] n. 예방책, 예방 조치
A precaution is an action that is intended to prevent something dangerous or unpleasant from happening.

prevent [privént] v. 막다, 예방하다, 방지하다
To prevent someone from doing something means to make it impossible for them to do it.

secure [sikjúər] a. 안전한; 안심하는; v. 얻어 내다; (단단히) 고정시키다
A secure place is tightly locked or well protected, so that people cannot enter it or leave it.

disclose [disklóuz] v. 밝히다, 폭로하다 (undisclosed a. 밝혀지지 않은, 비밀에 붙여진)
Undisclosed information is not revealed to the public.

locate [lóukeit] v. (특정 위치에) 두다; ~의 정확한 위치를 찾아내다 (location n. 장소, 위치)
The location of someone or something is their exact position.

unbeknownst [ʌ̀nbinóunst] a. ~가 모르는
If something happens unbeknownst to you, you do not know about it.

‍ transmit [trænsmít] v. 전송하다, 송신하다; 전염시키다; 전도하다
(transmission n. 전송, 송신)
A transmission is a program or signal that is broadcast or sent out.

handheld [hǽndhèld] a. 손에 들고 쓰는; 손바닥 크기의, 포켓용의; n. 소형기기
A handheld device such as a camera or a computer is small and light enough to
be used while you are holding it.

device [diváis] n. 장치, 기구; 폭발물; 방법
A device is an object that has been invented for a particular purpose, for example
for recording or measuring something.

clip [klip] n. 짧은 영상; 핀, 클립; v. 핀으로 고정하다; 깎다, 자르다
A clip from a film or a radio or television program is a short piece of it that is
broadcast separately.

cam [kæm] n. (= camera) 카메라
A cam is short for camera.

rescue [réskju:] n. 구출, 구조, 구제; v. 구하다, 구출하다
Rescue is help which gets someone out of a dangerous or unpleasant situation.

spring [spriŋ] v. (sprang-sprung) 휙 움직이다; 뛰다; n. 샘; 봄; 생기, 활기
If something springs in a particular direction, it moves suddenly and quickly.

take off idiom (서둘러) 떠나다; 날아오르다
To take off means to leave a place suddenly.

footage [fútidʒ] n. (특정한 사건을 담은) 장면
Footage of a particular event is a film of it or the part of a film which shows this
event.

fuzzy [fʌ́zi] a. 흐릿한, 어렴풋한; 솜털이 보송보송한
A fuzzy picture, image, or sound is unclear and hard to see or hear.

newscast [njú:zkæst] n. 뉴스 방송
A newscast is a news program that is broadcast on the radio or on television.

‍ static [stǽtik] n. (수신기의) 잡음; 정전기; a. 고정된; 정지 상태의
If there is static on the radio or television, you hear a series of loud noises which
spoils the sound.

‍ announce [ənáuns] v. 발표하다, 알리다; 선언하다 (announcement n. 발표)
An announcement is a statement made to the public or to the media which gives
information about something that has happened or that will happen.

warp [wɔːrp] v. (원래의 모습을 잃고) 틀어지다; a. 초광속의, 워프의
If something warps or is warped, it becomes damaged by bending or curving, often because of the effect of heat or water.

electronic [ilektránik] a. 전자의, 전자 장비와 관련된 (electronically ad. 전자적으로)
An electronic device has transistors or silicon chips which control and change the electric current passing through the device.

＊ **alter** [ɔ́ːltər] v. 변하다, 달라지다; 바꾸다, 고치다 (altered a. 바뀐)
If something alters or if you alter it, it changes.

lock [lak] v. 고정시키다; (자물쇠로) 잠그다; n. 잠금장치
If you lock something in a particular position or if it lock there, it is held or fitted firmly in that position.

whisper [hwíspər] v. 속삭이다, 소곤거리다; n. 속삭임, 소곤거리는 소리
When you whisper, you say something very quietly, using your breath rather than your throat, so that only one person can hear you.

＊ **anticipate** [æntísəpèit] v. 기대하다, 고대하다; 예상하다 (anticipation n. 기대, 고대)
Anticipation is a feeling of excitement about something pleasant or exciting that you know is going to happen.

gadget [gǽdʒit] n. (작은) 기계 장치; 도구
A gadget is a small machine or device which does something useful.

stretch [streʧ] v. (길이·폭 등을) 늘이다; 뻗어 있다; n. 뻗기, 펴기; (길게) 뻗은 구간
When something soft or elastic stretches or is stretched, it becomes longer or bigger as well as thinner, usually because it is pulled.

rooftop [rúːftap] n. (건물의) 옥상
A rooftop is the outside part of the roof of a building.

vault [vɔːlt] v. 뛰어넘다; n. 금고, 보관실; 뛰기, 도약
If you vault something or vault over it, you jump quickly onto or over it, especially by putting a hand on top of it to help you balance while you jump.

＊ **bother** [báðər] v. 신경 쓰다; 신경 쓰이게 하다, 괴롭히다; n. 성가심
If you do not bother to do something or if you do not bother with it, you do not do it, consider it, or use it because you think it is unnecessary or because you are too lazy.

save the day idiom 곤경을 면하게 하다; 궁지를 벗어나다
If you save the day, you do something that prevents a situation from becoming unpleasant, embarrassing, or unsuccessful.

★ **postpone** [poustpóun] v. 연기하다, 미루다
If you postpone an event, you delay it or arrange for it to take place at a later time than was originally planned.

복습 **defeat** [difíːt] n. 패배; v. 물리치다; 좌절시키다; 이해가 안 되다
Defeat is the experience of being beaten in a battle, game, or contest, or of failing to achieve what you wanted to.

go on idiom 말을 계속하다; (어떤 상황이) 계속되다; 자자, 어서
To go on means to continue speaking after a short pause.

rant [rænt] v. 고함치다, 큰소리로 불평하다; n. 고함
If you say that someone rants, you mean that they talk loudly or angrily, and exaggerate or say foolish things.

복습 **take care of** idiom ~을 돌보다; ~을 처리하다
If you take care of someone or something, you look after them and prevent them from being harmed or damaged.

복습 **grab** [græb] v. (와락·단단히) 붙잡다; 급히 ~하다; n. 와락 잡아채려고 함
If you grab something, you take it or pick it up suddenly and roughly.

snack [snæk] n. 간식; v. 간식을 먹다
A snack is something such as a chocolate bar that you eat between meals.

복습 **control** [kəntróul] n. 통제, 제어; (기계·차량의) 제어 장치; v. 지배하다; 조정하다
If you have control of something or someone, you are able to make them do what you want them to do.

복습 **fire** [faiər] v. 발사하다; (엔진이) 점화되다; 해고하다; n. 화재, 불; 발사, 총격
If you fire an arrow, you send it from a bow.

복습 **slingshot** [slíŋʃat] n. 새총
A slingshot is a Y-shaped stick or piece of metal with a piece of elastic attached to the top parts, used especially by children for shooting small stones.

antenna [ænténə] n. (pl. antennae) 안테나
An antenna is a device that sends and receives television or radio signals.

jut [dʒʌt] v. 돌출하다, 튀어나오다; 내밀다
If something juts out, it sticks out above or beyond a surface.

★ **mess** [mes] v. 엉망으로 만들다; n. (지저분하고) 엉망인 상태; (많은 문제로) 엉망인 상황
(mess with idiom ~을 (방해하다)
To mess with something means to bother or interfere with it.

destination [dèstənéiʃən] n. 목적지, 도착지; 행선지
The destination of someone or something is the place to which they are going or being sent.

cover [kʌ́vər] v. 덮다; 적당히 둘러대다; 씌우다, 가리다; n. 위장, 속임수; 몸을 숨길 곳; 덮개
If one thing covers another, it has been placed over it in order to protect it, hide it, or close it.

flatten [flǽtn] v. 납작하게 엎드리다; 납작하게 하다; 때려눕히다
If you flatten yourself against something, you press yourself flat against it, for example to avoid getting in the way or being seen.

slip [slip] v. 슬며시 가다; 미끄러지다; (옷 등을) 재빨리 벗다; n. (작은) 실수; 미끄러짐
If you slip somewhere, you go there quickly and quietly.

hallway [hɔ́ːlwèi] n. 복도; 통로; 현관
A hallway in a building is a long passage with doors into rooms on both sides of it.

snake [sneik] v. 구불구불 가다, 꿈틀꿈틀 움직이다; n. 뱀
Something that snakes in a particular direction goes in that direction in a line with a lot of bends.

messy [mési] a. 지저분한, 엉망인; (상황이) 엉망인, 골치 아픈
Something that is messy is dirty or untidy.

laboratory [lǽbərətɔ̀ːri] n. 실험실
A laboratory is a building or a room where scientific experiments, analyses, and research are carried out.

tool [tuːl] n. 도구, 연장; 수단
A tool is any instrument or simple piece of equipment that you hold in your hands and use to do a particular kind of work. For example, spades, hammers, and knives are all tools.

lens [lenz] n. 렌즈
A lens is a thin curved piece of glass or plastic used in things such as cameras, telescopes, and pairs of glasses.

mask [mæsk] n. 마스크; 가면; v. 가면을 쓰다; (감정·냄새·사실 등을) 가리다
A mask is a piece of cloth or other material, which you wear over your face so that people cannot see who you are, or so that you look like someone or something else.

strew [struː] v. 흩어지다, 흩뿌려져 있다; 흩뿌리다 (strewn a. 흩어진)
If a place is strewn with things, they are lying scattered there.

$^{복}_{습}$ **inspect** [inspékt] v. 면밀하게 살피다, 점검하다; 시찰하다
If you inspect something, you look at every part of it carefully in order to find out about it or check that it is all right.

$^{복}_{습}$ **scatter** [skǽtər] v. 흩뿌리다; 황급히 흩어지다; n. 흩뿌리기; 소수, 소량
If you scatter things over an area, you throw or drop them so that they spread all over the area.

$_{*}$ **sketch** [sketʃ] n. 스케치; v. 스케치하다; 개요를 제시하다
A sketch is a drawing that is done quickly without a lot of details.

$^{*}_{*}$ **scientific** [sàiəntífik] a. 과학의; 과학적인, 체계적인
Scientific is used to describe things that relate to science or to a particular science.

$_{*}$ **tatter** [tǽtər] v. 해지다; 갈가리 찢다; n. 넝마, 누더기 옷 (tattered a. 해진; 누더기를 두른)
If something such as clothing or a book is tattered, it is damaged or torn, especially because it has been used a lot over a long period of time.

$^{복}_{습}$ **notice** [nóutis] v. 알아채다, 인지하다; 주의하다; n. 신경 씀, 알아챔; 통지, 예고
If you notice something or someone, you become aware of them.

$^{복}_{습}$ **fabric** [fǽbrik] n. 직물, 천
Fabric is cloth or other material produced by weaving together cotton, nylon, wool, silk, or other threads. Fabrics are used for making things such as clothes, curtains, and sheets.

$^{복}_{습}$ **reveal** [rivíːl] v. (보이지 않던 것을) 드러내 보이다; (비밀 등을) 밝히다
If you reveal something that has been out of sight, you uncover it so that people can see it.

$^{복}_{습}$ **goggle** [gagl] n. (pl.) 보호 안경, 고글
Goggles are large glasses that fit closely to your face around your eyes to protect them from such things as water, wind, or dust.

$_{*}$ **strap** [stræp] v. 끈으로 묶다; 붕대를 감다; n. 끈, 줄, 띠
If you strap something somewhere, you fasten it there with a strap.

mannequin [mǽnəkin] n. (상점의) 마네킹
A mannequin is a life-sized model of a person which is used to display clothes, especially in shop windows.

$^{복}_{습}$ **slam** [slæm] v. 쾅 닫다; 세게 치다, 놓다; n. 쾅 하고 닫기; 탕 하는 소리
If you slam a door or window or if it slams, it shuts noisily and with great force.

wire [waiər] n. 철조망; 전선, (전화기 등의) 선; v. 전선을 연결하다; 배선 공사를 하다
A wire is a long thin piece of metal like a thread.

cage [keidʒ] n. 우리; 새장; v. 우리에 가두다
A cage is a structure of wire or metal bars in which birds or animals are kept.

zap [zæp] v. 제압하다, 해치우다; 재빠르게 하다
To zap someone or something means to kill, destroy, or hit them, for example with a gun or in a computer game.

flick [flik] v. (버튼·스위치를) 탁 누르다; 튀기다, 털다; n. 재빨리 움직임
If you flick a switch, or flick an electrical appliance on or off, you press the switch sharply so that it moves into a different position and works the equipment.

hypnotic [hipnátik] a. 최면을 일으키는, 최면성의
Something that is hypnotic holds your attention or makes you feel sleepy, often because it involves repeated sounds, pictures, or movements.

blink [bliŋk] v. (불빛이) 깜박거리다; 눈을 깜박이다; n. 눈을 깜박거림
When a light blinks, it flashes on and off.

swirl [swəːrl] v. 빙빙 돌다, 소용돌이치다; n. 소용돌이
If you swirl something liquid or flowing, or if it swirls, it moves round and round quickly.

mesmerize [mézməràiz] v. 마음을 사로잡다, 완전 넋을 빼놓다
If you are mesmerized by something, you are so interested in it or so attracted to it that you cannot think about anything else.

shield [ʃiːld] v. 보호하다, 가리다; (기계 등에) 보호 장치를 두르다; n. 보호 장치; 방패
If you shield your eyes, you put your hand above your eyes to protect them from direct sunlight.

battle [bætl] v. 싸우다, 투쟁하다; n. 싸움; 전투
To battle with an opposing group means to take part in a fight or contest against them.

crash [kræʃ] v. 부딪치다; 충돌하다; 굉음을 내다; n. (자동차·항공기) 사고; 요란한 소리
If something crashes somewhere, it moves and hits something else violently, making a loud noise.

activate [æktəvèit] v. 작동시키다; 활성화시키다
If a device or process is activated, something causes it to start working.

yank [jæŋk] v. 홱 잡아당기다; n. 홱 잡아당기기

If you yank someone or something somewhere, you pull them there suddenly and with a lot of force.

alarm [əlá:rm] n. 경보 장치; 불안, 공포; v. 불안하게 하다; 경보장치를 달다

(fire alarm n. 화재 경보기)

A fire alarm is a device that makes a noise, for example with a bell, to warn people when there is a fire.

blare [blɛər] v. (소리를) 요란하게 울리다; n. 요란한 소리

If something such as a siren or radio blares or if you blare it, it makes a loud, unpleasant noise.

ceiling [síːliŋ] n. 천장

A ceiling is the horizontal surface that forms the top part or roof inside a room.

sprinkler [spríŋklər] n. 물을 뿌리는 장치, 살수 장치

A sprinkler is a device used to spray water. Sprinklers are used to water plants or grass, or to put out fires in buildings.

chaos [kéias] n. 혼돈; 혼란

Chaos is a state of complete disorder and confusion.

chase [ʧeis] n. 추적, 추격; 추구함; v. 뒤쫓다, 추적하다; 추구하다

A chase is the action of following someone or something quickly because you want to catch them.

be about to idiom 막 ~하려는 참이다

If you are about to do something, you are going to do it immediately.

slide [slaid] v. (slid-slid/slidden) 미끄러지듯이 움직이다; 슬며시 넣다; n. 떨어짐; 미끄러짐

When something slides somewhere or when you slide it there, it moves there smoothly over or against something.

shaft [ʃæft] n. (보통 건물·지하의) 수직 통로, 수갱; 손잡이

A shaft is a long vertical passage, for example for an elevator.

roof [ruːf] n. 지붕; (터널·동굴 등의) 천장; v. 지붕을 씌우다

The roof of a building is the covering on top of it that protects the people and things inside from the weather.

leap [liːp] v. (서둘러) ~하다; 뛰다, 뛰어오르다; n. 높이뛰기, 도약; 급증

If you leap somewhere, you move there suddenly and quickly.

parachute [pǽrəʃùːt] n. 낙하산; v. 낙하산을 타고 뛰어내리다
A parachute is a device which enables a person to jump from an aircraft and float safely to the ground.

midair [midέər] n. 공중, 상공
If something happens in midair, it happens in the air, rather than on the ground.

float [flout] v. (물 위나 공중에서) 떠가다; (물에) 뜨다; n. 부표
Something that floats in or through the air hangs in it or moves slowly and gently through it.

go off idiom (경보기 등이) 울리다; 터지다
If something like an alarm goes off, it starts making a noise as a signal or warning.

explode [iksplóud] v. 폭발하다; 갑자기 ~하다; (갑자기 강한 감정을) 터뜨리다
If an object such as a bomb explodes or if someone or something explodes it, it bursts loudly and with great force, often causing damage or injury.

rip [rip] v. (거칠게) 떼어 내다, 뜯어 내다; (갑자기) 찢다; 빠른 속도로 돌진하다; n. (길게) 찢어진 곳
If you rip something away, you remove it quickly and forcefully.

evidence [évədəns] n. 증거, 흔적; v. 증거가 되다; 증언하다
Evidence is anything that you see, experience, read, or are told that causes you to believe that something is true or has really happened.

irritate [írətèit] v. 짜증나게 하다, 거슬리다; 자극하다 (irritated a. 짜증이 난)
If something irritates you, it keeps annoying you.

level [lévəl] v. 완전히 무너뜨리다; 평평하게 하다; n. 정도, 수준; (건물·땅의) 층; a. 평평한
If someone or something such as a violent storm levels a building or area of land, they destroy it completely or make it completely flat.

cop [kap] n. 경찰관
A cop is a policeman or policewoman.

handcuff [hǽndkʌ̀f] n. 수갑; v. 수갑을 채우다
Handcuffs are two metal rings which are joined together and can be locked round someone's wrists, usually by the police during an arrest.

puzzle [pʌzl] v. 어리둥절하게 하다; n. 퍼즐; 수수께끼 (puzzled a. 어리둥절해하는, 얼떨떨한)
Someone who is puzzled is confused because they do not understand something.

punk [pʌŋk] n. 불량한 남자, 불량 청소년
A punk is an aggressive and violent young criminal.

‡ **blame** [bleim] v. ~을 탓하다, ~의 책임으로 보다; n. 책임; 탓
If you blame a person or thing for something bad, you believe or say that they are responsible for it or that they caused it.

emblem [émbləm] n. 상징, 표상; 엠블럼
An emblem is a design representing a country or organization.

work like a charm idiom 기적같이 성공하다
If you say that something worked like a charm, you mean that it was very effective or successful.

* **genius** [dʒíːnjəs] n. 천재; 천재성; 특별한 재능
A genius is a highly talented, creative, or intelligent person.

shucks [ʃʌks] int. 이런, 어머
You can say shucks for an expression of modesty, embarrassment, disappointment, or anger.

복습 **chuckle** [ʧʌkl] v. 킬킬 웃다; 빙그레 웃다; n. 킬킬거림; 속으로 웃기
When you chuckle, you laugh quietly.

Check Your Reading Speed

1분에 몇 단어를 읽는지 리딩 속도를 측정해보세요.

$$\frac{1{,}008 \text{ words}}{\text{reading time ( ) sec}} \times 60 = (\qquad) \text{ WPM}$$

Build Your Vocabulary

daze [deiz] v. 멍하게 하다; 눈부시게 하다; n. 멍한 상태; 눈이 부심 (dazed a. 멍한)
If someone is dazed, they are confused and unable to think clearly, often because of shock or a blow to the head.

burst [bəːrst] v. (burst-burst) 불쑥 움직이다; 갑자기 ~하다; n. (갑자기) ~을 함; 파열, 폭발
To burst into or out of a place means to enter or leave it suddenly with a lot of energy or force.

fraction [frǽkʃən] n. 분수; 부분, 일부
A fraction is a number that can be expressed as a proportion of two whole numbers. For example, 1/2 and 1/3 are both fractions.

percentage [pərséntidʒ] n. 백분율
A percentage is a fraction of an amount expressed as a particular number of hundredths of that amount.

rub [rʌb] v. (손·손수건 등을 대고) 문지르다; (두 손 등을) 맞비비다; n. 문지르기, 비비기
If you rub a part of your body, you move your hand or fingers backward and forward over it while pressing firmly.

catch up idiom 따라잡다, 따라가다; (소식 등을) 듣다
To catch up means to improve in order to reach the same standard or rate as someone or something.

decimal [désəməl] n. 소수; a. 십진법의
A decimal is a fraction that is written in the form of a dot followed by one or more numbers which represent tenths, hundredths, and so on: for example .5, .51, .517.

flash [flæʃ] v. 획 나타나다; 획 내보이다; (잠깐) 번쩍이다; n. 순간; (잠깐) 반짝임
If a picture or message flashes up on a screen, or if you flash it onto a screen, it is displayed there briefly or suddenly, and often repeatedly.

announce [ənáuns] v. 선언하다; 발표하다, 알리다
If you announce something, you tell people about it publicly or officially.

gear [giər] n. (특정 활동에 필요한) 장비; 기어
The gear involved in a particular activity is the equipment or special clothing that you use.

billionaire [biljənέər] n. 억만장자, 갑부
A billionaire is an extremely rich person who has money or property worth at least a thousand million pounds or dollars.

smug [smʌg] a. 의기양양한, 우쭐해 하는
If you say that someone is smug, you are criticizing the fact they seem very pleased with how good, clever, or lucky they are.

gleam [gli:m] v. 희미하게 빛나다; 환하다; n. 어슴푸레한 빛 (gleaming a. 빛나는)
If an object or a surface gleams, it reflects light because it is shiny and clean.

stare [stɛər] v. 빤히 쳐다보다, 응시하다; n. 빤히 쳐다보기, 응시
If you stare at someone or something, you look at them for a long time.

tap [tæp] v. (가볍게) 톡톡 두드리다; 박자를 맞추다; n. 수도꼭지; (가볍게) 두드리기
If you tap something, you hit it with a quick light blow or a series of quick light blows.

hood [hud] n. (자동차 등의) 덮개; (외투 등에 달린) 모자
The hood of a car is the metal cover over the engine at the front.

amaze [əméiz] v. (대단히) 놀라게 하다; 경악하게 하다 (amazing a. 놀라운)
You say that something is amazing when it is very surprising and makes you feel pleasure, approval, or wonder.

vehicle [víːikl] n. 차량, 운송 수단; 수단, 매개체
A vehicle is a machine such as a car, bus, or truck which has an engine and is used to carry people from place to place.

turn up idiom 나타나다, 찾아오다
If something turns up, it is found, especially by accident, after being lost or not known about.

private [práivət] a. 사적인; 사유의; 은밀한; 사생활의
Private places or gatherings may be attended only by a particular group of people, rather than by the general public.

auction [ɔ́:kʃən] n. 경매; v. 경매로 팔다
An auction is a public sale where goods are sold to the person who offers the highest price.

yell [jel] v. 고함치다, 소리 지르다; n. 고함, 외침
If you yell, you shout loudly, usually because you are excited, angry, or in pain.

release [rilí:s] v. (감정을) 발산하다; 놓아 주다; 풀어 주다; n. 풀어 줌; 발표, 공개
To release feelings or abilities means to allow them to be expressed.

fury [fjúəri] n. (격렬한) 분노, 격분; 흥분 상태
Fury is violent or very strong anger.

bolt [boult] v. 달아나다; 빗장을 지르다; n. 번쩍하는 번개; 볼트
If a person or animal bolts, they suddenly start to run very fast, often because something has frightened them.

splash [splæʃ] n. 첨벙 하는 소리; (어디에 떨어지는) 방울; v. 첨벙거리다; (물 등을) 끼얹다
A splash is the sound made when something hits water or falls into it.

grumble [grʌmbl] v. 투덜거리다, 불평하다; n. 투덜댐; 불평
If someone grumbles, they complain about something in a bad-tempered way.

march [ma:rʧ] v. (단호한 태도로 급히) 걸어가다; 행진하다; n. 행군, 행진; 3월
If you say that someone marches somewhere, you mean that they walk there quickly and in a determined way, for example because they are angry.

den [den] n. 서재, 작업실; 굴
Your den is a quiet room in your house where you can go to study, work, or carry on a hobby without being disturbed.

soak [souk] v. 흠뻑 적시다; (지식 등을) 흡수하다; n. (액체 속에) 담그기
(soaking wet a. 완전히 다 젖은, 흠뻑 젖은)
If something is soaking or soaking wet, it is very wet.

rummage [rʌ́midʒ] v. 뒤지다; n. 뒤지기
If you rummage through something, you search for something you want by moving things around in a careless or hurried way.

remote [rimóut] n. (= remote control) 리모컨; 원격 조종; a. 먼; 외진, 외딴; 원격의
The remote control for a television or video recorder is the device that you use to control the machine from a distance, by pressing the buttons on it.

on one's heels idiom ~을 바짝 뒤따라
If you say that someone is hot on your heels, you are emphasizing that they are chasing you and are not very far behind you.

load [loud] v. 가득 안겨 주다; (짐·사람 등을) 싣다; n. (많은 양의) 짐; (수·양이) 많음
If you load a vehicle or a container, you put a large quantity of things into it.

gadget [gǽdʒit] n. (작은) 기계 장치; 도구
A gadget is a small machine or device which does something useful.

demonstrate [démənstrèit] v. (사용법을) 보여주다; (행동으로) 보여주다
If you demonstrate something, you show people how it works or how to do it.

figure out idiom ~을 이해하다, 알아내다; 계산하다, 산출하다
If you figure out someone or something, you come to understand them by thinking carefully.

press [pres] v. 누르다; (무엇에) 바짝 대다; 꾹 밀어 넣다; n. 언론
If you press a button or switch, you push it with your finger in order to make a machine or device work.

roar [rɔːr] v. 웅웅거리다; 굉음을 내며 질주하다; 고함치다; n. 함성; 울부짖는 듯한 소리
If something roars, it makes a very loud noise.

stun [stʌn] v. 깜짝 놀라게 하다; 어리벙벙하게 하다; 기절시키다
If you are stunned by something, you are extremely shocked or surprised by it and are therefore unable to speak or do anything.

spin [spin] v. (spun-spun) (빙빙) 돌다; 돌아서다; n. 회전
If something spins or if you spin it, it turns quickly around a central point.

snatch [snætʃ] v. 와락 붙잡다, 잡아채다; 간신히 얻다; n. 잡아 뺏음, 강탈; 조각
If you snatch something or snatch at something, you take it or pull it away quickly.

dive [daiv] v. (dove/dived-dived) 급히 움직이다; (물 속으로) 뛰어들다; 급강하하다;
n. 급강하; (물 속으로) 뛰어들기
If you dive in a particular direction or into a particular place, you jump or move there quickly.

dual [djúːəl] a. 이중의
Dual means having two parts, functions, or aspects.

rocket [rάkit] n. 로켓 추진 미사일; 로켓; v. 로켓처럼 가다, 돌진하다; 급증하다
A rocket is a missile containing explosive that is powered by gas.

launch [lɔːntʃ] v. 발사하다; 시작하다; n. 시작; 발사; 개시, 진수 (launcher n. 발사 장치)
To launch a rocket, missile, or satellite means to send it into the air or into space.

emerge [imɔ́ːrdʒ] v. 나오다, 모습을 드러내다; (어려움 등을) 헤쳐 나오다
To emerge means to come out from an enclosed or dark space such as a room or a vehicle, or from a position where you could not be seen.

retrieve [ritríːv] v. 되찾아오다, 회수하다; 수습하다
If you retrieve something, you get it back from the place where you left it.

retract [ritrǽkt] v. (속으로) 들어가다; 철회하다, 취소하다
When a part of a machine or a part of a person's body retracts or is retracted, it moves inward or becomes shorter.

gesture [dʒéstʃər] v. (손·머리 등으로) 가리키다; 몸짓을 하다; n. 몸짓; (감정·의도의) 표시
If you gesture, you use movements of your hands or head in order to tell someone something or draw their attention to something.

chant [tʃænt] v. 되풀이하여 말하다; 구호를 외치다, 연호하다; n. (연이어 외치는) 구호
If you chant something or if you chant, you repeat the same words over and over again.

distract [distrǽkt] v. (주의를) 딴 데로 돌리다, 집중이 안 되게 하다
If something distracts you or your attention from something, it takes your attention away from it.

grunt [grʌnt] v. 끙 앓는 소리를 내다; (돼지가) 꿀꿀거리다; n. (사람이) 끙 하는 소리
If you grunt, you make a low sound, especially because you are annoyed or not interested in something.

power down idiom 전원을 끊다, 정지하다
If a machine powers down, or someone or something powers it down, it is switched off and comes to stop.

blow [blou] v. 폭파하다; (휑하니) 떠나다; (바람·입김에) 날리다; n. 강타
To blow something out, off, or away means to remove or destroy it violently with an explosion.

sink [siŋk] v. (sank-sunk) 주저앉다; 가라앉다, 빠지다; 박다; n. 개수대
If you sink, you lower yourself or drop down gently.

achoo [aːtʃúː] int. 에취 (재채기 하는 소리)
Achoo is used for representing the sound that you make when you sneeze.

* **sneeze** [sni:z] v. 재채기하다; n. 재채기
When you sneeze, you suddenly take in your breath and then blow it down your nose noisily without being able to stop yourself, for example because you have a cold.

jet [dʒet] n. 분출; 제트기; v. 급속히 움직이다; 분출하다
A jet of liquid or gas is a strong, fast, thin stream of it.

intangible [intǽndʒəbl] a. 실체가 없는, 무형의; 만질 수 없는; 막연한
Something that is intangible is abstract or is hard to define or measure.

smolder [smóuldər] v. (서서히) 타다; (속으로) 들끓다
If something smolders, it burns slowly, producing smoke but not flames.

upstairs [ʌpstéərz] ad. 위층으로; 위층에; n. 위층
If you go upstairs in a building, you go up a staircase toward a higher floor.

shriek [ʃri:k] v. (날카롭게) 비명을 지르다; 악을 쓰며 말하다; n. (날카로운) 비명
When someone shrieks, they make a short, very loud cry, for example because they are suddenly surprised, are in pain, or are laughing.

show off idiom ~을 자랑하다; 돋보이게 하다
To show off someone or something means to try to make people pay attention to them because you are proud of them.

fang [fæŋ] n. (뱀·개 등의) 송곳니
Fangs are the two long, sharp, upper teeth that some animals have.

* **transform** [trænsfɔ́:rm] v. 변형시키다; 완전히 바꿔 놓다
To transform something into something else means to change or convert it into that thing.

stammer [stǽmər] v. 말을 더듬다; n. 말 더듬기
If you stammer, you speak with difficulty, hesitating and repeating words or sounds.

process [práses] v. (공식적으로) 처리하다; 가공하다; n. 과정, 절차; 공정
To process means to think about a difficult or sad situation so that you can gradually accept it.

uncool [ʌnkú:l] a. 멋지지 않은
If you say something is uncool, you mean that it is not good.

formulate [fɔ́ːrmjulèit] v. (세심히) 만들어 내다; (의견을 공들여) 표현하다
If you formulate something such as a plan or proposal, you invent it, thinking about the details carefully.

intense [inténs] a. 극심한, 강렬한; 치열한; 진지한 (intensity n. 강렬함, 강함)
If you describe a person as intense, you mean that they appear to concentrate very hard on everything that they do, and they feel and show their emotions in a very extreme way.

force [fɔːrs] v. 억지로 ~하다; ~를 강요하다; n. 작용력; 힘; 영향력
If a situation or event forces you to do something, it makes it necessary for you to do something that you would not otherwise have done.

explode [iksplóud] v. (갑자기 강한 감정을) 터뜨리다; 폭발하다; 갑자기 ~하다
If someone explodes, they express strong feelings suddenly and violently.

rant [rænt] n. 고함; v. 고함치다, 큰소리로 불평하다
A rant is a long loud and angry complaint about something.

vent [vent] v. (감정·분통을) 터뜨리다; n. 통풍구, 환기구
If you vent your feelings, you express them forcefully.

take in idiom 이해하다; ~을 눈여겨보다
If you take in something, you understand and remember something that you hear or read.

turn into idiom ~이 되다, ~으로 변하다
To turn or be turned into something means to change, or to make a thing change, into something different.

flame [fleim] v. 활활 타오르다; 시뻘게지다; n. 불길, 불꽃; 격정 (flaming a. 불타는)
Flaming is used to describe something that is burning and producing a lot of flames.

roll with the punches idiom 힘든 상황에 적응하다
If you roll with the punches, you are able to deal with a series of difficult situations.

thunder [θʌ́ndər] n. 천둥, 우레; v. (천둥소리같이) 우르릉거리다; 천둥이 치다
Thunder is the loud noise that you hear from the sky after a flash of lightning, especially during a storm.

crap [kræp] v. 배변하다; n. 허튼소리, 헛소리; 배변; a. 형편없는, 쓰레기 같은
To crap means to get rid of faeces from your body.

lightning [láitniŋ] n. 번개, 번갯불; a. 아주 빨리; 급작스럽게
Lightning is the very bright flashes of light in the sky that happen during thunderstorms.

mediocre [miːdióukər] a. 보통 밖에 안 되는, 썩 좋지는 않은
If you describe something as mediocre, you mean that it is of average quality but you think it should be better.

no way idiom 절대로 아니다; (강한 거절의 의미로) 절대로 안 돼, 싫어
If you say there's no way that something will happen, you are emphasizing that you think it will definitely not happen.

hiccup [híkʌp] v. 딸꾹질을 하다; n. (약간의) 문제; 딸꾹질
When you hiccup, you make repeated sharp sounds in your throat.

roof [ruːf] n. 지붕; (터널·동굴 등의) 천장; v. 지붕을 씌우다
The roof of a building is the covering on top of it that protects the people and things inside from the weather.

primal [práiməl] a. 원시의, 태고의
Primal is used to describe something that relates to the origins of things or that is very basic.

backyard [bækjáːrd] n. 뒷마당; 뒤뜰
A backyard is an area of land at the back of a house.

scramble [skræmbl] v. 재빨리 움직이다; 허둥지둥 해내다; n. (힘들게) 기어가기; 서로 밀치기
If you scramble to a different place or position, you move there in a hurried, awkward way.

pool [puːl] n. 수영장; 웅덩이; v. (자금·정보 등을) 모으다; 고이다
A pool is the same as a swimming pool which is a large hole in the ground that has been made and filled with water so that people can swim in it.

giggle [gigl] v. 피식 웃다, 킥킥거리다; n. 피식 웃음, 킥킥거림
If someone giggles, they laugh in a childlike way, because they are amused, nervous, or embarrassed.

coo [kuː] v. 정답게 소곤거리다; 구구 울다; n. 구구 (하고 새가 우는 소리)
When someone coos, they speak in a very soft, quiet voice which is intended to sound attractive.

Chapters 14 & 15

1. How did Bob get Jack-Jack to reappear?

A. He told Jack-Jack that they could play a game.

B. He sang Jack-Jack a lullaby.

C. He gave Jack-Jack a shiny toy.

D. He offered Jack-Jack a snack.

2. How did Edna first feel about babysitting Jack-Jack?

A. She was unwilling and annoyed.

B. She was eager and grateful.

C. She was hesitant but understanding.

D. She was interested but terrified.

3. What did Bob say to Violet about Tony?

A. He had no idea that Tony worked at a restaurant.

B. Boys like Tony were not worth the trouble.

C. What happened to Tony was unfair to Violet.

D. Tony should have never talked to Dicker about Violet.

4. What did Winston announce at the party?

A. Superheroes had just met with leaders at a summit.

B. Leaders had just agreed to keep Superheroes underground.

C. Superheroes and leaders would meet on a ship for a signing ceremony.

D. Leaders would meet on a ship to decide whether Superheroes were necessary.

5. What did Elastigirl wonder about the pizza guy who was arrested?

A. She wondered if he had had his own suit cam.

B. She wondered if he had been hypnotized by screens.

C. She wondered if he might escape from jail.

D. She wondered if he could still control people.

Check Your Reading Speed
1분에 몇 단어를 읽는지 리딩 속도를 측정해보세요.

$$\frac{1{,}304 \text{ words}}{\text{reading time ( ) sec}} \times 60 = (\qquad) \text{ WPM}$$

Build Your Vocabulary

ː assume [əsúːm] v. (사실일 것으로) 추정하다; (특질·양상을) 띠다
If you assume that something is true, you imagine that it is true, sometimes wrongly.

kid [kid] v. 놀리다, 장난치다; 속이다
You can say 'you've got to be kidding' or 'you must be kidding' to someone if they have said something that you think is ridiculous or completely untrue.

keep track of idiom ~에 대해 계속 알고 있다
If you keep track of someone or something, you continue to be informed or know about them.

⁎ insane [inséin] a. 제정신이 아닌; 정신 이상의, 미친
If you describe a decision or action as insane, you think it is very foolish or excessive.

복습 besides [bisáidz] ad. 게다가, 뿐만 아니라; prep. ~외에
Besides is used to emphasize an additional point that you are making, especially one that you consider to be important.

복습 handle [hǽndl] v. (사람·작업 등을) 처리하다; 들다, 옮기다; n. 손잡이
If you say that someone can handle a problem or situation, you mean that they have the ability to deal with it successfully.

복습 sarcastic [saːrkǽstik] a. 빈정대는, 비꼬는; 풍자적인 (sarcastically ad. 비꼬는 투로)
Someone who is sarcastic says or does the opposite of what they really mean in order to mock or insult someone.

복습 vanish [vǽniʃ] v. 사라지다, 없어지다; 모습을 감추다
If someone or something vanishes, they disappear suddenly or in a way that cannot be explained.

rush [rʌʃ] v. 급히 움직이다; 서두르다; n. (감정이 갑자기) 치밀어 오름; 혼잡; 기쁨, 흥분
If you rush somewhere, you go there quickly.

jar [dʒɑːr] n. 병; v. 불쾌감을 주다, (신경을) 거슬리다; 부딪치다
A jar is a glass container with a lid that is used for storing food.

num [nʌm] int. 냠냠
Num is used to express pleasure at eating, or at the prospect of eating.

freak [friːk] v. 기겁을 하다; n. 괴짜, 괴물 (freaky a. 기이한)
If you freak, you become so angry, surprised, excited, or frightened that you cannot control yourself.

tempt [tempt] v. (어떤 것을 제의하거나 하여) 유도하다; (좋지 않은 일을 하도록) 유혹하다
If you tempt someone, you offer them something they want in order to encourage them to do what you want them to do.

out of nowhere idiom 어디에선지 모르게, 난데없이
If you say that something or someone appears out of nowhere, you mean that they appear suddenly and unexpectedly.

gobble [gabl] v. 게걸스럽게 먹다
If you gobble food, you eat it quickly and greedily.

dimension [diménʃən] n. 차원; 관점; 크기; (상황의) 규모
A dimension is a mode of linear extension of which there are three in space and two on a flat surface, which corresponds to one of a set of coordinates specifying the position of a point.

flat [flæt] a. 생기가 없는; 평평한, 편평한; 납작한; ad. 평평하게, 반듯이
You use flat to describe someone's voice when they are saying something without expressing any emotion.

obvious [ábviəs] a. 분명한, 확실한; 명백한 (obviously ad. 분명히)
You use obviously when you are stating something that you expect the person who is listening to know already.

stable [steibl] a. 안정된, 안정적인; 차분한; n. 마구간 (unstable a. 불안정한)
If people are unstable, their emotions and behavior keep changing because their minds are disturbed or upset.

request [rikwést] v. 요청하다, 요구하다; n. 요구 사항; 요청, 신청
If you request something, you ask for it politely or formally.

复습 demonstrate [démənstrèit] v. (행동으로) 보여주다; (사용법을) 보여주다
If you demonstrate a particular skill, quality, or feeling, you show by your actions that you have it.

최최 demand [dimǽnd] v. 요구하다; 강력히 묻다, 따지다; n. 요구; 수요
If you demand something such as information or action, you ask for it in a very forceful way.

복습 pop [pap] n. 펑 (하는 소리); v. 불쑥 나타나다; 펑 하는 소리가 나다
Pop is used to represent a short sharp sound, for example the sound made by bursting a balloon or by pulling a cork out of a bottle.

복습 transform [trænsfɔ́:rm] v. 변형시키다; 완전히 바꿔 놓다
To transform something into something else means to change or convert it into that thing.

gnaw [nɔ:] v. 갉아먹다, 물어뜯다
If people or animals gnaw something or gnaw at it, they bite it repeatedly.

복습 panic [pǽnik] n. 극심한 공포, 공황; 허둥지둥함; v. 어쩔 줄 모르다, 공황 상태에 빠지다
Panic is a very strong feeling of anxiety or fear, which makes you act without thinking carefully.

복습 bite [bait] v. (이빨로) 물다; 베어 물다; n. 한 입; 물기; 소량
If you bite something, you use your teeth to cut into it, for example in order to eat it or break it.

복습 slump [slʌmp] v. 털썩 앉다; (가치·수량 등이) 급감하다; n. 부진, 슬럼프; 급감; 불황
If you slump somewhere, you fall or sit down there heavily, for example because you are very tired or you feel ill.

복습 couch [kauʧ] n. 긴 의자, 소파
A couch is a long, comfortable seat for two or three people.

복습 snack [snæk] v. 간식을 먹다; n. 간식
If you snack, you eat snacks between meals.

복습 frown [fraun] v. 얼굴을 찡그리다; 눈살을 찌푸리다; n. 찡그림, 찌푸림
When someone frowns, their eyebrows become drawn together, because they are annoyed, worried, or puzzled, or because they are concentrating.

복습 babble [bæbl] v. 지껄이다, 횡설수설하다; n. 횡설수설; 와글와글, 왁자지껄
If someone babbles, they talk in a confused or excited way.

conjure [kándʒər] v. 마술을 하다
If you conjure something out of nothing, you make it appear as if by magic.

smooth [smuːð] a. 매끈한; 순조로운; (소리가) 감미로운; v. 매끈하게 하다
A smooth surface has no roughness, lumps, or holes.

gum [gʌm] v. 잇몸으로 깨물다; n. 잇몸; 껌
If someone gums something, they chew it with toothless areas of firm, pink flesh inside your mouth.

crack [kræk] v. (목소리가) 갈라지다; 깨지다, 부서지다; n. 날카로운 소리; 금; (좁은) 틈
If your voice cracks when you are speaking or singing, it changes in pitch because you are feeling a strong emotion.

major [méidʒər] a. 주요한, 중대한; 심각한; n. (대학생의) 전공
You use major when you want to describe something that is more important, serious, or significant than other things in a group or situation.

realign [riəláin] v. 변경하다, 조정하다; 재편성하다 (realignment n. 재편성)
If a company, economy, or system goes through a realignment, it is organized or arranged in a new way.

solid [sálid] a. 확실한; 단단한; 고체의; n. 고체, 고형물
You use solid to describe something such as advice or a piece of work which is useful and reliable.

outside-the-box idiom 새로운 관점의, 고정관념에서 벗어난
If you think outside-the-box, you think in a fresh, inventive, unconventional way.

pull up idiom (차량·운전자가) 멈추다, 서다
If a vehicle or driver pulls up, they stop.

ornate [ɔːrnéit] a. 화려하게 장식된
An ornate building, piece of furniture, or object is decorated with complicated patterns or shapes.

security [sikjúərəti] n. 보안, 경비; 경비 담당 부서; 안도감, 안심
Security refers to all the measures that are taken to protect a place, or to ensure that only people with permission enter it or leave it.

suit [suːt] n. (특정한 활동 때 입는) 옷; 정장; 소송; v. ~에게 편리하다; 어울리다
A particular type of suit is a piece of clothing that you wear for a particular activity.

worn out [wɔːrn áut] a. 매우 지친
Someone who is worn out is extremely tired after hard work or a difficult or unpleasant experience.

narrow [nǽrou] v. (눈을) 찌푸리다; 좁히다; a. 좁은
If your eyes narrow or if you narrow your eyes, you almost close them, for example because you are angry or because you are trying to concentrate on something.

disapprove [dìsəprúːv] v. 탐탁찮아 하다, 못마땅해 하다 (disapprovingly ad. 마땅치 않게)
A disapproving action or expression shows that you do not approve of something or someone.

lean [liːn] v. 기울이다, (몸을) 숙이다; ~에 기대다; a. 군살이 없는, 호리호리한
When you lean in a particular direction, you bend your body in that direction.

screech [skriːʃ] v. 끼익 하는 소리를 내다; n. 끼익, 꽥 (하는 날카로운 소리)
When you screech something, you shout it in a loud, unpleasant, high-pitched voice.

unusual [ʌnjúːʒuəl] a. 특이한, 흔치 않은, 드문
If something is unusual, it does not happen very often or you do not see it or hear it very often.

entrance [éntrəns] n. 입구, 문; 입장, 등장 (entrance hall n. 입구 안에 있는 홀)
The entrance hall of a large house, hotel, or other large building, is the area just inside the main door.

ghastly [gǽstli] a. 몸이 안 좋은; 무시무시한, 소름끼치는; ad. 무섭게
If someone looks ghastly, they look very ill or very shocked, especially with a very pale face.

gigantic [dʒaigǽntik] a. 거대한
If you describe something as gigantic, you are emphasizing that it is extremely large in size, amount, or degree.

ramble [rǽmbl] v. 횡설수설하다; 걷다, 거닐다; n. 걷기; 횡설수설(하는 말·글)
If you say that a person rambles in their speech or writing, you mean they do not make much sense because they keep going off the subject in a confused way.

load [loud] n. (많은 양의) 짐; (수·양이) 많음; v. 가득 안겨 주다; (짐·사람 등을) 싣다
If you refer to a load of people or things or loads of them, you are emphasizing that there are a lot of them.

proper [prápər] a. 적절한, 제대로 된; 올바른, 정당한 (properly ad. 제대로, 적절히)
If something is done properly, it is done in a correct and satisfactory way.

parenting [péərəntiŋ] n. 육아
Parenting is the activity of bringing up and looking after your child.

heroic [hiróuik] a. 영웅적인, 용감무쌍한; 영웅의; n. (pl.) 영웅적 행동
If you describe a person or their actions as heroic, you admire them because they show extreme bravery.

fortunate [fɔ́:rʧənət] a. 운 좋은, 다행한
If you say that someone or something is fortunate, you mean that they are lucky.

afflict [əflíkt] v. 괴롭히다, 피해를 입히다
If you are afflicted by pain, illness, or disaster, it affects you badly and makes you suffer.

design [dizáin] v. 설계하다; 고안하다; n. 설계; 계획, 의도
When someone designs a garment, building, machine, or other object, they plan it and make a detailed drawing of it from which it can be built or made.

collapse [kəlǽps] v. 주저앉다; 붕괴되다, 무너지다; 쓰러지다; n. 실패; (건물의) 붕괴
If you collapse onto something, you sit or lie down suddenly because you are very tired.

toddle [tadl] v. (어린 아이가) 아장아장 걷다
When a child toddles, it walks unsteadily with short quick steps.

hardly [há:rdli] ad. 거의 ~아니다; ~하자마자; 거의 ~할 수가 없다
You use hardly to modify a statement when you want to emphasize that it is only a small amount or detail which makes it true, and that therefore it is best to consider the opposite statement as being true.

classify [klǽsəfài] v. 분류하다, 구분하다; 기밀 취급하다
To classify things means to divide them into groups or types so that things with similar characteristics are in the same group.

emergency [imə́:rdʒənsi] n. 비상
An emergency is an unexpected and difficult or dangerous situation, especially an accident, which happens suddenly and which requires quick action to deal with it.

cut off idiom (말을) 중단시키다; 단절시키다
To cut off means to prevent someone from continuing what they are saying.

irritate [írətèit] v. 짜증나게 하다, 거슬리다; 자극하다 (irritated a. 짜증이 난)
If something irritates you, it keeps annoying you.

edge [edʒ] n. 끝, 가장자리; 우위; v. 조금씩 움직이다; 테두리를 두르다
The edge of something is the place or line where it stops, or the part of it that is furthest from the middle.

robe [roub] n. 길고 헐거운 겉옷; 예복, 가운
A robe is a loose piece of clothing which covers all of your body and reaches the ground.

stuff [stʌf] v. 쑤셔 넣다; 채워 넣다; n. 일, 것, 물건
If you stuff something somewhere, you push it there quickly and roughly.

snatch [snætʃ] v. 와락 붙잡다, 잡아채다; 간신히 얻다; n. 잡아 뺏음, 강탈; 조각
If you snatch something or snatch at something, you take it or pull it away quickly.

facility [fəsílə ti] n. 재능; 시설; 기관; 기능
A facility is a natural ability to do something well.

involve [inválv] v. 관련시키다, 연루시키다; 수반하다, 포함하다
If you say that someone involves themselves in something, you mean that they take part in it, often in a way that is unnecessary or unwanted.

prosaic [prouzéiik] a. 따분한, 세속적인; 평범한, 상상력이 없는
Something that is prosaic is dull and uninteresting.

day-to-day [dei-tə-déi] a. (일이) 매일 행해지는, 그날그날의
Day-to-day things or activities exist or happen every day as part of ordinary life.

gaze [geiz] v. (가만히) 응시하다, 바라보다; n. 응시, (눈여겨보는) 시선
If you gaze at someone or something, you look steadily at them for a long time.

intense [inténs] a. 극심한, 강렬한; 치열한; 진지한 (intensely ad. 강렬하게)
If you describe the way someone looks at you as intense, you mean that they look at you very directly and seem to know what you are thinking or feeling.

inflate [infléit] v. (공기나 가스로) 부풀리다; 과장하다; (가격을) 올리다
If you inflate something such as a balloon or tire, or if it inflates, it becomes bigger as it is filled with air or a gas.

identical [aidéntikəl] a. 동일한, 꼭 같은
Things that are identical are exactly the same.

drift [drift] v. (물·공기에) 떠가다; (자신도 모르게) ~하게 되다; (서서히) 이동하다; n. 표류; 흐름
If sounds drift somewhere, they can be heard but they are not very loud.

absorb [æbsɔ́ːrb] v. (관심을) 빼앗다; (액체·가스 등을) 흡수하다 (absorbed a. ~에 몰두한)
If you are absorbed in something or someone, you are very interested in them and they take up all your attention and energy.

feature [fíːʧər] n. 특색, 특징; 특집; v. 특별히 포함하다, 특징으로 삼다
A feature of something is an interesting or important part or characteristic of it.

fascinate [fǽsənèit] v. 마음을 사로잡다, 매혹하다 (fascinating a. 대단히 흥미로운, 매력적인)
If you describe something as fascinating, you find it very interesting and attractive, and your thoughts tend to concentrate on it.

glance [glæns] v. 흘낏 보다; 대충 훑어보다; n. 흘낏 봄
If you glance at something or someone, you look at them very quickly and then look away again immediately.

sneeze [sniːz] v. 재채기하다; n. 재채기
When you sneeze, you suddenly take in your breath and then blow it down your nose noisily without being able to stop yourself, for example because you have a cold.

rocket [rákit] v. 로켓처럼 가다, 돌진하다; 급증하다; n. 로켓; 로켓 추진 미사일
If something such as a vehicle rockets somewhere, it moves there very quickly.

plummet [plʌ́mit] v. 곤두박질치다, 급락하다
If someone or something plummets, they fall very fast toward the ground, usually from a great height.

midair [midéər] n. 공중, 상공
If something happens in midair, it happens in the air, rather than on the ground.

hover [hʌ́vər] v. (허공을) 맴돌다; 서성이다; 주저하다; n. 공중을 떠다님
To hover means to stay in the same position in the air without moving forward or backward.

outstretched [àutstréʧt] a. 쭉 뻗은
If a part of the body of a person or animal is outstretched, it is stretched out as far as possible.

shoo [ʃuː] v. 쉬이하고 쫓아내다; 쉬이하다; int. 쉬, 쉿 (새 등을 쫓는 소리)
If you shoo an animal or a person away, you make them go away by waving your hands or arms at them.

overnight [óuvərnàit] ad. 밤사이에, 하룻밤 동안; a. 야간의; 하룻밤 동안의
If something happens overnight, it happens throughout the night or at some point during the night.

rapid [rǽpid] a. (속도가) 빠른; (행동이) 민첩한 (rapidly ad. 빠르게, 신속히)
A rapid movement is one that is very fast.

fill in idiom 대신 일을 봐주다
If you fill in for someone, you do their job for them while they are away.

challenge [ʧǽlindʒ] v. 도전하다; 도전 의식을 북돋우다; n. 도전; 저항
(challenging a. 도전적인)
A challenging task or job requires great effort and determination.

take care of idiom ~을 처리하다; ~을 돌보다
To take care of someone or something means to do what is necessary to deal with
a person or situation.

coo [kuː] v. 정답게 소곤거리다; 구구 울다; n. 구구 (하고 새가 우는 소리)
When someone coos, they speak in a very soft, quiet voice which is intended to
sound attractive.

impatient [impéiʃənt] a. 짜증난, 안달하는; 어서 ~하고 싶어 하는 (impatiently ad. 성급하게)
If you are impatient, you are annoyed because you have to wait too long for
something.

usher [ʌ́ʃər] v. 안내하다; n. (교회·극장 등의) 좌석 안내원
If you usher someone somewhere, you show them where they should go, often by
going with them.

doorstep [dɔ́ːrstep] n. 문간(의 계단)
A doorstep is a step in front of a door on the outside of a building.

confuse [kənfjúːz] v. (사람을) 혼란시키다; 혼동하다 (confused a. 혼란스러워하는)
If you are confused, you do not know exactly what is happening or what to do.

babysit [béibisit] v. (부모가 외출한 동안) 아이를 봐 주다
If you babysit for someone or babysit their children, you look after their children
while they are out.

grin [grin] v. 활짝 웃다; n. 활짝 웃음
When you grin, you smile broadly.

sigh [sai] n. 한숨; v. 한숨을 쉬다, 한숨짓다; 탄식하듯 말하다
A sigh is a slow breath out that makes a long soft sound, especially because you
are disappointed, tired, annoyed, or relaxed.

^복_습 **erase** [iréis] v. (완전히) 지우다; (지우개 등으로) 지우다
If you erase a thought or feeling, you destroy it completely so that you can no longer remember something or no longer feel a particular emotion.

pay the price idiom 대가를 치르다
if you pay the price for something, you have to deal with the bad effects of something that you have done.

^복_습 **realize** [rí:əlàiz] v. 깨닫다, 알아차리다; 실현하다, 달성하다
If you realize that something is true, you become aware of that fact or understand it.

^복_습 **wrap** [ræp] v. (무엇의 둘레를) 두르다; 포장하다; 둘러싸다; n. 포장지; 랩
If someone wraps their arms, fingers, or legs around something, they put them firmly around it.

^복_습 **hug** [hʌg] n. 포옹; v. 껴안다, 포옹하다
A hug is the act of holding someone or something close to your body with your arms.

^복_습 **snore** [snɔːr] v. 코를 골다; n. 코 고는 소리
When someone who is asleep snores, they make a loud noise each time they breathe.

^복_습 **fast asleep** idiom 깊이 잠들다
Someone who is fast asleep is completely asleep.

Check Your Reading Speed

1분에 몇 단어를 읽는지 리딩 속도를 측정해보세요.

$$\frac{837 \text{ words}}{\text{reading time ( ) sec}} \times 60 = (\quad) \text{ WPM}$$

Build Your Vocabulary

lavish [lǽviʃ] a. 호화로운; 풍성한; 아주 후한 (lavishly ad. 호화롭게)
If you describe something as lavish, you mean that it is very elaborate and impressive and a lot of money has been spent on it.

decorate [dékərèit] v. 장식하다, 꾸미다; (훈장을) 수여하다
If you decorate something, you make it more attractive by adding things to it.

in full swing idiom 한창 진행 중인, 무르익은
If something is in full swing, it is operating fully and is no longer in its early stages.

chat [ʧæt] v. 이야기를 나누다, 수다를 떨다; n. 이야기, 대화
When people chat, they talk to each other in an informal and friendly way.

display [displéi] v. (정보를) 보여주다; (자질·느낌을) 드러내다; 전시하다; n. 진열; 디스플레이
When a computer displays information, it shows it on a screen.

slow-motion [slou-móuʃən] a. 슬로 모션의; n. (영화·텔레비전에서) 슬로 모션
When film or television pictures are shown in slow motion, they are shown much more slowly than normal.

loop [lu:p] n. 순환 테이프; 고리; v. 고리 모양을 만들다; (필름·테이프이) 끊임없이 반복되다
A loop is an endless strip of tape or film allowing continuous repetition.

cam [kæm] n. (= camera) 카메라
A cam is short for camera.

footage [fútidʒ] n. (특정한 사건을 담은) 장면
Footage of a particular event is a film of it or the part of a film which shows this event.

capture [kǽpʧər] n. 생포; 구금, 억류; v. 붙잡다; 포로로 잡다, 억류하다
Capture is the act of catching someone so that they become your prisoner.

crowd [kraud] n. 사람들, 군중; v. 가득 메우다; 바싹 붙어 서다
A crowd is a large group of people who have gathered together, for example to watch or listen to something interesting, or to protest about something.

circle [sə́ːrkl] v. 에워싸다, 둘러싸다; 빙빙 돌다; n. 원형
To circle around someone or something, or to circle them, means to move around them.

celebrate [séləbrèit] v. 기념하다, 축하하다
If you celebrate, you do something enjoyable because of a special occasion or to mark someone's success.

support [səpɔ́ːrt] n. 지지, 지원; 버팀대; v. 지지하다; (넘어지지 않도록) 떠받치다
If you give support to someone during a difficult or unhappy time, you are kind to them and help them.

applaud [əplɔ́ːd] v. 박수를 치다; 갈채를 보내다
When a group of people applaud, they clap their hands in order to show approval, for example when they have enjoyed a play or concert.

crystal clear [krìstl klíər] a. 명명백백한, 아주 분명한; 수정같이 맑은
If you say that a message or statement is crystal clear, you are emphasizing that it is very easy to understand.

proclaim [proukléim] v. 선언하다, 선포하다; 분명히 보여주다
(self-proclaimed a. 자기 혼자 주장하는, 자칭의)
Self-proclaimed is used to show that someone has given themselves a particular title or status rather than being given it by other people.

threaten [θretn] v. 위협하다; 협박하다; (나쁜 일이 있을) 조짐을 보이다
If a person threatens to do something unpleasant to you, or if they threaten you, they say or imply that they will do something unpleasant to you, especially if you do not do what they want.

reign [rein] n. 통치, 지배; v. 통치하다; 군림하다
Reign is a period of time during which a particular person, group, or thing is very important or a powerful influence.

mask [mæsk] n. 마스크; 가면; v. 가면을 쓰다; (감정·냄새·사실 등을) 가리다
A mask is a piece of cloth or other material, which you wear over your face so that people cannot see who you are, or so that you look like someone or something else.

hood [hud] n. (외투 등에 달린) 모자; (자동차 등의) 덮개
A hood is a part of a coat which you can pull up to cover your head. It is in the shape of a triangular bag attached to the neck of the coat at the back.

roar [rɔ:r] v. 고함치다; 웅웅거리다; 굉음을 내며 질주하다; n. 함성; 울부짖는 듯한 소리
If someone roars, they shout something in a very loud voice.

approve [əprúːv] v. 찬성하다; 승인하다 (approval n. 찬성)
If someone or something has your approval, you like and admire them.

thanks to idiom ~의 덕분에, 때문에
If you say that something happens thanks to a particular person or thing, you mean that they are responsible for it happening or caused it to happen.

bashful [bǽʃfəl] a. 수줍음을 타는
Someone who is bashful is shy and easily embarrassed.

* **reluctant** [rilʌ́ktənt] a. 꺼리는, 마지못한, 주저하는 (reluctantly ad. 마지못해, 꺼려하여)
If you are reluctant to do something, you are unwilling to do it and hesitate before doing it, or do it slowly and without enthusiasm.

make one's way idiom 나아가다, 가다
When you make your way somewhere, you walk or travel there.

headgear [hédgiər] n. (머리에 쓰는 모자 등의) 쓸 것
You use headgear to refer to hats or other things worn on the head.

memento [məméntou] n. 기념품
A memento is an object which you keep because it reminds you of a person or a special occasion.

whisper [hwíspər] v. 속삭이다, 소곤거리다; n. 속삭임, 소곤거리는 소리
When you whisper, you say something very quietly, using your breath rather than your throat, so that only one person can hear you.

debt [det] n. 은혜를 입음, 신세를 짐; 빚, 부채
You use debt in expressions such as I owe you a debt or I am in your debt when you are expressing gratitude for something that someone has done for you.

pressure [préʃər] n. 압박, 스트레스; 압력; v. 강요하다; 압력을 가하다
If you are experiencing pressure, you feel that you must do a lot of tasks or make a lot of decisions in very little time, or that people expect a lot from you.

worldwide [wɔ́ːrldwaid] a. 전 세계적인
If something exists or happens worldwide, it exists or happens throughout the world.

summit [sʌ́mit] n. 정상 회담; (산의) 정상
A summit is a meeting at which the leaders of two or more countries discuss important matters.

legal [líːgəl] a. 법이 허용하는, 합법적인; 법률과 관련된
An action or situation that is legal is allowed or required by law.

enthusiastic [inθùːziǽstik] a. 열렬한, 열광적인
If you are enthusiastic about something, you show how much you like or enjoy it by the way that you behave and talk.

cheer [ʧíər] n. 환호(성), 응원; v. 환호성을 지르다, 환호하다
A cheer is a loud shout of happiness or approval.

gather [gǽðər] v. (사람들이) 모이다; (여기저기 있는 것을) 모으다
If people gather somewhere or if someone gathers people somewhere, they come together in a group.

televise [téləvàiz] v. 텔레비전으로 방송하다
If an event or program is televised, it is broadcast so that it can be seen on television.

sign [sain] v. 서명하다; 신호를 보내다; n. 표지판; 몸짓; 기색, 흔적
When you sign a document, you write your name on it, usually at the end or in a special space.

ceremony [sérəmòuni] n. 의식, 의례
A ceremony is a formal event such as a wedding.

swarm [swɔːrm] n. 군중; (곤충의) 떼, 무리; v. 많이 모여들다; 무리를 지어 다니다
A swarm of people is a large group of them moving about quickly.

congratulate [kəngrǽʧulèit] v. 축하하다; 기뻐하다, 자랑스러워하다
If you congratulate someone, you say something to show you are pleased that something nice has happened to them.

drift [drift] v. (서서히) 이동하다; (물·공기에) 떠가다; (자신도 모르게) ~하게 되다; n. 표류; 흐름
To drift somewhere means to move there slowly or gradually.

fixate [fíkseit] v. 응시하다; 정착하다, 고정하다
If you fixate on someone or something, you focus your gaze on them.

^{복습} **gut** [gʌt] n. 직감; 배; (pl.) 배짱; v. 내부를 파괴하다
A gut feeling is based on instinct or emotion rather than reason.

^{복습} **wind down** idiom (서서히) 종료되다; 긴장을 풀다
If something winds down, it ends gradually or in stages.

^{복습} **slip** [slip] v. 슬며시 가다; 미끄러지다; (옷 등을) 재빨리 벗다; n. (작은) 실수; 미끄러짐
If you slip somewhere, you go there quickly and quietly.

^{복습} **edit** [édit] v. 편집하다; 수정하다
If you edit a film or a television or radio program, you choose some of what has
been filmed or recorded and arrange it in a particular order.

^{복습} **suite** [swiːt] n. 잇달아 붙은 방; (호텔 등의) 스위트 룸; 한 벌
A suite is a set of rooms in a hotel or other building.

★ **review** [rivjúː] v. 재검토하다; 확인하다; n. 검토; 논평; 복습
If you review a situation or system, you consider it carefully to see what is wrong
with it or how it could be improved.

‡ **raw** [rɔː] a. 가공되지 않은; 익히지 않은; 다듬어지지 않은
Raw data is facts or information that has not yet been sorted, analysed, or
prepared for use.

‡ **definite** [défənit] a. 확실한, 확고한; 분명한, 뚜렷한 (definitely ad. 확실히, 분명히)
You use definitely to emphasize that something is the case, or to emphasize the
strength of your intention or opinion.

‡ **duty** [djúːti] n. 직무, 임무; (도덕적·법률적) 의무 (on duty idiom 일하는 중인)
If someone is on duty, they are working.

^{복습} **ignore** [ignɔ́ːr] v. 무시하다; (사람을) 못 본 척하다
If you ignore someone or something, you pay no attention to them.

^{복습} **costume** [kástjuːm] n. 의상, 복장; 분장
An actor's or performer's costume is the set of clothes they wear while they are
performing.

^{복습} **clink** [kliŋk] v. 쨍그랑 하는 소리를 내다; n. 쨍그랑 (하는 소리)
If objects clink or if you clink them, they touch each other and make a short,
light sound.

grip [grip] n. 꽉 붙잡음; 통제, 지배; v. 꽉 잡다, 움켜잡다; (마음·흥미·시선을) 끌다
(grip and grin idiom 악수·미소 공세)
A grip and grin is an event at which somone is expected to smile and shake hands
for a photograph.

stuff [stʌf] n. 일, 것, 물건; v. 쑤셔 넣다; 채워 넣다
You can use stuff to refer to things such as a substance, a collection of things,
events, or ideas, or the contents of something in a general way without mentioning
the thing itself by name.

invent [invént] v. 발명하다; (사실이 아닌 것을) 지어내다
If you invent something such as a machine or process, you are the first person to
think of it or make it.

please [pliːz] v. 기쁘게 하다, 기분을 맞추다; ~하고 싶다
If someone or something pleases you, they make you feel happy and satisfied.

engage [ingéidʒ] v. 관계를 맺다; 약속하다; (주의·관심을) 사로잡다
If you engage someone, you become involved, or have contact, with them.

trade [treid] v. 주고받다, 교환하다; 거래하다; n. 거래, 교역, 무역
If someone trades one thing for another or if two people trade things, they agree
to exchange one thing for the other thing.

quality [kwáləti] n. 질(質); 우수함; 특성; a. 고급의, 양질의
The quality of something is how good or bad it is.

crap [kræp] a. 형편없는, 쓰레기 같은; n. 허튼소리, 헛소리; 배변; v. 배변하다
If you describe something as crap, you think that it is wrong or of very poor
quality.

convenient [kənvíːnjənt] a. 편리한, 사용하기 좋은
If a way of doing something is convenient, it is easy, or very useful or suitable for
a particular purpose.

not sit right idiom ~에 받아들여지지 않다, 수긍되지 않다
If something that someone does or says does not sit right with you, you do not
agree with it or do not like it.

notice [nóutis] v. 알아채다, 인지하다; 주의하다; n. 신경 씀, 알아챔; 통지, 예고
If you notice something or someone, you become aware of them.

tune [tjuːn] v. (라디오·텔레비전 채널을) 맞추다; (악기의) 음을 맞추다; n. 곡, 선율; (마음의) 상태
If your radio or television is tuned to a particular broadcasting station, you are
listening to or watching the programs being broadcast by that station.

control [kəntróul] n. (기계·차량의) 제어 장치; 통제, 제어; v. 지배하다; 조정하다
A control is a device such as a switch or lever which you use in order to operate a machine or other piece of equipment.

rock [rak] v. (전후·좌우로) 흔들리다; n. 바위; 돌멩이
When something rocks or when you rock it, it moves slowly and regularly backward and forward or from side to side.

back and forth idiom 여기저기에, 왔다갔다; 좌우로; 앞뒤로
If someone moves back and forth, they repeatedly move in one direction and then in the opposite direction.

circuit [sə́:rkit] n. (전기) 회로; 순환, 순회 (closed circuit n. 폐쇄 회로)
A closed circuit television or video system is one that operates within a limited area such as a building.

hack [hæk] v. (컴퓨터) 해킹하다; (마구·거칠게) 자르다, 난도질하다
If someone hacks into a computer system, they break into the system, especially in order to get secret information.

sophisticated [səfístəkèitid] a. 지적인, 수준 높은; 정교한; 세련된
A sophisticated person is intelligent and knows a lot, so that they are able to understand complicated situations.

lock [lak] n. 잠금장치; v. (자물쇠로) 잠그다; 고정시키다
The lock on something such as a door or a drawer is the device which is used to keep it shut and prevent other people from opening it.

work out idiom 해결하다; ~을 계획해 내다; (일이) 잘 풀리다
To work out means to find the answer to a question or something that is difficult to understand or explain.

mystery [místəri] n. 수수께끼, 미스터리; 신비스러운 사람, 것
A mystery is something that is not understood or known about.

doubtful [dáutfəl] a. 확신이 없는, 의심을 품은; 불확실한
If you are doubtful about something, you feel unsure or uncertain about it.

make sense idiom 타당하다; 이해가 되다
If something makes sense, it is a sensible or practical thing to do.

brilliant [bríljənt] a. (재능이) 뛰어난; 아주 밝은, 눈부신; 훌륭한
A brilliant person, idea, or performance is extremely clever or skilful.

conceive [kənsíːv] v. (생각·계획 등을) 마음속으로 하다; 임신하다
If you conceive a plan or idea, you think of it and work out how it can be done.

technology [teknálədʒi] n. (과학) 기술; 기계, 장비
Technology refers to methods, systems, and devices which are the result of scientific knowledge being used for practical purposes.

jail [dʒeil] n. 교도소, 감옥; v. 수감하다
A jail is a place where criminals are kept in order to punish them, or where people waiting to be tried are kept.

patent [pætnt] n. 특허권; a. 특허의; 전매특허품인; v. 특허를 받다
A patent is an official right to be the only person or company allowed to make or sell a new product for a certain period of time.

clerk [kləːrk] n. 직원; 점원; v. 사무원으로 일하다
A clerk is a person who works in an office, bank, or law court and whose job is to look after the records or accounts.

race [reis] v. (머리·심장 등이) 바쁘게 돌아가다; 쏜살같이 가다; 경주하다; n. 경주; 인종, 종족
If your mind races, or if thoughts race through your mind, you think very fast about something, especially when you are in a difficult or dangerous situation.

hypnotize [hípnətàiz] v. 최면을 걸다; 혼을 빼놓다, 홀리다
If someone hypnotizes you, they put you into a state in which you seem to be asleep but can still see, hear, or respond to things said to you.

goggle [gagl] n. (pl.) 보호 안경, 고글
Goggles are large glasses that fit closely to your face around your eyes to protect them from such things as water, wind, or dust.

inspect [inspékt] v. 면밀하게 살피다, 점검하다; 시찰하다
If you inspect something, you look at every part of it carefully in order to find out about it or check that it is all right.

instant [ínstənt] n. 순간, 아주 짧은 동안; a. 즉각적인 (in an instant idiom 곧, 즉시)
An instant is an extremely short period of time.

lens [lenz] n. 렌즈
A lens is a thin curved piece of glass or plastic used in things such as cameras, telescopes, and pairs of glasses.

blaze [bleiz] v. 눈부시게 빛나다; 활활 타다; n. 불길; 휘황찬란한 빛
If something blazes with light or color, it is extremely bright.

hypnotic [hipnátik] a. 최면을 일으키는, 최면성의

Something that is hypnotic holds your attention or makes you feel sleepy, often because it involves repeated sounds, pictures, or movements.

state [steit] n. 상태; 국가, 나라; 주(州); v. 말하다, 진술하다

When you talk about the state of someone or something, you are referring to the condition they are in or what they are like at a particular time.

Chapters
16 & 17

1. How did Jack-Jack compare to other Super babies?

    A. He was more curious than them.

    B. He had more powers than them.

    C. He was more emotional than them.

    D. He had the same abilities as them.

2. What could Jack-Jack's tracker do?

    A. It could calm him down.

    B. It could control all of his movements.

    C. It could make him disappear.

    D. It could predict his physical changes.

3. What was one feature of Jack-Jack's suit?

    A. It could play music.

    B. It could put out fires.

    C. It could stick to walls.

    D. It could prepare meals.

4. What was NOT true about Evelyn?

    A. She had come up with the idea of the Screenslaver.

    B. She had made a pizza-delivery guy seem like the Screenslaver.

    C. She had told Winston about inventing the Screenslaver.

    D. She had no regrets about creating the Screenslaver.

5. How did Evelyn feel about Superheroes?

    A. She was thankful that they helped weak people.

    B. She was bitter that they helped only rich people.

    C. She was confident that they made the world stronger.

    D. She was certain that they made the world worse.

Check Your Reading Speed
1분에 몇 단어를 읽는지 리딩 속도를 측정해보세요.

$$\frac{921 \text{ words}}{\text{reading time ( ) sec}} \times 60 = (\quad) \text{ WPM}$$

Build Your Vocabulary

fog [fɔːg] n. 혼미, 혼란; 안개; v. 수증기가 서리다; 헷갈리게 하다
You can use fog to refer to a situation which stops people from being able to notice things, understand things, or think clearly.

dawn [dɔːn] v. 분명해지다, 이해되기 시작하다; 밝다; n. 새벽, 여명
If something dawns on you, you realize it for the first time.

remove [rimúːv] v. (옷 등을) 벗다; 없애다, 제거하다; 치우다, 내보내다
If you remove clothing, you take it off.

couch [kauʧ] n. 긴 의자, 소파
A couch is a long, comfortable seat for two or three people.

blanket [blǽŋkit] n. 담요, 모포; v. (완전히) 뒤덮다
A blanket is a large square or rectangular piece of thick cloth, especially one which you put on a bed to keep you warm.

pillow [pílou] n. 베개
A pillow is a rectangular cushion which you rest your head on when you are in bed.

cereal [síəriəl] n. 시리얼; 곡물, 곡류
Cereal or breakfast cereal is a food made from grain. It is mixed with milk and eaten for breakfast.

grin [grin] v. 활짝 웃다; n. 활짝 웃음
When you grin, you smile broadly.

lab [læb] n. (= laboratory) 실험실, 연구실
A lab is the same as a laboratory, which is a building or a room where scientific experiments, analyses, and research are carried out.

‡ imitate [ímətèit] v. 흉내내다; 모방하다, 본뜨다
If you imitate someone, you copy what they do or produce.

복습 appreciate [əprí:ʃièit] v. 고마워하다; 진가를 알아보다
If you appreciate something that someone has done for you or is going to do for you, you are grateful for it.

‡ gratitude [grǽtətjù:d] n. 고마움, 감사
Gratitude is the state of feeling grateful.

inexpressible [iniksprésəbl] a. 이루 말로 다 할 수 없는
An inexpressible feeling cannot be expressed in words because it is so strong.

‡ rate [reit] n. 요금; 속도; 비율; v. 평가하다; 등급을 매기다
A rate is the amount of money that is charged for goods or services.

stutter [stʌ́tər] v. 말을 더듬다, 더듬거리다; n. 말을 더듬기
If someone stutters, they have difficulty speaking because they find it hard to say the first sound of a word.

‡ joke [dʒouk] v. 농담하다; 농담 삼아 말하다; n. 농담; 웃음거리
If you joke, you tell someone something that is not true in order to amuse yourself.

복습 assign [əsáin] v. (일·책임 등을) 맡기다; (사람을) 배치하다 (assignment n. 임무, 과제)
An assignment is a task or piece of work that you are given to do, especially as part of your job or studies.

. stimulate [stímjulèit] v. 자극하다, 고무하다, 활성화시키다 (stimulating a. 자극이 되는)
If you are stimulated by something, it makes you feel full of ideas and enthusiasm.

‡ deserve [dizə́:rv] v. ~을 받을 만하다, ~을 누릴 자격이 있다; ~을 당해야 마땅하다
If you say that a person or thing deserves something, you mean that they should have it or receive it because of their actions or qualities.

복습 enormous [inɔ́:rməs] a. 막대한, 거대한
Something that is enormous is extremely large in size or amount.

. potential [pəténʃəl] n. 잠재력; 가능성; a. 가능성이 있는, 잠재적인
If you say that someone or something has potential, you mean that they have the necessary abilities or qualities to become successful or useful in the future.

복습 adore [ədɔ́:r] v. 흠모하다; 아주 좋아하다 (adoringly ad. 홀딱 반하여)
An adoring person is someone who loves and admires another person very much.

babble [bǽbl] v. 지껄이다, 횡설수설하다; n. 횡설수설; 와글와글, 왁자지껄
If someone babbles, they talk in a confused or excited way.

punch [pʌntʃ] v. (자판·번호판 등을) 치다; 주먹으로 치다; n. 주먹으로 한 대 침
If you punch something such as the buttons on a keyboard, you touch them in order to store information on a machine such as a computer or to give the machine a command to do something.

code [koud] n. 암호, 부호; (컴퓨터) 코드; v. 암호로 쓰다
A code is a system of replacing the words in a message with other words or symbols, so that nobody can understand it unless they know the system.

keypad [kíːpæd] n. 키패드(숫자가 적힌, 전화·텔레비전 등의 조작기)
The keypad is a small set of keys with numbers on them used to operate a television, phone, or calculator.

protocol [próutəkɔ̀ːl] n. (컴퓨터) 프로토콜; 외교 의례; (국가 간의) 협안
A protocol is a set of rules for exchanging information between computers.

pro [prou] n. (= professional) 전문가, 프로; prep. ~에 호의적인, ~을 지지하는; a. 전문적인
A pro is a professional.

scan [skæn] v. 정밀 촬영하다; (유심히) 살피다; 훑어보다; n. 정밀 검사
(scanner n. 판독 장치, 스캐너)
A scanner is a machine which is used to examine, identify, or record things, for example by using a beam of light, sound, or X-rays.

retina [rétənə] n. (눈의) 망막 (retinal a. 망막의)
Your retina is the area at the back of your eye. It receives the image that you see and then sends the image to your brain.

lack [læk] v. ~이 없다, 부족하다; n. 부족, 결핍
If you say that someone or something lacks a particular quality or that a particular quality is lacking in them, you mean that they do not have any or enough of it.

coherent [kouhíərənt] a. 일관성 있는; 조리 있게 말하는 (coherency n. 일관성)
Coherency is a state or situation in which all the parts or ideas fit together well so that they form a united whole.

affix [əfíks] v. 부착하다, 붙이다
If you affix one thing to another, you stick it or attach it to the other thing.

platform [plǽtfɔ̀ːrm] n. (장비 등을 올려놓는) 대(臺); 연단, 강단
A platform is a flat raised structure or area, usually one which something can stand on or land on.

INCREDIBLES 2

‡ exception [iksépʃən] n. 예외, 이례; 제외
If you make a general statement, and then say that something or someone is no exception, you are emphasizing that they are included in that statement.

복습 limit [límit] v. 제한하다; 한정하다; n. 한계, 한도; 제한, 허용치 (unlimited a. 무제한의)
If there is an unlimited quantity of something, you can have as much or as many of that thing as you want.

＊ creative [kriéitiv] a. 창의적인, 창조적인, 독창적인
A creative person has the ability to invent and develop original ideas, especially in the arts.

‡ fever [fíːvər] n. 열기; 열; 흥분, 초조
A fever is extreme excitement or nervousness about something.

복습 shift [ʃift] v. 바꾸다; (장소를) 옮기다; n. 교대 근무 (시간); 변화
If you shift something or if it shifts, it moves slightly.

‡ address [ədrés] v. 말을 걸다; 연설하다; 주소를 쓰다; n. 주소; 연설
If you address someone or address a remark to them, you say something to them.

stay up idiom 자지 않고 일어나 있다; (더 늦게까지) 깨어 있다
If you stay up, you remain out of bed at a time when most people have gone to bed or at a time when you are normally in bed yourself.

＊ fabulous [fæbjuləs] a. 기막히게 좋은; 엄청난, 굉장한
If you describe something as fabulous, you are emphasizing that you like it a lot or think that it is very good.

＊ chamber [ʧéimbər] n. (특정 목적용) -실(室); 회의실; (지하의) 공간
A chamber is a room designed and equipped for a particular purpose.

복습 multiple [mʌ́ltəpl] a. 많은, 다수의; 복합적인; n. 배수
You use multiple to describe things that consist of many parts, involve many people, or have many uses.

sum up idiom 요약하다
If something sums a person or situation up, it represents their most typical characteristics.

복습 specific [spisífik] a. 특정한; 구체적인, 명확한 (specifically ad. 특별히; 분명히)
You use specifically to add something more precise or exact to what you have already said.

press [pres] v. 누르다; (무엇에) 바짝 대다; 꾹 밀어 넣다; n. 언론
If you press a button or switch, you push it with your finger in order to make a machine or device work.

snap [snæp] v. 급히 움직이다; 툭 부러지다; 날카롭게 말하다; n. 탁 하는 소리
If you snap something into a particular position, or if it snaps into that position, it moves quickly into that position, with a sharp sound.

engage [ingéidʒ] v. (주의·관심을) 사로잡다; 관계를 맺다; 약속하다
If something engages you or your attention or interest, it keeps you interested in it and thinking about it.

blend [blend] v. 조합하다; 섞다; n. 조합
If you blend substances together or if they blend, you mix them together so that they become one substance.

durable [djúərəbl] a. 내구성이 있는, 오래가는 (durability n. 내구성, 내구력)
Something that is durable is strong and lasts a long time without breaking or becoming weaker.

duress [djuərés] n. 협박, 압력
To do something under duress means to do it because someone forces you to do it or threatens you.

comfort [kʌ́mfərt] n. 안락, 편안; 위로, 위안; v. 위로하다, 위안하다
If you are doing something in comfort, you are physically relaxed and contented, and are not feeling any pain or other unpleasant sensations.

sleek [sli:k] a. (모양이) 매끈한; 윤이 나는
Sleek vehicles, furniture, or other objects look smooth, shiny, and expensive.

interweave [intərwí:v] v. (interwove-interwoven) (실·털실 등을) 섞어 짜다
If two or more things are interwoven or interweave, they are very closely connected or are combined with each other.

fabric [fǽbrik] n. 직물, 천
Fabric is cloth or other material produced by weaving together cotton, nylon, wool, silk, or other threads. Fabrics are used for making things such as clothes, curtains, and sheets.

mesh [meʃ] n. 망사; 그물망, 철망; v. 꼭 들어맞게 하다; 맞물리다
Mesh is material like a net made from wire, thread, or plastic.

tiny [táini] a. 아주 작은
Something or someone that is tiny is extremely small.

sensor [sénsər] n. 센서, 감지기
A sensor is an instrument which reacts to certain physical conditions or impressions such as heat or light, and which is used to provide information.

physical [fízikəl] a. 신체의; 물질의, 물리적인
Physical qualities, actions, or things are connected with a person's body, rather than with their mind.

property [prápərti] n. (pl.) (사물의) 속성; 재산, 소유물
The properties of a substance or object are the ways in which it behaves in particular conditions.

replicate [répləkèit] v. (바이러스·분자가) 자기 복제를 하다; (정확히) 모사하다
(replication n. 복제)
If genetic material or a living organism replicates, it reproduces or gives rise to a copy of itself.

imminent [ímənənt] a. 금방이라도 닥칠 듯한, 목전의, 임박한
If you say that something is imminent, especially something unpleasant, you mean it is almost certain to happen very soon.

multiply [mʌ́ltəplài] v. 크게 증가하다; 곱하다; 증식하다
When something multiplies or when you multiply it, it increases greatly in number or amount.

lord [lɔːrd] int. 이런, 맙소사; n. 지배자, 주인; 국왕; 귀족
Lord is used in exclamations such as 'good Lord!' and 'oh Lord!' to express surprise, shock, frustration, or annoyance about something.

blame [bleim] v. ~을 탓하다, ~의 책임으로 보다; n. 책임; 탓
If you blame a person or thing for something bad, you believe or say that they are responsible for it or that they caused it.

track [træk] v. 추적하다, 뒤쫓다; n. (기차) 선로; 경주로, 트랙; 자국 (tracker n. 추적 장치)
A tracker is a device that follows and records the movements of someone or something.

anticipate [æntísəpèit] v. 예상하다; 기대하다, 고대하다
If you anticipate something, you do it, think it, or say it before someone else does.

alert [əlɔ́ːrt] v. (위험 등을) 알리다; n. 경계경보; a. 경계하는; 기민한
If you alert someone to a situation, especially a dangerous or unpleasant situation, you tell them about it.

mount [maunt] v. 끼우다, 고정시키다; (자전거·말 등에) 올라타다; n. (전시품을 세우는) 판; 산
If you mount an object on something, you fix it there firmly.

pole [poul] n. 막대, 기둥; 장대; 극
A pole is a long thin piece of wood or metal, used especially for supporting things.

chase [ʧeis] v. 뒤쫓다, 추적하다; 추구하다; n. 추적, 추격; 추구함
If you chase someone, or chase after them, you run after them or follow them quickly in order to catch or reach them.

slap [slæp] v. 털썩 놓다; (손바닥으로) 철썩 때리다; n. 철썩 때리기, 치기
If you slap something onto a surface, you put it there quickly, roughly, or carelessly.

merge [mə:rdʒ] v. 합치다; 어우러지다
If one thing merges with another, or is merged with another, they combine or come together to make one whole thing.

panic [pǽnik] v. 어쩔 줄 모르다, 공황 상태에 빠지다; n. 극심한 공포, 공황; 허둥지둥함
If you panic or if someone panics you, you suddenly feel anxious or afraid, and act quickly and without thinking carefully.

painful [péinfəl] a. (마음이) 괴로운; 고통스러운 (painfully ad. 극도로; 아플 정도로)
You use painfully to emphasize a quality or situation that is undesirable.

involve [inválv] v. 수반하다, 포함하다; 관련시키다, 연루시키다
If a situation or activity involves something, that thing is a necessary part or consequence of it.

inevitable [inévətəbl] a. 불가피한, 필연적인 (inevitably ad. 필연적으로)
If something will inevitably happen, it is certain to happen and cannot be prevented or avoided.

demon [díːmən] n. 악령, 악마
A demon is an evil spirit.

phase [feiz] n. (변화·발달의) 단계; v. 단계적으로 하다
A phase is a particular stage in a process or in the gradual development of something.

detect [ditékt] v. 발견하다, 알아내다, 감지하다
To detect something means to find it or discover that it is present somewhere by using equipment or making an investigation.

penetrate [pénətrèit] v. 뚫고 들어가다; 간파하다; 침투하다
If something or someone penetrates a physical object or an area, they succeed in getting into it or passing through it.

turn into idiom ~이 되다, ~으로 변하다
To turn or be turned into something means to change, or to make a thing change, into something different.

pad [pæd] n. 패드; (메모지 등의) 묶음; v. 소리 안 나게 걷다; 완충재를 대다
A pad is a flat area on the edge of an integrated circuit to which wires or component leads can be attached to make an electrical connection.

combustion [kəmbʌ́stʃən] n. 불이 탐; (물질의 화학적) 연소
Combustion is the act of burning something or the process of burning.

burst [bəːrst] v. (burst-burst) 갑자기 ~하다; 불쑥 움직이다; n. (갑자기) ~을 함; 파열, 폭발
To burst into something means to suddenly start doing it.

flame [fleim] n. 불길, 불꽃; 격정; v. 활활 타오르다; 시뻘게지다
If something bursts into flames or bursts into flame, it suddenly starts burning strongly.

countermeasure [káuntərmèʒər] n. 대책, 보호 조치
A countermeasure is an action that you take in order to weaken the effect of another action or a situation, or to make it harmless.

extinguish [ikstíŋgwiʃ] v. (불을) 끄다; 끝내다, 없애다
If you extinguish a fire or a light, you stop it burning or shining.

trip [trip] v. 작동시키다; 발을 헛디디다; n. 여행; 발을 헛디딤
To trip means to make a switch go on or off, especially by accident.

sprinkler [spríŋkləːr] n. 물을 뿌리는 장치, 살수 장치
A sprinkler is a device used to spray water. Sprinklers are used to water plants or grass, or to put out fires in buildings.

foam [foum] n. 거품; v. 거품을 일으키다
Foam consists of a mass of small bubbles that are formed when air and a liquid are mixed together.

erupt [irʌ́pt] v. 분출되다; (강한 감정을) 터뜨리다
When a volcano erupts, it throws out a lot of hot, melted rock called lava, as well as ash and steam.

put out idiom (불을) 끄다
If you put out something, especially a fire, you make it stop burning.

giggle [gigl] v. 피식 웃다, 킥킥거리다; n. 피식 웃음, 킥킥거림
If someone giggles, they laugh in a childlike way, because they are amused, nervous, or embarrassed.

lick [lik] v. 핥다; 핥아먹다; n. 한 번 핥기, 핥아먹기
When people or animals lick something, they move their tongue across its surface.

substance [sʌ́bstəns] n. 물질; 실체
A substance is a solid, powder, liquid, or gas with particular properties.

retardant [ritá:rdənt] n. 지연제; a. 저지하는 (flame retardant n. 방화(防火) 재료)
Flame retardant substances make the thing that they are applied to burn more slowly.

effective [iféktiv] a. 효과적인; 시행되는
Something that is effective works well and produces the results that were intended.

edible [édəbl] a. 먹을 수 있는
If something is edible, it is safe to eat and not poisonous.

relieve [rilí:v] v. 안도하다; (불쾌감·고통 등을) 없애 주다; 완화하다 (relieved a. 안도하는)
If you are relieved, you feel happy because something unpleasant has not happened or is no longer happening.

chuckle [ʧʌkl] n. 킬킬거림; 속으로 웃기; v. 킬킬 웃다; 빙그레 웃다
A chuckle is a quiet or suppressed laugh.

clutch [klʌʧ] v. (꽉) 움켜잡다; n. 움켜쥠
If you clutch at something or clutch something, you hold it tightly, usually because you are afraid or anxious.

doorstep [dɔ́:rstep] n. 문간(의 계단)
A doorstep is a step in front of a door on the outside of a building.

pish-posh [píʃ-paʃ] int. 말도 안 돼; n. 터무니없는 말, 허튼소리
You can use pish-posh to declare that someone's opinions or thoughts are absurd, irrelevant or redundant.

bill [bil] n. 고지서, 청구서; 계산서; 지폐; v. 청구서를 보내다
A bill is a written statement of money that you owe for goods or services.

deduct [didʌ́kt] v. (돈·점수 등을) 공제하다, 빼다
When you deduct an amount from a total, you subtract it from the total.

* **fee** [fiː] n. 요금; 수수료
A fee is the amount of money that a person or organization is paid for a particular job or service that they provide.

* **exclusive** [iksklúːsiv] a. 독점적인, 전용의; 고급의
Something that is exclusive is used or owned by only one person or group, and not shared with anyone else.

design [dizáin] v. 설계하다; 고안하다; n. 설계; 계획, 의도 (designer n. 디자이너)
A designer is a person whose job is to design things by making drawings of them.

universe [júːnəvəːrs] n. 우주; 은하계; (특정한 유형의) 경험 세계
The universe is the whole of space and all the stars, planets, and other forms of matter and energy in it.

buckle [bʌkl] v. 버클로 잠그다; 찌그러지다; n. 버클, 잠금장치
When you buckle a belt or strap, you fasten it.

babysit [béibisit] v. (부모가 외출한 동안) 아이를 봐 주다
If you babysit for someone or babysit their children, you look after their children while they are out.

caress [kərés] v. 애무하다, 어루만지다
If you caress someone, you stroke them gently and affectionately.

cheek [ʧiːk] n. 뺨, 볼; 엉덩이
Your cheeks are the sides of your face below your eyes.

Check Your Reading Speed

1분에 몇 단어를 읽는지 리딩 속도를 측정해보세요.

$$\frac{439 \text{ words}}{\text{reading time ( ) sec}} \times 60 = (\quad) \text{ WPM}$$

Build Your Vocabulary

blink [blɪŋk] v. 눈을 깜박이다; (불빛이) 깜박거리다; n. 눈을 깜박거림
When you blink or when you blink your eyes, you shut your eyes and very quickly open them again.

flicker [flíkər] v. (불·빛 등이) 깜박거리다; 움직거리다; n. (빛의) 깜박거림; 움직거림
If a light or flame flickers, it shines unsteadily.

go out idiom (불·전깃불이) 꺼지다; 외출하다
If the fire or the light goes out, it stops burning or shining.

trance [træns] n. 최면 상태; 실신; 무아지경
A trance is a state of mind in which someone seems to be asleep and to have no conscious control over their thoughts or actions, but in which they can see and hear things and respond to commands given by other people.

bind [baɪnd] v. (bound-bound) 묶다; 결속시키다; 굳다, 뭉치다
If you bind something or someone, you tie rope, string, tape, or other material around them so that they are held firmly.

intercom [íntərkɑm] n. 내부 통화 장치, 인터콤
An intercom is a small box with a microphone which is connected to a loudspeaker in another room.

resist [rizíst] v. 참다, 견디다; 저항하다; 굴하지 않다
If you resist doing something, or resist the temptation to do it, you stop yourself from doing it although you would like to do it.

tempt [tempt] v. (어떤 것을 제의하거나 하여) 유도하다; (좋지 않은 일을 하도록) 유혹하다
(temptation n. 유혹)
If you feel you want to do something or have something, even though you know you really should avoid it, you can refer to this feeling as temptation.

stretch [streʧ] v. (길이·폭 등을) 늘이다; 뻗어 있다; n. 뻗기, 펴기; (길게) 뻗은 구간
When something soft or elastic stretches or is stretched, it becomes longer or bigger as well as thinner, usually because it is pulled.

stare [stɛər] v. 빤히 쳐다보다, 응시하다; n. 빤히 쳐다보기, 응시
If you stare at someone or something, you look at them for a long time.

temperature [témpərəʧər] n. 온도, 기온; 체온
The temperature of something is a measure of how hot or cold it is.

freeze [fri:z] v. 얼다; (두려움 등으로 몸이) 얼어붙다; n. 동결; 한파
If a liquid or a substance containing a liquid freezes, or if something freezes it, it becomes solid because of low temperatures.

shiver [ʃívər] v. (몸을) 떨다; n. (추위·두려움 등으로 인한) 전율; 오한
When you shiver, your body shakes slightly because you are cold or frightened.

franchise [frǽnʧaiz] n. (회사의) 가맹점 영업권; 체인점, 프랜차이즈; v. 가맹점 영업권을 주다
A franchise is an authority that is given by an organization to someone, allowing them to sell its goods or services or to take part in an activity which the organization controls.

free enterprise [fri: éntərpràiz] n. 자유 기업 체제
Free enterprise is an economic system in which businesses compete for profit without much government control.

hypnosis [hipnóusis] n. 최면술; 최면 상태
Hypnosis is the art or practice of hypnotizing people.

technology [teknálədʒi] n. (과학) 기술; 기계, 장비
Technology refers to methods, systems, and devices which are the result of scientific knowledge being used for practical purposes.

sarcastic [sa:rkǽstik] a. 빈정대는, 비꼬는; 풍자적인 (sarcastically ad. 비꼬는 투로)
Someone who is sarcastic says or does the opposite of what they really mean in order to mock or insult someone.

jail [dʒeil] n. 교도소, 감옥; v. 수감하다
A jail is a place where criminals are kept in order to punish them, or where people waiting to be tried are kept.

height [hait] n. (사람의) 키; 최고조, 절정; 높이
The height of a person or thing is their size or length from the bottom to the top.

build [bild] n. (사람의) 체구; v. (건물을) 짓다
Someone's build is the shape that their bones and muscles give to their body.

bother [báðər] v. 신경 쓰이게 하다, 괴롭히다; 신경 쓰다; n. 성가심
If something bothers you, or if you bother about it, it worries, annoys, or upsets you.

innocent [ínəsənt] a. 무죄인, 결백한; 순진한; 무고한; 악의 없는
If someone is innocent, they did not commit a crime which they have been accused of.

surly [sɔ́:rli] a. 성질 못된, 무례한
Someone who is surly behaves in a rude bad-tempered way.

count on idiom 기대하다, 의지하다
If you count on someone, you depend on them to do what you want or expect them to do for you.

theme [θi:m] n. 주제, 테마
Theme music or a theme song is a piece of music that is played at the beginning and end of a film or of a television or radio program.

costume [kástju:m] n. 의상, 복장; 분장
An actor's or performer's costume is the set of clothes they wear while they are performing.

glove [glʌv] v. 장갑을 끼다; n. 장갑 (gloved a. 장갑을 낀)
To glove means to put gloves on your hands.

helpless [hélplis] a. 무력한, 속수무책인
If you are helpless, you do not have the strength or power to do anything useful or to control or protect yourself.

grand [grænd] a. 웅장한, 장려한; 원대한
Grand plans or actions are intended to achieve important results.

conflate [kənfléit] v. 융합하다, 합체하다
If you conflate two or more descriptions or ideas, or if they conflate, you combine them in order to produce a single one.

fool [fu:l] n. 바보; v. 놀리다, 속이다
If you call someone a fool, you are indicating that you think they are not at all sensible and show a lack of good judgment.

illegal [ilíːgəl] a. 불법적인; 비합법적인
If something is illegal, the law says that it is not allowed.

ignite [ignáit] v. 불을 붙이다, 점화하다
When you ignite something or when it ignites, it starts burning or explodes.

glaze [gleiz] v. (눈이) 게슴츠레해지다; 유리를 끼우다; n. 유약
If you or your eyes glaze over, you start to look bored or tired and it is obvious to other people that you have stopped listening.

wicked [wíkid] a. 못된, 사악한; 아주 좋은; 짓궂은
You use wicked to describe someone or something that is very bad and deliberately harmful to people.

spell [spel] n. 주문; 마법; v. (어떤 단어의) 철자를 쓰다; 철자를 맞게 쓰다
(fall under one's spell idiom ~의 통제를 받다)
If you fall under someone's spell, you are strongly influenced by someone, so that you do what you think they want, or you copy them in some way.

Chapters
18 & 19

1. **What happened when the hypnotized Supers first arrived at the Parr house?**

    A. They gave Frozone a pair of hypno-goggles.

    B. They threatened to destroy the house.

    C. They told Dash and Violet that they were not safe.

    D. They went upstairs to search for Jack-Jack.

2. **How did the Incredibile get to the house?**

    A. Dash used a remote to summon it.

    B. Frozone sent a signal to activate it.

    C. Violet pressed buttons to direct it.

    D. Bob drove it from Victor Cachet's mansion.

3. **What happened when Mr. Incredible went into the hydroliner ballroom?**

    A. He immediately noticed that Elastigirl was in a trance.

    B. He immediately sensed that Elastigirl was dangerous.

    C. Elastigirl hugged him when she saw him.

    D. Elastigirl attacked him when she saw him.

4. **How did Violet, Dash, and Jack-Jack get onto the ship?**

    A. They jumped from the dock to a ladder on the ship.

    B. They swam from the Incredibile to a ladder on the ship.

    C. They ejected themselves from the Incredibile onto the deck of the ship.

    D. They drove the Incredible right onto the deck of the ship.

5. **What was Jack-Jack trying to do on the ship?**

    A. Stop Evelyn

    B. Find his mom

    C. Rescue the Supers

    D. Protect Violet and Dash

Check Your Reading Speed

1분에 몇 단어를 읽는지 리딩 속도를 측정해보세요.

$$\frac{1{,}093 \text{ words}}{\text{reading time (\quad) sec}} \times 60 = (\quad) \text{ WPM}$$

Build Your Vocabulary

backyard [bækjá:rd] n. 뒷마당; 뒤뜰
A backyard is an area of land at the back of a house.

suit [su:t] n. (특정한 활동 때 입는) 옷; 정장; 소송; v. ~에게 편리하다; 어울리다
A particular type of suit is a piece of clothing that you wear for a particular activity.

demonstrate [démənstrèit] v. (행동으로) 보여주다; (사용법을) 보여주다
If you demonstrate a particular skill, quality, or feeling, you show by your actions that you have it.

concentrate [kánsəntrèit] v. (정신을) 집중하다; (한 곳에) 모으다; n. 농축물
If you concentrate on something, or concentrate your mind on it, you give all your attention to it.

ray [rei] n. 광선; 약간, 소량
Rays of light are narrow beams of light.

land [lænd] v. (땅·표면에) 내려앉다, 착륙하다; 놓다, 두다; n. 육지, 땅; 지역
When someone or something lands, they come down to the ground after moving through the air or falling.

target [tá:rgit] n. (공격의) 표적; 목표; v. (공격·비판의) 목표로 삼다
A target is something at which someone is aiming a weapon or other object.

wrap [ræp] v. 둘러싸다; (무엇의 둘레를) 두르다; 포장하다; n. 포장지; 랩
When you wrap something such as a piece of paper or cloth round another thing, you put it around it.

belly [béli] n. 배, 복부; (사물의) 볼록한 부분
The belly of a person or animal is their stomach or abdomen.

INCREDIBLES 2

fire [faiər] v. 발사하다; (엔진이) 점화되다; 해고하다; n. 화재, 불; 발사, 총격
If someone fires a gun or a bullet, or if they fire, a bullet is sent from a gun that they are using.

aim [eim] v. 겨누다; 목표하다; n. 겨냥, 조준; 목적
If you aim a weapon or object at something or someone, you point it toward them before firing or throwing it.

no way idiom 절대로 아니다; (강한 거절의 의미로) 절대로 안 돼, 싫어
You can say 'no way' as an emphatic way of saying 'no'.

control [kəntróul] v. 지배하다; 조정하다; n. (기계·차량의) 제어 장치; 통제, 제어
To control a piece of equipment, process, or system means to make it work in the way that you want it to work.

squeal [skwi:l] v. 꽤액 소리를 지르다; 끼익 하는 소리를 내다; n. 끼익 하는 소리
If someone or something squeals, they make a long, high-pitched sound.

alert [ələ́:rt] n. 경계경보; v. (위험 등을) 알리다; a. 경계하는; 기민한
An alert is a situation in which people prepare themselves for something dangerous that might happen soon.

morph [mɔːrf] v. 변하다, 바뀌다; 바꾸다
If one thing morphs into another thing, especially something very different, the first thing changes into the second.

imminent [ímənənt] a. 금방이라도 닥칠 듯한, 목전의, 임박한
If you say that something is imminent, especially something unpleasant, you mean it is almost certain to happen very soon.

playful [pleifl] a. 장난으로 한; 장난기 많은
A playful gesture or person is friendly or humorous.

vortex [vɔ́:rteks] n. (물·공기 등의) 소용돌이
A vortex is a mass of wind or water that spins round so fast that it pulls objects down into its empty center.

current [kə́:rənt] a. 현재의, 지금의; n. (물·공기의) 흐름, 해류; 전류
Current means happening, being used, or being done at the present time.

readout [rí:daut] n. (정보의) 해독, 판독; v. 정보를 송신하다
If an electronic measuring device gives you a readout, it displays information about the level of something such as a speed, height, or sound.

sweep [swi:p] v. (swept-swept) 훑다; 휩쓸고 가다; (빗자루로) 쓸다; n. 쓸기, 비질하기
To sweep means to look over every part of someone or something in one continuous movement of your eyes.

beep [bi:p] v. 삐 소리를 내다; (경적을) 울리다; n. 삑 (하는 소리)
If something such as a horn beeps, or you beep it, it makes a short, harsh sound.

click [klik] v. 딸깍 하는 소리를 내다; 분명해지다; n. 딸깍 (하는 소리)
If something clicks or if you click it, it makes a short, sharp sound.

dimension [diménʃən] n. 차원; 관점; 크기; (상황의) 규모
A dimension is a mode of linear extension of which there are three in space and two on a flat surface, which corresponds to one of a set of coordinates specifying the position of a point.

relate [riléit] v. 관계시키다; ~에 대하여 이야기하다 (relation n. 관련)
You can talk about something in relation to something else when you want to compare the size, condition, or position of the two things.

pan [pæn] v. (카메라로 찍어) 보여주다; n. (손잡이가 달린 얕은) 냄비
If you pan a film or television camera or if it pans somewhere, it moves slowly round so that a wide area is filmed.

device [diváis] n. 장치, 기구; 폭발물; 방법
A device is an object that has been invented for a particular purpose, for example for recording or measuring something.

exclaim [ikskléim] v. 소리치다, 외치다
If you exclaim, you cry out suddenly in surprise, strong emotion, or pain.

gobble [gabl] v. 게걸스럽게 먹다
If you gobble food, you eat it quickly and greedily.

cheer [ʧiər] v. 환호성을 지르다, 환호하다; n. 환호(성), 응원
When people cheer, they shout loudly to show their approval or to encourage someone who is doing something such as taking part in a game.

rush [rʌʃ] v. 급히 움직이다; 서두르다; n. (감정이 갑자기) 치밀어 오름; 혼잡; 기쁨, 흥분
If you rush somewhere, you go there quickly.

hang up idiom 전화를 끊다; ~을 중지하다
To hang up means to end a telephone conversation, often very suddenly.

immediate [imí:diət] a. 즉각적인; 당면한; 아주 가까이에 있는 (immediately ad. 즉시, 즉각)
If something happens immediately, it happens without any delay.

suit up idiom 유니폼을 입다
If you suit up, you put on the clothing that you wear to do a particular job, play, or a sport.

복
습 **weird** [wiərd] a. 기이한, 기묘한; 기괴한, 섬뜩한
If you describe something or someone as weird, you mean that they are strange.

복
습 **remote** [rimóut] n. (= remote control) 리모컨; 원격 조종; a. 먼; 외진, 외딴; 원격의
The remote control for a television or video recorder is the device that you use to control the machine from a distance, by pressing the buttons on it.

복
습 **hiss** [his] v. 쉿 하는 소리를 내다; (화난 어조로) 낮게 말하다; n. 쉭쉭거리는 소리
To hiss means to make a sound like a long 's.'

복
습 **reveal** [riví:l] v. (보이지 않던 것을) 드러내 보이다; (비밀 등을) 밝히다
If you reveal something that has been out of sight, you uncover it so that people can see it.

복
습 **mount** [maunt] v. 끼우다, 고정시키다; (자전거·말 등에) 올라타다; n. (전시품을 세우는) 판; 산
If you mount an object on something, you fix it there firmly.

복
습 **rip** [rip] v. 빠른 속도로 돌진하다; (갑자기) 찢다; (거칠게) 떼어 내다, 뜯어 내다; n. (길게) 찢어진 곳
To rip somewhere means to move forcefully and rapidly.

* **pier** [piər] n. 부두
A pier is a platform sticking out into water, usually the sea, which people walk along or use when getting onto or off boats.

nightstand [náitstænd] n. 침실용 탁자
A night stand is a small table or cupboard that you have next to your bed.

복
습 **drawer** [drɔːr] n. 서랍
A drawer is part of a desk, chest, or other piece of furniture that is shaped like a box and is designed for putting things in.

복
습 **blow** [blou] v. (blew-blown) (휑하니) 떠나다; 폭파하다; (바람·입김에) 날리다; n. 강타
To blow means to leave a place quickly.

dresser [drésər] n. 서랍장
A dresser is a chest of drawers, usually with a mirror on the top.

nonchalant [nànʃəlá:nt] a. 차분한; 태연한, 무심한 (nonchalantly ad. 태연하게, 무심하게)
If you describe someone as nonchalant, you mean that they appear not to worry or care about things and that they seem very calm.

toss [tɔːs] v. (가볍게) 던지다; (문제 등을) 가볍게 논하다; (고개를) 홱 쳐들다; n. 던지기
If you toss something somewhere, you throw it there lightly, often in a rather careless way.

renounce [rináuns] v. 포기하다; 그만두다, 끊다 (renunciation n. 포기)
If you renounce a claim, rank, or title, you officially give it up.

zip [zip] v. (어떤 방향으로) 쌩 하고 가다; 지퍼를 잠그다; n. 지퍼
If you say that something or someone zips somewhere, you mean that they move very fast.

downstairs [daunstéərz] ad. 아래층으로; n. 아래층
If you go downstairs in a building, you go down a staircase toward the ground floor.

glow [glou] v. 빛나다, 타다; (얼굴이) 상기되다; n. (은은한) 불빛; 홍조
If something glows, it produces a dull, steady light.

goggle [gagl] n. (pl.) 보호 안경, 고글
Goggles are large glasses that fit closely to your face around your eyes to protect them from such things as water, wind, or dust.

notice [nóutis] v. 알아채다, 인지하다; 주의하다; n. 신경 씀, 알아챔; 통지, 예고
If you notice something or someone, you become aware of them.

redundant [ridʌ́ndənt] a. 불필요한, 쓸모없는
Something that is redundant is no longer needed because its job is being done by something else or because its job is no longer necessary or useful.

driveway [dráivwèi] n. (주택의) 진입로
A driveway is a piece of hard ground that leads from the road to the front of a house or other building.

guard [gaːrd] v. 지키다, 보호하다; n. 경비 요원; 경비, 감시; 보호물
If you guard a place, person, or object, you stand near them in order to watch and protect them.

protective [prətéktiv] a. 보호하려고 하는; 보호용의 (protectively ad. 보호하려는 듯이)
If someone is protective toward you, they look after you and show a strong desire to keep you safe.

clutch [klʌʧ] v. (꽉) 움켜잡다; n. 움켜짐
If you clutch at something or clutch something, you hold it tightly, usually because you are afraid or anxious.

summon [sʌ́mən] v. 호출하다, (오라고) 부르다; (법원으로) 소환하다
If you summon someone, you order them to come to you.

managerial [mænidʒíəriəl] a. 경영의, 관리의
Managerial means relating to the work of a manager.

screw-up [skrúː-ʌp] n. 일을 망침, 실수
A screw-up is a situation in which someone makes a big mistake.

handle [hǽndl] v. (사람·작업 등을) 처리하다; 들다, 옮기다; n. 손잡이
If you say that someone can handle a problem or situation, you mean that they
have the ability to deal with it successfully.

mansion [mǽnʃən] n. 대저택, 저택
A mansion is a very large house.

power up idiom (기계가 작동하도록) ~에 전원을 넣다
If a machine powers up, or someone or something powers it up, it is switched on
and becomes ready to use.

take off idiom (서둘러) 떠나다; 날아오르다
To take off means to leave a place suddenly.

blast [blæst] v. 폭발시키다; 쾅쾅 울리다; 빠르게 가다; n. 폭발; (한 줄기의) 강한 바람
If someone blasts their way somewhere, they get there by shooting at people or
causing an explosion.

crack a smile idiom 미소를 짓다
If you crack a smile, you smile slightly.

knock [nak] v. 치다, 부딪치다; (문 등을) 두드리다; n. 문 두드리는 소리; 부딪침
To knock someone into a particular position or condition means to hit them very
hard so that they fall over or become unconscious.

cover [kʌ́vər] v. 덮다; 적당히 둘러대다; 씌우다, 가리다; n. 위장, 속임수; 몸을 숨길 곳; 덮개
If one thing covers another, it forms a layer over its surface.

slam [slæm] v. 쾅 닫다; 세게 치다; 놓다; n. 쾅 하고 닫기; 탕 하는 소리
If you slam a door or window or if it slams, it shuts noisily and with great force.

front door [frʌnt dɔ́ːr] n. (주택의) 현관
The front door of a house or other building is the main door, which is usually in
the wall that faces a street.

grab [græb] v. (와락·단단히) 붙잡다; 급히 ~하다; n. 와락 잡아채려고 함
If you grab something, you take it or pick it up suddenly and roughly.

crib [krib] n. 아기 침대; 구유, 여물통
A crib is a bed for a small baby.

shower [ʃáuər] n. 빗발침, 쏟아짐; 소나기; v. (작은 조각들을) 쏟아 붓다; 샤워를 하다
You can refer to a lot of things that are falling as a shower of them.

flash [flæʃ] n. 순간; (잠깐) 반짝임; v. 휙 내보이다; 휙 나타나다; (잠깐) 번쩍이다
If you say that something happens in a flash, you mean that it happens suddenly and lasts only a very short time.

hypnotize [hípnətàiz] v. 최면을 걸다; 혼을 빼놓다, 홀리다
If someone hypnotizes you, they put you into a state in which you seem to be asleep but can still see, hear, or respond to things said to you.

battle [bætl] v. 싸우다, 투쟁하다; n. 싸움; 전투
To battle with an opposing group means to take part in a fight or contest against them.

realize [ríːəlàiz] v. 깨닫다, 알아차리다; 실현하다, 달성하다
If you realize that something is true, you become aware of that fact or understand it.

force [fɔːrs] n. 작용력; 힘; 영향력; v. 억지로 ~하다; ~를 강요하다
Force is the power or strength which something has.

field [fiːld] n. ~장; 경기장; 들판, 밭
A magnetic, gravitational, or electric field is the area in which that particular force is strong enough to have an effect.

electrical [iléktrikəl] a. 전기에 관한, 전기의
Electrical energy is energy in the form of electricity.

crush [krʌʃ] v. 으스러뜨리다; 밀어 넣다; 좌절시키다; n. 홀딱 반함
To crush something means to press it very hard so that its shape is destroyed or so that it breaks into pieces.

dive [daiv] v. 급히 움직이다; (물 속으로) 뛰어들다; 급강하하다; n. 급강하; (물 속으로) 뛰어들기
If you dive in a particular direction or into a particular place, you jump or move there quickly.

secure [sikjúər] a. 안전한; 안심하는; v. 얻어 내다; (단단히) 고정시키다
If you secure a place, you make it safe from harm or attack.

‡ **command** [kəmǽnd] v. 명령하다, 지시하다; 지휘하다; n. 명령; 지휘, 통솔
If someone in authority commands you to do something, they tell you that you must do it.

‡ **identify** [aidéntəfài] v. (신원 등을) 확인하다; 찾다, 발견하다 (identification n. 식별; 신원 확인)
The identification of something is the recognition that it exists, is important, or is true.

₊ **horror** [hɔ́ːrər] n. 공포, 경악; ~의 참상
Horror is a feeling of great shock, fear, and worry caused by something extremely unpleasant.

₊ **restrain** [ristréin] v. 저지하다; (감정 등을) 억누르다
If you restrain someone, you stop them from doing what they intended or wanted to do, usually by using your physical strength.

struggle [strʌ́gl] v. 몸부림치다, 허우적거리다; 애쓰다; 힘겹게 나아가다; n. 투쟁, 분투; 몸부림
If you struggle when you are being held, you twist, kick, and move violently in order to get free.

lunge [lʌndʒ] v. 달려들다, 돌진하다; n. 돌진
If you lunge in a particular direction, you move in that direction suddenly and clumsily.

Check Your Reading Speed
1분에 몇 단어를 읽는지 리딩 속도를 측정해보세요.

$$\frac{1,819 \text{ words}}{\text{reading time } (\quad) \text{ sec}} \times 60 = (\quad) \text{ WPM}$$

Build Your Vocabulary

ballroom [bɔ́:lru:m] n. 무도회장
A ballroom is a very large room that is used for dancing.

physical [fízikəl] a. 신체의; 물질의, 물리적인 (physically ad. 신체적으로)
Physical qualities, actions, or things are connected with a person's body, rather than with their mind.

encounter [inkáuntər] n. 만남, 접촉; v. 맞닥뜨리다, 부딪히다; (우연히) 마주치다
An encounter with someone is a meeting with them, particularly one that is unexpected or significant.

crouch [krauʧ] v. (몸을) 쭈그리다, 쭈그리고 앉다; n. 쭈그리고 앉기
If you are crouching, your legs are bent under you so that you are close to the ground and leaning forward slightly.

ceiling [síːliŋ] n. 천장
A ceiling is the horizontal surface that forms the top part or roof inside a room.

notice [nóutis] v. 알아채다, 인지하다; 주의하다; n. 신경 씀, 알아챔; 통지, 예고
If you notice something or someone, you become aware of them.

fist [fist] n. 주먹
Your hand is referred to as your fist when you have bent your fingers in toward the palm in order to hit someone, to make an angry gesture, or to hold something.

punch [pʌnʧ] v. 주먹으로 치다; (자판·번호판 등을) 치다; n. 주먹으로 한 대 침
If you punch someone or something, you hit them hard with your fist.

react [riǽkt] v. 반응하다; 반응을 보이다
When you react to something that has happened to you, you behave in a particular way because of it.

^복_습 **block** [blak] v. 막다, 차단하다; 방해하다; n. 구역, 블록; 사각형 덩어리
To block a road, channel, or pipe means to put an object across it or in it so that nothing can pass through it or along it.

^복_습 **blur** [bləːr] n. 흐릿한 형체; v. 흐릿해지다; 모호해지다
A blur is a shape or area which you cannot see clearly because it has no distinct outline or because it is moving very fast.

^복_습 **spin** [spin] v. (빙빙) 돌다; 돌아서다; n. 회전
If something spins or if you spin it, it turns quickly around a central point.

^복_습 **jaw** [dʒɔː] n. 턱
Your jaw is the lower part of your face below your mouth.

^복_습 **snap** [snæp] v. 급히 움직이다; 툭 부러지다; 날카롭게 말하다; n. 탁 하는 소리
If you snap something into a particular position, or if it snaps into that position, it moves quickly into that position, with a sharp sound.

^복_습 **duck** [dʌk] v. (머리나 몸을) 휙 수그리다; 급히 움직이다; n. [동물] 오리
If you duck, you move your head or the top half of your body quickly downward to avoid something that might hit you, or to avoid being seen.

^복_습 **lunge** [lʌndʒ] v. 달려들다, 돌진하다; n. 돌진
If you lunge in a particular direction, you move in that direction suddenly and clumsily.

^복_습 **flip** [flip] v. 홱 뒤집다, 휙 젖히다; 툭 던지다; n. 회전; 툭 던지기
If something flips over, or if you flip it over or into a different position, it moves or is moved into a different position.

⁎ **doorway** [dɔ́ːrwèi] n. 출입구
A doorway is a space in a wall where a door opens and closes.

agile [ǽdʒəl] a. 날렵한, 민첩한; (생각이) 재빠른, 기민한 (agility n. 민첩)
Someone who is agile can move quickly and easily.

pit against idiom ~을 ~와 겨루게 하다
If you pit your skills, knowledge, or ability against someone, you use all your skill in order to deal successfully or compete with them.

^복_습 **whisper** [hwíspər] v. 속삭이다, 소곤거리다; n. 속삭임, 소곤거리는 소리
When you whisper, you say something very quietly, using your breath rather than your throat, so that only one person can hear you.

throw off guard idiom 방심하게 하다
If someone throws you off guard, they surprise you by doing something that you are not ready to deal with.

slap [slæp] v. 털썩 놓다; (손바닥으로) 철썩 때리다; n. 철썩 때리기, 치기
If you slap something onto a surface, you put it there quickly, roughly, or carelessly.

deck [dek] n. (배의) 갑판; 층; v. 꾸미다, 장식하다
A deck on a vehicle such as a bus or ship is a lower or upper area of it.

sign [sain] v. 서명하다; 신호를 보내다; n. 표지판; 몸짓; 기색, 흔적
When you sign a document, you write your name on it, usually at the end or in a special space.

ceremony [sérəmòuni] n. 의식, 의례
A ceremony is a formal event such as a wedding.

on board idiom 승선한, 탑승한
When you are on board a train, ship, or aircraft, you are on it or in it.

weird [wiərd] a. 기이한, 기묘한; 기괴한, 섬뜩한
If you describe something or someone as weird, you mean that they are strange.

shove [ʃʌv] v. (거칠게) 밀치다; 아무렇게나 놓다; n. 힘껏 떠밂
(shove off idiom 배를 물가에서 밀어내다)
If a boat shoves off, it moves away from the land into the water.

speed [spi:d] v. (sped-sped) 빨리 가다; 더 빠르게 하다; n. 속도
If you speed somewhere, you move or travel there quickly, usually in a vehicle.

lightning [láitniŋ] n. 번개, 번갯불; a. 아주 빨리; 급작스럽게
(like lightning idiom 번개처럼 빠르게)
Like lightning means very quickly.

pull over idiom (길 한쪽으로) 차를 대다
If a vehicle or driver pulls over, they stop by the side of the road.

figure out idiom ~을 이해하다, 알아내다; 계산하다, 산출하다
If you figure out someone or something, you come to understand them by thinking carefully.

challenge [ʧǽlindʒ] n. 도전; 저항; v. 도전하다; 도전 의식을 북돋우다
A challenge is something new and difficult which requires great effort and determination.

* **analyze** [ǽnəlàiz] v. 분석하다; 분해하다
If you analyze something, you consider it carefully or use statistical methods in order to fully understand it.

복습 **transform** [trænsfɔ́ːrm] v. 변형시키다; 완전히 바꿔 놓다
To transform something into something else means to change or convert it into that thing.

복습 **rapid** [rǽpid] a. (속도가) 빠른; (행동이) 민첩한 (rapidly ad. 빠르게, 신속히)
A rapid movement is one that is very fast.

복습 **confident** [kánfədənt] a. 확신하는; 자신감 있는
If you are confident that something is true, you are sure that it is true.

복습 **take on** idiom (일 등을) 맡다; (책임을) 지다; ~와 싸우다
If you take on something, you agree to be responsible for it.

복습 **pier** [piər] n. 부두
A pier is a platform sticking out into water, usually the sea, which people walk along or use when getting onto or off boats.

pull away idiom (차량이) 움직이기 시작하다
When a vehicle pulls away, it begins to move.

* **dock** [dak] n. 부두, 선창; v. (배를) 부두에 대다
A dock is an enclosed area in a harbor where ships go to be loaded, unloaded, and repaired.

복습 **disappoint** [disəpɔ́int] v. 실망시키다, 실망을 안겨 주다; 좌절시키다
(disappointed a. 실망한, 낙담한)
If you are disappointed, you are rather sad because something has not happened or because something is not as good as you had hoped.

복습 **launch** [lɔ:nʧ] v. 발사하다; 시작하다; n. 시작; 발사; 개시, 진수
To launch a rocket, missile, or satellite means to send it into the air or into space.

복습 **edge** [edʒ] n. 끝, 가장자리; 우위; v. 조금씩 움직이다; 테두리를 두르다
The edge of something is the place or line where it stops, or the part of it that is furthest from the middle.

복습 **jet** [dʒet] v. 급속히 움직이다; 분출하다; n. 제트기; 분출
If you jet somewhere, you travel there in a fast plane.

catch up idiom 따라잡다, 따라가다; (소식 등을) 듣다
If you catch someone or something up, you go faster so that you reach them in front of you.

pull up idiom (차량·운전자가) 멈추다, 서다
If a vehicle or driver pulls up, they stop.

alongside [əlɔ́ŋsàid] prep. ~옆에, 나란히; ~와 함께; ~와 동시에
If one thing is alongside another thing, the first thing is next to the second.

eject [idʒékt] v. 탈출하다; 쫓아내다, 내쫓다; 튀어나오게 하다 (ejector seat n. 비상 탈출 좌석)
An ejector seat is a special seat which can throw the pilot out of a fast military aircraft in an emergency.

dashboard [dǽʃbɔːrd] n. (승용차의) 계기판
The dashboard in a car is the panel facing the driver's seat where most of the instruments and switches are.

activate [ǽktəvèit] v. 작동시키다; 활성화시키다
If a device or process is activated, something causes it to start working.

urge [əːrdʒ] v. 충고하다, 설득하려 하다; 재촉하다; n. (강한) 욕구, 충동
If you urge someone to do something, you try hard to persuade them to do it.

max [mæks] a. (= maximum) (크기·빠르기 등이) 최대의; n. (양·규모·속도 등의) 최고
If you say that someone does something to the maximum, you are emphasizing that they do it to the greatest degree possible.

maximum [mǽksəməm] a. 최고의, 최대의
You use maximum to describe an amount which is the largest that is possible, allowed, or required.

be in for a treat idiom 좋아하게 되다
If you say someone is in for a treat, you know they are going to enjoy something.

accelerate [æksélərèit] v. 속도를 높이다, 가속화되다
When a moving vehicle accelerates, it goes faster and faster.

gigantic [dʒaigǽntik] a. 거대한
If you describe something as gigantic, you are emphasizing that it is extremely large in size, amount, or degree.

emerge [imɔ́ːrdʒ] v. 나오다, 모습을 드러내다; (어려움 등을) 헤쳐 나오다
To emerge means to come out from an enclosed or dark space such as a room or a vehicle, or from a position where you could not be seen.

hull [hʌl] n. (배의) 선체; v. (콩 등의) 껍질을 벗기다
The hull of a boat or tank is the main body of it.

surface [sə́:rfis] n. 수면, 표면, 지면; 외관; v. 수면으로 올라오다; (갑자기) 나타나다
The surface of something is the flat top part of it or the outside of it.

slip [slip] v. 슬며시 가다; 미끄러지다; (옷 등을) 재빨리 벗다; n. (작은) 실수; 미끄러짐
If you slip somewhere, you go there quickly and quietly.

corridor [kɔ́:ridər] n. 복도; 통로
A corridor is a long passage in a building or train, with doors and rooms on one or both sides.

vanish [vǽniʃ] v. 사라지다, 없어지다; 모습을 감추다
If someone or something vanishes, they disappear suddenly or in a way that cannot be explained.

suck it up idiom (좋지 않은 일을) 잘 받아들이다
If you suck it up, you accept something bad and deal with it well, controlling your emotions.

be up to idiom ~에 달려 있다; (특히 나쁜 짓을) 하고 있다
If something is up to you, you responsible for a particular duty.

amuse [əmjúːz] v. 즐겁게 하다, 재미있게 하다 (amused a. 재미있어 하는)
If you are amused by something, it makes you want to laugh or smile.

scowl [skaul] v. 노려보다, 쏘아보다; n. 노려봄, 쏘아봄
When someone scowls, an angry or hostile expression appears on their face.

sarcastic [saːrkǽstik] a. 빈정대는, 비꼬는; 풍자적인 (sarcastically ad. 비꼬는 투로)
Someone who is sarcastic says or does the opposite of what they really mean in order to mock or insult someone.

command [kəmǽnd] n. 명령; 지휘, 통솔; v. 명령하다, 지시하다; 지휘하다
A command is an order, especially one given by a soldier.

spot [spat] v. 발견하다, 찾다, 알아채다; n. (특정한) 곳; (작은) 점
If you spot something or someone, you notice them.

conference [kánfərəns] n. 회의, 학회; 회견
A conference is a meeting at which formal discussions take place.

^복^습 **track** [træk] v. 추적하다, 뒤쫓다; n. (기차) 선로; 경주로, 트랙; 자국 (tracker n. 추적 장치)
A tracker is a device that follows and records the movements of someone or something.

* **delegate** [déligət] n. 대표; v. (권한·업무 등을) 위임하다; (대표를) 뽑다
A delegate is a person who is chosen to vote or make decisions on behalf of a group of other people, especially at a conference or a meeting.

^복^습 **gather** [gǽðər] v. (사람들이) 모이다; (여기저기 있는 것을) 모으다
If people gather somewhere or if someone gathers people somewhere, they come together in a group.

^복^습 **massive** [mǽsiv] a. (육중하면서) 거대한; 엄청나게 심각한
Something that is massive is very large in size, quantity, or extent.

^복^습 **oversized** [óuvərsàizd] a. 너무 큰; 특대의
Oversize or oversized things are too big, or much bigger than usual.

^복^습 **spectacular** [spektǽkjulər] a. 장관을 이루는; 극적인; n. 화려한 쇼
Something that is spectacular is very impressive or dramatic.

waterline [wɔ́:tərlain] n. 수면과 선체와의 교차선
The waterline is a line, either real or imaginary, on the side of a ship representing the level the water reaches when the ship is at sea.

* **respective** [rispéktiv] a. 각각의, 각자의
Respective means relating or belonging separately to the individual people you have just mentioned.

lapel [ləpél] n. (양복 상의의 접혀 있는) 옷깃
The lapels of a jacket or coat are the two top parts at the front that are folded back on each side and join on to the collar.

^복^습 **mask** [mæsk] n. 마스크; 가면; v. 가면을 쓰다; (감정·냄새·사실 등을) 가리다
A mask is a piece of cloth or other material, which you wear over your face so that people cannot see who you are, or so that you look like someone or something else.

^복^습 **master** [mǽstər] a. 가장 큰, 주요한; n. 달인; 주인; v. ~을 완전히 익히다
Master means first in order of importance.

^복^습 **security** [sikjúərəti] n. 보안, 경비; 경비 담당 부서; 안도감, 안심
Security refers to all the measures that are taken to protect a place, or to ensure that only people with permission enter it or leave it.

INCREDIBLES 2

multiple [mʌ́ltəpl] a. 많은, 다수의; 복합적인; n. 배수
You use multiple to describe things that consist of many parts, involve many people, or have many uses.

vision [víʒən] n. 시력, 시야; 환상; 상상력; 통찰력 (night vision n. 야간 시력)
Night vision equipment enables people, for example soldiers or pilots, to see better at night.

capability [kèipəbíləti] n. 능력, 역량
If you have the capability or the capabilities to do something, you have the ability or the qualities that are necessary to do it.

cue [kju:] v. 신호를 주다; n. 신호; 실마리, 암시
If one performer cues another, they say or do something which is a signal for the second performer to begin speaking, playing, or doing something.

go time idiom ~을 할 시간이다
You can say 'It's go time,' when the time has arrived to undertake a task that is often unseemly, difficult, or requiring courage, at which point there is no going back.

broadcast [brɔ́:dkæst] v. 방송하다; 널리 알리다, 광고하다; n. 방송
To broadcast a program means to send it out by radio waves, so that it can be heard on the radio or seen on television.

globe [gloub] n. 세계; 구체; 지구
You can refer to the world as the globe when you are emphasizing how big it is or that something happens in many different parts of it.

momentous [mouméntəs] a. 중대한, 중요한
If you refer to a decision, event, or change as momentous, you mean that it is very important, often because of the effects that it will have in the future.

occasion [əkéiʒən] n. 특별한 일, 행사; 경우, 기회
An occasion is an important event, ceremony, or celebration.

accomplish [əkámpliʃ] v. 완수하다, 성취하다, 해내다
If you accomplish something, you succeed in doing it.

rare [rɛər] a. 드문, 보기 힘든; 진귀한, 희귀한
An event or situation that is rare does not occur very often.

crowd [kraud] n. 사람들, 군중; v. 가득 메우다; 바싹 붙어 서다
A crowd is a large group of people who have gathered together, for example to watch or listen to something interesting, or to protest about something.

^{복습} **chuckle** [tʃʌkl] v. 킬킬 웃다; 빙그레 웃다; n. 킬킬거림; 속으로 웃기
When you chuckle, you laugh quietly.

* **undo** [ʌndúː] v. 원상태로 돌리다, (묶인 것을) 풀다
To undo something that has been done means to reverse its effect.

* **extraordinary** [ikstrɔ́ːrdənèri] a. 보기 드문, 비범한; 기이한, 놀라운
(extraordinarily ad. 비상하게, 엄청나게)
If you describe something or someone as extraordinary, you mean that they have
some extremely good or special quality.

‡ **gift** [gift] v. (재능 등을) 부여하다; n. 재능, 재주; 선물 (gifted a. 재능이 있는)
Someone who is gifted has a natural ability to do something well.

‡‡ **treat** [triːt] v. (특정한 태도로) 대하다; 여기다, 치부하다; n. (대접하여 하는) 특별한 것, 대접
If you treat someone or something in a particular way, you behave toward them
or deal with them in that way.

^{복습} **benefit** [bénəfit] v. (~에서) 득을 보다; 유익하다; n. 혜택, 이득
If you benefit from something or if it benefits you, it helps you or improves your
life.

^{복습} **go on** idiom 말을 계속하다; (어떤 상황이) 계속되다; 자자, 어서
To go on means to continue speaking after a short pause.

^{복습} **ambassador** [æmbǽsədər] n. 대사
An ambassador is an important official who lives in a foreign country and
represents his or her own country's interests there.

^{복습} **support** [səpɔ́ːrt] n. 지지, 지원; 버팀대; v. 지지하다; (넘어지지 않도록) 떠받치다
If you give support to someone during a difficult or unhappy time, you are kind
to them and help them.

* **accord** [əkɔ́ːrd] n. (기관·국가 간의 공식적인) 합의; v. (권위·지위 등을) 부여하다
An accord between countries or groups of people is a formal agreement, for
example to end a war.

* **gasp** [gæsp] v. 헉 하고 숨을 쉬다; 숨을 제대로 못 쉬다; n. 헉 하는 소리를 냄
When you gasp, you take a short quick breath through your mouth, especially
when you are surprised, shocked, or in pain.

‡‡ **corner** [kɔ́ːrnər] v. (구석에) 가두다, (궁지에) 몰아넣다; n. 모퉁이; 구석
If you corner a person or animal, you force them into a place they cannot escape
from.

deflect [diflékt] v. 빗나가게 하다; ~를 막다; 모면하다
If you deflect something that is moving, you make it go in a slightly different direction, for example by hitting or blocking it.

realize [ríːəlàiz] v. 깨닫다, 알아차리다; 실현하다, 달성하다
If you realize that something is true, you become aware of that fact or understand it.

dart [daːrt] v. 쏜살같이 움직이다; 흘깃 쳐다보다; n. (작은) 화살; 쏜살같이 달림
If a person or animal darts somewhere, they move there suddenly and quickly.

be about to idiom 막 ~하려는 참이다
If you are about to do something, you are going to do it immediately.

take off idiom (서둘러) 떠나다; 날아오르다
To take off means to leave a place suddenly.

growl [graul] v. 으르렁거리다; 으르렁거리듯 말하다; n. 으르렁거리는 소리
When a dog or other animal growls, it makes a low noise in its throat, usually because it is angry.

fireball [fáiərbɔːl] n. 불덩이, 화구
A fireball is a ball of fire, for example one at the center of a nuclear explosion.

state [steit] n. 상태; 국가, 나라; 주(州); v. 말하다, 진술하다
When you talk about the state of someone or something, you are referring to the condition they are in or what they are like at a particular time.

set off idiom (경보 장치를) 울리다; 출발하다
If you set off something, you cause it to operate, especially by accident.

sprinkler [spríŋklə:r] n. 물을 뿌리는 장치, 살수 장치
A sprinkler is a device used to spray water. Sprinklers are used to water plants or grass, or to put out fires in buildings.

blaze [bleiz] v. 활활 타다; 눈부시게 빛나다; n. 불길; 휘황찬란한 빛
When a fire blazes, it burns strongly and brightly.

frustrate [frʌstreit] v. 좌절감을 주다, 불만스럽게 하다; 방해하다
(frustrated a. 좌절감을 느끼는)
If something frustrates you, it upsets or angers you because you are unable to do anything about the problems it creates.

put out idiom (불을) 끄다
If you put out something, especially a fire, you make it stop burning.

foam [foum] n. 거품; v. 거품을 일으키다
Foam consists of a mass of small bubbles that are formed when air and a liquid are mixed together.

ooze [uːz] v. (액체가) 흐르다; (특징·자질 등을) 줄줄 흘리다; n. (아주 조금씩) 스며 나오는 것
When a thick or sticky liquid oozes from something or when something oozes it, the liquid flows slowly and in small quantities.

extinguish [ikstíŋwiʃ] v. (불을) 끄다; 끝내다, 없애다
If you extinguish a fire or a light, you stop it burning or shining.

flame [fleim] n. 불길, 불꽃; 격정; v. 활활 타오르다; 시뻘게지다
A flame is a hot bright stream of burning gas that comes from something that is burning.

giggle [gigl] v. 피식 웃다, 킥킥거리다; n. 피식 웃음, 킥킥거림
If someone giggles, they laugh in a childlike way, because they are amused, nervous, or embarrassed.

lick [lik] v. 핥다; 핥아먹다; n. 한 번 핥기, 핥아먹기
When people or animals lick something, they move their tongue across its surface.

retardant [ritáːrdənt] n. 지연제; a. 저지하는
A retardant is any substance capable of reducing the speed of a given reaction.

vent [vent] n. 통풍구, 환기구; v. (감정·분통을) 터뜨리다
A vent is a hole in something through which air can come in and smoke, gas, or smells can go out.

relative [rélətiv] a. 비교적인; 상대적인; 관계가 있는; n. 친척 (relatively ad. 비교적)
Relatively means to a certain degree, especially when compared with other things of the same kind.

smash [smæʃ] v. 박살내다; (세게) 부딪치다; 부서지다; n. 박살내기; 요란한 소리
If you smash something or if it smashes, it breaks into many pieces, for example when it is hit or dropped.

squeeze [skwiːz] v. (꼭) 쥐다; (좁은 곳에) 비집고 들어가다; n. (손으로 꼭) 쥐기
If you squeeze something, you press it firmly, usually with your hands.

distance [dístəns] n. 먼 곳; 거리; v. (~에) 관여하지 않다
If you are at a distance from something, or if you see it or remember it from a distance, you are a long way away from it in space or time.

trap [træp] v. (위험한 장소에) 가두다; (함정으로) 몰아넣다; n. 함정; 덫
If you are trapped somewhere, something falls onto you or blocks your way and prevents you from moving or escaping.

whine [hwain] v. 징징거리다, 우는 소리를 하다; 낑낑거리다; n. 칭얼거리는 소리; 불평
If you say that someone is whining, you mean that they are complaining in an annoying way about something unimportant.

yell [jel] v. 고함치다, 소리 지르다; n. 고함, 외침
If you yell, you shout loudly, usually because you are excited, angry, or in pain.

burst [bəːrst] v. (burst-burst) 불쑥 움직이다; 갑자기 ~하다; n. (갑자기) ~을 함; 파열, 폭발
To burst into or out of a place means to enter or leave it suddenly with a lot of energy or force.

num [nʌm] int. 냠냠
Num is used to express pleasure at eating, or at the prospect of eating.

coax [kouks] v. 구슬리다, 달래다
If you coax someone into doing something, you gently try to persuade them to do it.

crash [kræʃ] v. 부딪치다; 충돌하다; 굉음을 내다; n. (자동차·항공기) 사고; 요란한 소리
If something crashes somewhere, it moves and hits something else violently, making a loud noise.

chase [ʧeis] v. 뒤쫓다, 추적하다; 추구하다; n. 추적, 추격; 추구함
If you chase someone, or chase after them, you run after them or follow them quickly in order to catch or reach them.

sight [sait] n. 광경, 모습; 보기; 시력; v. 갑자기 보다 (out of sight idiom 보이지 않는 곳에)
If someone or something is out of sight, you cannot see them.

crawl [krɔːl] v. 기어가다; 우글거리다; n. 기어가기
When you crawl, you move forward on your hands and knees.

peek [piːk] v. 살짝 보이다; (재빨리) 훔쳐보다; n. 엿보기
If someone or something peeks from somewhere, they stick out slightly and are partly seen.

toddle [tadl] v. (어린 아이가) 아장아장 걷다
When a child toddles, it walks unsteadily with short quick steps.

hallway [hɔ́ːlwèi] n. 복도; 통로; 현관
A hallway in a building is a long passage with doors into rooms on both sides of it.

get away idiom 도망치다; ~로부터 벗어나다
If you get away from someone or somewhere, you escape from them or there.

expand [ikspǽnd] v. 확대시키다, 팽창시키다; 더 상세히 하다
If something expands or is expanded, it becomes larger.

penetrate [pénətrèit] v. 뚫고 들어가다; 간파하다; 침투하다
If something or someone penetrates a physical object or an area, they succeed in getting into it or passing through it.

separate [sépərèit] v. 분리하다, 나누다; 갈라지다; a. 별개의; 분리된
If you separate people or things that are together, or if they separate, they move apart.

announce [ənáuns] v. 선언하다; 발표하다, 알리다
If you announce something, you tell people about it publicly or officially.

applaud [əplɔ́:d] v. 박수를 치다; 갈채를 보내다
When a group of people applaud, they clap their hands in order to show approval, for example when they have enjoyed a play or concert.

pose [pouz] v. 자세를 취하다; (위협·문제 등을) 제기하다; n. 포즈, 자세
If you pose for a photograph or painting, you stay in a particular position so that someone can photograph you or paint you.

historic [histɔ́:rik] a. 역사적으로 중요한, 역사적인
Something that is historic is important in history, or likely to be considered important at some time in the future.

hypnotic [hipnátik] a. 최면을 일으키는, 최면성의
Something that is hypnotic holds your attention or makes you feel sleepy, often because it involves repeated sounds, pictures, or movements.

instant [ínstənt] a. 즉각적인; n. 순간, 아주 짧은 동안 (instantly ad. 즉각, 즉시)
You use instant to describe something that happens immediately.

lock [lak] v. 고정시키다; (자물쇠로) 잠그다; n. 잠금장치
If you lock something in a particular position or if it lock there, it is held or fitted firmly in that position.

press [pres] v. 누르다; (무엇에) 바짝 대다; 꾹 밀어 넣다; n. 언론
If you press a button or switch, you push it with your finger in order to make a machine or device work.

^복_습 **switch** [swiʧ] v. 전환하다, 바꾸다; n. 스위치; 전환
If you switch to something different, for example to a different system, task, or subject of conversation, you change to it from what you were doing or saying before.

[*] **shot** [ʃat] n. (카메라가 담는) 장면; 사진; 시도; 발사
A shot is a photograph or a particular sequence of pictures in a film.

mandate [mǽndeit] v. 명령하다, 지시하다; 권한을 주다; n. 지시, 명령; 권한
To mandate means to order someone to do something.

[*] **bitter** [bítər] a. 억울해 하는; 신랄한; 쓰라린; 맛이 쓴
If someone is bitter after a disappointing experience or after being treated unfairly, they continue to feel angry about it.

^복_습 **serve** [səːrv] v. (어떤 조직·국가 등을 위해) 일하다; (음식을) 제공하다; (상품·서비스를) 제공하다
If you serve your country, an organization, or a person, you do useful work for them.

^복_습 **fit** [fit] a. 적합한, 알맞은; 건강한; v. (모양·크기가) 맞다; 어울리게 하다; 적절하다
If something is fit for a particular purpose, it is suitable for that purpose.

[*] **survive** [sərváiv] v. 살아남다, 생존하다
If a person or living thing survives in a dangerous situation such as an accident or an illness, they do not die.

^복_습 **static** [stǽtik] n. (수신기의) 잡음; 정전기; a. 고정된; 정지 상태의
If there is static on the radio or television, you hear a series of loud noises which spoils the sound.

^복_습 **signal** [sígnəl] n. 신호; 징조; v. (동작·소리로) 신호를 보내다; 암시하다
A signal is a series of radio waves, light waves, or changes in electrical current which may carry information.

Chapters
20 & 21

1. **What did Mr. Incredible do while he was hypnotized?**
   A. He communicated with Elastigirl by radio.
   B. He locked the ship's officers in a closet.
   C. He moved the delegates to the top deck.
   D. He broke the ship's steering wheel.

2. **What did Winston do when he came out of hypnosis?**
   A. He escaped from the jet.
   B. He followed Evelyn's orders.
   C. He ran away from the Supers.
   D. He continued the live broadcast.

3. **How did Evelyn try to fight off Elastigirl?**
   A. She pushed Elastigirl through portals.
   B. She covered Elastigirl's face with an oxygen mask.
   C. She moved the jet up to a high altitude.
   D. She made the jet fly backward.

4. **What was part of the Supers' plan to stop the ship from crashing?**
   A. Using their Super powers to fix the steering wheel
   B. Putting something big and heavy in front of the ship
   C. Destroying the engine by freezing it with ice
   D. Making the ship turn by pushing the rudder

5. **What happened when Evelyn fell out of the jet?**
   A. She begged Elastigirl to save her.
   B. She did not want Elastigirl to help her.
   C. Elastigirl flew the jet toward her.
   D. Elastigirl threw a parachute to her.

Check Your Reading Speed
1분에 몇 단어를 읽는지 리딩 속도를 측정해보세요.

$$\frac{1{,}075 \text{ words}}{\text{reading time (} \quad \text{) sec}} \times 60 = (\quad) \text{ WPM}$$

Build Your Vocabulary

shift [ʃift] v. 바꾸다; (장소를) 옮기다; n. 교대 근무 (시간); 변화
If you shift, you move your body or a part of your body slightly, for example because you are bored.

cover [kʌ́vər] v. 적당히 둘러대다; 덮다; 씌우다, 가리다; n. 위장, 속임수; 몸을 숨길 곳; 덮개
If you cover for someone who is doing something secret or illegal, you give false information or do not give all the information you have, in order to protect them.

interrupt [intərʌ́pt] v. 중단시키다; (말·행동을) 방해하다; 차단하다
If someone or something interrupts a process or activity, they stop it for a period of time.

broadcast [brɔ́:dkæst] n. 방송; v. 방송하다; 널리 알리다, 광고하다
A broadcast is a program, performance, or speech on the radio or on television.

alarm [əlá:rm] v. 불안하게 하다; 경보장치를 달다; n. 경보 장치; 불안, 공포
(alarming a. 걱정스러운, 두려운)
Something that is alarming makes you feel afraid or anxious that something unpleasant or dangerous might happen.

technical [téknikəl] a. 기술적인; 구체적인
Technical means involving the sorts of machines, processes, and materials that are used in industry, transport, and communications.

bear [bɛər] v. 참다, 견디다; (책임 등을) 떠맡다; (아이를) 낳다; n. [동물] 곰
(bear with idiom 참아주다)
If you bear with someone, you are patient and wait while they do something.

exit [égzit] v. 나가다, 떠나다; 퇴장하다; n. (고속도로의) 출구; (공공건물의) 출구; 퇴장
If you exit from a room or building, you leave it.

conference [kánfərəns] n. 회의, 학회; 회견
A conference is a meeting at which formal discussions take place.

INCREDIBLES 2

lock [lak] v. (자물쇠로) 잠그다; 고정시키다; n. 잠금장치
When you lock something such as a door, drawer, or case, you fasten it, usually with a key, so that other people cannot open it.

delegate [déligət] n. 대표; v. (권한·업무 등을) 위임하다; (대표를) 뽑다
A delegate is a person who is chosen to vote or make decisions on behalf of a group of other people, especially at a conference or a meeting.

hypnotize [hípnətàiz] v. 최면을 걸다; 혼을 빼놓다, 홀리다
If someone hypnotizes you, they put you into a state in which you seem to be asleep but can still see, hear, or respond to things said to you.

robotic [roubátik] a. 로봇 같은; 로봇식의 (robotically ad. 로봇같이)
You can use robotic for describing very stiff movements of someone's body, for example in some types of modern dancing.

march [maːrʧ] v. (단호한 태도로 급히) 걸어가다; 행진하다; n. 행군, 행진; 3월
If you say that someone marches somewhere, you mean that they walk there quickly and in a determined way, for example because they are angry.

deck [dek] n. (배의) 갑판; 층; v. 꾸미다, 장식하다
A deck on a vehicle such as a bus or ship is a lower or upper area of it.

command [kəmǽnd] n. 지휘, 통솔; 명령; v. 명령하다, 지시하다; 지휘하다
A command can refer to control over someone or something and responsibility for them.

disarm [disáːrm] v. 무장을 해제하다; 무력하게 하다
To disarm a person or group means to take away all their weapons.

officer [ɔ́ːfisər] n. 고급 선원; 경찰관; 순경; 장교
In the armed forces, an officer is a person in a position of authority.

guard [gaːrd] n. 경비, 감시; 경비 요원; 보호물; v. 지키다, 보호하다
(on guard idiom 경계근무 중인)
If someone is on guard, they are on duty and responsible for guarding a particular place or person.

radio [réidiòu] n. 무선 통신 장치, 무전기; 무전; 라디오; v. 무선 연락을 하다, 무전을 보내다
A radio is a piece of equipment that is used for sending and receiving messages.

hold off idiom 미루다, 연기하다; ~을 물리치다
If you hold off doing something, you deliberately delay doing it.

forcible [fɔ́:rsəbl] a. 물리력에 의한, 강제적인 (forcibly ad. 강제로)
Forcible action involves physical force or violence.

bridge [bridʒ] n. [항해] 선교, 함교; 다리; v. 다리를 놓다
The bridge is the place on a ship from which it is steered.

fling [fliŋ] v. (flung-flung) (힘껏) 던지다; (머리·팔 등을) 휘두르다; n. (한바탕) 실컷 즐기기
If you fling something somewhere, you throw it there using a lot of force.

rip [rip] v. (거칠게) 떼어 내다, 뜯어 내다; (갑자기) 찢다; 빠른 속도로 돌진하다; n. (길게) 찢어진 곳
If you rip something away, you remove it quickly and forcefully.

equipment [ikwípmənt] n. 장비, 용품; 준비, 채비
Equipment consists of the things which are used for a particular purpose, for example a hobby or job.

steer [stiər] v. (보트·자동차 등을) 조종하다; (특정 방향으로) 움직이다
When you steer a car, boat, or plane, you control it so that it goes in the direction that you want.

wheel [hwi:l] n. (배의) 타륜; (자동차 등의) 핸들; 바퀴; v. (바퀴 달린 것을) 밀다
The wheel of a car or other vehicle is the circular object that is used to steer it.

crush [krʌʃ] v. 으스러뜨리다; 밀어 넣다; 좌절시키다; n. 홀딱 반함
To crush something means to press it very hard so that its shape is destroyed or so that it breaks into pieces.

current [kə́:rənt] a. 현재의, 지금의; n. (물·공기의) 흐름, 해류; 전류
Current means happening, being used, or being done at the present time.

trajectory [trədʒéktəri] n. 궤도, 궤적; 곡선, 호(弧)
The trajectory of a moving object is the path that it follows as it moves.

barge [ba:rdʒ] v. 밀치고 가다; n. 바지선
If you barge into a place or barge through it, you rush or push into it in a rough and rude way.

think twice idiom 망설이다; 재고하다, 숙고하다
If you do not think twice, you do something immediately, without considering whether it is a good idea.

instant [ínstənt] a. 즉각적인; n. 순간, 아주 짧은 동안 (instantly ad. 즉각, 즉시)
You use instant to describe something that happens immediately.

field [fiːld] n. ~장; 경기장; 들판, 밭
A magnetic, gravitational, or electric field is the area in which that particular force is strong enough to have an effect.

deflect [diflékt] v. 빗나가게 하다; ~를 막다; 모면하다
If you deflect something that is moving, you make it go in a slightly different direction, for example by hitting or blocking it.

blow [blou] n. 강타; v. 폭파하다; (휑하니) 떠나다; (바람·입김에) 날리다
If someone receives a blow, they are hit with a fist or weapon.

stare [stɛər] v. 빤히 쳐다보다, 응시하다; n. 빤히 쳐다보기, 응시
If you stare at someone or something, you look at them for a long time.

curious [kjúəriəs] a. 궁금한, 호기심이 많은; 별난, 특이한 (curiously ad. 신기한 듯이)
If you are curious about something, you are interested in it and want to know more about it.

transparent [trænspɛ́ərənt] a. 투명한; 명쾌한, 명백한
If an object or substance is transparent, you can see through it.

recognize [rékəgnaiz] v. 알아보다; 인식하다; 공인하다
If you recognize someone or something, you know who that person is or what that thing is.

penetrate [pénətrèit] v. 뚫고 들어가다; 간파하다; 침투하다
If something or someone penetrates a physical object or an area, they succeed in getting into it or passing through it.

float [flout] v. (물 위나 공중에서) 떠가다; (물에) 뜨다; n. 부표
Something that floats in or through the air hangs in it or moves slowly and gently through it.

confuse [kənfjúːz] v. (사람을) 혼란시키다; 혼동하다 (confused a. 혼란스러워하는)
If you are confused, you do not know exactly what is happening or what to do.

upside down [ápsàid dáun] ad. (아래위가) 거꾸로
If something has been moved upside down, it has been turned round so that the part that is usually lowest is above the part that is usually highest.

gaze [geiz] v. (가만히) 응시하다, 바라보다; n. 응시, (눈여겨보는) 시선
If you gaze at someone or something, you look steadily at them for a long time.

frown [fraun] v. 얼굴을 찡그리다; 눈살을 찌푸리다; n. 찡그림, 찌푸림
When someone frowns, their eyebrows become drawn together, because they are annoyed, worried, or puzzled, or because they are concentrating.

glow [glou] v. 빛나다, 타다; (얼굴이) 상기되다; n. (은은한) 불빛; 홍조
If something glows, it produces a dull, steady light.

goggle [gagl] n. (pl.) 보호 안경, 고글
Goggles are large glasses that fit closely to your face around your eyes to protect them from such things as water, wind, or dust.

yank [jæŋk] v. 홱 잡아당기다; n. 홱 잡아당기기
If you yank someone or something somewhere, you pull them there suddenly and with a lot of force.

blink [bliŋk] v. 눈을 깜박이다; (불빛이) 깜박거리다; n. 눈을 깜박거림
When you blink or when you blink your eyes, you shut your eyes and very quickly open them again.

trance [træns] n. 최면 상태; 실신; 무아지경
A trance is a state of mind in which someone seems to be asleep and to have no conscious control over their thoughts or actions, but in which they can see and hear things and respond to commands given by other people.

furious [fjúəriəs] a. 몹시 화가 난; 맹렬한
Someone who is furious is extremely angry.

lunge [lʌndʒ] v. 달려들다, 돌진하다; n. 돌진
If you lunge in a particular direction, you move in that direction suddenly and clumsily.

spell [spel] n. 주문; 마법; v. (어떤 단어의) 철자를 쓰다; 철자를 맞게 쓰다
A spell is a situation in which events are controlled by a magical power.

rage [reidʒ] n. 격렬한 분노; v. 몹시 화를 내다; 맹렬히 계속되다
Rage is strong anger that is difficult to control.

get one's bearings idiom 주위를 살피다; 자신의 위치를 알다
If you get your bearings, you find out where you are or what you should do next.

defensive [difénsiv] a. 방어적인; 방어의 (defensively ad. 방어적으로)
Someone who is defensive is behaving in a way that shows they feel unsure or threatened.

^복^습 **toss** [tɔːs] v. (가볍게) 던지다; (문제 등을) 가볍게 논하다; (고개를) 홱 쳐들다; n. 던지기
If you toss something somewhere, you throw it there lightly, often in a rather careless way.

^복^습 **suit** [suːt] n. (특정한 활동 때 입는) 옷; 정장; 소송; v. ~에게 편리하다; 어울리다
A particular type of suit is a piece of clothing that you wear for a particular activity.

^복^습 **master** [mǽstər] a. 가장 큰, 주요한; n. 달인; 주인; v. ~을 완전히 익히다
Master means first in order of importance.

^복^습 **activate** [ǽktəvèit] v. 작동시키다; 활성화시키다
If a device or process is activated, something causes it to start working.

^복^습 **spring** [spriŋ] v. 휙 움직이다; 튀다; n. 샘; 봄; 생기, 활기
If something springs in a particular direction, it moves suddenly and quickly.

^복^습 **phase** [feiz] n. (변화·발달의) 단계; v. 단계적으로 하다
A phase is a particular stage in a process or in the gradual development of something.

^복^습 **announce** [ənáuns] v. 선언하다; 발표하다, 알리다
If you announce something, you tell people about it publicly or officially.

^복^습 **battle** [bætl] v. 싸우다, 투쟁하다; n. 싸움; 전투
To battle with an opposing group means to take part in a fight or contest against them.

^복^습 **remove** [rimúːv] v. (옷 등을) 벗다; 없애다, 제거하다; 치우다, 내보내다
If you remove clothing, you take it off.

electrocute [iléktrəkjùːt] v. 감전 사고를 입히다; 감전사시키다
If someone is electrocuted, they are accidentally killed or badly injured when they touch something connected to a source of electricity.

. **unfold** [ʌnfóuld] v. (어떤 내용이 서서히) 펼쳐지다; (접혀 있는 것을) 펴다
If a situation unfolds, it develops and becomes known or understood.

^복^습 **frustrate** [frʌ́streit] v. 좌절감을 주다, 불만스럽게 하다; 방해하다
(frustrated a. 좌절감을 느끼는)
If something frustrates you, it upsets or angers you because you are unable to do anything about the problems it creates.

spew [spju:] v. 뿜어져 나오다, 분출되다
When something spews out a substance or when a substance spews from something, the substance flows out quickly in large quantities.

melt [melt] v. 녹다; (감정 등이) 누그러지다; n. 용해 (molten a. 녹은)
Molten rock, metal, or glass has been heated to a very high temperature and has become a hot thick liquid.

lava [láːvə] n. 용암
Lava is the very hot liquid rock that comes out of a volcano.

block [blak] v. 막다, 차단하다; 방해하다; n. 구역, 블록; 사각형 덩어리
To block a road, channel, or pipe means to put an object across it or in it so that nothing can pass through it or along it.

put out idiom (불을) 끄다
If you put out something, especially a fire, you make it stop burning.

flame [fleim] n. 불길, 불꽃; 격정; v. 활활 타오르다; 시뻘게지다
A flame is a hot bright stream of burning gas that comes from something that is burning.

swoop [swuːp] v. 급강하하다, 위에서 덮치다; 급습하다; n. 급강하; 급습
When a bird or airplane swoops, it suddenly moves downward through the air in a smooth curving movement.

aim [eim] v. 겨누다; 목표하다; n. 겨냥, 조준; 목적
If you aim a weapon or object at something or someone, you point it toward them before firing or throwing it.

imminent [ímənənt] a. 금방이라도 닥칠 듯한, 목전의, 임박한
If you say that something is imminent, especially something unpleasant, you mean it is almost certain to happen very soon.

roof [ruːf] n. 지붕; (터널·동굴 등의) 천장; v. 지붕을 씌우다
The roof of a building is the covering on top of it that protects the people and things inside from the weather.

turn into idiom ~이 되다, ~으로 변하다
To turn or be turned into something means to change, or to make a thing change, into something different.

mission [míʃən] n. 임무; 사명; v. 길고 험난한 여정에 나서다
A mission is an important task that people are given to do, especially one that involves traveling to another country.

cut off idiom (말을) 중단시키다; 단절시키다
To cut off means to prevent someone from continuing what they are saying.

nod [nad] n. (고개를) 끄덕임; v. (고개를) 끄덕이다, 까딱하다
A nod is a movement up and down with the head.

shut down idiom (기계가) 멈추다; 종료하다
If a machine shuts down, or someone shuts it down, it stops working.

bow [bau] ① n. 뱃머리; (고개 숙여 하는) 인사; v. (고개를) 숙이다; 절하다 ② n. 활
The front part of a ship is called the bow or the bows.

confront [kənfrʌ́nt] v. 직면하다; (문제나 곤란한 상황에) 맞서다
If you confront someone, you stand or sit in front of them, especially when you
are going to fight, argue, or compete with them.

compact [kəmpǽkt] v. (단단히) 다지다; a. 조밀한, 촘촘한
To compact something means to press it so that it becomes more solid.

leap [liːp] v. (서둘러) ~하다; 뛰다, 뛰어오르다; n. 높이뛰기, 도약; 급증
If you leap somewhere, you move there suddenly and quickly.

debris [dəbríː] n. 파편, 잔해; 쓰레기
Debris is pieces from something that has been destroyed or pieces of rubbish or
unwanted material that are spread around.

rubble [rʌ́bl] n. (허물어진 건물의) 돌무더기, 잔해
When a building is destroyed, the pieces of brick, stone, or other materials that
remain are referred to as rubble.

hallway [hɔ́ːlwèi] n. 복도; 통로; 현관
A hallway in a building is a long passage with doors into rooms on both sides of it.

undo [ʌndúː] v. 원상태로 돌리다, (묶인 것을) 풀다
To undo something that has been done means to reverse its effect.

silly [síli] a. 어리석은, 바보 같은; 우스꽝스러운; n. 바보
If you say that someone or something is silly, you mean that they are foolish,
childish, or ridiculous.

forget it idiom 잊어버려, 별 거 아냐; 그만 지껄여
You say 'forget it' in reply to someone for showing that you are annoyed because
you think their comment or suggestion is completely unreasonable.

race [reis] v. 쏜살같이 가다; (머리·심장 등이) 바쁘게 돌아가다; 경주하다; n. 경주; 인종, 종족
If you race somewhere, you go there as quickly as possible.

meanwhile [míːnwàil] ad. (다른 일이 일어나고 있는) 그동안에
Meanwhile means while a particular thing is happening.

drag [dræg] v. 끌다, 끌고 가다; 힘들게 움직이다; n. 끌기, 당기기; 장애물
If someone drags you somewhere, they pull you there, or force you to go there by physically threatening you.

hypnosis [hipnóusis] n. 최면술; 최면 상태
Hypnosis is the art or practice of hypnotizing people.

freak [friːk] v. 기겁을 하다; n. 괴짜, 괴물
If you freak, you become so angry, surprised, excited, or frightened that you cannot control yourself.

launch [lɔːntʃ] n. 발사; 시작; 개시, 진수; v. 발사하다; 시작하다
A launch is the act of sending a missile, space vehicle, satellite, or other object into the air or into space.

release [rilíːs] v. 놓아 주다; 풀어 주다; (감정을) 발산하다; n. 풀어 줌; 발표, 공개
If you release a device, you move it so that it stops holding something.

strap [stræp] v. 끈으로 묶다; 붕대를 감다; n. 끈, 줄, 띠
If you strap something somewhere, you fasten it there with a strap.

glare [glɛər] v. 노려보다; 환하다, 눈부시다; n. 노려봄; 환한 빛, 눈부심
If you glare at someone, you look at them with an angry expression on your face.

shove [ʃʌv] v. (거칠게) 밀치다; 아무렇게나 놓다; n. 힘껏 떠밀
If you shove someone or something, you push them with a quick, violent movement.

for one's good idiom ~의 이익을 위하여
If something is done for the good of a person or organization, it is done in order to benefit them.

groan [groun] n. 신음, 끙 하는 소리; v. (고통·짜증으로) 신음 소리를 내다; 끙끙거리다
A groan is a long low sound that a person makes, especially when they are in pain or unhappy.

seal [siːl] v. 봉쇄하다; 봉인하다; 확정짓다; n. 도장; [동물] 바다표범
If you seal something, you close an entrance or container so that nothing can enter or leave it.

diplomat [dípləmæt] n. 외교관
A diplomat is a senior official who discusses affairs with another country on
behalf of his or her own country, usually working as a member of an embassy.

snap [snæp] v. 급히 움직이다; 툭 부러지다; 날카롭게 말하다; n. 탁 하는 소리
(snap out of idiom (기분·습관에서) 재빨리 벗어나다)
To snap out of something means to become suddenly freed from a condition.

ambassador [æmbǽsədər] n. 대사
An ambassador is an important official who lives in a foreign country and
represents his or her own country's interests there.

rush [rʌʃ] v. 급히 움직이다; 서두르다; n. (감정이 갑자기) 치밀어 오름; 혼잡; 기쁨, 흥분
If you rush somewhere, you go there quickly.

rear [riər] n. 뒤쪽; a. 뒤쪽의; v. 앞다리를 들어올리며 서다
The rear of something such as a building or vehicle is the back part of it.

brace [breis] v. (스스로) 대비를 하다; (몸에) 단단히 힘을 주다; n. 치아 교정기; 버팀대
If you brace yourself for something unpleasant or difficult, you prepare yourself
for it.

sprint [sprint] v. (짧은 거리를) 전력 질주하다; n. 전력 질주; 단거리 경기
If you sprint, you run or ride as fast as you can over a short distance.

in time idiom 제때에, 시간 맞춰, 늦지 않게
If you are in time for a particular event, you are not too late for it.

Check Your Reading Speed

1분에 몇 단어를 읽는지 리딩 속도를 측정해보세요.

$$\frac{826 \text{ words}}{\text{reading time ( ) sec}} \times 60 = (\quad) \text{ WPM}$$

Build Your Vocabulary

jet [dʒet] n. 제트기; 분출; v. 급속히 움직이다; 분출하다
A jet is an aircraft that is powered by jet engines.

exit [égzit] v. 나가다, 떠나다; 퇴장하다; n. (고속도로의) 출구; (공공건물의) 출구; 퇴장
If you exit from a room or building, you leave it.

spiral [spáiərəl] v. 나선형으로 움직이다, 나선형을 그리다; 급증하다; n. 나선, 나선형
If something spirals or is spiraled somewhere, it grows or moves in a spiral curve.

slip [slip] v. 슬며시 가다; 미끄러지다; (옷 등을) 재빨리 벗다; n. (작은) 실수; 미끄러짐
If you slip somewhere, you go there quickly and quietly.

powerful [páuərfəl] a. 강력한; 영향력 있는, 유력한
A powerful machine or substance is effective because it is very strong.

stretch [stretʃ] v. (길이·폭 등을) 늘이다; 뻗어 있다; n. 뻗기, 펴기; (길게) 뻗은 구간
When something soft or elastic stretches or is stretched, it becomes longer or bigger as well as thinner, usually because it is pulled.

belly [béli] n. (사물의) 볼록한 부분; 배, 복부
A belly can refer to the rounded underside of a ship or aircraft.

hatch [hætʃ] n. (배·항공기의) 출입구; v. 부화하다; (계획 등을) 만들어 내다
A hatch is an opening in the deck of a ship, through which people or cargo can go. You can also refer to the door of this opening as a hatch.

flash [flæʃ] v. 휙 나타나다; 휙 내보이다; (잠깐) 번쩍이다; n. 순간; (잠깐) 반짝임
If a picture or message flashes up on a screen, or if you flash it onto a screen, it is displayed there briefly or suddenly, and often repeatedly.

control [kəntróul] n. (기계·차량의) 제어 장치; 통제, 제어; v. 지배하다; 조정하다
A control is a device such as a switch or lever which you use in order to operate a machine or other piece of equipment.

^{복습} **panel** [pǽnl] n. (자동차 등의) 계기판; 판; 자문단; v. 판으로 덮다
A control panel or instrument panel is a board or surface which contains switches and controls to operate a machine or piece of equipment.

^{복습} **immediate** [imíːdiət] a. 즉각적인; 당면한; 아주 가까이에 있는 (immediately ad. 즉시, 즉각)
If something happens immediately, it happens without any delay.

^{복습} **aboard** [əbɔ́ːrd] ad. (배·기차·비행기 등에) 탄, 탑승한
If you are aboard a ship or plane, you are on it or in it.

^{복습} **spin** [spin] v. (빙빙) 돌다; 돌아서다; n. 회전
If something spins or if you spin it, it turns quickly around a central point.

^{복습} **dive** [daiv] v. 급강하하다; 급히 움직이다; (물 속으로) 뛰어들다; n. 급강하; (물 속으로) 뛰어들기
If an airplane dives, it flies or drops down quickly and suddenly.

^{복습} **cruise** [kruːz] v. 순항하다; 천천히 달리다; n. 순항
If a car, ship, or aircraft cruises somewhere, it moves there at a steady comfortable speed.

^{복습} **altitude** [ǽltətjuːd] n. (해발) 고도; 고도가 높은 곳, 고지
If something is at a particular altitude, it is at that height above sea level.

^{복습} **roam** [roum] v. (이리저리) 돌아다니다; (시선·손이) 천천히 훑다
If you roam an area or roam around it, you wander or travel around it without having a particular purpose.

^{복습} **cabin** [kǽbin] n. (항공기·배의) 선실; (나무로 된) 오두막집
A cabin is one of the areas inside a plane.

^{복습} **punch** [pʌnʧ] n. 주먹으로 한 대 침; v. 주먹으로 치다; (자판·번호판 등을) 치다
A punch is the action of hitting someone or something with your fist.

^{복습} **oxygen** [áksidʒen] n. [화학] 산소
Oxygen is a colorless gas that exists in large quantities in the air. All plants and animals need oxygen in order to live.

^{복습} **force** [fɔːrs] v. 억지로 ~하다; ~를 강요하다; n. 작용력; 힘; 영향력
If you force something into a particular position, you use a lot of strength to make it move there.

^{복습} **crash** [kræʃ] v. 부딪치다; 충돌하다; 굉음을 내다; n. (자동차·항공기) 사고; 요란한 소리
If something crashes somewhere, it moves and hits something else violently, making a loud noise.

remind [rimáind] v. 상기시키다, 다시 한 번 알려 주다
If someone reminds you of a fact or event that you already know about, they say
something which makes you think about it.

steer [stiər] v. (보트·자동차 등을) 조종하다; (특정 방향으로) 움직이다
When you steer a car, boat, or plane, you control it so that it goes in the direction
that you want.

exclaim [ikskléim] v. 소리치다, 외치다
If you exclaim, you cry out suddenly in surprise, strong emotion, or pain.

rudder [rʌ́dər] n. (배의) 키; (항공기의) 방향타
A rudder is a device for steering a boat. It consists of a vertical piece of wood or
metal at the back of the boat.

veer [viər] v. 방향을 홱 틀다; (성격을) 바꾸다
If something veers in a certain direction, it suddenly moves in that direction.

freeze [fri:z] v. 얼다; (두려움 등으로 몸이) 얼어붙다; n. 동결; 한파
If a liquid or a substance containing a liquid freezes, or if something freezes it, it
becomes solid because of low temperatures.

knock [nak] v. 치다, 부딪치다; (문 등을) 두드리다; n. 문 두드리는 소리; 부딪침
To knock someone into a particular position or condition means to hit them very
hard so that they fall over or become unconscious.

underwater [ʌndərwɔ́:tər] ad. 수면 아래로, 물속에서; a. 물속의, 수중의
Something that exists or happens underwater exists or happens below the surface
of the sea, a river, or a lake.

belowdeck [biloudék] ad. 주갑판 밑으로
If someone or something is belowdecks, they are inside a ship in the part of it that
is underneath the deck.

shield [ʃi:ld] n. 보호 장치; 방패; v. 보호하다, 가리다; (기계 등에) 보호 장치를 두르다
Something or someone which is a shield against a particular danger or risk
provides protection from it.

yell [jel] v. 고함치다, 소리 지르다; n. 고함, 외침
If you yell, you shout loudly, usually because you are excited, angry, or in pain.

anchor [ǽŋkər] n. 닻; (뉴스 등의) 진행자; v. 닻을 내리다; 고정시키다
An anchor is a heavy hooked object that is dropped from a boat into the water at
the end of a chain in order to make the boat stay in one place.

^복_습 **strap** [stræp] v. 끈으로 묶다; 붕대를 감다; n. 끈, 줄, 띠
If you strap something somewhere, you fasten it there with a strap.

^복_습 **massive** [mǽsiv] a. (육중하면서) 거대한; 엄청나게 심각한
Something that is massive is very large in size, quantity, or extent.

^복_습 **press** [pres] v. 누르다; (무엇에) 바짝 대다; 꾹 밀어 넣다; n. 언론
If you press a button or switch, you push it with your finger in order to make a machine or device work.

yelp [jelp] v. 비명을 지르다; n. (날카롭게) 외치는 소리, 비명
If a person or dog yelps, they give a sudden short cry, often because of fear or pain.

* **plunge** [plʌndʒ] v. (갑자기) 거꾸러지다; 급락하다; n. (갑자기) 떨어져 내림; 급락
If something or someone plunges in a particular direction, especially into water, they fall, rush, or throw themselves in that direction.

^복_습 **struggle** [strʌgl] v. 애쓰다; 몸부림치다, 허우적거리다; 힘겹게 나아가다; n. 투쟁, 분투; 몸부림
If you struggle to do something, you try hard to do it, even though other people or things may be making it difficult for you to succeed.

* **dodge** [dadʒ] v. (몸을) 재빨리 움직이다; 기피하다; n. 몸을 홱 피함
If you dodge, you move suddenly, often to avoid being hit, caught, or seen.

* **propeller** [prəpélər] n. 프로펠러
A propeller is a device with blades which is attached to a boat or aircraft. The engine makes the propeller spin round and causes the boat or aircraft to move.

^복_습 **concern** [kənsə́:rn] v. 걱정스럽게 하다; 관련되다; n. 우려, 걱정; 관심사
(concerned a. 걱정하는, 염려하는)
If something concerns you, it worries you.

^복_습 **meanwhile** [mí:nwàil] ad. (다른 일이 일어나고 있는) 그동안에
Meanwhile means while a particular thing is happening.

^복_습 **coherent** [kouhíərənt] a. 조리 있게 말하는; 일관성 있는
If someone is coherent, they express their thoughts in a clear and calm way, so that other people can understand what they are saying.

disorient [disɔ́:rièrnt] v. 어리둥절하게 하다; 방향 감각을 혼란시키다
(disoriented a. 혼란에 빠진; 방향 감각을 잃은)
If something disorients you, you lose your sense of direction, or you generally feel lost and uncertain, for example because you are in an unfamiliar environment.

lack [læk] n. 부족, 결핍; v. ~이 없다, 부족하다
If there is a lack of something, there is not enough of it or it does not exist at all.

land [lænd] v. (땅·표면에) 내려앉다, 착륙하다; 놓다, 두다; n. 육지, 땅; 지역
When someone or something lands, they come down to the ground after moving through the air or falling.

spot [spat] v. 발견하다, 찾다, 알아채다; n. (특정한) 곳; (작은) 점
If you spot something or someone, you notice them.

flare [flɛər] n. 신호탄, 조명탄; 확 타오르는 불길; v. 확 타오르다; (코를) 벌름거리다
A flare is a small device that produces a bright flame. Flares are used as signals, for example on ships.

chaos [kéias] n. 혼돈; 혼란
Chaos is a state of complete disorder and confusion.

fire [faiər] v. 발사하다; (엔진이) 점화되다; 해고하다; n. 화재, 불; 발사, 총격
If someone fires a gun or a bullet, or if they fire, a bullet is sent from a gun that they are using.

impact [ímpækt] n. 충돌, 충격; (강력한) 영향; v. 영향을 주다; 충돌하다
An impact is the action of one object hitting another, or the force with which one object hits another.

windshield [wíndʃiːld] n. (자동차 등의) 앞 유리
The windshield of a car or other vehicle is the glass window at the front through which the driver looks.

cockpit [kákpit] n. (비행기·우주선 등의) 조종석, 조종실
In an airplane or racing car, the cockpit is the part where the pilot or driver sits.

plummet [plʌ́mit] v. 곤두박질치다, 급락하다
If someone or something plummets, they fall very fast toward the ground, usually from a great height.

autopilot [ɔ́ːtoupàilət] n. (항공기·배의) 자동 조종 장치
An automatic pilot or an autopilot is a device in an aircraft that automatically keeps it on a particular course.

catch up idiom 따라잡다, 따라가다; (소식 등을) 듣다
If you catch someone or something up, you go faster so that you reach them in front of you.

^{복습} **midair** [midέər] n. 공중, 상공
If something happens in midair, it happens in the air, rather than on the ground.

^{복습} **grab** [græb] v. (와락·단단히) 붙잡다; 급히 ~하다; n. 와락 잡아채려고 함
If you grab something, you take it or pick it up suddenly and roughly.

^{복습} **expand** [ikspǽnd] v. 확대시키다, 팽창시키다; 더 상세히 하다
If something expands or is expanded, it becomes larger.

^{복습} **parachute** [pǽrəʃùːt] n. 낙하산; v. 낙하산을 타고 뛰어내리다
A parachute is a device which enables a person to jump from an aircraft and float safely to the ground.

_* **descend** [disénd] v. 내려오다, 내려가다; (아래로) 경사지다 (descent n. 하강, 강하)
A descent is a movement from a higher to a lower level or position.

^{복습} **propel** [prəpél] v. 나아가게 하다; 몰고 가다
To propel something in a particular direction means to cause it to move in that direction.

^{복습} **wrap** [ræp] v. (무엇의 둘레를) 두르다; 포장하다; 둘러싸다; n. 포장지; 랩
If someone wraps their arms, fingers, or legs around something, they put them firmly around it.

_* **spare** [spɛər] v. (시간·돈 등을) 할애하다; (불쾌한 일을) 겪지 않게 하다; a. 남는; 여분의
(to spare idiom (시간·돈 등이) 남는)
If you can spare time, you have it available.

^{복습} **surface** [sə́ːrfis] n. 수면, 표면, 지면; 외관; v. 수면으로 올라오다; (갑자기) 나타나다
The surface of something is the flat top part of it or the outside of it.

^{복습} **deck** [dek] n. (배의) 갑판; 층; v. 꾸미다, 장식하다
A deck on a vehicle such as a bus or ship is a lower or upper area of it.

iceberg [áisbəːrg] n. 빙산
An iceberg is a large tall mass of ice floating in the sea.

^{복습} **collapse** [kəlǽps] v. 붕괴되다, 무너지다; 주저앉다; 쓰러지다; n. 실패; (건물의) 붕괴
If a building or other structure collapses, it falls down very suddenly.

^{복습} **wave** [weiv] n. 물결; (손·팔을) 흔들기; v. (손·팔을) 흔들다; 손짓하다
A wave is a raised mass of water on the surface of water, especially the sea, which is caused by the wind or by tides making the surface of the water rise and fall.

snowbank [snóubæŋk] n. (바람에) 쌓인 눈더미
A snowbank is a large pile of snow.

barrier [bǽriər] n. 장벽; 장애물; 한계
A barrier is something such as a fence or wall that is put in place to prevent people from moving easily from one area to another.

run into idiom ~을 들이받다; ~와 우연히 마주치다
If you run into someone or something, you hit them by accident while you are driving.

cue [kjuː] n. 신호; 실마리, 암시; v. 신호를 주다 (on cue idiom 마침 때맞추어)
If you say that something happened on cue or as if on cue, you mean that it happened just when it was expected to happen, or just at the right time.

multiply [mʌ́ltəplài] v. 크게 증가하다; 곱하다; 증식하다
When something multiplies or when you multiply it, it increases greatly in number or amount.

burst [bəːrst] v. (burst-burst) 갑자기 ~하다; 불쑥 움직이다; n. (갑자기) ~을 함; 파열, 폭발
To burst into something means to suddenly start doing it.

Chapter 22

1. What was Bob's advice to Violet?

    A. To tell Tony that she was a Superhero

    B. To introduce herself to Tony again

    C. To let Tony know that she liked him

    D. To stop caring about Tony

2. What did a judge rule?

    A. Supers could go back to their secret lives.

    B. Supers could choose to reveal their identities.

    C. Supers could help the public again.

    D. Supers could work only when there was an emergency.

3. **What happened when the Parr family and Tony got to the movie theater?**

   A. Tony was left alone at the theater.

   B. Violet canceled her date with Tony.

   C. Bob gave Violet and and Tony some money for snacks.

   D. Helen told Tony that the family had to fight crime.

Check Your Reading Speed

1분에 몇 단어를 읽는지 리딩 속도를 측정해보세요.

$$\frac{479 \text{ words}}{\text{reading time ( ) sec}} \times 60 = (\quad) \text{ WPM}$$

Build Your Vocabulary

handcuff [hǽndkʌ̀f] v. 수갑을 채우다; n. 수갑
If you handcuff someone, you put handcuffs around their wrists.

* **escort** [éskɔːrt] v. 호송하다, 호위하다; n. 호위대
If you escort someone somewhere, you accompany them there, usually in order to make sure that they leave a place or get to their destination.

cart off idiom 데려 가다
To cart off means to take someone somewhere, especially to a prison or hospital.

grateful [gréitfəl] a. 고마워하는, 감사하는
If you are grateful for something that someone has given you or done for you, you have warm, friendly feelings toward them and wish to thank them.

clear one's throat idiom 목을 가다듬다; 헛기침하다
If you clear your throat, you cough once in order to make it easier to speak or to attract people's attention.

control [kəntróul] n. 통제, 제어; (기계·차량의) 제어 장치; v. 지배하다; 조정하다
If you have control of something or someone, you are able to make them do what you want them to do.

hug [hʌg] n. 포옹; v. 껴안다, 포옹하다
A hug is the act of holding someone or something close to your body with your arms.

pull up idiom (차량·운전자가) 멈추다, 서다
If a vehicle or driver pulls up, they stop.

remote [rimóut] n. (= remote control) 리모컨; 원격 조종; a. 먼; 외진, 외딴; 원격의
The remote control for a television or video recorder is the device that you use to control the machine from a distance, by pressing the buttons on it.

^복_습 **turn** [təːrn] n. 전환; 차례, 순번; 돌기; v. 돌다; 변하다
(take a turn for the better idiom 더 좋아지다)
If a situation takes a turn for the better, it suddenly becomes better.

courtroom [kɔ́ːrtrùːm] n. 법정
A courtroom is a room in which a legal court meets.

[:]_: **judge** [dʒʌdʒ] n. 판사; 심판; v. 판단하다; 심판을 보다; 짐작하다
A judge is the person in a court of law who decides how the law should be applied,
for example how criminals should be punished.

[:]_: **rule** [ruːl] v. 판결을 내리다; 다스리다, 지배하다; n. 규칙
When someone in authority rules that something is true or should happen, they
state that they have officially decided that it is true or should happen.

_* **restore** [ristɔ́ːr] v. 회복시키다; 돌려주다; 복원하다
To restore a situation or practice means to cause it to exist again.

^복_습 **legal** [líːgəl] a. 법이 허용하는, 합법적인; 법률과 관련된
An action or situation that is legal is allowed or required by law.

_* **status** [stéitəs] n. 신분, 자격; 상황
Your status is your social or professional position.

^복_습 **crowd** [kraud] n. 사람들, 군중; v. 가득 메우다; 바싹 붙어 서다
A crowd is a large group of people who have gathered together, for example to
watch or listen to something interesting, or to protest about something.

^복_습 **cheer** [ʧiər] v. 환호성을 지르다, 환호하다; n. 환호(성), 응원
When people cheer, they shout loudly to show their approval or to encourage
someone who is doing something such as taking part in a game.

^복_습 **applaud** [əplɔ́ːd] v. 박수를 치다; 갈채를 보내다
When a group of people applaud, they clap their hands in order to show approval,
for example when they have enjoyed a play or concert.

^복_습 **tap** [tæp] v. (가볍게) 톡톡 두드리다; 박자를 맞추다; n. 수도꼭지; (가볍게) 두드리기
If you tap something, you hit it with a quick light blow or a series of quick light
blows.

^복_습 **chuckle** [ʧʌkl] v. 킬킬 웃다; 빙그레 웃다; n. 킬킬거림; 속으로 웃기
When you chuckle, you laugh quietly.

^복_습 **chat** [ʧæt] v. 이야기를 나누다, 수다를 떨다; n. 이야기, 대화
When people chat, they talk to each other in an informal and friendly way.

^복_습 **front door** [frʌnt dóːr] n. (주택의) 현관
The front door of a house or other building is the main door, which is usually in
the wall that faces a street.

^복_습 **trot** [trat] v. 빨리 걷다; 총총걸음을 걷다; n. 속보, 빠른 걸음
If you trot somewhere, you move fairly fast at a speed between walking and
running, taking small quick steps.

* **curb** [kəːrb] n. 도로 경계석, 연석; v. 억제하다
The curb is the raised edge of a pavement or sidewalk which separates it from
the road.

^복_습 **limit** [límit] v. 제한하다; 한정하다; n. 한계, 한도; 제한, 허용치
If you limit something, you prevent it from becoming greater than a particular
amount or degree.

* **wink** [wiŋk] v. 윙크하다; (빛이) 깜박거리다; n. 윙크
When you wink at someone, you look toward them and close one eye very briefly,
usually as a signal that something is a joke or a secret.

^복_습 **rear** [riər] a. 뒤쪽의; n. 뒤쪽; v. 앞다리를 들어올리며 서다
(rearview mirror n. (자동차의) 백미러)
Inside a car, the rearview mirror is the mirror that enables you to see the traffic
behind when you are driving.

^복_습 **kid** [kid] v. 놀리다, 장난치다; 속이다
If you are kidding, you are saying something that is not really true, as a joke.

drop off idiom 내려 주다; 데려다 주다
If you drop someone off, you stop and let them get out of a car.

^복_습 **pull up** idiom (차량·운전자가) 멈추다, 서다
If a vehicle or driver pulls up, they stop.

siren [sáiərən] n. (신호·경보) 사이렌
A siren is a warning device which makes a long, loud noise.

^복_습 **blare** [blɛər] v. (소리를) 요란하게 울리다; n. 요란한 소리
If something such as a siren or radio blares or if you blare it, it makes a loud,
unpleasant noise.

^복_습 **race** [reis] v. 쏜살같이 가다; (머리·심장 등이) 바쁘게 돌아가다; 경주하다; n. 경주; 인종, 종족
If you race somewhere, you go there as quickly as possible.

＊ pursuit [pərsúːt] n. 뒤쫓음, 추적; 추구
Someone who is in pursuit of a person, vehicle, or animal is chasing them.

＊ suspect [səspékt] n. 용의자; v. 의심하다; 수상쩍어 하다
A suspect is a person who the police or authorities think may be guilty of a crime.

glance [glæns] n. 흘낏 봄; v. 흘낏 보다; 대충 훑어보다
A glance is a quick look at someone or something.

usher [ʌ́ʃər] v. 안내하다; n. (교회·극장 등의) 좌석 안내원
If you usher someone somewhere, you show them where they should go, often by going with them.

＊ row [rou] n. 열, 줄; 노 젓기; v. 노를 젓다
A row of things or people is a number of them arranged in a line.

hop [hap] v. 급히 움직이다; 깡충깡충 뛰다; n. 깡충깡충 뛰기
If you hop somewhere, you move there quickly or suddenly.

＊ halfway [hǽfwèi] ad. (거리·시간상으로) 중간에, 가운데쯤에
Halfway means in the middle of a place or between two points, at an equal distance from each of them.

mask [mæsk] n. 마스크; 가면; v. 가면을 쓰다; (감정·냄새·사실 등을) 가리다
A mask is a piece of cloth or other material, which you wear over your face so that people cannot see who you are, or so that you look like someone or something else.

transform [trænsfɔ́ːrm] v. 변형시키다; 완전히 바꿔 놓다
To transform something into something else means to change or convert it into that thing.

booster [búːstər] n. (우주선·미사일의) 추진 로켓; (사기·자신감 등을) 높이는 것; 후원자
A booster is an extra engine in a machine such as a space rocket, which provides an extra amount of power at certain times.

blast [blæst] v. 빠르게 가다; 폭발시키다; 쾅쾅 울리다; n. 폭발; (한 줄기의) 강한 바람
To blast means to move very quickly and loudly in a specified direction.

adventure [ædvénʧər] n. 모험; 모험심
If someone has an adventure, they become involved in an unusual, exciting, and rather dangerous journey or series of events.

수고하셨습니다!

드디어 끝까지 다 읽으셨군요! 축하드립니다! 여러분은 이 책을 통해 총 23,562 개의 단어를 읽으셨고, 1,000개 이상의 어휘와 표현들을 공부하셨습니다. 이 책에 나온 어휘는 다른 원서를 읽을 때도 빈번히 만날 수 있는 필수 어휘들입니다. 이 책을 읽었던 경험은 비슷한 수준의 다른 원서들을 읽을 때 큰 도움이 될 것입니다.

원서는 한 번 다 읽은 후에도 다양한 방식으로 영어 실력을 끌어올리는 데 활용할 수 있습니다. 일단 다 읽은 원서를 어떻게 활용할 수 있을지, 학습자의 주요 유형별로 알아보도록 하겠습니다.

리딩(Reading) 실력을 확실히 다지길 원한다면, 반복해서 읽어보세요!

리딩 실력을 탄탄하게 다지길 원한다면, 같은 원서를 2~3번 반복해서 읽을 것을 권합니다. 같은 책을 여러 번 읽으면 지루할 것 같지만, 꼭 그렇지도 않습니다. 반복해서 읽을 때 처음과 주안점을 다르게 두면, 전혀 다른 느낌으로 재미있게 읽을 수 있습니다.

처음 원서를 읽을 때는 생소한 단어들과 스토리로 인해 읽고 이해하기가 매우 힘듭니다. 전체 맥락을 잡고 읽어도 약간 버거운 느낌이지요. 하지만 반복해서 읽기 시작하면 달라집니다. 내용은 일단 파악해 둔 상황이기 때문에 문장 구조나 어휘의 활용에 더 집중하게 되고, 조금 더 깊이 있게 읽을 수 있게 됩니다. 좋은 표현과 문장을 수집하고 메모할 만한 여유도 생기게 되지요. 어휘도 많이 익숙해졌기 때문에 리딩 속도도 탄력이 붙습니다. 처음 읽을 때는 '내용'에서 재미를 느꼈다면, 반복해서 읽을 때는 '영어'에서 재미를 느끼게 되는 것입니다. 따라서 리딩 실력을 더욱 확고하게 다지고자 한다면, 같은 책을 2~3회 정도 반복해서 읽을 것을 권해드립니다.

리스닝(Listening) 실력을 늘리고 싶다면, 귀를 통해서 읽어보세요!

많은 영어 학습자들이 '리스닝이 안 돼서 문제'라고 한탄합니다. 그리고 리스닝 실력을 늘리는 방법으로, 무슨 뜻인지 몰라도 반복해 듣는 '무작정 듣기'를 선택합니다. 하지만 뜻도 모르면서 무작정 듣는 것은 엄청난 인내력이 필요합니다. 그래서 대부분 며칠 시도하다가 포기해버리고 말지요.

모르는 내용을 무작정 듣는 것보다는 어느 정도 알고 있는 내용을 반복해서 듣는 것이 더 효과적인 듣기 방법입니다. 그리고 이런 방식의 듣기에 활용할 수 있는 가장 좋은 교재가 오디오북입니다.

따라서 리스닝 실력을 향상시키길 원한다면, 이 책에서 제공하는 오디오북을 이용해서 듣는 연습을 해보세요. 오디오북의 활용법은 간단합니다. 그냥 MP3를 플레이어에 넣고 자투리 시간에 틈틈이 들으면 됩니다. 혹은 책상에 앉아 눈으로는 책을 보면서 귀로는 그 내용을 따라 읽는 것도 좋습니다. 보통 오디오북은 분당 150~180단어로 재생되는데, 재생 속도가 조절되는 MP3를 이용하면 더 빠른 속도로 재생이 가능하고, 이에 맞춰 빠른 속도로 듣는 연습을 할 수도 있습니다.

중요한 것은 내용을 따라가면서, 내용에 푹 빠져서 반복해 들어야 한다는 것입니다. 눈으로 책을 읽는 것이 아니라 '귀를 통해' 책을 읽는 것이지요. 이렇게 연습을 반복해서, 눈으로 읽지 않은 책도 '귀를 통해' 읽을 수 있을 정도가 되면, 리스닝으로 고생하는 일은 거의 사라질 것입니다.

이 책은 '귀로 읽기'와 '소리 내어 읽기'를 위해 오디오북을 기본으로 제공하고 있습니다.
오디오북은 MP3 파일로 제공되니 MP3 기기나 컴퓨터에 옮겨서 사용하시면 됩니다. 혹 오디오북에 이상이 있을 경우 helper@longtailbooks.co.kr로 메일을 주시면 안내를 받으실 수 있습니다.

스피킹(Speaking)이 고민이라면, 소리 내어 읽기를 해보세요!

스피킹 역시 많은 학습자들이 고민하는 부분입니다. 스피킹이 고민이라면, 원서를 큰 소리로 읽는 낭독 훈련(Voice Reading)을 해보세요!
'소리 내서 읽는 것이 말하기에 정말로 도움이 될까?'라고 의아한 생각이 들 수도 있습니다. 하지만, 인간의 두뇌 입장에서 봤을 때, 성대 구조를 활용해서 '발화'한다는 점에서는 소리 내서 읽기와 말하기는 큰 차이가 없다고 합니다. 소리 내서 읽는 것은 '타인의 생각'을 전달하고, 직접 말하는 것은 '자신의 생각'을 전달한다는 차이가 있을 뿐, 머릿속에서 문장을 처리하고 조음기관(혀와 성대 등)을 움직여 의미를 만든다는 점에서 같은 과정인 것이지요. 따라서 소리 내서 읽는 연습을 꾸준히 하는 것은 스피킹 연습에 큰 도움이 됩니다.

소리 내어 읽기를 하는 방법도 간단합니다. 일단 오디오북을 들으면서 성우의 목소리를 최대한 따라 하며 같이 읽어보세요. 발음 뿐 아니라, 억양, 어조, 느낌까지 완벽히 따라 한다고 생각하면서 소리 내어 읽습니다. 따라 읽는 것이 조금 익숙해지면, 옆의 누군가에게 이 책을 읽어준다는 생각으로 소리내서 계속 읽어나갑니다. 한 번 눈과 귀로 읽었던 책이라 보다 수월하게 진행할 수 있고, 자연스럽게 어휘와 표현을 복습하는 효과도 거두게 됩니다. 또 이렇게 소리 내어 읽는 것을 녹음해서 들어보면 스스로에게 좋은 피드백이 됩니다.

라이팅(Writing)까지 욕심이 난다면, 요약하는 연습을 해보세요!

최근엔 라이팅에도 욕심을 내는 학습자들이 많이 있습니다. 원서를 라이팅 연습에 직접적으로 활용하기에는 한계가 있지만, 역시 적절히 활용하면 유용한 자료가 될 수 있습니다.
특히 책을 읽고 그 내용을 요약하는 연습은 큰 도움이 됩니다. 요약 훈련의 방식도 간단합니다. 원서를 읽고 그날 읽은 분량만큼 혹은 책을 다 읽고 난 후에 전체 내용을 기반으로, 책 내용을 요약하고 나의 느낌을 영어로 적어보는 것입니다. 이때 그 책에 나왔던 단어와 표현을 최대한 활용해서 요약하는 것이 중요합니다.

영어 표현력은 결국 얼마나 다양한 어휘로 많은 표현을 해보았느냐가 좌우하게 됩니다. 이런 면에서 내가 읽은 책을, 그 책에 나온 문장과 어휘로 다시 표현해 보는 것이 가장 효율적인 방식입니다. 책에 나온 어휘와 표현을 단순히 읽고 무슨 말인지 아는 정도가 아니라, 실제로 직접 활용해서 쓸 수 있을 만큼 확실하게 익히게 되는 것이지요. 여기에 첨삭까지 받을 수 있는 방법이 있다면 금상첨화입니다.

또한 이런 '표현하기' 연습은 스피킹 훈련에도 그대로 적용할 수 있습니다. 책을 읽고 그 내용을 3분 안에 다른 사람에게 영어로 말하는 연습을 하는 것이지요. 순발력과 표현력을 기르는 좋은 훈련이 됩니다.

'스피드 리딩 카페'에서 함께 원서를 읽어보세요!

이렇게 원서 읽기를 활용한 영어 공부에 관심이 있으시다면, 국내 최대 영어원서 읽기 동호회 스피드 리딩 카페(http://cafe.naver.com/readingtc)로 와보세요. 이미 수만 명의 회원들이 모여서 '북클럽'을 통해 함께 원서를 읽고 있습니다.

단순히 함께 원서를 읽는 것뿐만 아니라, 위에서 언급한 다양한 방식으로 원서를 활용하여 영어 실력을 향상시키고 있는, 말뿐이 아닌 '실질적인 효과'를 보고 있는 회원들이 엄청나게 많이 있습니다. 여러분도 스피드 리딩 카페를 방문해보신다면 많은 자극과 도움을 받으실 수 있을 것입니다.

원서 읽기 습관을 길러보자!

일상에서 영어를 한마디도 쓰지 않는 비영어권 국가에서 살고 있는 우리에게 영어에 가장 쉽고, 편하고, 저렴하게 노출되는 방법은, 바로 '영어원서 읽기'입니다. 언제 어디서든 원서를 붙잡고 읽기만 하면 곧바로 영어를 접하는 환경이 만들어지기 때문이지요. 하루에 20분씩만 꾸준히 읽는다면, 1년에 무려 120시간 동안 영어에 노출될 수 있습니다.

영어원서를 꾸준히 읽어보세요. '원서 읽기 습관'을 만들어보세요! 이렇게 영어를 접하는 시간이 늘어나면, 영어 실력도 당연히 향상될 수밖에 없습니다.

아래 표에는 영어 수준별 추천 원서들이 있습니다. 하지만 이것은 절대적인 기준이 아니며, 학습자의 영어 수준과 관심 분야에 따라 달라질 수 있습니다. 이 책은 Reading Level 3에 해당합니다. 이 책의 완독 경험을 기준으로 삼아 적절한 책을 골라 꾸준히 읽어보세요.

영어 수준별 추천 원서 목록

리딩 레벨	영어 수준	원서 목록
Level 1	초 · 중학생	The Zack Files 시리즈, Magic Tree House 시리즈, Junie B. Jones 시리즈, Horrid Henry 시리즈, 로알드 달 단편들(The Giraffe and the Pelly and Me, Esio Trot, The Enormous Crocodile, The Magic Finger, Fantastic Mr. Fox)
Level 2	고등학생	Andrew Clements 시리즈 (Frindle, School Story 등), Spiderwick Chronicle 시리즈, 쉬운 뉴베리 수상작들 (Sarah Plain and Tall, The Hundred Dresses 등), 짧고 간단한 자기계발서 (Who Moved My Cheese?, The Present 등)
Level 3	특목고 학생 대학생	로알드 달 장편 (Charlie and the Chocolate Factory, Matilda 등), Wayside School 시리즈, 중간 수준의 뉴베리 수상작들 (Number the Stars, Charlotte's Web 등), A Series of Unfortunate Events 시리즈
Level 4	대학생 상위권	Harry Potter 시리즈 중 1~3권, Percy Jackson 시리즈, The Chronicles of Narnia 시리즈, The Alchemist, 어려운 수준의 뉴베리 수상작들 (Holes, The Giver 등)
Level 5	대학원생 이상 전문직 종사자들	Harry Potter 시리즈 중 4~7권, Shopaholic 시리즈, His Dark Materials 시리즈, The Devil Wears Prada, The Curious Incident of the Dog in the Night-Time, Tuesdays With Morrie 등등 (참고 자료: Renaissance Learning, Readingtown USA, Slyvan Learning Center)

'영화로 읽는 영어원서'로 원서 읽기 습관을 만들어보세요!

『인크레더블 2』를 재미있게 읽은 독자라면 「영화로 읽는 영어원서」 시리즈를 꾸준히 읽어보시길 추천해드립니다! 「영화로 읽는 영어원서」 시리즈는 유명 영화를 기반으로 한 소설판 영어원서로 보다 쉽고 부담 없이 원서 읽기를 시작할 수 있도록 도와주고, 오디오북을 기본적으로 포함해 원서의 활용 범위를 넓힌 책입니다.

『하이스쿨 뮤지컬』, 『업』, 『라푼젤』, 『겨울왕국』, 『메리다와 마법의 숲』, 『몬스터 주식회사』, 『몬스터 대학교』, 『인사이드 아웃』, 『빅 히어로』 등 출간하는 책들마다 독자들의 큰 사랑을 받으며 어학 분야의 베스트셀러를 기록했고, 학원과 학교들에서도 꾸준히 교재로 채택되는 등 영어 학습자들에게도 좋은 반응을 얻고 있습니다. (EBS에서 운영하는 어학사이트 EBS랑 www.ebslang.co.kr 교재 채택, 서초·강남 등지 명문 중고교 방과 후 보충교재 채택, 전국 영어 학원 정·부교재 채택, 김해 분성 초등학교 영어원서 읽기 대회 교재 채택 등등)

Prologue & Chapter 1

1. C The ground suddenly began to rumble and quake! The shaking became more and more violent—then an enormous armored vehicle with a powerful earthmover drill attached to the front exploded from the ground! It flipped cars out of its way, and Tony and his friends ran in different directions, trying to escape. Tony squatted behind a car and peered around it to watch as chaos enveloped the city.

2. B She pulled off her mask and threw it to the ground. Tony stared at her, taking in the sight of the Supersuit. He told Dicker he knew she had sounded familiar. . . . It was Violet! He couldn't believe it. Violet saw Tony. She tried to tell him everything was fine, but the situation was too weird for him to handle. So without knowing how to react, he just ran away.

3. C He pulled a long, wide tube from the tunneler and dragged it into the vaults. Planting himself in the center of the room, he turned on the powerful suction. Mountains of cash, bonds, and deeds were sucked up through the tube and into the tunneler!

4. A Mr. Incredible and the Underminer fought, tumbling around the tunneler until Mr. Incredible threw the Underminer against the control panel, breaking it! The massive machine began tunneling out of control, drilling upward, toward the surface.

5. D Elastigirl snaked her body through the tunneler's machinery, stretching to her limits, trying to spill the engine's coolant to force it to overheat. Mr. Incredible appeared. "Help me with the boiler!" Elastigirl urged. He rushed in to help her pry it loose, toppling it over. "That should do it!"

Chapters 2 & 3

1. C Dicker's face fell as they approached the van. "The program's been shut down," he said with a sigh. He knew how important the Super Relocation Program was to the Parr family. Ever since Supers were forced underground, it had helped them many times. "Politicians don't understand people who do good simply because it's right. Makes 'em nervous. They've been gunnin' for Supers for years. Today was all they needed. . . ." His voice trailed off. His sad eyes said it all: he genuinely felt bad about the whole situation. "Anyway . . . I'm done."

2. D It had been months since they'd moved in, and the motel room felt cluttered and crowded. It wasn't nearly big enough for a family of five.

3. D "We wanna fight bad guys!" exclaimed Dash. Jack-Jack babbled in approval and raised his fists, then slammed them down on the tray of his high chair. "No—you don't!" said Helen, finally weighing in. Violet turned to Helen. "You said things were different now." Helen explained that they were different when they were on the island with Syndrome. The rules weren't the same because they were all in danger, but since they were now back at home, everything was supposed to be normal again.

4. B "What are we gonna do?" asked Helen. "I don't know," said Bob with a shrug. "Maybe Dicker'll find something—" "Dicker is done, Bob," Helen said. "Any thought we had about being Supers again is fantasy. One of us has gotta get a job." Helen said she knew that Bob's job at the insurance company had been hard on him. She suggested that maybe it was her turn to get a job and he could stay home and take care of the kids. "NO," said Bob. "I'm the breadwinner."

5. A Then he told them about a man he had met on his way home from the Underminer attack. He pulled out a business card and handed it to Helen. He explained that the man represented a business tycoon named Winston Deavor, who wanted to meet the three of them to talk about "hero stuff."

Chapters 4 & 5

1. A "You're uncomfortable that I know your alter egos—that you two are married and have kids." He told them they had nothing to worry about. "You probably don't remember me," he added, "but I worked for Rick Dicker for a short period, right before you all went underground."

2. C One night, someone had broken into their family's home. "My mother wanted to hide, but my father insisted they call Gazerbeam—on the direct line. No answer. He called Fironic; no answer. Superheroes had just been made illegal, but somehow he was sure they'd answer his call. The robbers discovered him on the phone . . . and shot him."

3. D On the screen, Winston said, "We need you to share your perceptions with the world." Then Elastigirl asked her question. "How do we do that?" Evelyn clicked the

remote again, and a live feed appeared on the screen, showing the three Supers' faces. Simultaneously, they looked down at the security badges clipped to their suits. "With cameras," said Evelyn. She explained that they would sew tiny cameras into the fabric of their Supersuits.

4. B "Wait a minute—you're saying, what, I'm . . . messy?" said Mr. Incredible, still trying to process what was happening. Winston handed Mr. Incredible a folder. He looked at it, bewildered, as Winston explained that Evelyn had compared the costs and benefits of their last five years of crime fighting. "Elastigirl's numbers are self-explanatory," he said. Mr. Incredible shifted his weight uncomfortably. "Well, it's not a fair comparison . . . ," he said, feeling the need to defend himself. "Heavyweight problems need heavyweight solutions."

5. D "It's not a good time to be away," she said. "Dash is having trouble with homework. Vi is worried about her first date with that boy she likes—Tony. And Jack-Jack . . ." Her voice trailed off. Bob looked at her, waiting for her to finish the sentence. "Jack-Jack?" he said, prompting her to continue. "What's wrong with him?" "Okay, nothing is wrong with Jack-Jack," she said. "But even a normal baby needs a lot of attention. I'm just not sure I can leave."

Chapters 6 & 7

1. D "Ehhh, this is . . . homey," said Violet sarcastically, not nearly as taken as Dash. "I mean, look at this place," said Bob. "Winston bought it from an eccentric billionaire who liked to come and go without being seen, so the house has multiple hidden exits." Eager to explore, Dash zoomed away. "Good thing we won't stand out," said Violet, her voice still dripping with sarcasm. "Wouldn't want to attract any unnecessary attention." "IT'S GOT A BIG YARD!" screamed Dash from outside. Helen turned to Bob, a little uncertain. "This is . . . Isn't this a bit much?"

2. B Later that day, Bob held Jack-Jack as Elastigirl emerged from the bathroom wearing the new Supersuit the Deavors had sent. It was a shiny gray, and patterned with light black scales. "This isn't me . . . ," she said, looking at herself in a full-length mirror. She turned, assessing the suit from different angles. "I'm not all dark and angsty. I'm Elastigirl! I'm, ya

know, flexible!" "E designed this?" asked Bob. "No, some guy named Alexander Galbaki," she answered.

3. C "But I thought Superheroes were still illegal," said Violet. "They are," said Bob. "For now," he added. "So Mom is getting paid to break the law," Violet said, amazed that neither of her parents saw anything wrong with this idea. "She's an advocate for Superheroes," said Bob, trying to make it sound good. "It's a new job." "So Mom is going out, illegally, to explain why she shouldn't be illegal," said Violet.

4. A While a live band played boisterous music and a storm of flashbulbs went off, the doors to the hovertrain slid open. Passengers poured inside and the train rose up, hovering over the track. It began to pull out of the station, but then suddenly, it stopped, dropping back onto the track with a loud thud. The crowd murmured, confused, as the train slowly rose above the track again. Uncertain applause filled the station, and the train began to move . . . but it was going backward! As the train accelerated, the crowd's excitement turned to terror. "It's going in the wrong direction!" Elastigirl shouted.

5. A She crawled to the back of the train and she saw the engineer staring straight ahead. He didn't blink or move a muscle when she banged on the windshield, trying to get his attention.

Chapters 8 & 9

1. C Jack-Jack toddled to the door and pressed his hands against the glass . . . then passed right through it! Standing on his little feet, he grabbed the chicken leg from the raccoon and tossed it back into the garbage can. CLANG! He used his mind to make the lid float into the air and back onto the can. Jack-Jack unleashed multiple Super powers as he took on the raccoon, wrestling, punching, and kicking it. He giggled as laser beams suddenly came out of his eyes and shot at the raccoon.

2. D He sighed, sat up, and headed downstairs, determined to tackle the challenge. "'Wait for Mom.' What am I? A substitute parent?" A few minutes later, he was in the kitchen. He poured himself a cup of coffee and sat at the kitchen table with Dash's math book in front of him. He put on his glasses and began to read. Dash was sound asleep when Bob gently woke him a few hours later. "I think I understand your math assignment," he whispered.

3. A "Oh!" said Elastigirl. "Madam Ambassador, hello!" She was about to introduce herself when the ambassador pushed past her guards to shake Elastigirl's hand. "You are Elastigirl!" the ambassador said. She looked tickled to see her. "It was so sad when you went underground, and I am glad to see you are back in your shiny outfit!"

4. B "Do I have your attention?" asked Chad in a robotic voice. Elastigirl looked at her interviewer, trying to read his face, and noticed a strange flashing-light pattern reflected in his eyes. "Of course I do," said Chad mechanically. "I'm appearing on your screen. Reading the words I'm saying off another screen." Elastigirl followed his gaze to the teleprompter, where she caught a glimpse of hypnotic light patterns blazing across the screen. She started to fall under its spell, but averted her eyes just in time, breaking free.

5. A A security guard held a gun, with the terrified ambassador at his side. "Stand down!" insisted the ambassador. "It's Elastigirl!" The guard lowered his gun, and Elastigirl entered the cabin. Turning to the ambassador, she said, "Stay in your seat, ma'am!" Then she tried to open the door to the cockpit, but it was locked. She stretched to grab the security guard's gun and shot the lock off, opening it. Inside were two hypnotized pilots, sitting rigidly at the controls. She quickly punched the screens to break them, releasing the pilots from their trance.

Chapters 10 & 11

1. B "I can't tell you how many memories Dicker's had to erase over the years, when"— Bob pulled out the milk container and sniffed it, assessing whether it was still okay to drink—"someone figured out your mother's or my identity." He closed the refrigerator door and was surprised to see Violet standing right in front of him. "It was Dicker!" she growled, seething. "You told him about Tony!" "Honey—" started Bob, feeling guilty. "You had me erased from Tony's mind!" she yelled.

2. A Elastigirl exited the car, and a cheer erupted as the adoring crowd reached out, trying to shake her hand. She couldn't believe she had inspired so many people. "Thanks for coming!" she said. She crouched down to shake a little girl's hand and noticed her sign. It read THE SCREENSLAVER IS STILL OUT THERE. Suddenly, all the joy she felt from the outpouring of admiration disappeared. She knew it was true. She still had a villain to

catch.

3. B "I flew them in from all over," said Winston. "They've all been in hiding. They have powers, secret identities, and names they've given themselves." The Supers were ecstatic to meet Elastigirl and share their stories.

4. C The two continued to chat until an idea popped into Elastigirl's mind. She knew how to capture the Screenslaver! "I need to lock onto a signal and trace its origin." Elastigirl and Evelyn worked out the details. Evelyn would create a tracking device. Then they would schedule a remote interview with Chad Brentley and set a trap for the Screenslaver.

5. C "I thought Vi would want a change of pace from drive-in food," said Bob.

Chapters 12 & 13

1. A Unbeknownst to Chad, Elastigirl sat directly on top of the studio, on a large transmission tower.

2. B He went on to rant about how people use screens because they're lazy. And how they want Superheroes to take care of them so they don't have to take care of themselves.

3. D Moments later, Elastigirl watched as the cops took the Screenslaver away in handcuffs. "What's going on?" he asked, sounding puzzled.

4. C "It's the kind of thing you buy when you have everything else," said the smug billionaire, standing beside the gleaming Incredibile. "They said it was beyond repair," said Bob, staring at the television. "And hey, it was in perfect condition," added the billionaire, tapping the hood of the amazing vehicle. "You used to drive THAT?" asked Dash. "They said it was destroyed," said Bob, his anger growing by the second. "Long thought lost or destroyed, the famous car turned up at a private auction," said the reporter.

5. A "Jack-Jack has . . . powers?" asked Dash, completely shocked. "Well—yeah—but, um," Bob stammered as he nodded his head. "You knew about this?" asked Violet. She couldn't believe he hadn't told them. She asked him if he had told their mother. Bob put Jack-Jack into his playpen and answered nervously, "Yeah. I dunno—NO. Your mother is not—because I didn't want—because it's not the time—because—" "Why not?" asked Violet, shocked. "Why would you not tell Mom?" Dash, finally processing the

information, added, "We're your kids! We need to know these things! You'd want us to tell YOU, wouldn't you!"

Chapters 14 & 15

1. D Lucius started freaking out because Jack-Jack was gone, but Bob continued to try to tempt the baby back with cookies. Out of nowhere, Jack-Jack reappeared. He took a cookie, gobbled it down, and reached toward Bob for more.

2. A "Leave him? HERE?" said Edna, cutting him off. She looked down at Jack-Jack, irritated as he grabbed the edge of her robe and stuffed it into his mouth. She quickly snatched it from him. "I am not a baby person, Robert! I have no baby facilities! I am an artist; I do not involve myself in the prosaic day-to-day."

3. C "I'm sorry about Tony. I didn't think about Dicker erasing his memory, or about you having to pay the price for a choice you never made. It's not fair, I know. And then I made it worse at the restaurant by trying to—" He stopped himself, realizing he was rambling. He sighed before continuing. "Anyway, I'm sorry."

4. C "Just now at a worldwide summit, leaders from more than a hundred of the world's top countries have agreed to make Superheroes legal again!" Enthusiastic cheers filled the room. "We'll gather Superheroes and leaders from all over the planet on our ship, the EVERJUST, for a televised signing ceremony at sea!"

5. B "All the Screenslaver needs to do to hypnotize someone is get a screen in front of their eyes. But what if the screen doesn't look like a screen?" She lifted up the Screenslaver hood and goggles fell out. She picked them up and inspected them closely. "What if the pizza guy is really a pizza guy, but he was controlled by the screens built into his glasses?"

Chapters 16 & 17

1. B "Your child is a polymorph," she said. "Like all babies, he has enormous potential. It is not unknown for Supers to have more than one power when young, but this little one has many."

2. D Then she handed him a sleek monitor, its screen full of information. "Interwoven with these fabrics is a mesh of tiny sensors that monitor the baby's physical properties—"

Suddenly, the monitor lit up and read REPLICATION IMMINENT IN 3, 2, 1— Jack-Jack stood up and fell to the floor. As soon as he hit it, he multiplied into five Jack-Jacks, and they all happily danced around the chamber to the music. "Oh, lord," Bob said. "What's he doing?" "Well, it's Mozart, Robert!" said Edna. "Can you blame him? The important thing is that the suit and tracker anticipated the change and alerted you."

3. B Then the tracking pad lit up: COMBUSTION IMMINENT. "What does THAT mean?" asked Bob. Just then, Jack-Jack burst into flames and Bob screamed. "It means 'fire,' Robert," said Edna. "For which the suit has countermeasures. I suggest you extinguish the baby's flames before he trips the sprinkler system." Bob hit the tracker, and foam erupted from Jack-Jack's suit, quickly putting out the fire.

4. C "Let's say I created the character, and I own the franchises." "Does Winston know?" Elastigirl asked. "That I'm the Screenslaver? Of course not. Can you imagine what Mr. Free Enterprise would do with my hypnosis technology?" she said sarcastically. "Worse than what you're doing?" said Elastigirl. "I'm using the technology to destroy people's trust in it. Like I'm using Superheroes." "Who did I put in jail?" asked Elastigirl. "Pizza-delivery guy," Evelyn said. "Seemed the right height, build. He gave you a pretty good fight. I should say I gave you a good fight through him."

5. D "But why would you— Your brother—" "—is a child," Evelyn finished. "He remembers a time when we had parents and Superheroes. So, like a child, Winston conflates the two. Mommy and Daddy went away BECAUSE Supers went away. Our sweet parents were fools to put their lives in anybody else's hands. Superheroes keep us weak."

Chapters 18 & 19

1. C The doorbell rang, and Dash rushed downstairs to open it. Voyd, Brick, Reflux, He-lectrix, Screech, and Krushauer stood there, wearing glowing goggles. They were all being controlled by Evelyn. "You kids aren't safe," said Voyd. "The Deavors sent us—"

2. A Dash, still clutching the Incredibile remote behind his back, slowly found the button to summon the car.

3. D Mr. Incredible ran onto the hydroliner and quickly found Evelyn. "Good news and

bad news," she said as she led him toward the ballroom. "We've found her, she seems physically fine, but she's had an encounter with the Screenslaver and she's acting kind of strange. In here—" She opened the doors and Mr. Incredible went in. "Strange how?" he asked. He looked up to see Elastigirl crouched between the wall and ceiling, but before he even noticed her glowing eyes, her fists were in his face. She punched him four times before he could react.

4. C "Hey," said Dash, "what if the Incredibile has ejector seats?" The car responded with a message flashing across the dashboard: EJECTOR SEATS ACTIVATED. "Wait, what? No—" said Violet. "Yeah, baby!" said Dash, preparing for the ride. "NO! Don't say any more—" urged Violet. "MAX POWER!" said Dash. The message changed to read EJECTOR SEATS: MAXIMUM POWER. Violet tried to get Dash to stop, but he refused to listen. He ordered the car to launch the seats, and the kids shot into the air! Violet created a force field around them, and they safely landed on the deck of the ship.

5. B They hurried in to see Jack-Jack penetrating another wall! "Darn it!" said Dash. "He's heading for Mom!" said Violet.

Chapters 20 & 21

1. D Mr. Incredible crushed the steering wheel, locking it into its current trajectory. The ship was going to crash!

2. A Meanwhile, Evelyn grabbed Winston and dragged him toward her secret jet. He slowly came out of hypnosis and was confused. "Where are the delegates and the Supers?" he asked. "Still hypnotized," replied Evelyn. Winston started to freak out. "Oh, no, no, no—you're the Screenslaver!" he cried. Evelyn pressed a launch button, releasing the jet from the hydroliner. "Strap in NOW!" she yelled. Winston glared at her, then shoved her out of his way as he went for the stairs. Evelyn leaped to the controls and hit the thruster. The jet rose from the deck of the hydroliner as she yelled, "IT'S FOR YOUR OWN GOOD!" "NO!" Deavor yelled back. He opened the door to the jet. "THIS IS!" He jumped out and landed hard on the deck of the ship.

3. C Elastigirl pulled herself toward the controls and finally reached Evelyn. She went to deliver a punch, but Evelyn quickly placed an oxygen mask over her own face. As

she forced the jet directly up into the clouds, climbing higher and higher into the sky, Elastigirl became weaker and weaker.

4. D "Hey, what about turning the ship?" asked Dash. Both Mr. Incredible and Frozone reminded him that the steering had been destroyed. "Dash means from the outside!" exclaimed Violet. "If we break off one of the foils and turn the rudder, we can veer the ship away from the city." Frozone and Mr. Incredible agreed that it was their only option.

5. B The force of the impact sent Evelyn crashing through the windshield of the cockpit. She began to plummet toward the ocean! Elastigirl set the jet on autopilot and shot herself out the broken window toward Evelyn. She quickly caught up to her in midair, grabbed her, and expanded into a parachute. But Evelyn refused to be saved by a Super. She kicked Elastigirl to free herself and continued her descent toward the ocean. Elastigirl again propelled herself toward Evelyn and wrapped her arms around her.

Chapter 22

1. B "I've been thinking. Tony forgetting you isn't the worst thing. Just . . . take control. Reintroduce yourself. Go up to him and say, 'You don't know me, but I'm Violet Parr.' That'll be enough."

2. C Inside a courtroom, a judge ruled to restore the legal status of the Supers.

3. A But when they pulled up to the theater, sirens blared as police cars raced past in pursuit of a suspect. The Parrs exchanged glances, and Violet ushered Tony out of the car. "Here," she said, handing him some money. "Large popcorn, small soda. Save me a seat, center, about eight rows back." Violet hopped back into the car and stuck her head out the window. "Oh, and butter only halfway up, unless you like it all the way through!" Tony watched as the car drove off, wondering what had just happened.

인크레더블 2(INCREDIBLES 2)

1판 1쇄   2018년 7월 16일
1판 2쇄   2021년 8월 9일

지은이   Suzanne Francis
기획   이수영
책임편집   김보경 정소이
콘텐츠제작및감수   롱테일북스 편집부
번역   롱테일북스 편집부
마케팅   김보미 정경훈

펴낸이   이수영
펴낸곳   (주)롱테일북스
출판등록   제2015-000191호
주소   04033 서울특별시 마포구 양화로 113(서교동) 3층
전자메일   helper@longtailbooks.co.kr
(학원 · 학교에서 본도서를 교재로 사용하길 원하시는 경우 전자메일로 문의주시면
자세한 안내를 받으실 수 있습니다.)

ISBN 979-11-86701-84-3 14740

롱테일북스는 (주)북하우스 퍼블리셔스의 계열사입니다.

이 도서의 국립중앙도서관 출판시도서목록(CIP)은 서지정보유통지원시스템 홈페이지(http://seoji.nl.go.kr)와
국가자료공동목록시스템(http://www.nl.go.kr/kolisnet)에서 이용하실 수 있습니다. (CIP제어번호: CIP2018021374)